THE FOUNDATION OF THE LEAGUE OF ARAB STATES

Wartime Diplomacy and Inter-Arab Politics 1941 to 1945

AHMED M. GOMAA, D.Phil. (Oxon.)

Longman

LONGMAN GROUP LTD
LONDON AND NEW YORK

Associated companies, branches and representatives throughout the world

First published 1977

ISBN 0 582 78073 X

Library of Congress Cataloging in Publication Data

Gomaa, Ahmed Mahmoud H
The foundation of the League of Arab States

Originally presented as the author's thesis, Oxford.
Bibliography: p.
Includes index.
1. League of Arab States. I. Title.
DS36.2.G65 1977 341.24'77 77–21371
ISBN 0–582–78073–X

Printed in Great Britain by
Richard Clay (The Chaucer Press) Ltd., Bungay, Suffolk

THE FOUNDATION OF THE LEAGUE OF ARAB STATES

CONTENTS

Chapter Eight

PREFACE

This book does not attempt a detailed study of the question of Arab unity. Its main purpose is to throw fresh light on the circumstances which surrounded the establishment in March 1945 of the League of Arab States, and on the interplay of local and international factors which defined its shape and limited its scope. The main conclusion substantiated by a wealth of material from official British manuscript sources, is that the formation of the League was a purely Arab initiative, which had been encouraged, rather than inspired, by the British.

Four main factors are singled out as having contributed to the evolution of the Pact of the League. The first was the growing Arab solidarity concerning the Palestine problem and the wider issue of inter-Arab co-operation. The second factor was the increasing role of Egypt in Arab affairs. Egypt entertained no territorial ambitions in Arab Asia, and was not involved in the dynastic rivalries which had frustrated all past efforts towards Arab unity. It was, therefore, in a better position to play a conciliatory role. The third factor was the increasing realization by the British policy-makers of the need to deal with the area as an interrelated whole, both for the necessities of wartime and in response to Arab demands. A more sympathetic attitude to Arab aspirations for unity was favoured by Mr Churchill and some members of the War Cabinet as providing a chance for the settlement of the Palestine problem through the creation of a Jewish state within an Arab federation. The fourth factor was the favourable atmosphere created by the war for the promotion of economic regionalism, and for the end of French domination over Syria and Lebanon.

This book attempts to deal with each of these four factors in greater detail. It was thought necessary to include a brief introductory section dealing with Arab nationalism and Egypt's Arab policy during the inter-war period, in order to provide some historical perspective. The problem of Palestine and the struggle for the independence of Syria and Lebanon are dealt with in so far as they are relevant to the main issues of Arab co-operation. The year 1941 offered a convenient starting-point. It witnessed the collapse of the Rashid 'Ali movement in Iraq and the end of what came to be called the Iraqi phase of the Arab nationalist movement. Leadership of that movement passed to more moderate politicians, and Egypt started to play a more prominent role. The same year witnessed serious British reverses in the war, and the readiness of both the British and the Axis powers to propitiate the Arabs by issuing statements of sympathy with their aspirations for unity.

In view of the predominant role of Britain in the area before and during the Second World War, it was natural that British policy should be dealt with in greater detail. This was made easier by the availability of official British documents covering the period under study. With the paucity of such documents on the Arab side, it was necessary to rely on published memoirs, press statements of the Arab leaders at that time, and recollections of living Arab politicians.

Over thirty-two years have elapsed since the establishment of the Arab League. Its membership has risen to twenty fully independent Arab states in addition to the Palestine Liberation Organization, which has been granted full membership status as the legitimate representative of the Palestine Arab people. Its scope of activities has widened with the establishment of affiliated specialized agencies. As a regional organization, it has withstood the pressures of time, and survived several inter-Arab crises as well as four major Arab–Israeli wars. Alternative forms of closer co-operation or union attempted during the late fifties and the sixties have faltered. This in itself is a testimony to the sagacity of the initiators of the League, who had their feet on the ground, and who were able to devise a scheme well suited to Arab needs and circumstances. The present generation of Arab intellectuals and historians might find much to criticize in the methods and practices of the Arab leaders at the time the League was formed. These leaders were, however, living in very different times, and had to steer their course in a very delicate world situation, and under severe pressures compounded by foreign military presence. In spite of all this, they had a clear vision of the future. Their prescription is still relevant to Arab conditions today. The main issues involved in the establishment of the League did not lose their importance with the lapse of time. Arab unity is still a much-aspired-to ideal, and the Palestine problem still provides an impetus for Arab solidarity. It is therefore hoped that this study will contribute to a better understanding of present Arab politics and the underlying cause of the Arab–Israeli conflict.

The research work which went into the writing of this book took several years. It was during a three years' residence in Oxford as a graduate student, that I was finally able to complete it. It was originally presented as a D. Phil. thesis to Oxford University in May 1973. The Egyptian Government, the Secretariat of the Arab League, the British Council, the Board of Social Studies of Oxford University, and the Master and Fellows of Balliol College readily extended to me their invaluable assistance. To these institutions I owe a special debt of gratitude.

I am also deeply indebted to Mr Albert Hourani, Mr Wilfrid Knapp, Miss Elizabeth Monroe, Dr Roger Owen, Sir Harold Beeley, and the late Professor Trevor Evans for their constant encouragement and guidance. My thanks are also due to Mr Fikri Abaza, of Al Hilal Corporation, Mr Abu Seif Radi and Mr Wahid el-Daly of the Arab

League Secretariat, Dr Mohammad Salah el-Din, the former Egyptian Foreign Minister, as well as to the various Arab officials and writers with whom I had stimulating discussions about the subject of this book. I should also like to express my deep gratitude to the staffs of the Public Records Office in London, the Middle East Centre and Rhodes House in Oxford, and the Arab League, National, and University libraries in Cairo. I wish also to pay tribute to Mr Alan Gilchrist and the staff of Longman House for their keen interest and great assistance in preparing this book for publication.

I need hardly say that the orientation of this study and the views expressed in it are entirely my own, and should not be taken to represent those of the persons and institutions to whom tribute has been paid.

PART ONE

Arab Nationalism and Egypt's Arab Policy An Historical Background 1915 to 1941

Chapter One

Arab Nationalism: An Historical Review 1915 to 1941

Arab nationalism, and hence the general Arab aspiration for unity, is a phenomenon of relatively recent growth. It developed during the later part of the nineteenth century and the early part of the present century in reaction against Ottoman tyranny, and against the centralization policies of the Committee of Union and Progress. It gathered strength and some coherence during and after the First World War. The Great Arab Revolt of 1916 originated in that part of the Ottoman Empire least affected by the centralization policies, and least politically conscious. Sherif Hussein of Mecca, its leader, was actuated in the first place by fears of Turkish victimization and by personal ambition. It was through his contacts with the Arab nationalists in the Levant, and through their prompt positive response to his call for unified Arab action, that the Revolt gained significance as a national uprising. The Revolt was in essence an act of defiance against a long established authority whose very foundations had been shaken, and whose institutions had degenerated more than half a century earlier. It was also an alliance with a secular and strongly nationalistic West.

In his correspondence[1] with Sir Henry MacMahon, the British High Commissioner in Egypt, Sherif Hussein stated that he was speaking for the Arab nation and that his main goal was the independence of all the territories of Arab Asia. No mention was made of Arab unity at that early stage, since the area had always been considered as one unit for general political and economic purposes, and the continuation of that unity was taken for granted. It was only when the details of the Sykes–Picot agreement of 1916 became known that a greater stress began to be laid on Arab unity as a main goal of the Arab nationalist movement. There were many in the Levant who were willing and even eager to see independence qualified by recourse to foreign assistance, but none were

---

[1] The Hussein–MacMahon correspondence took place between 14 July 1915 and 10 March 1916. The official British text is in Cmd. 5957, HMSO, London, 1939; a study of the nature of British pledges embodied in Sir Henry's letters was conducted officially by a Joint Anglo-Arab Committee during the sittings of the London Round Table Conference of 1939: Cmd. 5974, HMSO, London, 1939

for the slightest compromise on the doctrine of unity.[1] Arab aspirations for unity were expressed in a persuasive way in a memorandum submitted to the Paris Peace Conference in January 1919 by Amir Faisal, the Sherif's son who led the Arab forces which took part in the conquest of Syria. He defined the Arabs as those people of "closely related Semitic stock, all speaking the one language, Arabic". The aim of the Arab nationalist movement, he stated, was "to unite the Arabs eventually into one nation". He referred to the Arabs' "splendid past", and their tenacity in resisting for centuries all Turkish attempts to absorb them. The unifying impact of a common religion was played down, and "the natural influences of race, language, and interest" were stressed as the moulding factors. He admitted that economic and social differences between the different parts of Arab Asia would make it "almost impossible to constrain them into one frame of government". He suggested, therefore, a decentralized form of administration with sufficient guarantees for the special status of the minorities, and with open frontiers, common railways and telegraphs, and a uniform system of education among the constituent parts.[2] Amir Faisal was in fact expressing the views of the Arab nationalists which were later affirmed during the meetings of the two Syrian Congresses of July 1919 and May 1920.

The dissection of the Arab East after the war and the imposition of British and French mandates over the Levant and Iraq shattered Arab hopes for both independence and unity. The Iraqi revolt of 1920 was the first serious reaction to the post-war settlement. The installing by the British of Amir Faisal as King of Iraq, and of his brother 'Abdullah as Amir of the newly constituted Emirate of Transjordan in 1921, was an imaginative response to the new situation. It was designed to allay Arab bitterness and to preserve effective British control behind a façade of national rule.

The French, on the other hand, went a long way in trying to stem the tide of Arab nationalism in Syria, from which they expelled Amir Faisal in 1920. Their policy aimed at strengthening the traditionally or potentially Francophile elements, the Christians, the Alawis, the Kurds, and other minorities; and at consolidating the position of Lebanon *vis-à-vis* the interior by adding to it in 1920 additional areas to the north and the south. This resulted in the establishment from 1925 to 1936 of four states: Greater Lebanon, Syria, the Alawis, and Jebel al-Druze.[3]

---

[1] George Antonius *The Arab Awakening*, London 1938, p. 304. The Anglo-French–Russian understanding for the partition of the territories of the Ottoman Empire into spheres of influence of each of these powers, which is commonly known as the Sykes–Picot agreement, was published by the new Russian regime following the Communist revolution in 1917; text in J. C. Hurewitz *Diplomacy in the Near and Middle East*, vol. II 1914–56, New York 1956, pp. 18–22

[2] Text in J. C. Hurewitz, op. cit., pp. 38–9

[3] A. H. Hourani *Syria and Lebanon: A Political Essay*, London 1946, p. 167

Syrian nationalists were victimized and excluded from office up to 1936, and some of them went into exile into Europe, Egypt, and Iraq.

The conquest of Hejaz by Ibn Sa'ud in 1925 dealt a final blow to the grandiose schemes of Sherif Hussein. It ushered in a new phase in Arab politics in which Ibn Sa'ud began to assume a leading role in the Arab World. His action was positive in so far as it accomplished the unity of the greater part of the Arabian Peninsula. It did not fail, however, to intensify Hashimite antipathy. Sa'udi-Hashimite feuds and rivalries became a main feature of inter-Arab politics. No common action based on mutual trust, even on general Arab issues, became possible for a long time between Ibn Sa'ud and his Hashimite rivals.

The Arab nationalists tended, in view of these obstacles and as was natural in the circumstances, to concentrate on the immediate goal of independence. The more pragmatic among them saw in the achievement of independence a necessary first step towards unity. Others saw that the achievement of unity even on a modest scale, starting perhaps with the Greater Syria states or with the union of Iraq and Syria, was necessary for the success of the nationalist struggle for independence. The Arab nationalist movement was then in its formative stage, with no solid ideological basis and no clear vision of the future. It was involved too soon for its own good in active hostilities, first against the Turks, and later against the British (Iraq 1920) and the French (Syria 1925), and had to formulate its ideals in an improvised way.

It was in the early thirties, after a brief halt, that Arab nationalists in the Levant began to think of a plan for future action. They were worried at the preoccupation of the Arab countries with their internal problems, which was accompanied by the concentration on parochial tendencies, especially among the minorities. The movement lacked encouragement and guidance from its original leader Amir (now King) Faisal and from his brother 'Abdullah, who, in accepting the thrones of Iraq and Trans-jordan in 1921, pledged to confine their activities to their two countries, and to curtail and withhold support from any anti-British or anti-French activities.[1] The regulation of Anglo-Iraqi relations, following the conclusion of the 1930 treaty ending the mandate, removed some of the constraints on King Faisal. The Arab nationalists in Syria and Palestine, for their part, took advantage of their presence in Jerusalem during the sittings of the Islamic Congress of December 1931 to meet and discuss the Arab question in general. An "Arab Covenant" was formulated which stressed that the Arab lands "are a complete and indivisible whole" and that all efforts in every Arab country should be directed towards the single goal of the complete independence, "in their entirety and unified", of all the Arab states. It deprecated any call for concen-

[1] PRO, Foreign Office Political Files, series 371, vol. 16855: memorandum on British attitude towards Arab unity dated June 1933

trating all efforts on local issues in each country, and asserted that the Arab nation rejected colonialism in all its forms, and was determined to combat it with all its forces.[1] It was decided to revive the activities of the Independence *Istiqlal* Party, which was founded in 1918 by some members of the pre-war Arab secret societies. An executive committee was set up to plan future action. At its first meeting, it was agreed to call for the convocation of an Arab Congress to discuss the necessary means for the propagation and the achievement of the ideals formulated in the Arab Covenant.[2]

The Arab nationalists pinned great hopes on King Faisal and on Iraq after its independence. They had the support of the leading Iraqi politicians, most of whom had had their affiliations in the past with the pre-war secret societies, and were veterans of the Great Arab Revolt. For these politicians, as for King Faisal, the pan-Arab movement offered a chance for the consolidation of Hashimite hegemony over the Levant. They had their eyes set on Syria, from which Faisal and his supporters had been evicted by the French in 1920. The Iraqi-championed pan-Arab activities centred on two main issues: the meeting of an Arab Congress in Baghdad to rally Arab nationalists under Faisal's leadership, and the attempt to secure the Syrian throne for a Hashimite candidate.

King Faisal's activities were resented by the French, who suspected British instigation behind his moves, and who were determined to prevent any extension of British influence through Iraq to Syria. They gave the impression at times, however, that a Hashimite candidate for the Syrian throne would not be unwelcome to them. Their purpose was to gauge Faisal's motives, to induce Iraq to settle outstanding border and trade issues, and to favour Syria over Palestine for the proposed oil pipeline to the Mediterranean.[3]

The British were also strongly opposed to any union between Iraq and Syria for fear that this might open Iraq to French influence and weaken the position of Faisal in Iraq, leading to the usurpation of power by the extreme nationalists. Any wider Arab union was found objectionable on the grounds that it was bound to conflict with the mandatory systems in the area. The British were aware of Ibn Sa'ud's objections to King Faisal's activities, which he considered inimical to his own interests. They were eager to maintain the stability of the area, and to avoid antagonizing the French or upsetting their friendly relations with Ibn Sa'ud. They discouraged King Faisal from identifying himself with, or

---

[1] A. J. Toynbee *Survey of International Affairs, 1934* [hereafter referred to as *Survey*], London, Royal Institute of International Affairs (RIIA), 1935, p. 107

[2] Muhamad Izzat Darwaza *Al Wihda al 'Arabiya: Mabahith Fi Ma'alim al Watan al 'Arabi al Kabir wa Muqawimat Wihdath*, Beirut 1957, pp. 124–5

[3] FO 371–15364: statement by King Faisal to Sir Francis Humphreys about French overtures and his comments, 20 January 1931

committing himself to, "any policy designed to bring about the political unity of the Arabs". They stressed in the meantime that they would be sympathetic towards any general policies of friendly inter-Arab relations and co-operation, especially in the cultural and economic fields.[1]

The death of King Faisal in 1933 put a temporary stop to the Iraqi-sponsored pan-Arab activities. King Ibn Sa'ud began to come to the fore as the leading Arab ruler. Many Arab nationalists in Syria and in Palestine were attracted by his personality, by the valour of his forces, and by the fact that he owed his position of prominence to his own efforts and not to the action of any foreign power. His successful war with the Yemen in 1934 was followed by the conclusion of a Treaty of Islamic Friendship and Arab Brotherhood with the Imam. The Treaty of Arab Brotherhood and Alliance of 1936 with Iraq, to which the Yemen acceded in 1937, provided for more comprehensive collective security arrangements and for closer co-operation in all fields.[2] Both treaties were concluded and given their pan-Arab colour on the initiative of Ibn Sa'ud. His attitude was governed mainly by his worries over the growing Italian menace in the Red Sea, and partly by his wish to play to the Arab gallery. His treaty with Iraq was highly praised all over the Arab World, and was described by him as providing "the foundation for the union of the Arab nation". He expressed his hope that the collective security arrangements embodied in the said treaty would be extended to include the other Arab countries.[3] Both treaties were based, however, on mutual respect for the territorial integrity and sovereignty of the contracting states, and no surrender, in part or in full, of that sovereignty was envisaged in the near or distant future. They provided, however, a good starting-point and were commended by Arab nationalists on this basis.

THE ARAB NATIONALIST MOVEMENT AND PALESTINE 1936 to 1939

The Arab struggle against Zionist designs and British policies in Palestine was rightly described as the most important of all the factors which

---

[1] FO 371–16855: memorandum on Arab unity, 14 June 1933

[2] Arnold Toynbee *Survey*, 1936, p. 803

[3] FO 371–20056: Foreign Office comments on a strong Sa'udi draft which provided for mutual assistance in case of aggression and for co-ordination of policies towards the other Arab countries. This strong draft was criticized by the British in view of their defence commitments to Iraq, and their unwillingness to allow any concerted Sa'udi–Iraqi intervention in the affairs of Palestine, Syria, or the Arabian Gulf Sheikhdoms. The draft was modified to remove the objectionable provision. The Iraqis were rather lukewarm, and Yassin Pasha al Hashimi, the Prime Minister, described the treaty as "little more than a gesture" of common sympathy between the Arab nations, of which the practical benefits would, in the far greater measure, accrue to Saudi Arabia. The Iraqis were obviously resentful of this attempt by Ibn Sa'ud to assert his role as the leader of the Arabs.

had stimulated the sense of Arab unity.[1] The dynamic nature of the Zionist movement became clear from 1933 onwards, with the rapid increase in Jewish immigrants and their settlement in the coastal and most fertile parts of Palestine. The Arabs began to realize the full implications of the Zionist programme. They had their fears of Jewish domination politically of Palestine and economically of the rest of the Arab countries. The Palestine Arab revolt of 1936 was the most serious expression of Arab discontent made so far, and had its repercussions all over the Arab World.

The attempt by the Arab rulers to emulate and outbid each other in support of the Arab cause in Palestine was indicative of the strength of public feeling on the issue. In Egypt, the Islamic and Arab organizations were very active in mobilizing public support for the Palestine Arabs. In Iraq public feeling ran high on the matter, and the government was to issue the strongest denunciation ever made by an Arab government of British policies in Palestine.[2] Even in Saudi Arabia, the King was under pressure from the *'Ulema* and his Syrian advisers to champion the Arab cause in Palestine. The situation was compounded for the British by the increasing Italian menace and by the attempt of Italian propaganda to capitalize on British difficulties in Palestine. Things became more difficult as a result of Zionist pressures both in Britain and in the United States. Considerations of prestige and the fear of possible Jewish reactions precluded any major concessions to the Arabs with regard to the cessation of Jewish immigration and land purchases, and to the establishment of self-government in Palestine.[3]

Two main aspects of the Palestine disturbances, which lasted intermittently until 1939, are of special relevance to our theme.

The first was the recognition by H.M.G. of the weight of neighbouring Arab reactions in a dangerous world situation and of the gradual erosion of the traditional policy of insulating Palestine from external influences. The Arabs, stated George Rendel, the head of the Eastern Department of the Foreign Office, were "a single race" whose "strong racial and cultural unity" made it "unreasonable" to expect them to be indifferent to the fate of their kin in Palestine.[4] The "most striking and

[1] A. H. Hourani *Syria and Lebanon*, p. 106

[2] Hikmat Suleiman, the Iraqi Premier, declared to the Press that "the hour has struck for the Arab nation everywhere to rise and form one united body". He lodged an official protest against the partition policy both with the British Ambassador in Iraq and, through his envoy in London, with Mr Eden, the Foreign Secretary. *Al Bilad*, 11 July 1937 and FO 371–20809

[3] These considerations were stated during the Cabinet meeting of 2 September 1936, which decided that measures must be taken to crush the revolt and that H.M.G. should not yield to disorders and violence. All requests by the Arab rulers for a conciliatory gesture were turned down and they were told that there must be unconditional cessation of violence. Cab 23/85—Cabinet Conclusions 56 (36) on 2 September 1936 and FO 371–20026

[4] FO 371–20806: letter of Rendel to Downie (CO) on 28 April 1937

far reaching" feature of the Palestine disturbances, stated the Report of the Royal Commission (Peel) in 1937, was the manner in which they roused the feeling of the Arab World at large against Zionism and its defenders. The Palestine Arabs were addressed by the Arab rulers as "our sons", and the solidarity of Arab interests was stressed by those rulers.[1] The views of the Foreign Office about the necessity of not treating the Palestine problem in isolation were to prevail after a tussle with the Colonial Secretary, Ormsby-Gore,[2] whose resignation in May 1938, to go to the House of Lords on the death of his father, paved the way for the evolution of a more conciliatory policy in Palestine.

A Cabinet Committee on Palestine was formed. In its first meeting, in October 1938, the idea of an Arab-Jewish conference was commended by the new Colonial Secretary, Malcolm MacDonald. The participation in this conference of the neighbouring Arab countries was, in his view, necessary, since a settlement "would never be reached" if Palestine was treated in isolation. Neville Chamberlain, the Prime Minister, expressed agreement with this view, adding that Palestine "has now become a pan-Arab question and the Arab 'princes' would be more likely to form a united front if they were omitted from the conference than if they were invited to attend it".[3] The logic of the new approach was summed up by MacDonald, who explained that if war broke out in Europe Britain would be fighting for her life, and every other consideration would have to be subordinated to that of winning the war. A conciliatory move was therefore necessary to alleviate Arab hostility and to secure British vital interests in the Middle East.

The meeting of the London Round Table Conference on Palestine took place in February 1939. It was attended by top-level representatives, from Egypt, Iraq, Transjordan, Saudi Arabia, and the Yemen, as well as by Jewish and Arab representatives from Palestine. The convening of the Conference was designed mainly to placate the Arabs by giving them the chance to air their grievances, and to create the impression that

---

[1] *The Palestine Commission Report*, Cmd. 5479, HMSO, London July 1937, p. 67

[2] Mr Ormsby-Gore, who was exasperated at the Foreign Office opposition to partition, sent a letter to Neville Chamberlain, the Prime Minister, on 9 January 1938 in which he argued that the establishment of a Jewish state in Palestine would "by its position as a bridge under predominantly British influence between the uncertain Arab world of Asia and North Africa, enable us to break up any potential pan-Islamic bloc." FO 371–21862. Ormsby-Gore's letter was strongly criticized by the Foreign Office but Eden was not in favour of preparing any answer to it. He realized no doubt that the Colonial Secretary's position in the Cabinet was already very weak. Neville Chamberlain, the Prime Minister, stated Oliver Harvey, the private secretary of Eden, "hates him [Gore] and the whole Cecil connection". Ormsby-Gore was in fact "pushed out" of the Cabinet by Chamberlain and was reluctant to go following the death of his father. *The Diplomatic Diaries of Oliver Harvey 1937–1940*, edited by John Harvey, London 1970, p. 140

[3] FO 371–21865: minutes of the first meeting of the Cabinet Committee on Palestine [P. (38) 1st Meeting]

due regard had been given to their fears and susceptibilities. It was also an attempt by the British to encourage the formation of an Arab front as a counterforce to the Jewish Agency and its Zionist supporters abroad. The Report of the Royal Commission (Peel) stressed the need for the establishment, as an alternative to partition, of an Arab Agency participated in by the neighbouring Arab countries as a counterweight to the Jewish Agency.[1] This became all the more important in the late thirties and early forties with the absence of any Arab body to represent Arab interests in Palestine at a time when almost all the important Arab leaders were either interned or driven into exile.

The British did not have any illusions about the chances of success of the Conference in reaching a Palestine settlement.[2] They had made up their minds some months earlier about dropping partition, and the need to make a conciliatory move towards the Arabs. The Conference failed to reach any agreement owing to the widely divergent views of the Arab and Jewish representatives. It was significant all the same, since it offered the chance for close contacts between the Arab leaders, and for informal contacts between them and the Zionist leaders. The meetings of the Arab delegates in Cairo before and after the Conference were the first official high level Arab gatherings of their nature. The Arab delegates in the Conference were able, in spite of their mutual suspicions and antagonisms, to represent a unified front on the issue. The White Paper issued by the British government in May 1939 went a long way to satisfying some Arab demands. It provided for the restriction of Jewish immigration and land purchases, and envisaged self-government in Palestine. It was strongly opposed by the Jews, who considered it a betrayal of British pledges to them. The Palestine Arabs found some of its terms objectionable, especially those making the establishment of self-government dependent upon Jewish approval. Many moderate

---

[1] *The Palestine Commission Report*, pp. 133–5

[2] FO 371–21865. In a memorandum submitted to the Cabinet Committee on Palestine on 20 October 1938, Malcolm MacDonald, the Colonial Secretary, stated that it was "of course, very doubtful whether the proposed Conference would succeed in reaching an agreement. But even if it ends in failure, I think it will do good and strengthen our position." The Zionist leaders understood correctly British motives for calling the meeting. They were of the view that the talks would almost certainly end in failure and that the British would be able later to enforce their policy. They fought the participation of the neighbouring Arab representatives. They realized that the Arabs had clearly won a victory and were given "what is virtually official status in Palestine", and that the world situation was playing into the hands of the Arabs. Ben Gurion, *Letters to Paula*, London 1971, pp. 223–6. George Antonius, the secretary of the Arab delegations to the Conference, described it as a conference of consultation between the Arabs and the British rather than a round table conference. He added that it was not a complete failure, since it provided the chance for close and frank consultations. (Antonius' letter to Walter Rogers of the Institute of Current World Affairs, of which Antonius was the Middle Eastern correspondent: Private Papers, St Antony's, Oxford)

Arabs found the White Paper, however, the best that could be achieved in the circumstances.[1]

The second aspect of the Palestine problem was the evolution, by some prominent Arab, Jewish, and British personalities, of schemes for its settlement through the creation of an Arab federation. It is not within the scope of this study to go into each of these schemes in detail, since they are numerous and have been current since the days of King Faisal I of Iraq. They were all based on the belief that by the satisfying of Arab aspirations for unity, the Arabs' fears of Jewish domination in Palestine would be allayed, and their objections to Jewish immigration diminished. The most vocal proponents of such schemes from 1937 onwards were Lord Samuel, the first High Commissioner for Palestine, and Nuri Pasha al Sa'id, the Iraqi leader. Lord Samuel's scheme[2] provided for the formation of a Great Arab Confederation which would include Saudi Arabia, Iraq, Transjordan, Syria, and Palestine. This would be established eventually with the assent of France and the full co-operation of the Zionist movement. Jewish immigration would be restricted in order to maintain the existing ratio of Arabs to Jews for an interim period of ten years, during which the Jewish population should not exceed forty percent of the total population of Palestine. Transjordan would be opened for development and settlement, both by the Arabs and by the Jews of Palestine, with British financial assistance. An Arab Agency would be formed side by side with the Jewish Agency and would have the power to prohibit land sales in the Arab areas. A Central Council for Palestine would be set up as a kind of federal body in which British members would act in an advisory capacity. Arab and Jewish representatives would participate on a basis other than election or proportional representation. A solemn guarantee in perpetuity of the Holy Places in Palestine would be given by the League of Nations.

Nothing came out of Lord Samuel's scheme. It was not favourably received by the Colonial Office, who had their minds set on partition.[3] The Zionist leaders were to show interest in schemes of Arab federation allowing for unrestricted Jewish immigration. David Ben Gurion, the chief executive of the Jewish Agency, proposed to Philby, the unofficial

---

[1] Tawfiq al-Suwaidi *Mudhakkirati: Nisf Qarn Min Tarikh al'Iraq wal-Qadiya al 'Arabiya*, Beirut 1969, p. 328

[2] The scheme was outlined by Lord Samuel during the debate in the House of Lords on the Report of the Royal Commission on 20 July 1937: Parl. Deb., H. of L., 5th ser., vol. CVI, cols. 641–3. Lord Samuel had in fact called for the establishment of a loose confederation of Arab states for economic and common purposes as far back as 1920, which idea was then rejected by Lord Curzon, the Foreign Secretary. Viscount Samuel *Memoirs*, London 1945, pp. 149–50, 284–5

[3] Samuel's proposals were strongly opposed by Ben Gurion, who sent a circular to all Zionist organizations and parties outside Palestine asking them "to protest vigorously against Samuel's treacherous conduct". He was critical in particular of Samuel's acceptance of a temporary minority status for the Jews in Palestine. David Ben Gurion *Letters to Paula*, p. 135

adviser to King Ibn Sa'ud, early in 1937 for communication to the Sa'udi government, a scheme which would have the mandate over Palestine and Transjordan terminated and the Balfour Declaration rescinded. The two countries would then be handed over to Ibn Sa'ud "in full sovereignty". This was made conditional on Ibn Sa'ud's approval of unlimited Jewish immigration to Palestine and Transjordan.[1] These proposals were rejected by Ibn Sa'ud, however, and were described by the Foreign Office as "absurd", and nothing came out of them. Dr Weizmann was also to express interest early in 1938 in a scheme for the solution of the problem through the creation of Arab federation, which was then being mooted in Egypt. Such schemes, he stressed, would be acceptable to the Jews only if they provided the possibility of a further increase in the Jewish population in Palestine to two millions. He considered it "inconceivable" for the Jews to accept a minority status in Palestine.[2]

Nuri's scheme, on the other hand, called for the formation of a federation comprising Iraq, Palestine, and Transjordan. Its head, he stressed, had to be one of the current Arab rulers. This meant, in effect, that such a federation would be under Hashimite leadership. His scheme provided also for the acceptance of the Jewish National Home within the federation, with local autonomy for the predominantly Jewish areas of Palestine. He stressed, however, that the Jewish population had to be fixed, on a permanent basis, at its current ratio of four Jews to seven Arabs.[3] Nuri conveyed his proposals to the British, who did not see anything of interest in them. He had talks about his scheme with Lord Samuel, who showed interest in its general outlines while raising objections to the limitation of Jewish immigration and the permanent minority status for the Jews. This was the main bone of contention in the Palestine controversy. For the Jews as well as for the British, schemes of

---

[1] FO 371–20806. It should be noted that high level Arab delegations including Amir Faisal, son of Ibn Sa'ud, were in London at that time (May 1937) to attend the coronation ceremony of King George VI. Ben Gurion stated that he got busy at that time trying to get in touch with the Sa'udi officials in particular, and that he had a talk with Philby. He added, however, that it was Philby who then suggested to him that the Zionists should reach an agreement with Ibn Sa'ud, since they would get a better deal from him than from the British. Ben Gurion stated that he replied that not only the Jews but also the Arabs would not agree that Ibn Sa'ud, "who is nothing but a Bedouin, should rule over Palestine". The account given by Sheikh Yusuf Yassin to the Foreign Office did not mention any suggestion made by Philby in this regard. David Ben Gurion, op. cit., pp. 116–17

[2] FO 371–21874: statement by Dr Weizmann during an interview with Prince Muhammad 'Ali in February 1938. The reference here is to the scheme proposed by the Prince in 1937 for the creation of an Arab federation in the Levant with autonomy for the minorities.

[3] FO 371–20028: record of Nuri's talks with Samuel in Paris in October 1936 conveyed to the Foreign and Colonial Offices. Also 20813–E5338/22/31 about the details of Nuri's scheme which he handed to the Oriental Secretary of the British Embassy in Cairo on 6 September 1937 for transmission to Eden.

Arab federation had their appeal only as providing the chance of Arab acceptance of continued Jewish immigration and settlement. The British argued that if the restriction of immigration and the maintenance of the current ratio of Jews to Arabs were to be found acceptable, this would solve the problem immediately. Schemes of federation would therefore become "rather irrelevant" to the issue. They were also highly sceptical about the possibility of the achievement of such a scheme in view of the possible strong objections of King Ibn Sa'ud to the creation of a Hashimite-led federation, and the legal difficulties of terminating the mandate over Palestine and Transjordan.

Nuri was not, however, the only Arab leader to advocate such solutions. Amir 'Abdullah was to devise his own scheme, which limited the federation to Palestine and Transjordan. The head would be an Arab sovereign "who is capable of carrying out his duties and executing his obligations", by which he obviously meant himself.[1] He naturally resented an association with his strong neighbours, Iraq and Saudi Arabia, which would have undermined his own chances of leadership. The British, recognizing the Amir's personal motives, did not give his scheme any serious consideration. Prince Muhammad 'Ali, the Egyptian Regent, was also to propose in May 1937, as a solution for the Palestine problem, that an Arab Empire to include Palestine, Transjordan, and Syria should be established. His ideas, conveyed to Sir Arthur Wauchope, the High Commissioner for Palestine, and to the Foreign Office, leaked to the Egyptian press, which gave them the most favourable comment. Lord Samuel, who showed interest in the idea, was to have talks with the Prince on the issue in 1938.[2]

The idea of a Palestine settlement through the creation of an Arab federation was therefore widely current from 1937 onwards. The new development was in the gradual shift in the attitude of the British policy-makers from scepticism to cautious support for this idea. They were told by Sir Archibald Clark-Kerr, the Ambassador in Baghdad, as far back as 1936 that H.M.G. "shall certainly have to reckon with the formation of some kind of Arab Confederation probably sooner than later". He considered it inexpedient to appear to wish to resist it and thus to throw away the friendship of the Arabs, "a thing of no small value".[3] They were warned at the same time, by Sir Miles Lampson, that as long as British policy in Palestine remained entirely unacceptable to the Arabs, any sort of Arab unification must result in stronger

---

[1] FO 371–21885: a memorandum prepared by the Amir and forwarded by the Palestine High Commissioner on 11 June 1938. The scheme envisaged the limitation of Jewish immigration and land purchases to the predominantly Jewish areas.

[2] FO 371–20806: letters of the Prince to Sir Arthur Wauchope, the Palestine High Commissioner and the Foreign Office in May 1937; and 21875: record of the meeting between the Prince and Samuel in March 1938

[3] FO 371–20029–E7217/94/31

Arab support for the Palestine Arabs against British Zionist policy.[1] The Palestine issue and that of Arab federation came to be viewed in the wider context of Anglo-Arab relations. Serious consideration was given to Ibn Sa'ud's warning in 1937 that the Arabs, if not given "reasonable satisfaction" with regard to Palestine, might turn in desperation to the Axis. The British policy-makers were obviously in a dilemma and were caught between Arab and Zionist pressures. They had to steer their course without risking a major break with either side.[2]

The acceptance by the British Government of the recommendations of the Royal Commission of 1937 meant in fact a veering on the official plane towards a limited federal solution to the Palestine problem. The whole question was viewed by the Commission as one of resurgent nationalism. The proposals were obviously based on the belief that Arab aspirations for unity were strong and genuine. By realizing for the Palestine Arabs some form of unity, of which their incorporation in Transjordan was to be the first step, a scheme of partition favouring the Jews in the coastal and more fertile parts of Palestine might be made acceptable to them. The idea of a federal solution to the Palestine problem had its supporters within the British Cabinet even after a decision was taken in 1938 to drop partition. Malcolm MacDonald was to state, early in November 1938, that in the long run any satisfactory solution for the Palestine problem would "probably" depend upon Palestine being joined in some kind of federation with "certain neighbouring countries". He envisaged the inclusion of Syria and Lebanon in such a federation, and considered as "unfortunate" the refusal of the French to allow representatives from either country to attend the proposed London Round Table Conference. The prospect of the formation of such a federation would, he maintained, make the Arabs more likely to

---

[1] FO 371–20806–E2158/22/31

[2] It should be noted that this was also a period of mounting world tensions following Hitler's annexation of Austria and claims on Czechoslovakia. The British government were eager to avert the eruption of a world war unless their interests were directly threatened. The Jews had their fears of a British let-down, and the new Colonial Secretary, MacDonald, did not rule out the possibility of the cessation of Jewish immigration if war broke out, in order to placate the Arabs. In his meeting with Chaim Weizmann and David Ben Gurion on 19 September 1938, MacDonald pointed to the strength of neighbouring Arab reactions and the threat involved to British vital interests in the area. He was worried in particular about the attitude of King Ibn Sa'ud in view of his "tremendous influence in the Moslem world and in India". If Ibn Sa'ud declared a holy war, MacDonald stated, "he could rock the Empire". He stressed the necessity of getting Ibn Sa'ud to reconcile himself to the Jewish National Home. An agreement was therefore necessary with him. The Colonial Secretary then suggested that the Zionist leaders should try to reach such an agreement with the King on the model of the Faisal–Weizmann abortive agreement of January 1919. Both Weizmann and Ben Gurion were strongly against any deference to the wishes of the neighbouring Arab leaders, for obvious reasons, and thought that Ibn Sa'ud was only after territorial expansion while the other Arabs were busy with their own affairs. David Ben Gurion *Letters to Paula*, pp. 167–79

agree to allow the Jews to have control over a larger area of Palestine than they would otherwise be prepared to concede. This long-term solution would be supplemented by an immediate one providing for local autonomy for the Jews and the Arabs in Palestine.[1] This was in fact the general tenor of Nuri's and Lord Samuel's proposals, except with regard to Jewish immigration, which he suggested should be regulated by a federal authority controlled by the British.

French opposition to the inclusion of Syria and Lebanon in any scheme of Arab federation represented the first real difficulty for the British. Syria was the original centre of the Arab nationalist movement. She was the most developed country in Arab Asia both culturally and economically. It was on her rather than on the backward Emirate of Transjordan that the eyes of the Palestine Arabs were set. Any scheme which excluded her was bound, therefore, to lose much of its appeal to them. An eventual association with Syria was envisaged both in the Report of the Royal Commission (Peel), and in MacDonald's statements to the Cabinet in November 1938. The idea of an Arab federation including Syria was also commended in the British press as providing the best solution for the Palestine problem.

The contents of the Report of the Royal Commission and British press reports did not fail to arouse French objections and suspicions. Several representations were made to the British Government in this regard. Pan-Arabism, they argued, was a "serious danger". They were against an Arab federation even if Syria was to be excluded, since such a federation, if established, "would act as a magnet and augment disquiet and agitation in Syria".[2] They were hardly convinced by the British argument that Pan-Arabism as an idea would grow in strength, making it "both ineffective and imprudent" to show lack of sympathy with it. They were not ready to compromise their position in Syria in order to help the British to solve their problems in Palestine. The preoccupation of the Arab nationalists with the Palestine issue provided a not unwelcome diversion for the French. The French, who were always placed at a disadvantage by the more liberal British policies in Iraq, Egypt, and Transjordan, did not fail to play on the fears of the Syrian nationalists of Jewish expansion to Syria within a British-dominated federation.[3]

The second real difficulty for the British was in the strong Sa'udi objections to the creation of any federation under Hashimite domination. These objections were to be expressed forcefully in February 1939

---

[1] FO 371–21865: Cabinet conclusions 52 (38), 2 November 1938

[2] FO 371–20814: conversation in Geneva on 13 September 1937 between Sir John Shuckburgh (CO) and a senior member of the French delegation; and 21883–E6341/6389/65: meeting between the French Ambassador and Sir Lancelot Oliphant (FO) on 28 October 1938

[3] Sir Harold MacMichael, the High Commissioner for Palestine, was to convey in 1941 reports about large-scale Jewish infiltration into Syria organized by the Jewish Agency's satellite organizations. Sir Harold to CO, 27 August 1941, FO 371–24124

in reaction to Nuri's attempt to advocate, while in London to attend the Round Table Conference, a Palestine settlement through the establishment of an Arab federation. Nuri, Ibn Sa'ud stated, wanted to add other territories to Iraq so as to attain preponderance over the other Arab states. This would, the King maintained, be objectionable, since it would disturb the current balance of power in the Arab World. His picture of the Arab World as it eventually ought to be was a group of independent states united by some such alliance as then "united" Iraq and Saudi Arabia. He wanted Palestine to be independent, "but not independent of H.M.G.". He added that if H.M.G. were prepared to accept Nuri's scheme, then they should give him a secret intimation "so that he may adjust his policy accordingly". Ibn Sa'ud's views were known to the British even before that, and his attitude was one of the main factors weighing on their consideration of the various federal schemes put forward by Nuri, Lord Samuel, and others. Lord Halifax, the Foreign Secretary, in an attempt to reassure Amir Faisal, who was then in London, went so far as to state that H.M.G. had never entertained such an idea, if only for the reason that they regarded a Palestine settlement as urgent, and any future creation of an Arab federation as a matter for a "distant and unforeseeable future".[1]

THE AFTERMATH OF THE PALESTINE ARAB REVOLT 1939 to 1941

An uneasy truce prevailed in Palestine following the outbreak of the war in September 1939. The Arabs and the Jews agreed to stop all disturbances for the duration of the war. Both sides continued in the meantime to press for the modification of the provisions of the White Paper. The assumption by Winston Churchill of the Premiership of Britain in May 1940 aroused fresh Arab apprehensions. Churchill was known for his pro-Zionist sympathies, and was one of the strong critics of the White Paper policy. One of his early decisions was to take no action to carry out the constitutional provisions of the White Paper; no public reference was to be made to this, so as not to provoke the Jews or to arouse fresh controversies. Its cancellation was not considered expedient, in view of possible Arab reactions. The general trend was to play it down until such time as it could be dropped altogether.

In Syria and Lebanon, the nationalists had a serious setback with the refusal of the French early in 1939 to ratify the 1936 treaties. This was followed by the resignation of the nationalist regimes and the instalment in power of pro-French governments. The French, unaffected by the

[1] FO 371–21869: Sir Reader Bullard to Lord Halifax, 28 November 1938; and 23224: Sir Reader to Lord Halifax on 18 February 1939 and record of meeting between Amir Faisal and Lord Halifax on 20 February 1938

wider considerations of imperial interests which dictated the British conciliatory move in Palestine, saw in the rising world tensions their chance to tighten their control over the two states. The picture did not look at all bright to the Arab nationalists, whose efforts during the past twenty-five years to achieve Arab independence and unity had come to naught. There was a general feeling of despondency and frustration, which developed among the young militant elements into a desire to adopt alternative methods of action and to look for alternative sources of support. It was the fate of Iraq to be the testing ground for this new approach. Iraq had been, since the days of King Faisal I, the centre of the Arab nationalist movement. She was viewed as the Prussia of the Arab East, which, in view of her early independence and the relative strength of her army, was thought to be in a position to help in the achievement of Arab aspirations. Several factors accounted for the drift towards extremism and the gradual weakening and isolation of the moderate and pro-British elements in Iraq.[1]

There was first the increasing intervention of the Iraqi army in politics. The four powerful Colonels known as "the Golden Square", led by Salah ud-Din As-Sabbagh, emerged from 1938 onwards as the real power in Baghdad. Nuri Pasha, in his conspiratorial meetings with them late in 1938, assured them, in return for engineering his return to office, of his loyalty to the pan-Arab ideals and his agreement that the army "should decide on the appointment and formation of Cabinets".[2] Nuri's efforts later on to curb their influence, by a combination of intrigue and divisive tactics, came to naught.

The four Colonels and their supporters inside and outside the army represented a new generation of Arab nationalists, with all their frustrations and craving for change. They had no serious grievances against the British in Iraq herself. Their eyes were set, however, on the Arab World at large. Salah ud-Din As-Sabbagh was born in Iraq in 1899 of a Lebanese father and a Nejdi mother. The facts of his birth and upbringing contributed to the evolution of his pan-Arab orientation. He was an idealist with great ambitions, a fertile imagination, and a strong belief in the possibility of the establishment of an Arab Empire. The

---

[1] The extreme elements saw in the circumstances of the war and British need for Arab support a unique chance to try to extract concessions with regard to Palestine and Syria. They argued that if Britain responded favourably to their demands, they would support her actively in the war. Failing that, Iraq should adopt a neutral line similar to that of Turkey, at least until the outcome of the war in North Africa and the attitude of Russia became clear. Nuri, on the other hand, had no doubts about an eventual Allied victory. He appreciated in 1940 that America would soon enter the war on the side of Britain and that Hitler would soon turn against Russia, leaving the Allies in a better position. Osman Kamal Haddad *Harakat Rashid 'Ali al Kilani 1941*, Sidon (n.d.), p. 7; and Mahmud al-Durra *Al Harb al 'Iraqiya al Biritaniya 1941*, Beirut 1969, pp. 141–2

[2] Salah ud-Din As-Sabbagh *Fursan al 'Uruba fi al 'Iraq*, Damascus 1956, p. 70

Iraqi army occupied a central position in his scheme[1], and he was responsible for supplying arms and training facilities to the Palestine Arabs during their revolt, behind the back of the Iraqi Government. He also tried to induce the Syrian nationalists to stage a revolt against the French with Iraqi military assistance. As an idealist, he tended to overlook many facts about the weakness of the Iraqi army and the fragmented nature of Iraqi society, with its minority and tribal problems. He did not have much experience in foreign politics, and had little knowledge of the configuration of forces on the world scene.

The second factor was the general pan-Arab effervescence in Iraq and the espousal by the general public of the pan-Arab ideals. Several Muslim and Arab societies had proliferated since the mid-thirties, foremost among which was the Muthana Club, founded in 1935 with a strong following from among the Syrian and Palestinian teachers in Baghdad. The educational authorities were very much attracted by the rising power of Germany, for which the Nazi methods of indoctrinating the youth were credited. The Iraqi youth movement *Al Futuwa* was reorganized in 1937 on lines similar to those of the Nazi *Jugend*, adopting the same uniform. Pan-Arab ideas and ideals were fostered in the educational curricula.[2] The Palestine Arab revolt stimulated public interest in Arab affairs in general. Pan-Arabism ceased to be the sole game of Iraqi veteran politicians like Nuri Pasha al-Sa'id, who were actuated mainly by the desire to gain political prestige for themselves and to further Hashimite ambitions in Syria and Palestine. An increasing number of Iraqis of radical views were drawn into the movement, which began to have a firm basis on the grass root level of Iraqi society.

The third factor was the arrival in Baghdad in October 1939 of the Mufti of Jerusalem, Haj Amin al-Husseini, from his enforced residence under French surveillance in Lebanon. The Mufti was well received by the Iraqi Government, and the four Colonels found him in agreement with them "on Arab ideals and national goals". They were attracted by his personality and were soon to establish "brotherly ties" with him, pledging to follow his path.[3] A year after his arrival in Baghdad, the

---

[1] Fritz Grobba, the German Minister in Baghdad, stated that As-Sabbagh believed that the Iraqi army could, with German air support and its own weapons, not only drive the British out of Iraq, but also occupy Palestine and Transjordan. Translated parts of Grobba's *Memoirs* in Najda Fathi Safwat *Al 'Iraq fi Mudhakkirat ad Diplumasiyin al Ajanib*, Sidon 1969, p. 165

[2] George Kirk, "The Middle East in War" in *The Survey 1939–1946*, London, RIIA, 1953, p. 58; and Majid Khadduri *Independent Iraq: A Study of Iraqi Politics since 1932*, London 1951, pp. 160–1. Of the said societies we can mention the Muslim Guidance Society, the Palestine Defence Society, the Arab Rover Society. *A Short History of Enemy Subversive Activities in Iraq 1935–1941*, published by the American Christian Defence Committee, New York (n.d.), p. 33

[3] Salah ud-Din As-Sabbagh *Fursan al'Uruba*, p. 109

Mufti was described by the American Minister in Baghdad as "the most highly respected and influential individual in Iraq today, both in religious and political circles".[1]

The Mufti had his serious grievances against the British, and it was mainly due to his influence that the Iraqi-centred pan-Arab movement began to take a strong anti-British turn. He had made up his mind before coming to Baghdad about the necessity of resorting to the Axis powers for assistance. He did not find much difficulty in winning the four Colonels to his plan for future action. An Arab Committee was formed in Baghdad early in 1940 under his chairmanship, with the membership of the four Colonels, Rashid 'Ali al-Kilani, Naji al-Suwaidi, Naji Shawkat, and Yunus al-Saba'awi. They decided to initiate contacts with the Axis powers and laid the bases for future Arab–Axis collaboration.[2] The assumption by Rashid 'Ali of the premiership on 31 March strengthened the Mufti group, from which all moderate elements like Nuri Pasha were excluded.

The fall of France in June 1940 and the entry of Italy into the war on the side of Germany removed all doubts and hesitations and gave the impression of an assured Axis victory. In all their subsequent contacts with the Axis powers, the Mufti group tried to obtain support for specific demands approved by the Arab Committee. They asked for a recognition of the full independence of the Arab countries already independent or under the mandate, as well as the non-independent colonies or protectorates such as Kuwait, Oman, Musqat, and Hadramawt. They also asked for an Axis pledge to recognize the right of these countries to establish their national unity, and to abstain from imposing any mandates over the area. They demanded the non-recognition of the Jewish National Home in Palestine and support for the right of the Arabs to find a just settlement for the Palestine problem in accordance with Arab national interests. They asked the Axis powers, moreover, to renounce any imperialist designs on Egypt and the Sudan and to recognize the independence of these two countries. They offered, in return, to restore diplomatic relations, severed in 1939, between Iraq and Germany, and to give German interests preference in the exploitation of Iraqi oil. They also offered to adhere first to strict neutrality, and to attempt later to spur from Syria a general uprising in Palestine and Transjordan, for which arms from the stocks of the French army in Syria would be

[1] State Department, *Foreign Relations of the United States*, 1940 vol. III, Washington D.C., Government Printing Office, 1959, p. 713 (hereafter referred to as F.R. of U.S.)

[2] *Documents on German Foreign Policy*, series D, vol. X, London, HMSO, 1957, p. 560 (hereafter referred to as D.G.F.P.): a statement by the Mufti's Secretary Haddad to Grobba in Berlin on 27 August 1940. Both Naji Shawkat and Naji al-Suwaidi became Ministers in Rashid 'Ali's Cabinet of March 1940. Yunus al-Saba'awi was one of the most militant deputies in the Iraqi Parliament and was to become a Minister in Rashid 'Ali's Government of National Defence of April 1941.

needed.[1] This confirmed the outward-looking nature of the movement and showed the strong influence of the Mufti over the whole group.

The fourth factor was the eagerness of the Axis powers to gain influence in the Middle East, if only to threaten British vital interests and to disrupt the British lines of communications with the rest of their Empire. The Germans were, up to September 1939, rather reluctant to play an active role in the area, first out of regard for British susceptibilities and uncertainty about the strength of the anti-British elements in Baghdad, and later out of regard for Italian desire to have absolute precedence in dealing with the Arabs.[2] The failure of the Italians to make any headway in their efforts to gain influence in the area because of Arab suspicions of their imperialist designs was coupled with serious Italian reverses on the Libyan front. It was at that time that Germany had abandoned the idea of the invasion of England. With the invasion of Russia being put off until the spring, there was time to conduct operations in the Middle East. It was then that the Germans decided to intervene militarily on the side of the Italians on the Libyan front.

The Germans began to have second thoughts about their earlier policy of giving "absolute precedence" to Italy in the area. The Italians realized the necessity of German support to avert the defeat of their forces in Libya. They yielded on 23 October 1940 to German wishes and agreed reluctantly to issue, together with Germany, a declaration, couched in very general and non-committal terms, of sympathy with the Arab struggle for independence.[3] This declaration fell far short of what the Arabs had asked for, and the Mufti did not hide his disappointment at its contents.

It was from December 1940 onwards that the Germans began to take the whole matter into their hands. The British had by then consolidated their position in Egypt following the ousting of 'Ali Maher Pasha from power in June, and were intensifying their pressure on Rashid 'Ali. A German Foreign Ministry memorandum prepared in December stressed that German strategic interests in the Eastern Mediterranean required that Germany, without giving up the principle of Italian precedence,

---

[1] *D.G.F.P.*, series D, vol. X, pp. 558–60, and Osman Kamal Haddad *Harakat* pp. 29–31

[2] The Germans counted until 1939 on British acceptance of their expansion in Central Europe and stressed the necessity "under no circumstances" to put Anglo-German relations under an unnecessary strain. Another factor was what they considered as "the political unreliability of the Arabs", who were torn by dynastic and sectarian feuds with their prominent rulers like Ibn Sa'ud being viewed as subservient to the British. After the outbreak of the war they decided to give absolute precedence to Italy and to renounce "any German claim to leadership in the Arabian area or a division of that claim with Italy". *D.G.F.P.*, series D, vol. X, p. 261 and vol. V, pp. 761–4

[3] Lukasz Hirszowicz, *The Third Reich and the Arab East*, London 1966, pp. 79–91 for a detailed study of the Arab–Axis contacts during this period

should become more active in the area. Germany, it was stated, had always seen in Arab nationalism "her natural ally", whereas Italy found it "irksome" and refused to recognize in writing the full independence, and the right to unite, of the Arab countries. All Italian public statements of sympathy with Arab aspirations were described as "merely propaganda".[1] The fall of Rashid 'Ali from power on 30 January 1941, as a result of British pressure, was a blow to the Mufti group. It was feared that measures would soon be taken to liquidate the power of the four Colonels. It was then that the Germans prepared a plan for action in support of the anti-British elements in Baghdad. Direct military assistance was ruled out at that stage because of Turkish neutrality, and the fact that the area was beyond the effective range of the German air force. Other alternatives were favoured. These included public expressions of Axis sympathy with Arab aspirations and the renunciation by Germany of any territorial ambitions in the area. They also included the provision of financial assistance and military supplies, and the stepping up of propaganda and intelligence activities.

A declaration of support for the establishment of a Great Arab Empire was ruled out for the time being because of Arab rivalries, Italian opposition, Turkish aversion, and the need to give no impetus to the Gaullist movement by appearing to favour an end to French presence in the Levant. It was stressed in the meantime that an open rebellion against Britain in Iraq "should not be actively promoted until the moment is conducive to success". A letter was handed to the Mufti on 8 April expressing readiness to support the Arabs militarily and financially "in so far as is possible" if they were forced to fight Britain in order to achieve their national aims. Italy, in agreeing reluctantly to the text of this letter, stressed that she should enjoy in the Arab World the position then enjoyed by Britain.[2]

It was at that time that the four Colonels had engineered the resignation of Taha al-Hashimi, the new Prime Minister, and pressed the Regent, who refused and left Baghdad, to reappoint Rashid 'Ali to the post. The German letter came a week after the crisis had started and was obviously intended to strengthen the position of the Iraqi nationalists, who went a step further by deposing the Regent and setting up a provisional National Defence Government under Rashid 'Ali. This triggered off prematurely the crisis which was to destroy the hopes of the Iraqi pan-Arabs.

The fifth factor was the refusal of the British to make any concessions with regard to Palestine and Arab aspirations in general. The British were naturally worried at the drift into extremism in Iraq. They had had several warning signals from their representatives in the area since 1939. Nuri Pasha was equally worried, and saw the danger to himself from

[1] *D.G.F.P.*, series D, vol. XI, pp. 826–9
[2] *D.G.F.P.*, series D, vol. XII, pp. 234–43, 489

the growing power of the Mufti group, from which he was excluded as being too pro-British to be of any real help. He pressed the British to issue a "clear and unambiguous" pronouncement guaranteeing immediately, or at the end of the war, the execution of promises already given with regard to self-government in Palestine and Syria. He saw in this the only way to counter Axis intrigues and to check the pro-Axis trend in Iraq. The British Cabinet under Churchill were against any concessions and refused even to make any public reaffirmation of their White Paper policy on Palestine.[1]

With political concessions being ruled out, the only alternative left was to intensify propaganda activities. Colonel Stewart Newcombe, an old hand on Arab affairs with many friends in Baghdad, was sent to Iraq in July 1940 at the suggestion of Lord Lloyd, the then Colonial Secretary. Newcombe's visit was welcomed both by Nuri and by Rashid 'Ali. Hopes were aroused about a more conciliatory British policy in the area. Newcombe went to Baghdad, however, with his hands tied. His visit was to be unofficial, but "a considerable sum of money" was placed at his disposal "to assist him in securing influence over certain newspapers and important personalities and over the Baghdad broadcasting station". He was instructed "to deal firmly" with any suggestion about the modification of the White Paper, and was told that the Mufti and his associates would be excluded "indefinitely" from Palestine.[2] Newcombe was therefore given no other means of persuasion and political influence except bribes and subsidies.

It was then that Nuri had intensified his pan-Arab activities in an attempt to outbid and take the wind out of the sails of the Mufti group. He urged the British again to issue a declaration of sympathy with Arab aspirations for unity, or to take an initiative "to set the closer-union ball rolling". He proposed a comprehensive scheme for Arab federation which included Iraq, Palestine, and Transjordan. Syria was excluded, but he felt that if the federation took shape she would drop into it "like a ripe date". He also suggested some modifications in the constitutional

---

[1] Cab. 67/6–W.P.G. (40) 149: memorandum by the Foreign Secretary dated 12 June 1940 on *The Arab States and Palestine*, in which it was stated that any renunciation of the White Paper policy at this juncture of the war would be "fatal". The Foreign Secretary, Lord Halifax, was in favour of giving assurances to Nuri regarding H.M.G.'s intention to carry it out. He was soon, however, to change his attitude, presumably as a result of Churchill's objections, and to take a stiffer line, avoiding any reference to the White Paper. This new line was approved by the War Cabinet in July 1940. (Minute by Luke, CO 733–444–75872/85/1940)

[2] FO 371–24549: Lord Lloyd to Sir Harold MacMichael, 22 June 1940. Colonel Newcombe was described by Rendel as one of the closest associates of T. E. Lawrence in the Great Arab Revolt. He conducted in 1914 a survey of Southern Palestine and was appointed in 1921 as senior British representative in the Syrio-Palestine Boundary Commission. In 1936 he tried unsuccessfully with Philby to get Foreign Office support for a scheme for a transport monopoly in Saudi Arabia. He had evolved ever since several schemes for a Palestine settlement. FO 371–21885

provisions of the White Paper to allow of the earlier establishment of self-government and the choice of an Arab ruler for Palestine. Nuri stated that Iraq, in return, would be ready to make a gesture of solidarity with the British by sending an Iraqi division led by Colonel As-Sabbagh to the Libyan front, which would keep the army busy and thus ease the internal situation.[1]

Colonel Newcombe, in communicating the results of his contacts with Nuri, Rashid 'Ali, and the other members of the Mufti group, urged his government to take "some positive and constructive steps" to conciliate the Arabs. He suggested that H.M.G. should at least declare their support for a closer union, federal or economic, of any Arab states which might eventually desire it. In such a union, Iraq and Saudi Arabia, he argued, would be able to use their influence to silence anti-British propaganda regarding Palestine. Sir Basil Newton, the Ambassador in Baghdad, as well as Sir Miles Lampson, expressed agreement with this suggestion.

The British Government took a completely negative attitude. They were worried at the possible Jewish reactions to any conciliatory policy towards the Arabs. The British military in the area were likewise against any concessions on Palestine at that stage for fear of Jewish disorders. Colonel Newcombe, by suggesting some concessions to the Arabs, seemed to have gone too far, and his mission was terminated on 20 August 1940. Sir Basil Newton was instructed to make it clear to all concerned that the British policy in Palestine was "fixed" and "cannot be changed to meet Jewish or Arab wishes".[2]

The collapse of the Newcombe mission further weakened the moderate and pro-British elements, leaving the Mufti group more resolute than ever to proceed further with their contacts with the Axis powers. Nuri did not achieve any success either in his efforts to win support for his ideas during his visits to Syria, Transjordan, and Egypt late in June

---

[1] FO 371–24549: Sir Basil Newton on 3 August 1940. Nuri had in fact put forward his scheme to the British after the conclusion of the meetings of the London Round Table Conference as an alternative in case the White Paper terms were rejected by the Arabs. [CO 733–410–75872/80/1939] Colonel As-Sabbagh stated that Nuri's ideas appealed to him but that he mistrusted British policy and was doubtful of an eventual British victory in view of the Soviet and Japanese attitude and American reluctance to enter the war. He added, however, that he would have agreed to send an Iraqi division to Syria if adequate promises regarding Palestine and Syria were given by the British. Salah ud-Din As-Sabbagh *Fursan al'Uruba*, pp. 148–56

[2] FO 371–24549: the Foreign Office were in fact not at all happy about the visit to Baghdad of Newcombe, who was described by Sir Harold MacMichael as "an ardent advocate of the Arab cause". They thought that it could do more harm than good, which was borne out by later events. The Arabs of the Mufti group and even Nuri spoke of an understanding with Newcombe on a Palestine settlement, which H.M.G. went back on. This was also mentioned by Musa al-'Alami, the Palestine Arab delegate during the Preparatory Committee meeting in Alexandria in October 1944, to which reference will be made later.

and early in July. British representations were made to the Egyptian and Sa'udi Governments to throw cold water on Nuri's pan-Arab schemes. When he returned to Baghdad, he was found by Sir Basil "depressed and uncommunicative".[1]

The Rashid 'Ali *coup* of April 1941 was the outcome of these five factors combined. The new Provisional Government of National Defence excluded Nuri Pasha and all pro-British elements. It was described by the Germans as "the most nationalist and pro-Axis thus far".[2] Yet it was, as rightly noted by Sir Kinahan Cornwallis, the new British Ambassador, the government of the "Golden Square" and not one of Rashid 'Ali relying on the unqualified support of the army. As a politician of practised cunning and a considerable following, Rashid 'Ali was, however, more than a figurehead. Yet indispensable as he was to the four Colonels, he was far from all-powerful.[3]

The British decision to intensify political and economic pressure on Rashid 'Ali and to intervene militarily in May 1941 forestalled the moves of the Iraqi nationalists. Rashid 'Ali's appeals for urgent German assistance were not promptly responded to at a time when the Axis powers were heavily engaged in Greece and later in Crete. His downfall was brought about at the end of May, with himself, the four Colonels, and the Mufti and his associates leaving the country in haste. Sir Kinahan was to report that the Iraqi resistance was "unexpectedly vigorous" and that feelings in the towns "ran high in support of the movement".[4]

The Rashid 'Ali movement was the first Arab national uprising of note since the First World War. It was a movement in which nationalists from Palestine and Syria took an active part, and which had the general support of the Arab public all over the area. Resort to the Axis powers for assistance was meant as a temporary expedient. All contacts with these powers centred on the need to obtain double assurances of support for Arab independence and unity. The whole situation was reminiscent of that which had preceded the Great Arab Revolt in 1916. This time the Arab nationalists were more careful, and insisted on having clear and definite pledges covering all the territories of Arab Asia as well as Egypt and the Sudan. They had their suspicions of Italian designs and counted more on German assurances and support. They were impressed by the Axis' profuse expressions of sympathy for Arab aspirations and were sure at least to achieve a favourable solution

---

[1] FO 371–24593: Sir Basil Newton on 24 August 1940

[2] *D.G.F.P.*, series D, vol. XII, p. 527

[3] FO 371–31371. Salah As-Sabbagh drew his pistol, threatening Rashid 'Ali, in mid-May when he suggested that they should come to terms with Britain. Osman Kamal Haddad *Harakat*, p. 120

[4] FO 371–31371: Annual Report for 1941, and Sir Llewellyn Woodward *British Foreign Policy in the Second World War*, vol. I, London, HMSO, 1970, pp. 575–81

for the Palestine problem in case of Axis victory, which seemed to be certain after the collapse of France. The Mufti hoped that he might get a fair share of the spoils. He exercised great influence over the four Colonels and was sure to gain a position of prominence both in Palestine and in any future Arab federation.[1] The Arab nationalists in Baghdad were not unique in their efforts to seek Axis assistance. Some overtures to the Axis powers were made earlier by King Farouq of Egypt and in 1939 by King Ibn Sa'ud.[2] Even Nuri Pasha was to make some unsuccessful overtures to the Italian Minister in Baghdad and the Mufti group in an attempt to know what kind of assurances were given by the Axis powers.[3] Some Arab leaders thought it expedient, in view of the British reverses in the war, to reinsure and to keep an open channel of contact with the Axis to guard against all eventualities.

The Rashid 'Ali movement was also a gesture of defiance to Britain and to the existing state of affairs, which seemed to perpetuate Arab weakness and divisiveness. It was an attempt by the Arabs to convince themselves that they were capable of resolution and action. On its positive side, it was an attempt to reconstruct the Arab East and to provide its people with effective leadership and a sense of purpose. Its main weakness was in the fact that it was based on high ideals espoused by rather rash army officers and amateur politicians, who had so little grasp of the limitations of their own power, and of the disintegrative forces in the Arab World. Their action did not fail to turn Iraq into an arena for the deadly struggle between Britain and the Axis powers. Several errors were committed in timing the movement and in underestimating the resolve and the ability of the British to take effective counter-action. The failure of the Rashid 'Ali movement destroyed the myth of Iraqi Prussianism and marked the end of the Iraqi phase of the Arab nationalist movement.

BRITISH DIPLOMACY AND ARAB NATIONALISM

1921 to 1941

When faced with Arab nationalist resurgence in the immediate post-war period, the British adopted a policy which was resourceful and imaginative. They were quick to realize the negative nature of the movement which centred on opposition to Anglo-French domination

---

[1] Lord Harlech (formerly Ormsby-Gore) in a debate in the House of Lords on 8 December 1938 described the Mufti as "a man of quite unlimited political ambition" and said that his ultimate objective was "the foundation of a dynasty of the Husseinis" and "the domination of the Arab World". *Parliamentary Debates*, H. of L., 5th ser., vol. CXI, col. 442

[2] *D.G.F.P.*, series D, vol. V, pp. 800–10

[3] Majid Khadduri, "General Nuri's Flirtations with the Axis Powers" in *Middle East Journal*, vol. 16, no. 3, Summer 1962

and the balkanization of Arab Asia. They were determined at the same time to preserve their effective control with the least possible military and financial commitment. The Churchill–Faisal–'Abdullah understanding of 1921 was designed to ensure, through the lure of high office, the containment of the Arab nationalist movement, and the stabilization of the *status quo*. By installing nationalist regimes in Baghdad and Amman, they avoided focusing public discontent against their policies, and were placed in a more favourable position *vis-à-vis* the French, who were more for direct control and openly hostile to Arab nationalism.

The British line of policy during the inter-war period was based on a rather curious paradox. Arab nationalism was regarded as essentially a negative and disruptive force in Middle Eastern politics, which could easily assume dangerous xenophobic and strongly exclusive qualities. The consolidation of local nationalisms was seen as less dangerous to British interests. King Faisal I was discouraged from the pursuit of any policy designed to bring about the unification of the Arabs. They were eager at the same time to avoid showing any lack of sympathy with the idea of Arab unity as long as it remained an ideal and a dream. They were convinced that its realization was almost impossible, but they were careful to lay the blame on French objections and Ibn Sa'ud's opposition, as well as on the lack of agreement among the Arabs themselves as to the form it should take and the question of leadership within any future Arab union.

The revival of the pan-Arab activities in relation to Palestine from 1936 onwards introduced a new factor into the situation. Jewish and Arab pressures gave the problem its wider pan-Arab and international Jewish implications. The idea of an Arab federation under British influence began to have its appeal to some British officials as offering the best solution for the Palestine problem. This was a misconception which overlooked many basic factors in the situation. It ignored the fact that the aim of the Zionist movement at that stage was to ensure unlimited Jewish immigration and settlement in Palestine and, if possible, in Transjordan as well. This meant that the problem, rather than disappearing in a federation, would be more intense, and trouble would spread over a wider area. It also ignored the fact, stressed in the Report of the Royal Commission (Peel), that national independence within Palestine, on an equal footing with Iraq, Egypt, and Transjordan, was the main aim of the Palestine Arabs. Arab unity was to them the ultimate rather than the immediate goal. From a theoretical point of view, it would have been an anomaly in political thinking to devise a scheme of a general nature to solve a problem of so many ramifications as that of Palestine. The sponsors of the federal schemes ignored also the fact that Arab nationalism, like any nationalist movement, would militate against foreign influence and domination. British sponsorship and Zionist support would have been enough to make any scheme objectionable to the Arabs.

It was also in relation to Palestine that there began to emerge a new outlook to the area as an interrelated whole. The Arabs, stated George Rendel in 1937, were "notoriously improvident and disunited", but Arab nationalism was nevertheless "a reality of growing importance".[1] The French were told in 1937 that to attempt to oppose the idea of pan-Arabism or to show open lack of sympathy with it "would be likely to prove a policy as ineffective as it was imprudent".[2] There was definitely a change, which was noticeable even in the Colonial Office, which at least until the departure of Ormsby-Gore in May 1938 was traditionally suspicious of all pan-Arab activities, and anxious to insulate Palestine from neighbouring Arab influence. The change was, however, one of emphasis and did not imply any radical shift in the attitude towards Arab nationalism.

This new change of emphasis, rather than of policy, was discernible in a Foreign Office memorandum prepared in September 1939, which attempted a reassessment of British policy towards Arab unity.[3] This was the first detailed study of the issue, which makes it worthwhile to go into its contents and conclusions in some detail. It excluded Egypt, whose leaders were thought to have no interest in joining any Arab federation. It started by enumerating the positive and negative factors. On the positive side reference was made to the cohesive impact of a common religion, language, and culture as well as to the fact that the existing boundaries between Syria, Lebanon, Palestine, and Trans-jordan did not conform to natural geographical or economic divisions. The growing sense of Arab solidarity was attributed to the impact o these factors, and to more extensive education and easier communi-cations.

On the negative side reference was made to dynastic rivalries, sec-tarian and racial frictions, and the prevalence of loyalty to a certain tribe or area over loyalty to an Arab homeland. There were also the strong French objections based on the belief that in view of the more sympathetic attitude of Britain towards Arab aspirations, French influence in an Arab federation would be much less powerful than that of Britain. Turkey had also its expansionist designs on Syria and Iraq, and was thought likely to oppose the creation of an Arab federation as representing an obstacle in this regard.

---

[1] FO 371–20816: memorandum by George Rendel on "Palestine Policy of H.M.G." dated 25 October 1937

[2] FO 371–21839: Eden's note handed to the French Ambassador in London on 20 October 1939, whose contents were conveyed again to the French government during Lord Halifax's visit to Paris late in 1938

[3] FO 371–23239: memorandum on "Arab Federation" prepared by Lord Bag-gallay on 28 September 1939

As for the British attitude, it was stated that H.M.G. had their own reservations with regard to the formation of an Arab federation. The protection of British vital interests in communications and oil required that Britain should continue to conduct her relations with the Middle Eastern states "through varying degrees of protection, alliance, and friendship". It also required the maintenance of effective control over certain vital points such as Haifa, the Suez Canal, Aden, the Persian Gulf, and the Basra–Haifa air route. The memorandum admitted that there was some truth in the argument that a single greater-Arab state would be less amenable to British influence than a number of small and weak states. It was therefore considered unlikely that Britain would of her own accord ever wish actively to promote and encourage pan-Arab ideas even if there were no dynastic rivalries involved, and even if the attitude of the French Government left her free to do so.

Pan-Arabism was considered, however, a phenomenon in Middle Eastern politics "which has probably come to stay". This being so, any attempt to oppose the idea which it embodied, as opposed to any particular manifestation of that idea, would be "not only ineffective but also extremely unwise". H.M.G., it was added, had therefore taken the line that while they would be unwilling to take any initiative which they believed should come from the Arabs themselves, they would endeavour to avoid displaying active opposition or open lack of sympathy for Arab unity, and try instead to guide the movement on lines friendly to Britain. This policy, the memorandum concluded, represented "the least and also the most" that H.M.G. could decide or do for the moment. Any positive declaration of sympathy with Arab unity should be avoided "as long as possible".

These conclusions were endorsed by British representatives in the area and by the War Office, which cast doubts on the existence of a common Arab culture or a common racial origin.[1] Even the most sympathetic among them, like Sir Basil Newton, the Ambassador in Baghdad, were not ready to go as far as to recommend a British initiative at that stage. All of them underlined the adverse effects of a policy unacceptable to the Arabs in Palestine. Such a policy, stated Sir Reader Bullard, the former Minister in Jedda who was then Ambassador in Tehran, would make it difficult for the British to exercise much influence on the Arab nationalist movement since "anti-Jewish" feeling "will to a large extent take the form of pan-Arabism". This, he maintained, would "hasten the time when the problem of Arab federation, which we should like to postpone, must be faced".[2]

No departure from previous policies was recommended, and the paradox underlying the British attitude, which was negative with a sympathetic cover, was maintained. Having stressed the necessity for

[1] FO 371–23195: letter from the War Office, October 1939

[2] FO 371–24548: Sir Reader Bullard to Viscount Halifax, 11 January 1940

the continuation of British presence and effective control in the area, this was only natural, since any encouragement of Arab nationalism would certainly endanger foreign interests and influence. There was, however, a noticeable change of emphasis. The Arab nationalist movement began to be taken more seriously as a force in Arab politics. The prescription was, rather than attempt to obstruct its path, to try to guide it along lines friendly to H.M.G.

Chapter Two

Egypt's Arab Policy 1915 to 1941

Some writers trace Egypt's interest in Arab affairs to the days of Ibrahim Pasha, son of Muhammad 'Ali, who led the Egyptian invasion of the Levant in 1831, and who expressed the desire to unite all the Arabs under his father's leadership. This overlooks the fact that Muhammad 'Ali himself was not an Arab, never spoke Arabic, and used to look down on Egyptians and Arabs alike. Sheer personal ambition was his main motive, and the conquest of the Levant was for him a political, strategic, and economic necessity.

Other writers discern in the 'Urabi movement of 1881–2 some pan-Arab tendencies, for the demonstration of which they quote one of its leaders, Mahmoud Sami al-Barudi, as saying that their aim was to establish a republic with which Syria and later the Hejaz could be united. Yet it was this same movement which took as its slogan "Egypt for the Egyptians" and which stressed more than once its loyalty to Ottoman authority. The main emphasis was on achieving equality between the Egyptians, relegated to second-class citizens in their own country, and the privileged non-Egyptian minorities.

Active Egyptian interest in Arab affairs was in fact a rather recent phenomenon. The distinct national evolution of Egypt, with its unique dependence on the Nile, distinguished her from the territories of Arab Asia, whose national identities were blurred since the Islamic conquest. In its modern history Egypt had maintained direct and constant contacts with Europe, which contributed to the evolution of a secular and rather exclusive basis for its nationalist movement. The British occupation of Egypt in 1882 confirmed this trend by imposing a separate path for the Egyptian national struggle for independence. The Egyptian leaders were against any diversions. Their main preoccupation was with the consolidation of national unity. Solidarity with the Arabs, who were weak, fragmented, and with no distinct national status, was ruled out since it was not likely to be of much help and would antagonize Turkey, which was sympathetic towards the Egyptian nationalist movement. The Great Arab Revolt was viewed in Egypt with suspicion for its break with Ottoman authority, which preserved at least a semblance of unity in the Arab World, and for its collaboration with the British. The pro-British leanings of the prominent members of the Syrian and Lebanese communities in Egypt, who owned most of the leading newspapers, were a constant source of irritation and resentment.[1] Having suffered from European encroachments long before the territories of Arab Asia, the Egyptians were more aware of the nature and extent of foreign ambitions in the area. The strong Islamic undercurrent in Egypt manifested itself in loyalty to the Caliphate as a symbol of Muslim unity. Arab unity was viewed by some, especially within Al-Azhar, as contrary to Islam's basic universalism. Islamic solidarity was seen by many as essential for effective resistance to European encroachments.

Prominent Arab visitors and expatriates in Egypt were struck by the unsympathetic and rather hostile attitude of Egyptian leaders towards the Arab nationalist movement. Shukri al-'Asali, the Syrian nationalist, did not find any support in Egypt in 1911 for his call for the unity of Syria and Egypt. The idea was dismissed by Ahmad Lutfi al-Sayyed, the Egyptian nationalist leader, as "impossible to achieve" and not in Egypt's interest to pursue.[2] Sa'ad Zaghlul Pasha was to tell the Arab leaders who approached him in 1919 with a view to concerting efforts in the Paris Peace Conference, that "our case is an Egyptian and not an Arab one". He was also to make his famous remark to 'Abdul Rahman 'Azzam, who was trying to win him to the idea of closer ties with Arab Asia, that "if you add zero to zero what will be the result?"[3] Sati' al-Husri found the Egyptians in 1920 "indifferent" to the developments in the neighbouring Arab countries, with some going even further and denouncing the Great Arab Revolt, "cursing its leaders and advocates".[4]

The post-war settlement and the subsequent national uprisings in Iraq (1920) and in Syria (1925) helped to clear the ground from some of the old suspicions. A new basis for mutual sympathies and community of interest in the struggle against foreign domination was established. Egypt was still, however, too much preoccupied with her own problems. Her nominal independence was declared by the British in February 1922, and the bases for democratic rule were laid down in the 1923 constitution. It soon became clear, however, that the British were far from ready to relinquish their effective control over Egypt, and that King Fu'ad was determined to assert his absolute authority.

[1] Criticism of the attitude of some prominent Syrians, especially the owners of *Al-Muqattam* newspaper, was voiced by Mustafa Kamel; Hafiz Ibrahim; Sheikh 'Ali Yusuf, editor of *Al Mua'yad*; and 'Abdullah al Nadim, editor of *Al 'ustaz*: Anis Sayigh *Al Fikrah al 'Arabiya fi Misr*, Beirut 1959, pp. 142–6

[2] Ahmed Lutfi al-Sayyed *Al Muntakhabat*, Cairo 1937, pp. 250–1

[3] Anis Sayigh *Al Fikrah*, p. 142

[4] Sati' al-Husri *'Ara' wa Ahadith fil Qawmiya al'Arabiya*, Beirut 1959, p. 17

Egyptian politics began to be dominated by a triangle of forces represented at one corner by the Wafd, the majority party in the country led by Sa'ad Zaghlul and after his death in 1927 by Mustafa al-Nahas, at the second corner by the Palace, with the British Residency representing the third and most powerful force and holding the balance, tipping it in favour of the Palace whenever the Wafd's agitation for independence was intensified, and in favour of the Wafd whenever the need for a treaty normalizing Anglo-Egyptian relations was felt in Whitehall. This configuration of forces imposed new strains on the Egyptian nationalist movement. The Wafd was kept out of office for most of the time and the 1923 Constitution was abrogated in 1930. The struggle against British domination was accompanied and sometimes overshadowed by the struggle against Palace autocracy. This did not leave much room for pursuing an active policy in the Arab World, especially since the Arab countries were not in a position to respond to any Egyptian initiative. Syria and Lebanon were under direct and effective French control. Iraq was too much occupied with her internal problems, while relations with Sa'udi Arabia were far from good after the Mahmal incident of 1926.[1]

It was only during the early thirties that issues related to Egypt's Arab orientation began to be raised by intellectuals and religious divines. The traditional religious centres of the time, represented by Al-Azhar, the Sufi sects, and the neo-Salafites of Al Manar school, stressed the Islamic, and hence the Arab, aspect of Egypt's culture and life. The secular elements such as Ahmed Lutfi al-Sayyed, Dr Taha Hussein, and Salama Mousa favoured a western orientation and stressed the historical impact of Mediterranean influences on Egyptian culture and life. They argued also for an equal emphasis on Egypt's Phara'onic past on the grounds that "a nation which has no past can have no future". Dr Taha Hussein called for a synthesis which should draw equally from Egypt's Phara'onic past with its persisting environmental influences, as well as from the Arabic heritage which had been "absorbed and Egyptianised" throughout the years, and the Western impact, which was strong in Egypt's modern life. Their argument revolved in essence around the glorification of Egypt, with its distinct national identity, its vitality, and its ability to absorb all other cultures without losing its specificity.

The secular elements were subject to fierce criticism at a time when the religious centres were still very strong. Ahmed Hassan al-Zayat, the

---

[1] Relations were actually severed on the official level with Sa'udi Arabia following that incident, during which some fanatic Wahhabi tribes attacked the Egyptian force guarding the Mahmal (the holy carpet for the Ka'ba), and the subsequent refusal of King Ibn Sa'ud to allow the Mahmal to proceed beyond Jedda. H. St. J. B. Philby *Arabian Jubilee*, 1st edn., New York 1953, pp. 89–90; *Al-Muqattam*, 11, 12, 13 May 1934

editor of *Al-Risalh*, blamed the Egyptian writers for carrying the controversy to extremes. This, he added, had worried the neighbouring Arabs, who thought that the Phara'onic idea had become an established belief; that three writers were speaking for a whole nation; and that Egypt, "the leader of the Arab World", had turned its minarets into obelisks, its mosques into temples, and its *'Ulema* into monks. Sheikh Rashid Rida, the editor of *Al Manar*, argued, on the other hand, that an Arab orientation for Egypt would assure her of leadership of the Arab World with all that this would mean in moral, political, and economic benefits. The renunciation of the Arab connection in favour of Phara'onism would, on the other hand, do Egypt no good either morally or materially.[1] The controversy, as stated earlier, was one in which intellectuals rather than politicians were interested. It helped, however, to clarify many issues, and the veering of many of the secular writers towards the admission of an Arab cultural orientation for Egypt in the subsequent years was reconciled with their firm belief in the necessity for establishing a secular and westernized basis for Egyptian culture and life.

The most impressive contribution to the promotion of Egyptian interest in Arab affairs was made, however, by the numerous pan-Eastern, Arab, and Islamic societies which were active during the thirties. There were strong Islamic and pan-Arab elements in the early societies, of which we may mention the Eastern Bond Association,[2] formed in 1922 under the presidency of the head of the Sufi sects, the General Arab Union,[3] founded in 1933, and the Arab Unity Society,[4] formed in 1930. A significant contribution was also made by the Arab professional congresses, foremost among which were the annual Arab Medical Congresses.[5] The periodical meetings, discussions, and publications sponsored by these societies were given wide coverage in the press. They contributed much towards the education of the general public in Arab affairs.

The Islamic organizations were also very effective in this regard. They had their strong appeal to the public at a time when the masses,

[1] For material on this controversy see Dr Muhammad Hussein Haykal *Thawrat al-Adab*, 3rd edn., Cairo 1965, p. 134; *Al Manar*, Part 6, vol. 31, p. 465; *Al Siasa*, Literary Supplement, 29 September 1933; *Al-Hilal*, vol. 6, 39th year, 1 April 1931, pp. 818–21; *Al-Risalh*, no. 11, 1st year, 15 June 1933 and no. 18, 1st year, 1 October 1933

[2] *Majallat al Rabita al Sharqiya*, 1st issue, 1st year, 15 October 1929 and 6th issue, 15 June 1929, for a detailed account of the constitution and activities of this Association

[3] *Al-Muqattam*, 4 November 1933

[4] Ibid., 15 June 1931

[5] The Medical Congress was exclusively Egyptian up to 1931, when it was decided to hold the fifth Congress in Beirut and to invite medical doctors from the other Arab countries to participate. Its name became henceforth the "Arab Medical Congress".

and especially the politically conscious among them, were disenchanted with the existing system, which meant nothing but deprivation for the majority while the privileged few consolidated their wealth and influence. For them the democratic experiment in Egypt had proved an utter failure, and they were ready to espouse alternative ideologies and methods of action. The Islamic movements, with their comprehensive economic and social reform programmes and their radical approach, provided the alternative for most of these elements.[1]

The first of these organizations was the Young Men's Muslim Association, founded in 1927 by Dr 'Abdul Hamid Sa'id, with a prominent Syrian journalist, Muhib ul-Din al-Khatib, as its Secretary-General. Its aims included the teaching of Islamic ethics, the discouragement of dissension, and the fight for the revival of the glories of Islam through the adoption of its rules. Its founders were keen on extending its activities to the neighbouring Arab countries. By 1929, it had twenty branches in Syria, Iraq, and Palestine.[2] It was very active in marshalling support for the Arab cause in Palestine, Syria, and in North Africa.

The second and largest Islamic organization was the Muslim Brotherhood. Founded in 1928 by a non-Azharite teacher, Hasan al-Banna, it had by 1934 fifty branches in Egypt with a following that was estimated in 1946 at one and a half million.[3] Its main principles were the return to the Shari'a (Muslim law), the establishment of an Islamic state with an Islamic constitution, a pure life for the individual, and the abolition of all political parties as sources of strife. The impact of the Muslim Brotherhood on the enhancement of Egyptian interest in Arab affairs was twofold: conceptual and practical.

On the conceptual side, Al-Banna tried to reconcile the basic universalism of Islam with the modern ideas of nationalism. Loyalty to one's homeland, or *Qawmiya*, was commended as a necessary first step. Loyalty to the Arab nation or Arab unity represented the next stage of development. The Arabs, he stressed, occupy a privileged position among the Muslim peoples by virtue of their early espousal of the Islamic faith and their struggle for its propagation. The Arab bond, he maintained, was based on the two factors of common religion and common language. Arab unity should, therefore, include all the Arabic-speaking Muslims living in the area stretching from the Arabian

---

[1] For a good study of the internal situation in Egypt during the early thirties and the rise into popularity of the Islamic organizations, see Christina Phelps Harris *Nationalism and Revolution in Egypt: the Role of the Muslim Brotherhood*, London 1964, pp. 136–42; Nadaf Safran *Egypt in Search of Political Community*, London 1961, pp. 187–208; Richard P. Mitchell *The Society of the Muslim Brothers*, London 1969, p. 16

[2] J. Heyworth-Dunne *Religious and Political Trends in Modern Egypt*, Washington D.C. 1950, pp. 11–13

[3] Ibid., p. 68

Gulf to the Atlantic coast of Morocco.[1] Arab unity, for him, was essential for the restoration of the glory of Islam. The third and wider circle was that of Islamic unity. This was for him the ultimate and supreme objective. Islam, he maintained, was a belief, *Aqida*, as well as a homeland, *Watan*, and a nationality, *Jinsiya*. As such it did not admit of any boundaries or racial distinctions between the Muslim peoples. His immediate goal was therefore defined as that of seeking the establishment in Egypt of an Islamic system of government which would "uphold the cause of Islam; work for the unity of the Arab nation; protect all Muslims in all parts of the world from aggression; and spread the word of God".[2]

On the practical side, the impact of the Brotherhood was more impressive. It had an extensive organizational network covering virtually every city and town, and most of the villages. Directives were issued to the local branches providing their minor leaders with a lead on all issues of importance as they cropped up. In this way, when it was decided from 1936 onwards to make the Palestine question a main issue, messages were relayed and great efforts were made to mobilize public support for the Palestine Arabs. The Brotherhood was solidly on the side of the Palace in its conflict with the Wafd, and was used by the Palace politicians such as 'Ali Maher in their efforts to undermine the Wafd's popularity. The establishment of several branches of the Brotherhood in Palestine, Syria, and Iraq underlined the wider scope of the movement.[3]

Misr al-Fatat, renamed in 1940 The National Islamic Party, was founded in 1933 by Ahmed Hussein. Its leader was a great admirer of the fascist ideology and methods of action. *Misr al-Fatat* had a very small following in the country and was more radical than the other two Islamic organizations. It was strongly nationalistic in outlook. Ahmed Hussein called for the revival of Egypt's glorious past, the end of all vestiges of foreign domination, and the establishment in Egypt of a strong Islamic state which would assume the leadership of the Arab and the Muslim countries. He saw that the independence of Egypt could no longer satisfy the aspirations of its people, and that the ultimate goal should be the establishment of an Arab and, if possible, of an Islamic empire. Arab unity was, in his view, a necessity for Egypt socially, economically, and politically. The first line of defence for Egypt, he maintained, was along the Taurus Mountains on the borders of Asia

---

[1] Hasan al-Banna *Majmu'at Rasa'il al Imam al-Shahid*, Beirut 1965, pp. 71, 281

[2] Ibid., p. 73. Al-Banna's views on Arab unity carried the impact of the teachings of Rashid Rida, who went to great pains to stress the compatibility of Arab and Islamic unity and whose ideas had a great influence on Al-Banna. Richard P. Mitchell *The Society of the Muslim Brothers*, pp. 267–9

[3] Ishak Musa Husaini, *The Moslem Brethren: The Great Modern Islamic Movements*, Beirut 1956, pp. 74–80

Minor, and the second line was in Palestine. If both lines were to collapse, Egypt would lie open before any invading force. The Syrian question was for him "in essence an Egyptian question".[1] Arab Asia was for him, therefore, a mere "lebensraum" for Egyptian influence.

THE ACTIVE PHASE IN EGYPTIAN–ARAB RELATIONS 1936 to 1940

This period was marked by substantial changes in Egypt's domestic and foreign politics. The conclusion in August 1936 of the Treaty of Friendship and Alliance with Britain was followed in 1937 by the end of the Capitulations, and the admission of Egypt into the League of Nations. This seemed to settle, for the time being at least, the hitherto burning national issue. The death of King Fu'ad in April 1936 came just a few weeks after the restoration of the 1923 Constitution, and was followed by the return of the Wafd to power in May. With the heir to the throne, King Farouq, still a minor, the royal factor in Egyptian politics seemed to have been removed for some time.

The earlier period was characterized by a slow but steady increase in public interest in Arab affairs. It was also characterized by the indifference of Egyptian politicians to the issue of closer relations with the Arab countries. This was to change in 1936. The Egyptian leaders, proud of their country's independence and enhancement of status, were eager to establish closer relations with the other Arab states. The old feud with Saudi Arabia was ended, and a treaty normalizing the relations between the two countries was concluded in April 1936. Arab Affairs sections were established for the first time in the Ministry of Foreign Affairs and in the Publications Department. A special committee was formed in the Ministry of Commerce to discuss ways of promoting economic co-operation with the Arab countries. 'Abdul Rahman 'Azzam, the ardent pan-Arabist, was appointed Minister Plenipotentiary in Baghdad. Two other Ministers were appointed, in Jedda and Damascus. The speech from the throne in 1936 stressed the need for consolidating relations with the "sister" Arab countries.[2] The rather vague term "the Eastern countries", used in the pre-1936 press articles and news items to refer to the Arab countries, began to disappear, and more stress began to be laid on the Arab orientation of Egypt.

The Palestine Arab revolt of 1936 introduced a new factor, the importance of which was accentuated by the contiguity of Palestine, and

---

[1] Ahmed Hussein *Imani*, 1st edn., Cairo 1936, pp. 84–92; J. Heyworth-Dunne *Religious and Political Trends in Modern Egypt*, p. 104; *Misr al-Fatat* (newspaper), 27 March 1941

[2] *Majallat al Rabita al-Arabiya*, No. 29, 1st year, 9 December 1936

by the fact that the Arab cause there merited support both on Arab and on Islamic grounds. A Higher Committee for the Relief of the Palestine Victims was formed late in 1936. It included in its membership such impressive figures as Hasan al-Banna; Dr 'Abdul Hamid Sa'id; Hamad al-Basel, the former Vice-President of the Wafd; Dr Muhammad Hussein Haykal, the prominent writer and leading figure in the Liberal Constitutional Party; in addition to a number of prominent Arabs then living in Egypt.[1] The fact that this Committee had strong anti-Wafdi elements turned it into a semi-opposition pressure group ready to attack the government whenever it showed any slackening in its support for the Palestine Arabs. The question of Palestine began to intrude into Egyptian domestic politics.

The settlement of the national and constitutional questions left the Wafd with no other live issue to use in rallying the masses and in sustaining their support for the party. The Islamic organizations were attracting an increasing number of disenchanted Wafdi youths, and were using the Palestine issue to embarrass the Wafdist government.[2] Nahas Pasha saw the benefit to himself and to the Wafd in championing the Arab cause in Palestine. He was eager at the same time not to antagonize the British, and responded to their representations by urging the press and the Islamic organizations to tone down their anti-British campaign on the grounds that this would prejudice his own efforts to bring about a settlement of the problem.[3] He also refrained until July 1937 from any public utterances on the subject. He made at the same time numerous representations to the British on the issue. The urgency of the matter to him, he argued, was caused by the fact that Muslim feeling "was getting worked up and manifestations were only not occurring by a miracle".[4] He offered his mediatory efforts in settling the issue, yet he abstained from participating in the Joint Arab Appeal of October 1936 on the grounds that this would leave Egypt as a card to be played later in case the Appeal should prove fruitless.[5] As the leader of the wealthiest and most populous Arab country, Nahas wanted to be the sole arbiter and mediator, which would have greatly enhanced his own prestige *vis-à-vis* the opposition minority parties and the Palace elements within Egypt.

Nahas, while always careful not to let the agitation in support of the Palestine Arabs get out of hand, and while maintaining towards the British an attitude which was described by them as "absolutely correct", did "take every opportunity of passionately advocating the Arab

---

[1] *Al-Muqattam*, 27 May 1936

[2] FO 371–20023: Sir Miles Lampson to Eden, 16 August 1936

[3] FO 371–20021: the Acting High Commissioner noted that in doing so Nahas was "risking some loss of popularity".

[4] FO 371–20110: Sir Miles Lampson to Eden, 7 June 1936

[5] FO 371–20026: Sir Miles Lampson to Eden, 2 October 1936

cause in private conversations, using on one occasion the phrase, 'We, too, are Arabs'."[1] In voicing his opposition to partition in July 1937, he argued that Egypt could not regard with equanimity the prospect of the creation of a Jewish state at its borders for, "apart from questions of defence . . . etc., who would say the voracious Jews would not claim Sinai next?" He entreated the British to pause before proceeding with what he could only regard as their fatal policy, and offered again his help "in trying to devise ways out of this impasse".[2] The maiden speech of the Egyptian Minister of Foreign Affairs after Egypt's admission to the League of Nations in 1937 dealt almost entirely with the Palestine question. It stressed that the issue was of interest to Egypt in view of the contiguity of Palestine and the historic brotherly ties based on common religion, language, and culture between its Arab people and the Egyptian people.[3] As the position of Nahas grew weaker in the later part of 1937, following the coronation of King Farouq, the reassertion of Palace authority, and the strong anti-Wafdi campaign supported by the Islamic organizations, his representations to the British increased in intensity. His dismissal from office in December 1937 freed him from all constraints. The Palestine issue was effectively used by the Wafd in its anti-British and anti-Palace campaign. The new government of Muhammad Mahmoud Pasha, which was more Arab-oriented and more eager to demonstrate its support for the Arab cause in Palestine, was accused of half-heartedness and at times of subservience to the British on the issue. Nahas was to declare in November 1938 that his party would continue to co-operate with "our Palestinian brothers" and that it was about time "that all oppressed Eastern peoples should close their ranks in a united front against imperialist designs".[4] The Wafd was, however, to abstain from participating in the Cairo Inter-Parliamentary Congress for the Defence of Palestine, merely because it was sponsored by the opposition elements.[5]

Active Egyptian interest in Arab affairs during this period was, however, only partly due to the wave of public support for the Arab cause in Palestine. It was a deliberate act of policy on the part of the Palace elements who wanted to achieve for Egypt, after its independence, a position of prominence in a constellation of Arab and Muslim states.

---

[1] FO 371–19980: David Kelly to Eden, 4 September 1936. David Kelly commented "He is not [an Arab], but as the prevailing doctrine in Germany illustrates, the importance assumed by racial myths need not bear any relevance to the degree of truth contained in them, and there is, of course, much Arab blood in the fellaheen".

[2] FO 371–20810: Sir Miles Lampson to Eden, 25 July 1937

[3] *Al Misri*, 25 July 1937 and 2 July 1938

[4] Ibid., 14 November 1938

[5] Nahas Pasha received the Arab delegates to the Congress and explained to them that the non-participation of the Wafd was due to considerations of internal politics and did not in any way imply any coolness in the party's support for the Palestine Arabs. FO 371–21883: Sir Miles Lampson to Viscount Halifax, 24 October 1938

This policy was espoused by the young King and masterminded by 'Ali Maher Pasha and Sheikh Muhammad Mustafa al-Maraghi.

'Ali Maher was an original member of the Wafd under Sa'ad Zaghlul. He was soon to cede from the party in the early twenties. He developed throughout the years a great hatred for party politics and for the Wafd in particular, with its mass appeal and its leaders' somewhat demagogic methods. This hatred manifested itself in a desire to undermine all parties in favour of Palace autocracy, for which he would be the chief instrument. After the death of King Fu'ad in April 1936 and the temporary eclipse of the Palace role in domestic politics, 'Ali Maher was able to establish close contacts with the young King, and to win his confidence. He had, however, to contend with the power of Sheikh Mustafa al-Maraghi, the rector of Al-Azhar and the tutor of the young monarch, who was a close friend of Muhammad Mahmoud Pasha, the leader of the Liberal Constitutional Party. 'Ali Maher had one thing in common with Al-Maraghi. This was the determination to reassert Palace authority *vis-à-vis* the Wafd, to dislodge Nahas from office, and to keep him out of power for as long as possible. This was soon to be achieved, in December 1937. Muhammad Mahmoud Pasha was appointed Prime Minister of a coalition government from which the Wafd was excluded. 'Ali Maher himself was appointed two months earlier head of the King's Cabinet.

The appointment of Muhammad Mahmoud to the Premiership was a big boost for Al-Maraghi, who started to revive his old ideas about the Caliphate. He sent Egyptian *'Ulema* to the Muslim countries to carry out propaganda for an Egyptian Caliph with vice-Caliphs in each of these countries. He also advocated the idea of establishing a permanent supreme Islamic Council in Cairo, participated in by representatives from all the Muslim countries, to discuss and formulate a common policy on all questions of interest to these states.[1] Al-Maraghi hoped thereby to cash in on King Farouq's popularity inside Egypt for his youth, good looks, and alleged piety. He wanted secondly to spread Egyptian influence throughout the Muslim world. His third aim was, through the assumption by King Farouq of the Caliphate, to enhance his own prestige by the possible assumption of a position of great authority similar to that of Sheikh al Islam in the Ottoman Empire, and thus to be a power behind the throne. It was with this end in view that he, as well as the leaders of the Islamic organizations, supported in June 1937 the idea of a religious coronation ceremony for the young

[1] FO 371–21878: Sir Miles Lampson to Viscount Halifax, 25 March 1938, enclosing a report from the government of India on the activities of Al-Maraghi's emissaries, and the record of an interview between Lord Lloyd and Al-Maraghi, who conveyed his views regarding the formation of a Supreme Muslim Council. Also: Elie Kedourie *The Chatham House Version and Other Middle Eastern Studies*, London 1970, pp. 204–5

monarch. The idea was then rejected by Nahas as implying that the King derived his authority from a source other than the Constitution, and as likely to antagonize the sizeable Coptic minority. The argument then put forward in support of the idea was that such a ceremony "would enhance Egypt's prestige in the Muslim countries, which prestige we wish to see all our Ministers keen on consolidating in the interests of Egypt and Islam".[1]

Al-Maraghi was to approach the British Embassy early in 1938 through his friend Muhammad Mahmoud, inviting their views on the matter. It was then that Al-Maraghi's activities began to engender sharp reactions from King Ibn Sa'ud and the Turkish Government. The British were afraid lest they be thought to be the instigators of these activities. They considered it undesirable for them to be implicated in any form of religious dissension among the Arab and Muslim states. Their objections were conveyed to the Egyptian Government. The Foreign Office, in the meantime, inspired an article in *Great Britain and the East* which deprecated all activities aimed at the revival of the Caliphate, attributing them to "hotheadedness, national pride, and short-sightedness". The Caliphate was described as "an outworn institution" which would "unnecessarily accentuate divisions within Islam".[2]

The pursuit by Al-Maraghi of the Caliphate idea did not stop, however, in spite of British objections. The meeting of the Arab and Islamic Inter-Parliamentary Congress for the Defence of Palestine in Cairo in October 1938 offered a unique chance to propagate it. The Congress, to which members of Parliament from most of the Arab and Muslim countries were invited, was described by the Egyptian press as a manifestation of Muslim and Arab solidarity. The reading of the delegates' names at the opening session ended with shouts of "Long live the King of Egypt, Farouq I, the Commander of the Faithful". The last episode in the Caliphate campaign took place early in 1939. Some of the Arab delegates, assembled in Cairo on their way to attend the London Round Table Conference on Palestine, accompanied the King for the Friday prayers. The royal entourage prevented the Imam from officiating as usual. Farouq himself led the congregation in prayers as was the

---

[1] *Al Balagh*, 24 June 1937; Muhammad al-Tabi'i *Min Asrar al-Sasa wal Siasa*, Cairo (n.d.), pp. 57–8, 69–70, for an account of Nahas—the Palace relations with regard to this and other issues. Al-Tabi'i's view is that Nahas mishandled the whole affair by allowing the Wafdist newspapers to engage in polemics over the issue with the pro-Palace newspapers, which were exploited by the Palace elements like Al-Maraghi and 'Ali Maher to sow discord between Nahas and the young King.

[2] FO 371–22004: minute by Cavendish-Bentinck on 9 May 1938. The article referred to was written by Kenneth Williams, entitled "Islam Does Not Need Another Caliph: Ambitious Divines in Egypt" in *Great Britain and the East*, 2 June 1938

prerogative of a Caliph. On leaving the Mosque, Farouq was greeted by shouts of "Long live the Caliph".[1]

The Caliphate campaign did not get very far, however, because of British opposition and the hostile reaction of some Muslim countries. The insinuation was made by Muhammad Mahmoud Pasha in 1938[2] and again in 1939 by Taqla Pasha, the owner of *Al-Ahram*,[3] that 'Ali Maher Pasha and not Al-Maraghi was the chief sponsor of the idea. It is possible that 'Ali Maher did give it his support in view of the appeal it had for the King. 'Ali Maher was, however, far from being its chief sponsor, since it was Al-Maraghi who had espoused it as far back as 1915 and had pursued it consistently ever since.[4] It was, moreover, quite natural for such an idea to be sponsored by a religious divine rather than by a secular politician such as 'Ali Maher. What concerns us more here is that it was a manifestation of the new outward-looking policy of the Palace. The religious nature of the Caliphate campaign had its negative aspects as far as the issue of closer ties with the Arab countries was concerned. Al-Maraghi was to declare early in 1938 that he did not believe in Arab unity and that he was not one of its supporters. He added that he was for Islamic unity, which does not distinguish between Arabs and non-Arabs.[5] Support for Arab unity was therefore thought of by Al-Maraghi and his fellow Azharites as contrary to Islam's basic universalism, and as likely to antagonize the non-Arab Muslims, whose support for the Caliphate idea he was keen on securing.

'Ali Maher, on the other hand, was to declare that he believed in Arab unity provided the independence and national identity of each country were preserved. He envisaged early in 1938 the establishment of a general Council, participated in by all the independent Arab states, whose purpose would be to provide a forum for the discussion of matters of common concern and to consolidate inter-Arab relations.[6] This was in fact the only arrangement to be found possible and acceptable six years later, when the idea of the Arab League was agreed upon. He told the British during his visit to London in February 1939 that he had "never liked the Caliphate idea and that he considered it now dead". He thought that it would only divide the Muslim world, adding that he had managed to get Al-Maraghi to accept this fact.[7]

---

[1] FO 371–23304: Sir Miles Lampson to Viscount Halifax, 25 January 1939 and Elie Kedourie *The Chatham House Version*. p. 204

[2] FO 371–22004: Sir Miles Lampson to Viscount Halifax, 4 July 1938

[3] FO 371–23304: a record of an interview in Cairo between Bateman and Taqla on 28 February 1939

[4] Elie Kedourie *The Chatham House Version*, pp. 179–81

[5] Muhammad Shaker al-Khardhji *Al 'Arab fi Tariq al Ittihad*, vol. I, Damascus 1947, p. 79

[6] Muhammad Shaker al-Khardhji *Al 'Arab fi Tariq al Ittihad*, p. 78

[7] FO 371–23304: minute by D. Kelly on 28 February 1939

'Ali Maher was finally to achieve his aim by replacing Muhammad Mahmoud Pasha as Prime Minister in August 1939, after months of intensive intrigues. His Cabinet had the strongest representation yet of the pan-Arab and Islamic elements. 'Abdul Rahman 'Azzam was given the Portfolio of Awqaf and later of Social Affairs. He was also given charge of the formation of a Territorial Army for internal security purposes.[1] 'Azzam was the most enthusiastic of all the Egyptian pan-Arabists. He had called as far back as 1934 for the restoration of the Arab Empire, arguing that in a world dominated by big blocs there was no place for small countries with limited resources.[2] Muhammad 'Ali 'Allouba, a life-long advocate of closer inter-Arab co-operation and the sponsor of the Cairo Inter-Parliamentary Congress of 1938, was appointed Minister of State for Parliamentary Affairs. Saleh Harb Pasha, who was to become late in 1940 the head of the Young Men's Muslim Association, was appointed Minister of War. The post of the Army Chief of Staff went to 'Aziz 'Ali al-Misri. Al-Misri had prominent service in the Ottoman Army and was the founder of one of the pre-First World War Arab secret societies (*Al-'Ahd*). He was described by T. E. Lawrence as "an idol of the Arab officers" to many of whom he stood as "the father of the Arab nationalist movement".[3]

'Ali Maher set for his Cabinet a policy with three main objectives. The first was to consolidate Egypt's independence and to make use of the circumstances of the war for this purpose. Diplomatic relations were severed with Germany following the outbreak of the war. Lines of communication were kept open, however, with the Axis through the Italian Minister in Cairo, whom 'Ali Maher used to see quite often. One of Maher's early decisions was to put on the retirement list a group of high Egyptian officials known for their pro-British leanings, such as Amin 'Osman and Abdul Razeq Abul Keir, both of whom were recent recipients of high British honours.[4] He also refused to declare

---

[1] This army was formed of non-conscript soldiers with the purpose of performing defence duties behind the battle lines. Sir Miles Lampson had his misgivings about its formation and described it as an "ill-thought of scheme" and worthless from the military point of view though it was thought well of by the British military in Cairo. The anti-government elements, on the other hand, were very suspicious of the idea and thought that 'Ali Maher intended to use it to establish his authority and to crush opposition. FO 371–23335 Sir Miles Lampson on 20 September 1939 FO 371–24623 Sir Miles Lampson on 5 February 1940

[2] *Al-Hilal*, 42nd year, No. 4, February 1934

[3] T. E. Lawrence *Seven Pillars of Wisdom: A Triumph*, London 1935, p. 59; also Majid Khadduri, "Aziz 'Ali al Misri and the Arab Nationalist Movement" in *St Antony's Papers: Middle Eastern Affairs*, No. 17, p. 140

[4] Azzam stated that 'Ali Maher's Cabinet was determined to pursue an independent policy and "not to allow it to be said that Egypt was still a British protectorate". It was for this reason that Maher sought to curtail the powers of the British military mission attached to the Egyptian Army and raised the issue of treaty revision after the war. FO 371–24623

war on the Axis, as urged by the British Ambassador and as promised earlier by himself. This was due to the forceful intervention of King Farouq,[1] who had his pro-Axis sympathies and who was not so sure about an eventual British victory in the war. His second objective was to pursue an active policy in the Arab World. This was reflected in his choice of Ministers and in his frequent representations to the British with regard to Palestine. He was won to the ideas of 'Azzam about closer Arab ties and the political, economic, and strategic advantages to Egypt from establishing close connections with the neighbouring Arab countries. It should be remembered that the Wafd at that time was intensifying its own anti-British and anti-Palace propaganda. Representatives from the neighbouring Arab countries were invited to the Wafdist Convention of 1938, and the unity of the Arab people in their struggle against imperialist designs was called for by Nahas.[2] 'Ali Maher and the Palace considered it in their interest to try to outbid the Wafd in this regard. In this 'Ali Maher was rightly described as the first Egyptian Prime Minister to envisage the possibility of making Egypt the champion of the Arab World.[3] His third objective was to pursue a more active policy in the Muslim world in order to enhance Egypt's prestige and influence. He had his early connections with the Islamic movements, whose popularity in the country was seen by the Palace as a useful counterforce to the mass appeal of the Wafd. In this 'Ali Maher was responding to pressures from the leaders of these movements, and from the King, whose imagination was captured by the Caliphate idea sponsored by Sheikh al-Maraghi.

'Ali Maher, as the most resourceful and experienced of the Egyptian politicians of the time, knew full well that this policy would put him at loggerheads with the British. He had throughout his political career never had any illusions about the real centres of power in Egypt, and had always maintained good relations both with the British and with the Palace. His appointment as chief of the King's Cabinet in 1937 was in fact suggested by the British, who wanted to see a man "of real character" beside the young King.[4] Yet he was after all a Palace man, and this was the policy favoured by the King at the time. The war situation and the apparent ascendancy of the Axis forces everywhere seemed to offer a unique chance to pursue that policy.

Sir Miles Lampson admitted more than once that 'Ali Maher had

---

[1] Statement of King Farouq to the outgoing American Minister in March 1941. F.R. of the U.S., vol. III, 1941, p. 264. The Foreign Office noted that Sir Miles "naturally feels strongly about the collapse of his efforts to get the Egyptians to declare war". The British military decided later, however, that this step was convenient but not essential since they were having all the facilities needed. FO 371–23307 and 24625

[2] *Al Misri*, 8 and 14 August 1939

[3] J. Heyworth-Dunne *Religious and Political Trends in Modern Egypt*, pp. 23–6

[4] FO 371–23304: a note on 'Ali Maher by David Kelly (FO) on 9 March 1939

"great qualities: energy, determination, and quickness of action—none of them very common characteristics in this country".[1] He also admitted that Maher had responded promptly and positively to all British requests with regard to communication and supply facilities for their troops in Egypt. He realized the pressures being exerted on him by the Wafd, the Islamic organizations, and the Palace. He argued in April 1940 that the Syrian and Palestinian questions seemed likely to play in Egypt's domestic politics "the same role as in Iraq", and thought that in view of the Wafd's championship of the Arab cause, 'Ali Maher might be involved in "difficulties similar to those with which Nuri Pasha has been continually beset".[2] The Ambassador was incensed, however, at 'Ali Maher's refusal at the last minute to declare war or to expedite the liquidation of the Italian mission in Cairo. He attributed the anti-British leanings of the Palace and the Islamic organizations to his influence. He represented him to his superiors in Whitehall as the "evil genius" of King Farouq, his ministry as an "unhealthy growth"[3] composed of an "unreliable clique" who were "without statesmanship and full of fantastic ideas". He went at one time so far as to state that he "should several times of late have liked to shake him by the scruff of the neck".[4]

The Foreign Office were struck by the rancour and personal antipathy which characterized the Ambassador's relations with 'Ali Maher and King Farouq. They attributed this to the influence of Walter Smart, the Oriental Counsellor, who had local connections and who had been kept for so long in his post. They suggested the introduction of "fresh blood and a fresh method" in the Oriental Secretariat in Cairo. The Ambassador insisted, however, on retaining Smart in his post.[5] It was only in 1940 that the Foreign Office began to take the Ambassador's warnings seriously. The Axis forces were on the ascendant everywhere, and no security risks however slight were to be tolerated. They went, on the Ambassador's advice, so far as to prepare contingency plans for deposing the King himself should he refuse to dismiss 'Ali Maher from office,[6] a step which he reluctantly agreed to take in June 1940.

---

[1] FO 371–23307: Sir Miles Lampson to Kelly (FO), 20 September 1939

[2] FO 371–24625: Sir Miles Lampson to Viscount Halifax, 26 April 1940

[3] FO 371–23307: Sir Miles Lampson on 2 October 1939

[4] FO 371–23307: Sir Miles Lampson to Kelly, 18 September 1939

[5] FO 371–27428: minutes by Thompson and Sir Orme Sargent, the Deputy Under-Secretary of State in January 1941. This suggestion, it was minuted, had been made repeatedly in the past. Eden was, however, for leaving the handling of the situation to the Ambassador since "he knows the people with whom he is dealing very well" and since "it is difficult for anyone to have dealings with King Farouq and not agree with Sir Miles Lampson".

[6] FO 371–24625: Sir Miles somehow regretted not deposing the King at that time. He was to state in December 1940 that he had for long felt that there would be "no true stability" in Anglo-Egyptian relations with King Farouq on the throne. FO 371–27428

'Ali Maher had to leave, then, with the impression of him as a "confirmed intriguer" who "not only looks foxy but acts like it" having stuck in Whitehall. Even his activities out of office were not tolerated by the Ambassador, who saw that his influence over the King remained "constant and pernicious".[1] Several representations were therefore made for his internment. 'Ali Maher was envied and even hated by the other politicians, and the Wafdist leaders in particular, for his influence in the Palace, which undermined their own chances. His ousting from office put an end, for the time being, to the Palace-sponsored outward-looking policy and was followed by the temporary eclipse of its supporters among the leaders of the Islamic organizations whose activities were suppressed. It was also a setback for the first attempt, at the official level, to play an active role in Arab affairs.

EGYPT AND THE PAN-ARAB CONFERENCES

One of the distinctive features of the late thirties was the recurrence of general Arab meetings in connection with the Palestine issue. The Bludan Conference of 1937 was the first of such meetings. It was co-chaired by Muhammad 'Ali 'Allouba Pasha and attended by Dr Abdul Hamid Sa'id, the head of the Young Men's Muslim Association. The Inter-Parliamentary Congress of the Arab and Islamic Countries for the Defence of Palestine was, however, a more impressive gathering. It was sponsored and called by 'Allouba Pasha and attended by sixty Egyptian members of Parliament led by the Speaker of the Chamber of Deputies. King Farouq showed great interest in its proceedings, and the delegates were entertained in the Palace and received at lunch by the Prime Minister. The Egyptian press gave wide coverage to its meetings and the Congress was represented as a manifestation of Arab and Islamic solidarity.

The Congress met at a time when the Palestine disturbances were at their height and when British troops were being reinforced to crush Arab resistance. The world situation retained its explosive nature after Munich, and the Axis anti-British activities in the Middle East did not cease. The Congress was therefore bound to be accompanied by some anti-British propaganda and to provide material for the Axis powers in their anti-British campaign. Several representations were made by the British to Muhammad Mahmoud Pasha to disallow the meeting of the Congress. This he agreed to do only if war broke out before its convocation. He pointed in the meantime to the strength of public feeling with regard to Palestine, and to the difficulty of taking a negative attitude towards the Congress without antagonizing the Palace and the

---

[1] FO 371–24627: Sir Miles Lampson, 7 October 1940

religious divines, and without providing a chance for the Wafd to attack the government on this count. The British then urged him and 'Ali Maher to exercise their influence with the organizers and the members of the Congress in the direction of moderation.[1] Both promised to do so, and it was noted by a Foreign Office official after the conclusion of the meetings that the Congress "was not more venomous and Anglophobe than we had expected—in fact rather less so". Its resolutions were described as "very moderate and sensible".[2] The British also asked the Egyptian Prime Minister to avoid giving the Congress any form of official recognition.[3] He promised to do so but was soon to change his mind when King Farouq insisted, in spite of British representations, on giving a tea party to the delegates and suggested to the Prime Minister that he should also receive the delegates. The King argued that as the head of an Arab state it was quite proper that he should extend hospitality to such a distinguished gathering of Arab delegates.[4]

The idea of the Congress had in fact the blessing of the Palace right from the start. Its sponsor 'Allouba Pasha was a close friend of 'Ali Maher Pasha. Sheikh al-Maraghi, though not a member of Parliament, asked and was allowed to attend the meetings. The Prime Minister was to stress that Egypt felt that she "should have more to say" about Palestine than any other Muslim country and was only held back by her loyalty to her ally[5] (Britain). The Wafd boycotted the Congress, and its organs were attacking the government and accusing the Prime Minister of subservience to the British on the issue. The Prime Minister, on the other hand, urged the British to refer to his contacts with them in any policy statement with regard to Palestine since this would "greatly help him politically".[6]

The Congress, as explained earlier, provided the chance for Al-Maraghi to propagate his ideas with regard to the revival of the Caliphate. The stress during the proceedings was on Arab and Islamic solidarity. The delegates did not respond favourably, however, to a proposal by Faris al-Khouri, the Speaker of the Syrian Chamber of Deputies, calling for the union of Syria with Palestine in one state in treaty relations with Britain and France. The Iraqi and the Palestinian

---

[1] FO 371–21881: Sir Miles Lampson to Viscount Halifax, 3 October 1938

[2] FO 371–21881: minute by Colville (FO); 21882: minute by Colville

[3] FO 371–21879: record of an interview between Viscount Halifax and Muhammad Mahmoud Pasha on 4 August 1938

[4] FO 371–21881: Sir Miles Lampson, 10 October 1938

[5] Ibid., Sir Miles Lampson, 6 October 1938

[6] FO 371–21881: Sir Miles Lampson, 6 October 1938. Sir Miles was in favour of making such a gesture since Muhammad Mahmoud "has played the game well by us". The Foreign Office were unresponsive since this might antagonize other Arab leaders by giving the impression that the Egyptian Premier, rather than any of them, was taken into the confidence of H.M.G.

delegates pointed out that negotiations with these two "imperialistic powers" would only render more difficult the settlement of the Palestine question. The Congress called for the immediate cessation of Jewish immigration, general amnesty for all the interned or convicted Arabs in connection with the Palestine disturbances, the preservation of the unity of Palestine as an Arab state, and the establishment of self-government in Palestine. It gave a stern warning that if this solution was not adopted, the British and the Jews would incur the enmity of the Arab and Muslim peoples throughout the world.[1]

Two practical steps were decided upon by the Congress. The first was the formation of a permanent committee to follow up the implementation of its resolutions. The committee included 'Allouba Pasha and Dr Abdul Hamid Sa'id from Egypt; Mauloud Mukhlis, the Speaker of the Iraqi Chamber of Deputies; Faris al-Khouri; and Jamal al-Husseini and Awni 'Abdul Hadi, both of whom were members of the Arab Higher Committee in Palestine. The second step was the formation of a delegation led by 'Allouba Pasha, whose task was to visit Britain to present the Arab case to its officials and members of Parliament. The British Government were not ready to receive the delegation. 'Allouba Pasha went to London all the same and was received by the Foreign Office officials and by the Colonial Secretary "not as head of the delegation, but as a prominent member of the Egyptian Senate".[2]

A sequel to the Parliamentary Congress was the Eastern Women's Congress held on 15 October 1938 to discuss the Palestine question. It was sponsored and called by Huda Sha'rawi, the Egyptian feminist leader. Its resolutions called on the Arab and Muslim rulers to intervene in order to find a solution to the Palestine problem. They stressed that the Arab struggle in Palestine "is a struggle for the existence and the future of the Arab nation as a whole". The Congress urged the Arab people everywhere to encourage Arab goods and to favour them over foreign products.[3] Its proceedings and resolutions were more emotional and less well-directed than those of the Inter-Parliamentary Congress. Its significance was underlined, however, by the British Ambassador, who noted that "the power of women in the East, as in France, is far greater than their legal disabilities indicate".[4]

The meeting of the two Congresses in Cairo underlined the leading role of Egypt in the Arab World. The resolutions of the Inter-Parlia-

---

[1] *Kuras al Mu'tamar al Barlamani al 'Alami lil Dowal al 'Arabiya wal Islamiya*, Cairo, 1938; *Al-Muqattam*, 12 October 1938

[2] FO 371–21883: Viscount Halifax to Sir Miles, 17 November 1938 and record of the interview between 'Allouba and MacDonald on 21 November 1938

[3] *Al Mara' al Arabiya wa Qadiyat Filistin: Al Mu'tamar al Nisai' al Sharqi*, Cairo, 1939, pp. 13–19, 170

[4] FO 371–21883: Sir Miles, 24 October 1938

mentary Congress were described by a leading Egyptian newspaper as "the Magna Carta of the Near East and of the Arab Near East in particular".[1] Faris al-Khouri declared that the Inter-Parliamentary Congress had "confirmed the need for Arab co-operation and integration in an Arab–Islamic bloc capable of resisting imperialist designs, and of protecting the Arabs and Muslims from oppression".[2] 'Allouba Pasha stated that the Congress had two beneficial results: a limited one related to Palestine, and a general one related to the promotion of mutual understanding and co-operation between the Muslim and Arab peoples. He added that such gatherings were "necessary first steps" in the road towards Arab unity.[3]

Sir Miles Lampson, by way of comment on the proceedings of both Congresses, stated that Cairo was increasingly becoming "the nerve centre of the Muslim world". The establishment of a permanent committee in Cairo was, in his view, indicative of the move towards closer Arab and Muslim co-operation. He underlined the dangers to British positions in the Eastern Mediterranean in view of the fact that this manifestation of Arab and Muslim solidarity centred on opposition to British policy in Palestine. This was also stressed by David Kelly, the then head of the Egyptian Department in the Foreign Office. He added that the Egyptians might not be Arabs in race but "as Muslims and speakers of Arabic as well as from political vanity" they were rapidly coming to regard themselves as such and to aspire to moral leadership.[4]

A third and more significant official Arab meeting was held early in 1939 when the Arab delegates to the London Round Table Conference assembled in Cairo on their way to, and back from, London. The delegates met under the chairmanship of the Egyptian Prime Minister, and managed to evolve a unified Arab attitude towards the London talks. 'Abdul Rahman 'Azzam, who was a member of the Egyptian delegation to that Conference, stated that "the seeds of Arab unity had been sown in the London Conference".[5] A pro-government newspaper stressed that, in spite of the failure of the Conference to reach any solution to the Palestine problem, the Arabs had gained much from its convocation. The Conference testified to their ability to form a solid united front and made the British realize that Arab solidarity was a force to be reckoned with, and that co-operation with the Arabs was the best course to follow.[6]

---

[1] *Al-Muqattam*, 22 October 1938
[2] *Al-Muqattam*, 28 October 1938
[3] *Al-Hilal*, No. 6, April 1939, pp. 50–1
[4] FO 371–21883: Sir Miles, 24 October 1938 and minute by Kelly on 11 November 1938
[5] *Al Balagh*, 18 March 1939
[6] *Al Balagh*, 18 March 1939

ARAB CO-OPERATION VERSUS ARAB UNITY: THE EGYPTIAN ATTITUDE

The participation of Egypt in any political union with the neighbouring Arab countries was favoured only by very few of its politicians and intellectuals. Hasan al-Banna, Ahmed Hussein, and Dr 'Abdul Hamid Sa'id conceived of Arab unity not as an end in itself, but as a step towards the wider Islamic unity. The religious divines of Al-Azhar, on the other hand, considered Arab unity as incongruous with Islam's basic universalism. Both groups thought of unity, whether Arab or Islamic, in terms of complete integration, and they talked about the restoration of the Arab, and, if possible, the Islamic Empires. The revival of the Caliphate was a central issue for all of them. By appearing to favour the assumption by King Farouq of the title of Caliph, they were obviously thinking of an Empire under Egyptian hegemony.

For the majority of the Egyptian politicians and intellectuals, political union between Egypt and the neighbouring Arab countries was ruled out as not falling within the realm of practical politics. Much confusion was caused, however, by the use of the term "Arab unity" to mean Arab solidarity in the general sense or mere co-operation between independent states. Unity was thought of by many in moral rather than in political terms.[1] The meeting of the Bludan and the Cairo Inter-Parliamentary Congresses as well as the secondment of Egyptian teachers to Iraq were all represented as manifestations of Arab unity.

Nahas Pasha, the leader of the Wafd, was to describe the idea of Arab unity in 1938 as a good idea. What he was thinking of, however, was the promotion of economic and cultural inter-Arab relations. If this could be achieved, he added, then steps aiming at political co-operation could be initiated "with each country retaining its political identity in accordance with its special circumstances and needs".[2] The idea of an Egyptian–Iraqi alliance, suggested by Nuri Pasha al-Sa'id and later by Hikmat Suleiman in 1936, was not enthusiastically received by Nahas at the time. He argued that he did not wish to get involved in general complications and wished first to consolidate Egypt's position.[3]

---

[1] Mustafa Fahmi, a prominent Egyptian writer, noted that the term "Arab unity" had been subject to much misunderstanding. He did not see it as possible for Egypt to join any political Arab union, stressing that the Arab League was the more accurate description of the form of association favoured between Egypt and the Arabs. Egypt, he added, was the centre of this League, which was based on the cultural, historical, and emotional ties between Egypt and her Arab neighbours. *Al Siasa*, Literary Supplement, 29 September 1933. The Eastern Bond Association considered the achievement of political unity as impossible and defined its aim as that of calling for "a spiritual bond" based on cultural and economic co-operation. *Majallat al Rabita al Sharqiya*, 3rd year, No. 3, December 1930

[2] Muhammad Shaker al-Khardhji *Al 'Arab fi Tariq al Ittihad*, p. 76

[3] FO 371–20801: Sir Miles Lampson to Eden, 26 March 1937

Even when the Wafd decided from 1938 onwards to intensify its campaign against the British and the Palace government, the main emphasis was on the solidarity of the Arab and the Eastern peoples against imperialist designs. Nahas called upon these peoples to rally their ranks and to rise against their oppressors. Makram 'Ubaid, his second-in-command in the Wafd, stressed that the Egyptians were Arabs and that Arab unity was already in existence. What it needed, he stated, was organization aiming at welding the Arab countries into a united front whose purpose would be "to resist imperialism, to preserve national identities, to achieve the welfare, and to enhance the economic resources" of these countries. This organization, he added, had already started with the various steps taken to promote the exchange of benefits, goods, and ideas and to bring about general inter-Arab meetings.[1]

Muhammad Mahmoud Pasha, the successor of Nahas to the Premiership in December 1937, stressed only the need for Arab co-operation. Dr Muhammad Hussein Haykal, his second-in-command in the Liberal Constitutional Party, considered the harmonization of culture as "the first step and the solid foundation" for Arab unity.[2] 'Allouba Pasha dismissed the idea of an Arab Empire as "impossible to achieve" and a "waste of time" even to discuss. He described it as a "faulty" outmoded idea whose disadvantages far outweighed its advantages. Each Arab state, he stressed, wanted to retain its full sovereignty and independence. The most appropriate course, he maintained, was to promote inter-Arab co-operation in cultural, economic, and defence matters, that is "in everything that does not infringe upon the political independence of each of the Arab countries".[3] This was also the view of the great majority of 184 leading politicians, writers, and university professors interviewed in 1938.[4]

By 1939 the Egyptians came to regard their country as an integral part of the Arab World. Some of them tended to stress the cultural basis of Egypt's Arab orientation, while others stressed the political, economic, and strategic advantages to Egypt from closer relations with the neighbouring Arab countries. They all envisaged a leading role for Egypt in the area. 'Allouba Pasha was to state in 1936 that Egypt, by virtue of her wealth, population, and cultural prominence, should assume the leadership as of right. He talked about "the sacred mission" of Egypt in the Arab World and favoured a kind of relationship between her and these countries similar to that between Britain and the English-speaking dominions such as Australia and Canada. He stressed, however, that each state should retain its full political independence.[5] The

---

[1] *Al-Hilal*, No. 6, April 1939, p. 32 [2] Ibid., p. 12
[3] *Al-Hilal*, December 1940, p. 2
[4] Muhammad Shaker al-Khardhji, *Al 'Arab fi Tariq al Ittihad*, pp. 76–189
[5] *Majallat al Rabita al-'Arabiya*, 1st year, No. 9, 22 July 1936; Muhammad 'Ali 'Allouba *Mabadi' fil Siasa al-Misriya*, Cairo 1942, pp. 313–15

leading role of Egypt was also stressed by Hasan al-Banna, Ahmed Hussein, Nahas Pasha, 'Abdul Rahman 'Azzam, and Dr Haykal.

It should be noted, however, that for most Egyptians the leadership they envisaged was a moral one based on culture and learning, and a vague political one based on solidarity against foreign domination. This was summed up by Karim Thabit, the co-owner of the Wafdist organ *Al Misri*, when he stated that material assistance was the last thing required by the neighbouring Arabs from Egypt. What interested them most, he added, was the evolution of a spiritual, moral, and racial sense of community feeling between Egypt and the rest of the Arab World. By assuming a leading role in the area, Egypt, he argued, could consolidate her international position and contribute much to the Arab national struggle.[1] Dr Taha Hussein was to add a rather cynical note to the argument by stating that the Arab countries "for some reason told Egypt that it is the leader, and Egypt for some reason believed that". He considered the establishment of Egyptian primary and secondary schools in the Levant and the Hejaz as more beneficial both to Egypt and to these countries than many of the Egyptian consulates and legations. He stressed that this leadership in order to be credible had to be sustained by serious efforts towards the promotion of cultural co-operation with the neighbouring Arab countries.[2]

How then did the Arabs conceive of an Egyptian connection? The Arabs felt that an Arab orientation for Egypt would provide an additional source of strength to the Arab nationalist movement. They realized that the central position, international standing, wealth, population, and cultural development of Egypt gave her a prominent position in the area. They were willing to concede the leadership to her, provided her leaders would show readiness to lend their support and put their country's resources at the service of the Arab cause.

The Arab nationalists were to approach Sa'ad Zaghlul Pasha in 1919 with a view to concerting efforts in the Paris Peace Conference. King Faisal I of Iraq was to deprecate in the early twenties all the ideas then prevalent in Egypt about the need to avoid any diversions and to concentrate on the Egyptian struggle for independence. Egypt was for him an integral part of the Arab World and was in need of the Arabs as much as the Arabs were in need of her. He hoped that Zaghlul would take a bold step and extend his activities to the neighbouring Arab countries, in which case he would be "the national leader of the whole Arab World".[3] The same views about Egyptian leadership of the Arab World were reiterated by many Arab politicians and intellectuals,

[1] *Al Misri*, two articles on 24 and 25 November 1938 by Karim Thabit, following a visit he paid to the Levant

[2] Taha Hussein *Mustaqbal al Thaqafa Fi Misr*, Cairo 1944, pp. 386–8

[3] *Majallat al Thaqafa*, 2nd year, No. 87, 27 August 1940, an article by 'Awni Abdul Hadi entitled "Sa'ad and the East"

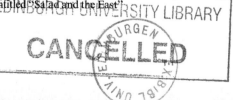

foremost among whom were Nuri Pasha al-Sa'id[1] and Sa'adullah al-Jabri.[2]

Prominent Egyptian visitors to the neighbouring Arab countries during the twenties and the thirties were impressed by the wide knowledge and the keen interest with which the Arabs followed political and cultural developments in Egypt. They were told that the Arabs recognized the leadership of Egypt and considered her their "eldest sister", and would like the Egyptians to take as much interest in their affairs as they took in Egyptian affairs. They expressed concern at the call by some Egyptian intellectuals in the early thirties for an equal stress on Egypt's Phara'onic heritage. They feared lest this should develop into a drift towards isolationism on the part of Egypt.[3] Sati' al-Husri, the prominent Iraqi writer, expressed his firm belief, as far back as 1936, in the emergence of a strong Arab orientation for Egypt, and lent his pen to the advocacy of the idea.[4] The Arab delegates to the ninth Arab Medical Congress held in Cairo in December 1936 called upon Nahas Pasha to dedicate his efforts to the service of the Arab cause. One of them expressed in a public speech his hope to see Nahas as the Prime Minister of an Arab Empire with Cairo as its capital and centre.[5] It should be noted, however, that most of the Arab leaders and intellectuals did not think of Egyptian leadership within the framework of a political association. Egypt was excluded from all their schemes for Arab federation. The Iraqi leaders had their fears of Egyptian domination within any Arab union, which would undermine the leading role they had envisaged for their country in Arab Asia. They conceived of Egyptian leadership therefore in a moral, and not in a political, sense.

THE BRITISH ATTITUDE TO EGYPTIAN INVOLVEMENT IN ARAB AFFAIRS

The question of Egyptian involvement in Arab affairs did not present itself in any serious form to the British policy-makers prior to 1936. It was from then onwards that the growing public support for the Arab cause in Palestine coincided with the eagerness of both the Wafd and the Palace to play an active role in the Arab World. The activities of the Islamic organizations, and the anti-British tone of the press in connection with Palestine gave further cause for alarm to the British.

---

[1] *Al-Muqattam*, 15 June 1933

[2] *Al Misri*, 24 November 1938. Al-Jabri was then Deputy Prime Minister of Syria.

[3] Dr Muhammad Hussein Haykal in *Al Siasa*, Literary Supplement, 17 September 1932; Muhammad 'Abdullah Inan in *Al Siasa*, 14 October 1932; Karim Thabit in *Al Misri*, 24 and 25 November 1938

[4] Abu Khaldun Sati' al-Husri *Mudhakkirati fil 'Iraq*, vol. II, 1926–41, 1st edn., Beirut, 1968, pp. 476–7

[5] *Majallat al Rabita al- 'Arabiya*, 1st year, No. 30, 16 December 1936

This came at a time when they had begun to have their serious apprehensions about Italian designs in the area, and when they were pinning much hope on the development of more harmonious relations with Egypt following the conclusion of the 1936 treaty.

The British representatives in Egypt tended at the beginning to underestimate the nature and extent of Egyptian interest in Arab affairs. Egypt, stated Sir Miles Lampson in August 1936, "both geographically and psychologically is much isolated from its neighbours, and its sympathy for the Arab World has always had to be artificially stimulated". The pan-Arab movement, he added, had "very little real strength" in Egypt, where it had always been "a very academic business fostered by men of letters and a few old fashioned religious pundits". Public sympathy for the Palestine Arabs was attributed mainly to the strength of the religious bond and partly to the propaganda activities of the Palestine Arab notables living in Egypt.[1]

They were soon to realize, however, that there was more to the Egyptian attitude than just that. A new trend had been gathering strength since the early thirties, the main manifestation of which was the rise into popularity of the fundamentalist Islamic movements. The apparent failure of the democratic experiment in Egypt, and the appeal of the rising power of the totalitarian regimes in Germany and Italy provided an additional boost for this trend. The Palestine question provided the chance for it to evolve itself in the form of active support for the Palestine Arabs. Egyptian public sympathy for the Arab cause in Palestine had strong religious as well as pan-Arab undertones. The argument put forward by the Islamic organizations was not very different from that used by Jamal ud-Din al-Afghani half a century earlier. The plight of the Palestine Arabs was attributed to the disunity and weakness of the Arab people as a whole.

David Kelly, the Acting High Commissioner in Egypt, was to state in September 1936 that there were definite signs of a change in the Egyptian approach to Arab affairs. He added that, however vague and theoretical the new gospel of Arab solidarity might be when it came to concrete action, it was "a sufficiently definite and shaping state of mind to be a factor with which to reckon". He warned that "whether it turns to our advantage or creates a new source of friction depends on how we deal with it".[2] Sir Miles Lampson was to state in 1938 that "every Egyptian is pro-Arab"[3] and that the Egyptians felt a natural sympathy for the Palestine Arabs "as Arabs", which had been "reinforced by the fact that they are fellow Muslims".[4] The Foreign Office were well aware

---

[1] FO 371–20023: Sir Miles Lampson to Eden, 12 August 1936

[2] FO 371–19980: Kelly to Eden, 9 September 1936

[3] FO 371–21876: Sir Miles Lampson to Eden, 3 May 1938

[4] FO 371–28801: record of interview between Sir Miles and the Colonial Secretary in London on 31 August 1938

of the dangers of the new movement towards Arab solidarity taking an anti-British turn. They realized that Egypt, with the great influence of its press throughout the area, its large population and wealth, and its cultural prominence, would lend more weight to that movement and hence increase its potential threat to British influence and military presence in the Arab World.

The British line of policy up to 1938 was, therefore, to discourage any Egyptian involvement in Arab affairs, and to keep Egypt "isolated" from its Arab neighbours. Egyptian participation in the Joint Arab Appeal of October 1936 was not encouraged, on the grounds that this would "increase the weight" of the general Arab attitude, and would bring Egypt directly into Palestinian and Arab affairs, "which we have so far succeeded in avoiding".[1] All Nahas' offers of mediation in the Palestine conflict were turned down. The idea of an Egyptian–Iraqi alliance suggested by Nuri Pasha and later by Hikmat Suleiman, the new Iraqi Prime Minister, in 1936 was not warmly received. It was pointed out that such alliances would "tend to intensify external co-operation" with the Palestine Arabs against Britain and Zionism. Even David Kelly, the British Counsellor in Cairo, who saw "nothing intrinsically fantastic" in the vision of a Near Eastern "Little Entente" headed by Egypt and working in close harmony with Britain, warned that this could be a double-edged weapon which might contain elements of serious trouble.[2] Objections were raised by the Foreign Office to some parts of Nahas' proposed statement on Palestine in the Senate in July 1937. It was stressed that "it is important that the impression should not be given that Egypt is entitled to have a voice in the solution reached".[3] Prince Muhammad 'Ali's proposals for a Palestine settlement in 1937 were ignored, and his interest in the problem was attributed merely to the desire to play to the Muslim gallery, and thus to further King Farouq's ambitions to the Caliphate.[4] Serious objections were raised with regard to the meeting of the Inter-Parliamentary Congress in Cairo.

By 1938 the British had realized that the active Egyptian interest in Arab affairs could no longer be contained, and was likely to increase with time. Sir Miles Lampson pointed out as far back as February 1937 that it seemed "inevitable" that Egypt and the neighbouring Arab countries "must sooner or later get together with a view to international co-operation". He considered it "undesirable" in principle "to oppose tendencies which have in them such elements of inevitability",

---

[1] FO 371–20021: Sir Miles' views conveyed on 8 July 1936 and endorsed by the Cabinet [Cabinet Conclusions 51 (36) of 9 July 1936]

[2] FO 371–19980: Kelly to Eden, 4 September 1936

[3] FO 371–20809: Eden to Sir Miles, 19 July 1937

[4] FO 371–21874: minute by Lord Baggallay (FO) on the record of the meeting of Dr Weizmann and the Prince on 7 February 1938

and suggested that the British attitude should be one of benevolent expectancy rather than of discouragement.[1] The new line of policy adopted from 1938 onwards was designed, as stated by a Foreign Office official, not to discourage the movement towards Arab solidarity, but to try to show sympathy towards it, for "it will only be by so doing that we may be able to shape its course a little". The Egyptians, stressed another senior official, might not be predominantly Arabs in race, "but as Muslims and speakers of Arabic as well as from political vanity, they are rapidly coming to regard themselves as such and to aspire to moral leadership".[2] Even Egyptian interest in the Palestine situation, so far attributed mainly to the activities of the Islamic organizations and the Palestine Arab expatriates, began to be viewed as based also on considerations of national interest. The Egyptians, it was realized, had their serious apprehensions of future Jewish encroachments on the territories of the neighbouring countries, and fears lest the creation of a powerful Jewish state in Palestine would seriously affect Egypt's economic primacy in the area, and establish a land barrier between her and the Levant.[3]

The decision of the British Cabinet in November 1938 to invite the Arab governments, including that of Egypt, to the proposed London Round Table Conference was a clear admission that Egypt was an integral part of the Arab World, and that the Palestine problem could no longer be treated in isolation. The idea of holding such a meeting was in fact suggested by Muhammad Mahmoud Pasha, the Egyptian Prime Minister, to the Colonial Secretary some months earlier.[4] When the Egyptian Government showed reluctance to take part in the Conference because of the British refusal to give them any intimation as to their future line of policy, several representations were made by the British Ambassador to secure Egyptian participation at the highest possible level of representation. The Colonial Secretary stressed that the British Government would regard it "as unfortunate in the extreme if the Egyptian Government were to refuse the invitation".[5]

The British were in the meantime very sceptical about the willingness of Egypt to participate in any political union with the Arab countries. Egypt was excluded from all the general studies prepared by the Foreign Office on Arab unity. It was stressed that the danger of pan-Arabism in general was in the shape of a mental attitude rather than in that of political union, the possibility of which they discounted for a long time

---

[1] FO 371–20801: Sir Miles Lampson to Eden, 1 February 1937

[2] FO 371–21883: minutes by Etherington Smith and David Kelly in November 1938

[3] FO 371–22304: Sir Miles Lampson to Viscount Halifax, 16 January 1939

[4] FO 371–21879: interview in London on 29 July 1938

[5] FO 371–21867: Sir Miles to Viscount Halifax on 26 and 28 November 1938 and MacDonald to Sir Miles on 28 November 1938

to come.[1] They did not see anything objectionable, on the other hand, in closer co-operation between Egypt and her Arab neighbours in cultural and economic matters as long as this did not take an exclusive and anti-British turn.

The change in the British attitude towards Egyptian involvement in Arab affairs was connected with the change of outlook on the area as an interrelated whole from 1938 onwards. This change was brought about partly as a result of the Palestine disturbances and the intensity of neighbouring Arab reactions. The main factor was, however, the rising world tension and the threat to British interests as a result of the growing anti-British feeling in connection with the Palestine situation, which was effectively exploited by Axis propaganda. Egyptian interest in Arab affairs was recognized and tolerated. Efforts were made at the same time to keep it within acceptable limits.

[1] FO 371–21883: minute by Kelly, 11 November 1938

PART TWO

British Policy towards the Arabs in Wartime 1941 to 1944

Chapter Three

Arab Leadership and Politics 1941 to 1944

The outbreak of the war introduced a new important factor into Middle Eastern politics. The decision of Churchill during the Battle of Britain in August 1940 to give top priority to the defence of Egypt, making it second in importance to the defence of the United Kingdom itself, meant many things. It meant the transformation of Egypt into a war base both for offensive and for defensive purposes, and a large concentration of British troops on Egyptian soil. This imposed many strains both on the British with regard to supply and shipping facilities, and on the Egyptian economy, communication facilities, and labour force. It also meant the necessity of having in Egypt a friendly government and an acquiescent population. Egyptian internal politics became in effect, and more than ever before, a matter of direct concern to the British.

In Iraq, Transjordan, and Palestine, no direct confrontation was envisaged with the Axis forces at that stage. These countries retained their importance, however, in terms of communications and oil supplies and as providing the strategic depth for the defence of Egypt and the Suez Canal. In Syria and Lebanon, the French saw in the worsening international situation their chance to tighten their hold and to make known their decision early in 1939 not to ratify the 1936 treaties even as modified in 1938. They considered it "folly", in the existing world circumstances, to grant independence to the Syrians, who were "apart from the Christian minorities, a soft race, incapable of defending themselves".[1]

For the Arabs, as for the British, the victory at Al-'Alamain in November 1942 was a major turning-point. It put an end to Arab doubts and hesitations bred from their mistrust of British and French policies, and from frustrations over their failure in the inter-war period to achieve any of their national goals.

The British were able to hold the area in the end by a combination of resourceful diplomacy and forceful methods (Iraq 1941, Egypt 1940 and 1942, Syria and Lebanon 1941). Several factors helped the British to

---

[1] FO 371–23194: statement by M. Bonnet, the French Foreign Minister, to the British Ambassador in Paris on 26 April 1939

pacify the area for the duration of the war. Foremost among them was the presence of a large concentration of troops, especially in Egypt. The Middle East was to the British an area of vital strategic importance, and it was the only area in which the Axis forces could be engaged directly in battle. The Middle East was, on the other hand, never viewed by the Axis powers, or at least by Germany, as a major field of war operations, and it was topped in their scale of priorities by operations in Europe and against the Soviet Union.

A victory for the Axis powers would have meant the ascendancy of the extreme nationalist and pseudo-fascist groups in Egypt, Iraq, Syria, and Palestine. This would have involved a threat to the privileged classes and to the old politicians who had monopolized the scene of Arab politics for too long, and who were against any change in the *status quo* perpetuated under British influence. The Axis powers responded to contacts from King Farouq of Egypt and made some unsuccessful overtures to King Ibn Sa'ud, the bastion of conservatism in the area. It is doubtful, however, whether what was sought as a temporary expedient would have acquired permanence. The shouts of "forward Rommel" in the streets of Cairo late in January and early in February 1942[1] came from an odd combination of dissatisfied and frustrated groups including the supporters of Misr al-Fatat; the ultra-conservative followers of the Muslim Brotherhood; and the extreme elements of the Wafdist youth. The Egyptian peasants started, with the advance of Rommel across the Egyptian borders, to talk about parcelling out the big estates of their rich landlords. The Rashid 'Ali movement was masterminded by extreme nationalist young officers who were hostile to veteran politicians like Nuri al-Sa'id and Jamil al-Madfa'i. The *status quo* forces in the Arab World were, therefore, apprehensive of an Axis victory and solidly on the side of the Allies out of a keen sense of self-preservation.

The war situation forced upon Arab intellectuals a dilemma, since it involved a choice between totalitarian ideologies, the manifestation of which they saw in an odious fashion in Egypt in the street fighting and chaos spread by the extremist groups of Misr al-Fatat and the Wafdist Blue Shirts, and liberal democracy. They were disenchanted at the failure of the democratic experiment in the Arab World, but they did not accept totalitarian methods of government as the only alternative.[2] The veteran Arab nationalists were, on the other hand, strongly suspicious of Italian motives. Their experience during the First World War had left a deep mark on them. Collaboration with the British had led to the balkanization of the Arab East and its subjection to foreign domination.

---

[1] Muhammad Hussein Haykal *Mudhakkirat fil Siasa al Misriya*, p. 225; *The Killearn Diaries 1934–1946*, edited and introduced by Trefor E. Evans, London 1972, p. 209

[2] Muhammad Hussein Haykal *Mudhakkirat*, pp. 46–50; Abbas Mahmoud Al-Aqqad's article in *Al Dustour*, 28 July 1939

Collaboration with the Axis powers, they feared, would only lead to another and more odious type of foreign domination. King Ibn Sa'ud was to advise the Iraqi nationalists in 1941 to seek an understanding with the British, adding that the company of the well-fed lion (meaning the British) was safer than the company of the hungry vulture (meaning the Germans).[1]

EGYPTIAN POLITICS AND THE WAR: THE WAFD, THE PALACE, AND THE BRITISH 1942 TO 1944

The Wafd was brought back to power following the famous crisis of 4 February 1942, during which the British, by a military demonstration and a pre-drafted document of abdication in case of refusal, forced King Farouq to appoint Nahas Pasha as Prime Minister.[2] Nahas Pasha paid his debt by unflinching loyalty to the Anglo-Egyptian alliance and by the use of emergency powers, including press-censorship, imposed after the outbreak of the war, to combat fifth columnists and to intern Axis sympathizers. He managed, through the extensive party machinery, to sway waverers, and stood solidly on the side of the British throughout the most critical months of the summer of 1942, when their forces were driven back to Al-'Alamain, some seventy miles from Alexandria. The victory at Al-'Alamain strengthened his position internally *vis-à-vis* the opposition and the Palace. Egyptian politics remained, however, governed by the interaction of the Palace forces, the Wafd, and the British. In Nahas Pasha the Palace had a formidable foe, while the British had, during a critical war situation, a powerful ally whose mass appeal and strong party organization secured the stability of Egypt during the following two and a half years.

Nahas Pasha started his political career in 1919, when he participated in the Sa'ad Zaghlul movement. He was second only to Sa'ad Pasha in the Wafdist First High Command of 1921, and was chosen as Minister of Communications in Zaghlul's Cabinet of 1924. He was debarred, however, from participation in Adli Yakan's coalition government of June 1926, as a result of British objections on the grounds that he had "always stood for a policy of uncompromising hostility to Great Britain and the British Connexion".[3] On the death of Sa'ad Zaghlul in 1927, Nahas was elected president of the Wafd, a post for which he got the support of the young and rather extreme elements led by Makram 'Ubaid against his more moderate opponent Fathalla Barakat. The ascendance of the young and extreme elements was a foregone

---

[1] Mahmud al-Durra, *Al Harb al 'Iraqiya al Biritaniya*, p. 308

[2] Muhammad Hussein Haykal: *Mudhakkirat*, pp. 227–46 for a detailed account of the British intervention; *The Killearn Diaries*, pp. 211–14

[3] Lord Lloyd *Egypt since Cromer*, vol. II, London 1934, p. 165

conclusion after the secession from the Wafd, in 1921 and the following years, of most of the moderates and the representatives of big business and landed aristocracy. Under the leadership of Nahas, the Wafd tried to sustain its popularity by taking an extreme position on the ever-popular national issue: opposition to British occupation. Lord Lloyd, the then High Commissioner, was to note that the Wafd, under Nahas, had "reverted to a condition of irresponsible extremism". Nahas, in his view, was devoid of "the peculiar gifts of mind and character which had made Zaghlul so powerful a leader", and had become completely at the mercy of "the wild men of his left wing".[1]

Nahas, in spite of his appeal to the masses, his indisputable role in the nationalist struggle, and his eloquence as an orator, was rather weak *vis-à-vis* his leading supporters, and was easily swayed, both in and out of office, by the competing elements in the Wafd's inner circle.[2] His innate vanity was played on by his more resourceful supporters such as Makram 'Ubaid, who presented him to the masses as the true and only nationalist leader, on whose shoulders the mantle of Sa'ad Zaghlul had fallen. The leadership of the Wafd became captive to the belief that they alone represented the real interests of the nation. The glorification of the personality of Nahas and the strong influence over him of the extreme elements were soon to alienate many prominent Wafdist leaders, and to drive opponents to extreme hostility towards the Wafd. As a result of successive splits, all the twenty-two members of the Wafdist High Command of 1927, with the exception of Nahas and Makram 'Ubaid, had left the party by 1938.[3] The Wafd lost in the process the services of some of its strong leaders such as Dr Ahmed Maher, Mahmoud Fahmi al-Nuqrashi, Bahi-ul Din Barakat, and Hamad al-Basel. This vain and rather arrogant attitude of the Wafd's leadership was also to alienate the young King Farouq in 1937, and to play into the hands of its rivals led by 'Ali Maher Pasha.

The second major weakness of the Wafd was its lack of a comprehensive programme for economic and social reform. This was due mainly to the rather limited social outlook of its leadership. Many prominent Wafdists had acquired wealth throughout the years, and some elements from the landed aristocracy and big business were allowed to infiltrate into the party's leadership. The Wafd's popularity was sustained throughout the years by its consistent opposition to the British occupation and to the Palace's encroachments on the constitution. When both the national and the constitutional issues were settled for the time being in 1936, the Wafd had to resort to pseudo-fascist tactics to silence its opponents, as manifested by its formation of the "Blue Shirts" affiliated

[1] Ibid., p. 269

[2] FO 371-35532: J 1916/2/16

[3] Zaheer Masood Quraishi *Liberal Nationalism in Egypt: Rise and Fall of the Wafd Party*, Delhi, 1967, pp. 223–5

para-military organization and its disruptive activities in 1937.[1] This was a betrayal of the party's claim to be the guardian of liberal democracy and the constitution. There was in fact little or no manifest conflict of economic interest among the groups which provided the leadership of the various political parties at the time. Bitterly as they fought against each other on political grounds, they all presented a common front against the unprivileged groups in the social field.[2] The Islamic organizations, with their radical social reform programmes, offered the alternative to the masses, and attracted many from the ranks of the Wafd.

The third weakness was the corruption, nepotism, and abuse of authority which seeped into the Wafd's leadership while in office. This was not unique to the Wafd in fact, but the Wafd, as the majority party, had more leading members to favour, and more vested interests to protect. Nahas' yielding to the influence of his young and pretty wife from the late thirties onwards was to create frictions between him and his chief lieutenant, Makram 'Ubaid. Matters came to a head in 1942 when Makram, as Minister of Finance and Supply, resented the unusual promotion and the grant of import licences to Nahas' relatives. With his consequent ousting from the Cabinet, the party, and the Parliament, the Wafd lost another powerful figure. Makram was driven into extreme hostility towards Nahas and his Cabinet, publishing early in 1943 a "Black Book" containing allegations of nepotism and corruption against Nahas and the leading members of his Cabinet. The King saw in this his chance to dismiss Nahas from office, a step which he was precluded from taking both in April 1943 and in April 1944 by the British. The Wafd was in fact kept in power until October 1944 as a result of British pressure and forceful intervention, a fact which was rather embarrassing to the more sincere elements in the party.

As for the Palace, it had remained throughout the reign of King Fu'ad the dominant centre of power in Egypt. A coalition of forces between the Palace and the opposition minority parties, all of which were splinter groups from the Wafd with no big following in the country, managed to dominate the scene for most of the time. The death of King Fu'ad in 1936 removed the royal factor in Egyptian politics for some time. The Wafd was able to stay in power from May 1936 until December 1937,

---

[1] James P. Jankowski, "The Egyptian Blue Shirts and the Egyptian Wafd: 1935–1938" in *Middle Eastern Studies* Vol. VI, No. 1, January 1970, p. 81. The Blue Shirt units were formed in January 1936. Each unit was composed of eleven Wafdist members from among the youth, especially the students and the workers, with a High Command of five members. Military drills were conducted, and members were given lectures on patriotism and religion. These units were soon to be involved in Wafdist campaigns against the opposition. Nahas Pasha, in the face of growing criticism, had to decide on 5 December 1937 to subordinate these units to himself and to forbid their members from carrying any weapons or sticks and from wearing their uniform except at functions approved by the party.

[2] Nadav Safran *Egypt in Search of Political Community*, p. 194

and thus to have the longest term in office so far in its history. The popularity which King Farouq acquired in the country after his coronation in July 1937 was a potential threat to the Wafd. Nahas' rather tactless manner in dealing with the young King combined with the influence of the anti-Wafd groups to alienate him from Nahas Pasha and the Wafd. British intervention in February 1942 and the acceptance of office by Nahas "on the head of British bayonets"[1] further incensed King Farouq. Persistent efforts were made by the British to bring about better relations between the King and his Prime Minister, but all were in vain. The King complained that Nahas wanted to usurp his position and to cast himself in the role of a head of state instead of that of the leader of a political party. To the British contention that under a constitutional monarchy the king rules but does not govern, Farouq argued for a role which included both ruling and governing. This was, in his view, more conducive to stability in the Egyptian scene, since the monarchy outlasts any single government.

King Farouq's flirtations with the Italians, known to the British, coloured their judgment and increased their mistrust of his motives. Nahas, stated the British Foreign Secretary in May 1944, "is not our enemy, Farouk is".[2] King Farouq kept himself well-informed on politics and the movement of opinion. He was far from sure that the British would win the war and had therefore kept open some line of retreat to the Axis.[3] His antagonism to the Wafd meant the recurrence of the normal pattern of Egyptian politics, with the Palace forces always pitted against the Wafd.

The British, through their Ambassador, represented the third corner of the triangle. Sir Miles Lampson (later Lord Killearn) was a career diplomat, who was transferred to Cairo in 1934 to become the last of the High Commissioners and the first British Ambassador to Egypt in 1936. He managed to bring to an end a long drawn out period of tension in Anglo-Egyptian relations through the conclusion of the 1936 treaty. He remained on good terms with the Wafd and Nahas Pasha, about whom he conveyed approvingly a remark made by Amir 'Abdullah of Trans-jordan in 1940, that he (Nahas) was a man who "fills his clothes".[4] He was quite aware, however, of the weaknesses of the Wafd and the corruption of some of its leaders. As the majority party, always suppressed and kept out of office for most of the time by an intriguing

[1] Muhammad Hussein Haykal *Mudhakkirat*, p. 243: a remark made by Ahmed Maher Pasha on 4 February 1942

[2] FO 371–41327–J 12081/31/16. For King Farouq's contacts with Germany through his father-in-law, Zulfiqar Pasha, the then Egyptian Ambassador in Tehran, see: *D.G.F.P.*, series D, vol. XIII, pp. 55–78 and vol. XII, pp. 558–681, during the period 14 April 1941–3 July 1941

[3] Lord Chandos *Memoirs of Lord Chandos*, London 1962, p. 238

[4] FO 800/398—e. g./40/10

monarch, the Wafd was the underdog towards which Sir Miles' sympathies went.

He knew King Farouq as a boy, and after his accession to the throne in July 1937 continued to refer to him as "a boy" and to treat him from time to time to long lectures on how to discharge his responsibilities or to handle particular issues. Farouq resented the patronizing and rather condescending attitude of the British Ambassador. Relations between the two became worse and worse as 'Ali Maher's influence in the Palace grew stronger. A member of the British Embassy at the time noted that the frequent public expressions of Sir Miles' bitter antipathy to the King were a source of embarrassment to the members of his Embassy, and were resented even by the Egyptians least disposed towards the King. Sir Miles was described as "physically and temperamentally incapable of giving any convincing impression of change" in Anglo-Egyptian relations after the conclusion of the 1936 treaty.[1]

The Ambassador's forceful interventions, in June 1940 in order to have 'Ali Maher dismissed from office and in February 1942 in order to have Nahas installed in office, incensed the King, who was described by the Ambassador as "an overgrown, over-developed boy who had been given his head for too long (mainly by Ali Maher)".[2] Sir Miles saw the conflict between the Palace and the Wafd as essentially one between two concepts: Palace autocracy, and popular government. He believed that if there was "a more responsible" monarch in Egypt, a clash between the two concepts would have been less probable.[3]

Sir Miles Lampson was very much concerned about the rise of anti-British feelings in Egypt and in the other Arab countries in connection with the Palestine problem. He had persistently urged his government not to treat the Palestine issue in isolation, and warned of the possible threat to British vital interests from the continuation of the conflict in Palestine. He was eager to keep Egypt away from any involvement in the more complicated Arab issues.

The Ambassador drew attention also to Egyptian fears lest Jewish predominance in Palestine might constitute an economic danger to Egypt, with the possibility of Haifa supplanting Alexandria and thus shifting the economic weight from Egypt to Palestine. He considered it "probably to the interest of both the Arabs and the British" that Egypt's interest in Arab problems should remain "as academic as possible" and that "we and the Arabs should settle Arab problems among ourselves". Egypt, in his view, was "not really an Arab country in spite of her claims to be one". Her participation in Arab problems tended to give them a more religious colour than was necessary. He considered it would be

---

[1] Laurence Grafftey-Smith *Bright Levant*, London 1970, pp. 138, 238. Also Barrie St Clair MacBride *Farouk of Egypt; A Biography*, London 1967, p. 117

[2] FO 371–23304–J 941/1/16

[3] FO 371–41326–J 180 and 190/31/16

harmful to British interests if Egypt were to become the champion of Islam "against western 'imperialism' ". This would intensify national bitterness and retard the progress of what he called "the Egypto–Arab World" towards inclusion in "the western comity of nations".[1]

The Ambassador's views are very interesting, since they were expressed just a few weeks before the start of the Arab unity consultations which led to the formation of the Arab League. They seem to falsify the charge made so often that the idea of the League was inspired by the British, presumably through their Ambassador.[2]

IRAQ IN THE AFTERMATH OF THE RASHID 'ALI PUTSCH: NURI AL-SA'ID

The history of Iraq since the early thirties cannot be separated from the versatile career of Nuri Pasha al-Sa'id. Nuri Pasha was born in 1888 and had his military education in Constantinople, where he joined *Al'Ahd*, the secret Arab society founded by Aziz 'Ali al-Misri. He joined the Great Arab Revolt in 1916 and accompanied Amir (later King) Faisal in the Syrian campaign. He belonged to a group of Iraqi nationalists whose political outlook was shaped during the pre-war critical period, and who were embittered at the balkanization and the imposition of foreign mandates over the Arab East after the war. This group included Yassin al-Hashimi, Ja'afar al-Askari, Jamil al-Madfa'i, and Taha al-Hashimi. Of all of them, Nuri proved to be the most determined pan-Arabist, and the most astute politician. By 1944, he had assumed the Premiership eight times and for periods longer than any of his colleagues.[3] His strong loyalty to, and connections with, the Iraqi Royal Family made him no less influential when out of office.

He was known for his strong loyalty to the Anglo-Iraqi alliance and for his firm belief in the benefit to Iraq and the Arab countries from continued friendship and co-operation with the British. The British connection was for him the best guarantee against a hostile French policy in Syria and an expansionist policy on the part of Turkey and Persia. It was this attitude which made him suspect in the eyes of the extreme Iraqi nationalists, by whom he was stigmatized as a pliable tool for the British.

Yet Nuri was known more as a born intriguer, a man who did not know a straight line. His biographer, Lord Birdwood, was to note his skill as a politician for whom "every move in the political game, the reactions of supporters or opponents to each move, the play of shifting

---

[1] Cab. 95/1—M.E.W.C. (43) 15

[2] See, for instance, Abdul Rahman al-Rafi'i *Fi Aa'qab al-Thawra al-Misriya*, vol. III, Cairo 1951, p. 141

[3] Majid Khadduri *Independent Iraq*, pp. 278–9

loyalties, were studied with the care of the chess player".[1] He was able to rule Iraq in his own way, which was almost similar to that of Sir Robert Walpole in England in the early part of the eighteenth century. He used to play on his opponents' weak points, keeping them contented in a way that did not conflict with his own drive for power.[2] This was all the more important in Iraq, where internal politics was based on personalities rather than on parties as was the case in Egypt. Relations among the old influential politicians were far from harmonious. Politics to them was an art of intrigue, manoeuvre, and skill. They all had a common interest in the preservation of the existing system, since any radical change would have involved a threat to their position and prestige. This lesson was driven home to them after the Bakr Sidqi *coup* of 1936, which, by the injection of a new force, namely that of the Iraqi army, had upset the normal pattern of Iraqi politics. It was driven home to Nuri in particular, since by intriguing with the four Colonels to bring him back to power in December 1938 he had unwittingly contributed to the increase in the army's intervention in politics, and had unleashed forces which he was not able to control. The monarchy in Iraq did not involve itself too much in the rivalries among this group of veteran politicians. The preclusion of the monarch, according to the Iraqi constitution, from dismissing incumbent Prime Ministers was always a limiting factor. The competing elements in Iraqi politics observed certain rules of conduct towards one another, thus avoiding the bitter acrimonies and victimizations which characterized the relations between the Wafd and the minority parties in Egypt. They all belonged to the socially if not economically privileged class, and were keen on maintaining the *status quo*.

Nuri was also an ardent Arab nationalist, with a fertile imagination and a broader outlook on Arab affairs. He did not go to extremes, however, and tried always to achieve a compromise between British policies and Arab aspirations. The methods he used ranged from persuasion to mild pressure. He used always to stress that the realization of Arab aspirations in independence and unity would consolidate, rather than weaken, British prestige and influence in the area. His espousal of pan-Arab ideals was motivated by his belief in the economic and political benefits to Iraq from an Arab association. He also saw the benefit to himself both inside and outside Iraq from championing the cause of Arab unity. His pan-Arab activities did often put him at loggerheads with the British, who had to contend with Sa'udi and French objections, and who resented Nuri's attempt to have a say in the settlement of the Palestine problem. Nuri was described as "a devious intriguer with a passion for having his finger in every pie".[3] To them Nuri, was,

---

[1] Lord Birdwood *Nuri as Sa'id: A Study in Arab Leadership*, London 1959, p. 190

[2] 'Abdul Rahman Al-Bazzaz *Safahat Min al-Ams al-Qarib*, Beirut 1960, p. 170

[3] FO 371–21872–E257/10/31: a minute by Lord Cranborne, the then Parliamentary Under-Secretary of State in the Foreign Office, in January 1938

however, a person to be trusted and relied on at least in Iraqi internal politics.

Nuri's pan-Arab activities were resented by the French, who were keen on insulating Syria and Lebanon from the pan-Arab effervescence in Iraq, and who suspected British instigation behind Nuri's moves. He came to realize in 1941 the difficulty of including Syria in any Arab federation, because of French objections. He thought, however, that once such a federation took shape, Syria would drop in "like a ripe date". To Ibn Sa'ud, Nuri was anathema, and was suspected of trying merely to further Hashimite designs in Syria and to enhance his own personal prestige. Nuri did not in fact conceal, at least from the British, his wish to see a Hashimite, and Amir 'Abdul Ilah, the Iraqi Regent, in particular, at the head of any prospective federation. Ibn Sa'ud also resented Nuri's attempt to take the lead, which he thought belonged to himself, in Arab affairs. He was rather disdainful of this encroachment on the part of a politician, who was subject to removal from office, on his own prerogatives as an established monarch of great prestige in the Arab World. Amir 'Abdullah also resented Nuri's activities, which he thought were aimed at furthering the ambitions of the Iraqi Royal Family at his own expense. He considered himself, as the senior surviving Hashimite ruler, more worthy of leadership in the area.

After the collapse of the Rashid 'Ali movement late in May 1941, Jamil al-Madfa'i assumed the premiership for a little over four months. He was found by the British rather lax in dealing with the former supporters of that movement. Nuri Pasha was therefore summoned from Cairo early in October 1941 to become the Prime Minister and Minister of Defence. Once in office, Nuri followed a tough policy, which included the internment and trial of the participants in, and the sympathizers with, the Rashid 'Ali movement. This was done in response to British requests. The internment list was furnished by the British Ambassador. Pan-Arab and extreme nationalist items were deleted from the educational curricula, and more British officials were appointed in the government and in the Ministry of the Interior in particular. The Iraqi army was purged of all the former sympathizers with Rashid 'Ali and the four Colonels. Nuri responded to all British demands in this regard since there was no room for refusal with their troops in effective hold over the whole country. He realized that this was a necessary price to pay for the Rashid 'Ali putsch, and he was eager to restore relations with the British to their previously friendly state. By the end of 1941, Sir Kinahan Cornwallis was to note that the attitude of the Iraqi Government had been "extremely exemplary" and that all British requests had been complied with.[1]

Nuri tried also to associate Iraq with the Allied war effort, hoping

---

[1] FO 371–35010–E1667/489/93: Sir Kinahan Cornwallis to FO, December 1941

thereby for his country to have a say in the post-war settlement. Iraq adhered to the United Nations Declaration and in January 1943 was the first Arab country to declare war on the Axis. In preparing Iraqi public opinion for this step, Nuri stressed the third provision of the Atlantic Charter with regard to the right of self-determination and self-government for those countries which had been forcibly deprived of them. In his reply to Churchill's message welcoming Iraq as a co-belligerent, Nuri reminded the British Prime Minister that the Arab countries which had not yet achieved their independence still looked to the British to fulfil their past promises. When reproached by the British for advancing such demands without making any contribution to the war effort, he offered to send some Iraqi troops for service under the British Command in Syria, which offer was turned down by the British.[1]

Nuri was to develop during this period his scheme for Arab unity, which he embodied in a long Note on Arab Independence and Unity, which he forwarded in January 1943 to Richard Casey, the Minister of State in Cairo. He called for an initiative on the part of the United Nations by declaring:

"1. That Syria, Lebanon, Palestine, and Transjordan shall be united into one state.
2. That the form of government of this state, whether monarchical or republican, whether unitary or federal, shall be decided by the peoples of this state themselves.
3. That there shall be created an Arab League to which Iraq and Syria will adhere at once and which can be joined by the other Arab states at will.
4. That this Arab League shall have a permanent Council nominated by the member states and presided over by one of the rulers of the states, who shall be chosen in a manner acceptable to the states concerned.
5. That this Arab League Council shall be responsible for the following: (*a*) defence; (*b*) foreign affairs; (*c*) currency; (*d*) communications; (*e*) customs; (*f*) protection of minority rights.
6. That the Jews in Palestine shall be given semi-autonomy. They shall have the right to their own rural and urban district administration including schools, health institutions, and police, subject to general supervision by the Syrian state.
7. That Jerusalem shall be a city to which members of all religions shall have free access for pilgrimage and worship. A special commission composed of representatives of the three theocratic religions shall be set up to ensure this.
8. That if they demand it, the Maronites in the Lebanon shall be granted a privileged regime such as they possessed during the last

[1] FO 371–40041–E1143/37/93

years of the Ottoman Empire. This special regime, like those to be set up in paragraph 6 and 7 above, shall rest on an international guarantee."

Nuri excluded Saudi Arabia and Egypt from his scheme. Iraq's relations with Syria, Lebanon, Palestine, and Transjordan, he stated, had always been close. The Arabian Peninsula states, on the other hand, had a different economy, while Egypt had a larger population and was preoccupied more with her own problems in the Sudan and elsewhere. He assumed therefore that neither Egypt nor the Arabian Peninsula states would be inclined at first to join, though they might wish to do so if such a union succeeded.[1]

Nuri pointed out that his scheme would remove a great many of the difficulties which had confronted Britain and France in the area in the past. He added that it would also allay the fears of the Arabs in Palestine of being a minority, and would enable the Jews to establish their National Home in the predominantly Jewish parts of Palestine with a greater feeling of security. He did not envisage unlimited Jewish immigration and settlement in Palestine, and thought of the development of a National Home on the basis of the White Paper of 1939. He was against partition or a federal structure inside Palestine, since in a small state this would be difficult and expensive.

Nuri based his scheme on the principles of the Atlantic Charter and on the assumption that the post-war settlement would endeavour to group the smaller countries together in some form of regional leagues and alliances able to protect themselves. It was natural, therefore, for Nuri to envisage the realization of his scheme as a result of a United Nations initiative, which was a novel idea in itself, and which meant in effect a federal scheme imposed by the great powers.

Nuri's exclusion of Egypt and Saudi Arabia was significant. It was obvious that what was envisaged was an Arab League under a Hashimite ruler. His scheme had many snags. It ignored French opposition, Ibn Sa'ud's objections, and Jewish refusal to accept a minority status in Palestine. The British doubted the possibility of the achievement of Nuri's scheme. Casey confined his comment to the request embodied in Nuri's covering letter that the Allies should make a definite declaration immediately to the effect that they would not support the creation of a Jewish state in Palestine and that they would adhere to the White Paper policy. Such a declaration was ruled out both by Casey and by the

---

[1] General Nuri al-Sa'id *Arab Independence and Unity: A Note on the Arab Cause with Particular Reference to Palestine and Suggestions for a Permanent Settlement of which are Attached Texts of All the Relevant Documents*, Baghdad, Government Printing Press, 1943. The *Note* was in fact prepared by Lloyd, Nuri's private secretary, on lines laid down by Nuri himself. C. Edmonds, the British adviser to the Ministry of the Interior, read the draft and suggested certain modifications of asperities of language. FO 371–24957–E2307/506/65

Foreign Office. Casey suggested, however, that in view of the sympathetic British attitude towards the ideal of Arab unity, the effect of this "discouraging" reply to Nuri's request could be alleviated by authorizing the British Ambassador to make, at his discretion, some constructive comment on Nuri's proposals. The Foreign Office did not see any necessity for replying to Nuri's Note, which was presented to Casey on an unofficial basis.[1]

The main reaction to Nuri's scheme was to come from Ibn Sa'ud. Nuri conveyed to the King the main tenor of his proposals, avoiding any reference to the exclusion of Saudi Arabia. He indicated that he sought no personal advantage, nor did he intend to set up any particular king on the Syrian throne, leaving it to the Syrians themselves to decide on any form of government they wanted. He expressed the hope that Ibn Sa'ud would support his scheme and thus ensure its success. Ibn Sa'ud's initially favourable reaction was soon to change, however, when the Sa'udi Chargé d'Affaires in Baghdad was told by the Iraqi Foreign Minister "in strict confidence" that the aim of his government was to secure the Syrian throne for the Iraqi Regent. The Iraqi Minister added that they had reason to suppose that this would be welcomed by the Syrians. He then appealed for Ibn Sa'ud's support on this point, noting that if, by Ibn Sa'ud's help, a Hashimite prince became King of Syria, the old Sa'udi–Hashimite feud would be removed for ever. Ibn Sa'ud considered Hashimite domination over Syria a direct threat to his country. He warned that if the British refused to intervene to put a stop to Nuri's activities, then his hands would be free and he would know how to safeguard his own interests.

Nuri, on his part, denied that the Iraqi Foreign Minister had ever made such statements, which he considered an obvious ruse on the part of their author to discover the views of H.M.G. on the issue. He gave a categorical assurance to the British that he was not working to secure the Syrian throne for the Iraqi Regent. He added, however, that his personal opinion was that the Syrians wanted a Hashimite as king, and "time will show if he is right".[2] It is not clear whether Ibn Sa'ud invented the story in an attempt to gauge British views, as suggested by Nuri, or whether the Iraqi Foreign Minister had made such statements in an attempt to sabotage Nuri's scheme. It is also possible that the Sa'udi Chargé might have invented the story, since he was very suspicious of Nuri's motives, and tried on previous occasions to prejudice the judgment of Ibn Sa'ud with regard to Nuri's proposals.[3]

---

[1] FO 371–34955–E1196/506/65: Nuri's *Note* was received favourably by L. Amery, the Secretary of State for India, who reiterated his belief that an Arab federation offered the only solution to the Palestine problem. FO 371–34958–E2810/506/65

[2] FO 371–34955: Wikeley (Jedda) to Eden on 23 February 1943, and Sir Kinahan to Eden on 5 March 1943

[3] FO 371–34955–E1050/506/65

Nuri conveyed the contents of his Note to Amir 'Abdullah, hoping for his support and inviting him, if he had any alternative scheme, to produce it. The Amir's reaction, as reported by Sir Harold MacMichael, the British High Commissioner, was "as usual" based entirely on the personal aspects of the matter and showed itself in jealousy at this attempt to take the lead, which he thought belonged to himself, in the Arab World.[1]

Nuri's preoccupation with Arab affairs resulted in his neglect of the pressing internal problems in Iraq. Sir Kinahan Cornwallis criticized him for his "subservience to vested interests", his "ignorance of detail", his "failure to grasp the economic nettle", and "his tendency to indulge in high political dreaming". A British Intelligence Report described the Iraqi Government as "an oligarchy of racketeers".[2] As was the case in Egypt in 1943, it fell to the British Ambassador to speak to Nuri "in no uncertain terms" about "the persistent failure" of his government to deal with the economic crisis and the steady deterioration in the morale and capabilities of the administration services. This criticism was not to disappear after Nuri reconstituted his Cabinet in December 1943. The new Cabinet, the Ambassador noted, contained "no progressive elements and was representative of the old ruling class of established families".[3]

There might be some truth in the argument made quite often in recent years that pan-Arab activities were often conducted by politicians to divert public attention from internal problems. With Nuri, this was only partly true, since the role he envisaged for himself was one which transcended frontiers, a role of an architect of a powerful regional grouping, and the Prime Minister of a Greater Arab federation.

IBN SA'UD AND THE WAR

Ibn Sa'ud emerged after the death of King Faisal of Iraq in 1933 as the leading figure in the Arab World. He was described as a man of commanding presence who made little parade of royalty, preferring the dignified simplicity of a great Arab personage.[4] He was also described as a benevolent despot who had the administration tightly centralized in his own hands. He was a ruler who remained throughout his reign accessible to his subjects, disposing personally of their complaints,[5] and who was very well versed in Arab lore and tribal affairs. As a leader who had suffered deprivation and exile in his youth, and who had established

---

[1] FO 371–34955–E1193/506/65
[2] FO 371–35010–E489/489/93
[3] FO 371–40041–E1143/37/93
[4] Sir Andrew Ryan *The Last of the Dragomans*, London 1951, pp. 274–7
[5] David Howarth *The Desert King: A Life of Ibn Saud*, London 1964, pp. 117–18

his authority through years of fighting, raiding, and sacrifices, Ibn Sa'ud was keen on preserving the independence and sovereignty of his country. In statesmanship Ibn Sa'ud was described by Sir Andrew Ryan, the first British Minister in Jedda, as "very shrewd",[1] and by Dr Chaim Weizmann as "astute".[2] By 1936 he had consolidated his authority within his domains; reduced his unruly followers to order; normalized his relations with Yemen, Transjordan, and Iraq; and cast himself in the role of a good neighbour and a conciliator of the Arabs. The rise of Sa'udi power was hence rightly described as the positive pole of the movement towards Arab solidarity.[3]

In conducting his foreign relations, Ibn Sa'ud was assisted by a trio of specialists, namely Sheikh Fu'ad Hamza, Sheikh Hafiz Wahba, and Sheikh Yusuf Yassin. Fu'ad Hamza was a Syrian Druze who had entered into Ibn Sa'ud's service late in the twenties. He was soon to become Deputy Minister of Foreign Affairs, a post which he retained until the late thirties, when he was appointed as Sa'udi Minister in Paris. Hafiz Wahba was an Egyptian, who joined Ibn Sa'ud's service in the twenties and was appointed early in the thirties as Sa'udi Minister in London, a key post which he maintained for several years. Yusuf Yassin, the King's Syrian private secretary, had been a permanent member in the King's entourage since the twenties. With Hafiz Wahba in London and Fu'ad Hamza in Paris, it was left to him to conduct most of the King's contacts with foreign representatives in Jedda, and he was to represent Ibn Sa'ud in the Arab unity consultations of 1943 and in the Alexandria Conference of 1944. These three officials had in common a strong loyalty to the King. Apart from that they had their own ambitions, jealousies, and intrigues against one another, and were always in competition for the King's favours. None of them was, however, anything but an adviser. Ibn Sa'ud was the only authority in the country, and his advisers were his most obedient servants in a literal sense.[4]

Ibn Sa'ud was very realistic in his approach to world politics. He based his foreign policy on the necessity for continued close relations with the British, whom he trusted and used to consult on all Arab and

---

[1] Sir Andrew Ryan, op. cit., p. 275

[2] Norman Rose: "The Debate on Partition 1937–38: The Anglo-Zionist Aspect II: The Withdrawal" in *Middle Eastern Studies*, vol. 7, January 1971, No. 1, p. 21 (footnote). Also: Amin al-Rihani *Muluk al-'Arab*, vol. II, 3rd edn., Beirut 1951, pp. 43–4, 53–4, for an interesting and detailed account of Ibn Sa'ud's handling of the internal affairs of his kingdom

[3] Arnold Toynbee *Survey of International Affairs: 1936*, Royal Institute of International Affairs, London 1937, p. 785

[4] Sir Andrew Ryan, op. cit., p. 277. We can cite the attempts of Sheikh Hafiz to prejudice Ibn Sa'ud and the British against Sheikh Fu'ad in January 1939 by alleging that Fu'ad was in the pay of the Italians: FO 371–23268–E174/174/25. Also: Khair ud-Din al-Zurkally *Shibh al-Jazira fi 'Ahd al-Malik 'Abdul 'Aziz*, vol. III, Part 3, Beirut 1970, p. 981

international issues. This was coupled with profuse flattery, which captivated all British officials who came in touch with him.[1] In taking this line of policy Ibn Sa'ud was guided by several practical considerations. Britain was the world power most interested in the region which had a strong military presence in the areas surrounding his kingdom. Britain had assisted him consistently even before his conquest of the Hejaz, and recognized "the complete and absolute independence" of his domains in 1927, at a time when most Arabs and Muslims were apprehensive of his power and hostile to the extension of the orthodox Wahhabi authority over the Holy Places in the Hejaz. Britain was, moreover, through its hold over Iraq and Transjordan, the only power capable of restraining the Hashimites from pursuing or encouraging anti-Sa'udi activities, and which had readily intervened to bring about a stabilization of the *status quo* in his favour. Britain was also, through its control over most of the Muslim countries in the Middle East, Africa, and India, in a position to ensure the continued inflow of pilgrims, whose contributions formed, up to the late thirties, the main source of income for Saudi Arabia. Britain was finally the country on whose financial assistance he relied most when the number of pilgrims decreased during the depression years of the early thirties and during the Second World War.

The British, on the other hand, saw in the establishment of a strong and friendly regime in Saudi Arabia a stabilizing factor in the area, and a guarantee for the safety of the Muslim pilgrims. Ibn Sa'ud's great prestige and popularity in the Arab World were a great asset to the British, in view of his moderating influence on the extreme Arab nationalists in Palestine, Syria, and Iraq. Ibn Sa'ud was, however, far from being the willing tool of the British in the area. His pragmatic approach to world politics was coupled with excessive caution and far-sightedness. The failure of the British to offer any serious resistance to the Italian invasion of Abyssinia in 1935 was, in his view, a blow to British prestige in the area. His reaction was to avoid as much as possible antagonizing Italy, and to work for the formation of a compact alliance system between the Arab states to withstand a similar Italian attack on his country or on Yemen. When the British were unable in 1938 to provide him with small arms to control irredentist tribes, or enough financial assistance and food-stuffs to stave off starvation in some parts of his kingdom, he decided to resort to the Germans for help. He expounded to Dr Grobba, the German representative in Baghdad who was also accredited to Saudi Arabia, in February 1939, his grievances against the British.

---

[1] Of this we can cite his statement in 1939 when he heard of the sinking by the Germans of a British warship that he felt as if one of his sons had died, or his statement later that Britain was like a big tree of which the Arab countries were the leaves which would dry and fall off if the tree were to fall. FO 371–35147–E140/69/25; FO 371–23271–E7604/549/25

The British, Ibn Sa'ud maintained, had supported the Hashimites, his rivals, and had kept to themselves Bahrein and Kuwait, which had previously belonged to his country. The British had therefore greatly impeded his freedom of action. British attitudes with regard to the question of Palestine and to the annexation by Turkey of Alexandretta belied any "alleged friendship" for the Arabs. He added that his aim was to free himself gradually from British influence in a manner which should not be noticeable as long as he was not in a position to check their excessive influence in the area. For this reason, his country was seeking friends in the world in order to strengthen her own position. He then asked for German moral support, and for urgent supplies of small arms.[1] The King's overtures at first found no response from the Germans, who thought that he had yielded completely to British tutelage, was remaining aloof from the pan-Arab movement and the Arab struggle in Palestine, and wanted merely to play Germany off against Britain and on occasion against Italy too.[2] The Germans were soon to change their attitude in view of the failure of Italy to make any headway in her efforts to gain influence in the area. Khalid al-Hud al-Qarqani, the King's adviser, who paid an unsuccessful visit to Germany in the summer of 1938, was to pay a second visit to Berlin in June 1939. He was warmly received by the Germans, and had a long interview with Hitler. Axis propaganda gave wide publicity to the visit, leaving the impression that Ibn Sa'ud was turning against Britain. It was then that Ibn Sa'ud began to draw back. He realized that he was being used by the Germans for their own purposes. He felt rather embarrassed at the excessive publicity given to the visit of Khalid al-Hud, which was obviously intended to strain his relations with the British, and thus to force him to throw himself completely into the Axis camp. He was eager from the start not to arouse British suspicions, and kept them informed of the general tenor and purpose of his contacts with the Germans, indicating his readiness to accept any alternative British offer of arms and assistance. The deal agreed upon between Khalid al-Hud and the Germans was cancelled by the King at the last minute soon after the outbreak of the war, "lest his action should be exaggerated by the Germans or misinterpreted by others".[3] This incident served only to increase his suspicions of Axis motives and to draw him closer to the British. He refused to allow Dr Grobba to take up residence in Jedda, and rejected all subsequent German overtures.

The serious drop in the King's two sources of income—pilgrimage, and advance payments of oil royalties—because of the war situation, left him with a revenue of approximately ten percent of his expenditure.

---

[1] *Documents on German Foreign Policy*, series D, vol. V, pp. 800–10

[2] Ibid., vol. VI, p. 556

[3] FO 371–23272–E6913/735/25

Export restrictions imposed by all the neighbouring countries, and the scarcity of shipping space made it very difficult to supply his country with sufficient food, motor transport, and other necessities. He appealed persistently for British help to stave off the danger of famine and consequent troubles in his kingdom. The Foreign Office managed to convince a reluctant and war-strained Treasury to increase financial assistance to Saudi Arabia. It went up as a result from £396,582 in 1940, to £3,840,836 in 1943.[1] Ibn Sa'ud became no less dependent upon the British than was Amir 'Abdullah of Transjordan. Yet the King, with his known tact and resourcefulness, avoided compromising his position. While profuse in expressions of support for the British, he abstained till 1945 from declaring war on the Axis powers. He was not in fact pressed by the British to change his attitude of benevolent neutrality. Such a change, they thought, might be attributed to British pressure and financial inducements, and might compromise his position and influence in the area as a truly independent Arab leader. The King was, moreover, not in a position to render any material help to the Allies in the war.[2]

Ibn Sa'ud's relations with the other Arab countries were governed to a great extent by his antagonism to the Hashimites, and his resentment of any single state or leader taking the lead over himself or his country in Arab affairs. There was much to arouse his suspicions in the Arab nationalist movement which was led by King Faisal I and whose leaders tended, at least until the death of King Faisal, to favour Hashimite rule over Syria. The rising popularity and prestige of Ibn Sa'ud appealed to many Arab nationalists. His exploits in his war against the Hashimites in 1925 and against the Yemen in 1934 captured their imagination. They saw in him, after the death of King Faisal, the only leader of note in the Arab World. The King realized the extreme difficulties facing the Arab nationalists. He also realized that any increased involvement on his part in Arab affairs was bound to worsen his relations both with the British and the French, and would be viewed with suspicion by the Hashimite rulers in Iraq and Transjordan. He therefore confined himself to a negative role, and exerted all his efforts to prevent the formation either of a Greater Syria or the union of Iraq and Syria. He kept a watchful eye on Hashimite intrigues and manoeuvres, and managed to frustrate their schemes at times by inviting British intervention, and at other times through the counter-activities of his supporters in Syria and Palestine. His contacts with the Syrian, Lebanese, and Palestinian nationalists were designed mainly to serve this negative end.

He was opposed to any union between two or more countries in the Arab East under Hashimite leadership, since this would upset the bal-

---

[1] FO 371–40265–E1775/128/25

[2] FO 371–31450–E1237/13/25. Also: Khair ud-Din al-Zurkally *Shibh al-Jazira fi 'Ahd al-Malik 'Abdul 'Aziz*, pp. 961–4

ance in the Arab World and be contrary to his own interests.[1] He was even opposed to the idea of an Arab federation itself even if the participation of Saudi Arabia was envisaged and his prominent role was recognized. As the leader of one of the least advanced of the Arab states, he could only play a minor role, with the possibility of his country, if not during his reign then after his death, being engulfed by its more advanced and more powerful neighbour Iraq, joined by Transjordan. The King used to stress, once and again, that his aim was to be secure within his own possessions, and that he had no designs or ambitions in Syria or Palestine. He wanted every Arab country to gain and retain its independence, and saw no reason why the Arabs in Syria and Palestine should throw off French and British tutelage "only to fall under that of Hashimites or the Egyptians".[2]

His idea of the Arab World as it should be was a group of states, each retaining its independence, and combined by a comprehensive alliance system which should provide for collective security arrangements. The role of Britain was central in his scheme, since no single Arab state or leader was, in his view, strong or disinterested enough to command the respect of the rest. Britain, on the other hand, enjoyed the respect of all the Arabs. As such, she could help them "to compose their differences" and thus to promote their unity "by guaranteeing the protection of the interests of each state in relation to the others".[3] A British arbitratory and conciliatory role was, in Ibn Sa'ud's view, essential even with regard to closer inter-Arab economic co-operation. This was so, he maintained, because the economic interests of the Arab countries were not necessarily in harmony, and each state would "naturally and inevitably" try to get the best bargain for herself.[4] The King's views were no doubt determined by his suspicions of Hashimite intrigues, which could only be held in check by a British guarantee. The concept of political unity or integration was unacceptable to him, and he used quite often to confuse the idea of unity with the alliance system which he favoured and which proved a failure in strengthening ties between his country and Iraq.

Ibn Sa'ud took an active interest in the Palestine problem.[5] He was keen on playing to the Arab gallery in view of the pressures which were being exerted on him by the *'Ulema* in Nejd, by his Syrian advisers, and by the Arab nationalists in the Levant. His support for the Arab cause in Palestine was seasoned, however, by his realization of the general

[1] Ibn Sa'ud's statement to Sir Reader Bullard in October 1939. FO 371–23271–E7604/549/25

[2] FO 371–35147–E140/69/25; 23281–E6959/6697/89: Ibn Sa'ud's statements to Lord Moyne in December 1941

[3] FO 371–23195–E7813/7697/65

[4] FO 371–35147–E140/69/25

[5] Al-Zurkally, op. cit., pp. 1071–1125 for an account of Ibn Sa'ud's contacts with the British and American governments with regard to Palestine

weakness of the Arabs, and of the necessity to proceed with caution and through persuasion and mild pressure rather than through extremism. He therefore refrained from making any public statements on the issue and continued to counsel moderation and the need to reach an understanding with the British.[1] He made, in the meantime, several representations to the British, warning them at one time that the Arabs might turn in desperation to the Axis powers, if the British continued their negative and repressive policies in Palestine, which warning was vindicated by the Rashid 'Ali movement of 1941. In this, his efforts were more effective with the British than were those of the other Arab leaders.

He took interest also in the situation in the Levant following the Anglo-Free-French invasion in June 1941. He expressed disappointment at the establishment there of the authority of the Free French, whom he considered as "just a slice from the same old loaf".[2] Yet he was soon to recognize the regimes installed by the Free French in Syria and Lebanon late in 1941, when he was asked by the British to do so in spite of the fact that these regimes were denounced as unconstitutional by the Iraqi and the Egyptian Governments. He played a great and positive role in removing British suspicions of Axis leanings on the part of the Syrian nationalists. He also advised the nationalists in the Levant to co-operate with the British in order to secure the achievement of their goals.

In all this Ibn Sa'ud was actuated primarily by self-interest. He wanted to foil the moves of the Hashimites, and to vindicate, by his favourable influence on the neighbouring Arabs, his worth as a good friend of the British. He played a valuable moderating role in the area during the war and was consistent in his friendship with H.M.G.

AMIR 'ABDULLAH'S AMBITIONS IN SYRIA

Amir 'Abdullah, the son of Sherif Hussein of Mecca, was the first to contact the British in February 1914, explaining to them Arab grievances against the Turks. This was a prelude to the subsequent contacts between his father and Sir Henry MacMahon and to the Great Arab Revolt. He took a daring step in November 1920 following the eviction of his brother Faisal by the French from Syria. The Amir proceeded to

[1] Stonehewer-Bird, the British Minister in Jedda, was to note in his annual report for 1940 that Ibn Sa'ud "stands almost alone in his sympathetic understanding of the difficulties which face H.M.G. in the matter of Palestine. Whereas Amir Faisal and Sheikh Yusuf Yassin hanker for further declarations of British intentions after the war and for the immediate grant of a greater share for Palestine Arabs in the administration, the King realised and has advised Arab statesmen 'that present efforts must be concentrated on winning the war'." FO 371–27261–E1766/114/25

[2] FO 371–27267–E4326/4326/25. Also: Al-Zurkally, op. cit., pp. 1236–8

Ma'an and established himself in Amman in March 1921. His purpose was to mobilize forces to fight the French, and to re-establish the Arab kingdom of his brother in Syria. He had to change his plans, however, following his meeting with Churchill, the then Colonial Secretary, in Jerusalem on 29 March 1921. In that meeting the Amir accepted the Emirate of Transjordan on a temporary basis. It was pointed out to him that if he succeeded in checking anti-French action for six months, he might convince the French of his good intentions and willingness to co-operate with them. He would in this way reduce their opposition to Faisal's candidature for the Kingship of Iraq, and greatly improve his own chances of being installed by the French as Amir of Syria in Damascus. It was made "perfectly clear" to him, however, that "while H.M.G. would do everything to assist him towards the attainment of this object, they would not in any way guarantee that it would be achieved".[1] It was on the basis of this understanding that the Amir continued throughout the following years to entertain hopes of the Syrian throne and to consider himself, of all the candidates, the most worthy of that throne.

The French were strongly against the extension of the Amir's authority to Syria, which would have meant in effect an extension of British influence to that country. The Amir had another rival in the person of King Faisal of Iraq, and later in the person of the Iraqi Regent Amir 'Abdul Ilah. King Ibn Sa'ud was also against any extension of Hashimite rule to Syria, for the prevention of which he was ready to resort to the use of force if necessary. The Syrian and Lebanese nationalists were determined to preserve the republican regimes in both countries. There was no love lost between them and the Amir, who was too traditional and backward for the sophisticated and secularized Syrians and Lebanese, and who was too subservient to the British to be of any real help to them.

The Amir was therefore left in Transjordan, an arid country artificially constituted, and dependent for its survival on an annual British subsidy. He was obliged, under the 1928 agreement with Britain, to accept British advice in all matters of finance, defence, and foreign affairs. He was never satisfied with his reduced status, and considered himself, after the death of King Faisal, as the most legitimate contender for the leadership of the Arabs by virtue of his being the senior surviving Hashimite, and of his role in the Great Arab Revolt. His obsession with the issue of the Syrian throne was coupled with his antagonism towards Ibn Sa'ud and the Wahhabis, who had dislodged his family from the Hejaz and threatened his rule in Transjordan. He never concealed his hope for the re-establishment of his father's kingdom in the Hejaz, and never stopped his intrigues against Ibn Sa'ud. It was for this reason that Ibn Sa'ud was opposed to the emancipation of Transjordan, since as

[1] FO 371–23281–E6880/6697/89. Also: King 'Abdullah *Mudhakkirat al Malik 'Abdullah*, 2nd edn., Amman 1947, pp. 241–4

long as the British were in effective control he was sure that they would check all hostile activities on the part of the Amir.[1] In dealing with this situation, the British tried to bring a normalization of relations between Saudi Arabia and Transjordan. They managed to get the countries to conclude a treaty in 1933, in which both the Amir and Ibn Sa'ud recognized each other's regimes. The emancipation of Transjordan was ruled out at that time because of the financial dependence of Transjordan on Britain, and because of what was considered as "the unsatisfactory personality of the Amir" who was "far too preoccupied with petty and parochial intrigues".[2]

The Amir was the first and only Arab ruler to accept the recommendations of the Palestine Royal Commission in 1937 regarding partition and the annexation of the Arab part of Palestine to Transjordan. His attitude enraged Arab nationalists everywhere, and drew sharp reactions from Ibn Sa'ud and the Iraqi Prime Minister Hikmat Suleiman. He was also to draw up his own scheme for Arab federation in 1938, which provided for the union of Palestine and Transjordan under one sovereign.[3] The Amir excluded his two bigger neighbours, Iraq and Saudi Arabia, since their participation would have undermined his own chances of leadership in the proposed union.

The Amir saw in the outbreak of the war his chance for pressing further his claims in Syria and his request for the emancipation of Transjordan from the mandate. He was eager to play a greater role in the Arab World, similar to that played by his father during the First World War. He expressed to the British his dissatisfaction with what he regarded as the minor role assigned to him, of keeping Transjordan quiet. He reminded the British of the promises made by Churchill in 1921 with regard to Syria, adding that pro-Axis activities in the area could only be combated if Arab aspirations in Syria and Palestine were to be realized, and if his army, the Arab Legion, was strengthened in order to become the bulwark of British influence in Arab Asia.[4] He intensified, in the meantime, his propaganda and contacts with Syrian notables in Hauran and Jebel al-Druze.

---

[1] The objections of Ibn Sa'ud to the emancipation and the enlargement of the territory of Transjordan were voiced forcefully and repeatedly following the issue of the Report of the Royal Commission (Peel) in July 1937. Major J. Glubb, who was then in charge of the Arab Legion in Transjordan, reported alarming Sa'udi frontier activities including the arming of the frontier tribes and active recruiting among the anti-Amir Transjordan tribes. FO 371–20810, 20818. Ibn Sa'ud had in fact established contacts with Fawzi al-Qawaqji, who took an active part in the Palestine revolt, and promised arms assistance provided a revolt was staged first in Transjordan to topple Amir 'Abdullah. *Mudhakkirat Taha al-Hashimi: 1919–1943*, ed. by Sati' al-Husri, Beirut, 1968, pp. 229–30. For an example of Amir 'Abdullah's antagonism towards Ibn Sa'ud see: *Mudhakkirat al Malik 'Abdullah*, pp. 216–18

[2] FO 371–18965–E6911/6911/31

[3] FO 371–21885–E3866/38/31

[4] FO 371–23281–E7102/6697/89

News began to appear in the Egyptian press about an imminent agreement between the British and the French Governments to give the throne of Syria to the Amir. It was stated that this was intended as a counter-move to Ibn Sa'ud's overtures to the Axis powers and the visit of Khalid al-Hud to Berlin. This news was echoed also in some British and Jewish newspapers.[1] Ibn Sa'ud was terribly annoyed at the Amir's activities. He sought and got British assurances against any further moves by the Amir on the issue. He stressed that he did not want anything outside his dominions but feared lest the addition of Syria either to Iraq or Transjordan would facilitate Hashimite designs against his kingdom. As for Amir 'Abdullah, he noted, if it were not for British support he would not be even the Amir of Transjordan for another day.[2] Nuri Pasha al-Sa'id was also to express to the British his resentment of the Amir's activities. The strongest objections came, however, from the French Government. The Amir, for them, was a mere "willing tool" for the British, who would wish, through him, to extend their influence as widely as possible. The British, on the other hand, were rather embarrassed at the Amir's activities, and informed Ibn Sa'ud, Nuri, and the French that it was not their policy to support the Amir's claims to the Syrian throne. Their attitude was, rather than to use the Amir to extend their influence, "to keep his ambitions within the narrowest limits compatible with a reasonable recognition of the services he has rendered to them in the past twenty years".[3]

The Amir's activities did not stop, however, in spite of British discouragement, and they were to take a new turn after the fall of France in June 1940. He considered that the French mandate over Syria and Lebanon had fallen with the fall of France. He declared his intention to issue a public statement to the effect that Syria and Transjordan would henceforth be one country in alliance with Britain, and to prepare enough forces to occupy any part of Syria from which the French could be ejected. He sent emissaries to his supporters in Syria to inform them of his plans. The British, however, opposed any action against the French in the Levant at that stage, since they were not ready to open a new front at a time when their forces were occupied on the Libyan front. The Amir yielded to British pressure but he did not fail to remind them once more of Churchill's promises, and to urge them to bear them in mind when the policy *vis-à-vis* Syria was decided upon.[4]

When the Anglo-Free-French operations in the Levant started in June 1941, the Amir offered the participation of the Arab Legion in these operations in order to establish for himself some rights in Syria. He suggested that he should issue a manifesto calling upon the Syrians

[1] *Al Misri*, 30 July and 3–6 August 1939; *Al-Muqattam*, 21 August 1939
[2] FO 371–23271–E7604/549/25
[3] FO 371–24547–E1588/225/65; 24548–E2027/953/65
[4] FO 371–24592–E2227/2170/89. Sir Harold MacMichael to CO on 1 July 1940

to welcome the invading armies. The British realized the Amir's real intentions, and urged him to abstain from all intervention in the operations in Syria, which were "the concern of the military authorities and no one else". They did not respond to his advice that the "pro-Axis politicians" in Syria should be interned since they would "make a settlement impossible".[1] This was an obvious reference to the leaders of the National Bloc who were strongly committed to a republican regime in Syria, and who had affiliations with King Ibn Sa'ud. The Amir's subsequent representations to the British with regard to the Syrian throne included the forwarding to them of two long Cabinet resolutions, in July 1941 and January 1942, and several letters and oral messages.[2] In a letter to Churchill in November 1941, he called for the establishment of a Syrian union. He referred to the settlement after the First World War, and expressed the hope that Churchill's "dexterous hands" would lay down a structure for the future which would make him (the Amir) this time "luckier than I was at the last peace".[3]

The Amir was never taken seriously by the British, who knew that, with his financial dependence on them and with the wide powers they had in Transjordan under the 1928 agreement, he would not be able to make any move without their knowledge and consent. They were annoyed, however, at his indiscretions and antagonism to Ibn Sa'ud, whom he continued to refer to as the King of Nejd. They were also annoyed at his persistent agitation for the Syrian throne. He was described, however, as "a very loyal and whole-hearted supporter (of H.M.G.), charming, astute and amusing, but wisdom and discretion unfortunately have passed him by".[4] The Colonial Office were impressed by his loyalty and helpful attitude with regard to the Palestine situation. They were always rather sympathetic towards his aspirations, especially those related to the emancipation of Transjordan. Yet the realization by the British in 1938 that the Amir's kingship over Transjordan and the Arab part of Palestine was the main reason for Sa'udi and Iraqi opposition to partition made the Amir appear to them as a liability rather than an asset. Ormsby-Gore, the then Colonial Secretary, thought that perhaps the Amir could be "bought out", thus removing a serious obstacle in the way of partition.[5]

The Amir's strong loyalty to the British, for which he had in fact no alternative considering his financial dependence on them, did not fail to

---

[1] FO 371–27044–E4225/53/65. Also: *Al Kitab Al Urduni al-Abiad: Al Watha'iq al Qawmiya fil Wihda al-Suriya al Tabi'iya:* issued by the Government of Transjordan, Amman (n.d.), pp. 21–35

[2] Ibid., pp. 58–63

[3] FO 371–31338–E7278/49/65

[4] CO 733–444–75872/115/41, from a report by Sir Harold MacMichael, the High Commissioner for Palestine and Transjordan in 1941

[5] FO 371–20807–E3527/22/31; 20808–E3906/22/31: minute by George Rendel (Foreign Office) on 3 July 1937

antagonize Arab nationalists. He alienated the Palestine Arab nationalists of the Mufti group by his support for the so-called moderate Nashashibi faction. His ambitions in Syria alienated Syrian nationalists, and he found supporters only from among the traditional notables of Jebel al-Druze and the Hauran. The Amir was in fact regarded by Arab nationalists everywhere as being too pro-British to be of any effective help to the Arab cause. The inferior status of Transjordan under the British mandate, together with its backwardness and poverty, did not lend any credibility to the Amir's claims to a leading role in Arab Asia. His attempt to draw all the time on the great contributions of his family during the Arab Revolt did not impress the new generation of Arab nationalists, who saw in the settlement after the First World War the root of all present trouble in the area.

THE INDEPENDENCE OF SYRIA AND LEBANON: ANGLO-FRENCH FRICTIONS 1941 TO 1945

The refusal of the French early in 1939 to ratify the 1936 treaties with Syria and Lebanon was a setback for the national movement in the Levant. The French attitude stood in sharp contrast to British efforts at just the same time to propitiate the Arabs by adopting a more conciliatory policy in Palestine. To the British, the Arab nationalist movement was a genuine force in Middle East politics. The French, on the other hand, doubted the strength of that movement in view of the parochial and sectarian dissensions which they themselves did much to foster. The best policy for them was "to divide and rule", and, in the then prevailing illusions about France's impregnable defences in Europe, even resort to forceful measures to quell any national uprising was not ruled out. French suspicions of British motives were deeply rooted, and British views on the necessity of conciliating the Arabs[1] were not welcomed even at that time of close Anglo-French collaboration.

The fall of France in June 1940 and the rallying of the French forces in the Levant to the Vichy regime created a new set of problems for the British. They were ready, however, to compromise, and even to co-operate with the French in the Levant just to buy time, as long as no Axis activities were allowed against British positions in the area. The

---

[1] The most forceful British representations to the French government were those made on instructions from the Foreign Office by Sir Eric Phipps in Paris in April 1939. The British expressed their misgivings at the new line the French were taking in the Levant, which they felt would provide a profitable field for Axis propaganda and intrigues. The French were told that "upon a larger view H.M.G. cannot help feeling that the day has passed when the clock can be put back in a country like Syria, which was moreover the first home of Arab nationalism". Reference was made to possible neighbouring Arab reactions and to the necessity, in the present world conditions, of remaining "on terms of close friendship with the various Arab states". FO 371–23194

British attitude changed in April 1941. This was due to the worsening situation in Iraq following the Rashid 'Ali *coup*, and the yielding of the Vichy regime to German pressure and requests to allow German aircraft sent to Iraq to land for refuelling on Syrian airfields. It was also due to the temporary lull in the war on the Libyan front, which made possible some minor operations elsewhere. Action against Vichy French forces in the Levant, for so long being urged by General de Gaulle, the leader of the Free French movement, was finally decided upon. The defeat of these forces was brought about in July 1941 in a joint Anglo-Free-French operation in which the British troops had the overwhelming numbers and bore the main brunt of the fighting.

The Allied operation was supplemented by a political initiative designed to secure the support and co-operation of the population with the invading forces, and to placate the feelings of the neighbouring Arabs as well. A declaration was issued on 8 June 1941 on the entry of Allied troops into Syria, by General Catroux, in the name of Free France, promising an end to the mandate and independence for Syria and Lebanon in treaty relationship with France. Sir Miles Lampson, on behalf of the British Government, issued simultaneously a statement associating his government with Free French assurances with regard to the independence of these two states.[1] The issue of this statement was strongly resented by General de Gaulle, who considered it "unnecessary" and likely to engage the responsibility of the British in any settlement, which in his view fell only within the province of the Free French, jointly with the Syrians and the Lebanese. Churchill saw it necessary, however, to issue a British guarantee to the French declaration, and stressed that in any settlement of the Syrian question the stability of the Middle East should not be endangered and "everything possible should be done to meet Arab aspirations and susceptibilities".[2]

A divergence of views developed, therefore, before the start of the joint Anglo-Free-French operation. The British, for so long resented by the French in their efforts to conciliate the Arabs, and very conscious of the inroads which Axis propaganda was able to make in the area, found their chance at last to have their way. The French saw in this a prelude to increased British intervention in the affairs of the Levant, and an attempt to supplant them in the area. General de Gaulle was very suspicious of British motives and was determined to keep French authority and control over the Levant if only to ward off any criticism against his movement by the Vichy French and any accusations of having surrendered parts of the French Empire to the British. He saw that the only difficulty in the way of the establishment of Free French authority would

[1] Text of General Catroux's Proclamation and Sir Miles' declaration in: Sir Llewellyn Woodward *British Foreign Policy in the Second World War*, pp. 584–6

[2] Charles de Gaulle *War Memoirs: The Call to Honour 1940–1942*: Documents, translated by Jonathan Griffin, London 1955, p. 159

come from the British side, "where there is a team of Arabophiles sprinkled over the General Staff, the Embassy in Cairo, the Palestine High Commissioner's Office, etc., who have always played against France in the Arab World and would be inclined to continue".[1]

The British were, however, eager to avoid any clash with the Free-French at that stage. An agreement was therefore concluded between General de Gaulle and Oliver Lyttelton, the Minister of State in Cairo, on 25 July 1941 defining in more detail the British role in the Levant. In an accompanying note, the Minister of State assured de Gaulle that H.M.G. "recognize the historic interests of France in the Levant". The note stated that while H.M.G. have "no interest in the Levant except to win the war, they together with the Free French were pledged to the independence of Syria and Lebanon". It added that "when this essential step has been taken, and without prejudice to it, we freely admit that France should have the dominant privileged position in the Levant among all European nations". In his reply, General de Gaulle did not emphasize the prior commitment to independence and took note of British recognition "in advance" of the dominant and privileged position of France.[2]

The British were not ready, however, in spite of their assurances, to leave the field to the Free French. They were soon (in August) to ask that General Spears, the head of their mission in the Levant, should be present at conferences at which the negotiation of treaties with Syria and Lebanon was to be discussed. General de Gaulle considered this request "incompatible with the sovereign rights of France", and described it as "meddling" by England in French political affairs, which could only lead to "some very grave complications". He directed his attack against what he called "the fanatical group of British Arabophiles supported by the Prime Minister and the Colonial Office", who saw in the Syrian affair "the opportunity for driving the French out". He deprecated the role of General Spears in particular, whose part was, in his view, "altogether mischievous and disquietening".[3]

General Sir Edward Spears, the head of the British mission and later the accredited Minister to the Levant States, was a member of Parliament and a close friend of Churchill, whom he assisted early in the war by acting as a liaison officer with the French Government. He had been the first to bring General de Gaulle to the attention of Churchill and had assisted de Gaulle to leave France after her defeat. He was appointed head of the British mission to de Gaulle when the latter was officially recognized by the British Government. He was soon to clash with de Gaulle, however, and from that moment, his views, generally considered

[1] Charles de Gaulle, op. cit., p. 177; also Sir Llewellyn Woodward, op. cit., vol. I, pp. 568–70, about Anglo-Free-French frictions during this early period

[2] Texts in Sir Llewellyn Woodward, op. cit., pp. 586–93

[3] Ibid., p. 209

strongly Francophil, had undergone a fundamental change. He became "the most violently Francophobe of all British politicians".[1] He was described by Oliver Lyttelton, however, as a representative "who missed nothing" and whose views were "not only well-informed but generally original and imaginative".[2]

It is not within our scope here to dwell on Anglo-Free-French frictions in the Levant in greater detail. Suffice it to state that the seeds of conflict were sown from the start, and that the root of the trouble went back in history to the early twenties and to old French suspicions of British policy in the area. It was also due to the divergence in the main assumptions on which the Free French and the British had based their policies in the Middle East. Under the stress of the war, the French saw the British role as confined to military requirements, whereas the British saw the difficulty of separating the military from the political aspects. They felt, on the strength of the reports of their representatives in the area, that the pacification of the local population and the stability of the Arab East could only be secured by making good the Allied promises about Syrian and Lebanese independence. Their experience in Palestine made them more conscious of the possible adverse reactions in the neighbouring Arab countries to any reversion by the Free French to their previous policy of repression and direct control. Anglo-Free-French frictions could not therefore be attributed simply to the machinations of a single official or group of officials, however influential they were. The Free French, as rightly noted by George Kirk, could never face the fact that they owed their return to the Levant entirely to British favour, and that they could not conduct their affairs in such a vital region as an exclusive prerogative independent of the wider British interests.[3]

The nationalists in both Syria and Lebanon were quick to realize the underlying causes of the Anglo-Free-French conflict. They began to concentrate their efforts and to rely more on British support. They had their previous sympathies with the pan-Arab leaders of the Mufti circle and their serious grievances against British and French policies in the area. They had also their fears of a British promise to cede parts of northern Syria and Iraq to Turkey in return for Turkish military support.[4] They were branded by the Free French as pro-Axis. Their main

---

[1] Duff Cooper *Old Men Forget*, London 1953, p. 322

[2] Lord Chandos *Memoirs*, p. 259. Richard Casey, Lyttelton's successor as Minister of State in Cairo, also thought highly of Spears. Lord Casey *Personal Experience: 1939–1946*, London 1962, p. 148

[3] George Kirk *The Middle East in the War: Survey of International Affairs 1939–1946*, Royal Institute of International Affairs, London 1954, p. 113

[4] F.R. of the U.S., vol. III—1941, Washington 1959, p. 695. Shukri al-Qwatli, the leader of the Syrian National Bloc, expressed these fears to Consul Engert, who imputed them to Axis propaganda. The British did in fact envisage the possibility of the cession of some parts of Syria to Turkey in 1941. FO 371–27043–E2685/53/65

objective was to convince the British of their pro-Allied stand, and to enlist British support for their aspirations. This was done effectively through the neighbouring Arab rulers and Ibn Sa'ud in particular. The British gave assurances to the nationalists through Ibn Sa'ud that they would have nothing to fear as long as they were prepared to co-operate with the Allies, and stressed "the categorical nature" of the Allied pledges with regard to independence.[1]

It soon became clear, however, that the nationalists had no place in the new order envisaged by the Free French in the Levant. General Catroux, the French Delegate General, in approaching the question of the future government in the Levant based himself on several assumptions. He considered that his proclamation of independence made the end of the mandate conditional upon the conclusion of treaties recognizing the privileged and predominant position of France in the Levant. He assumed that a nationalist government would not be in the best interests of the population. The leaders of the National Bloc in Syria were, in his view, torn with dissensions and were discredited during their period in office (1936–9) because of their "inexperience, conceited evasiveness, and maladministration". A new leadership was therefore required. This only meant a leadership subservient to the French, which fact became clear after the appointment of Sheikh Taj ud-Din, known for his long association with France, as President of the Syrian Republic. A declaration of Syrian independence, subject to the exigencies of the war and with all public services being placed at the disposal of the Allied Command, was issued on 27 September 1941. A significant paragraph was inserted in the declaration stressing the political and territorial indivisible unity of the Syrian state and favouring political, cultural and economic bonds between the different parts of Syria, which were to be subordinated to the central power in Damascus.

In Lebanon, the French position, General Catroux maintained, was much stronger. Nationalism, in his view, had never struck deep roots in Lebanon, with its diversified heterogeneous structure. Lebanon remained "an artificial construction" of French policy. Public opinion was against the assumption of power by either of the leaders of the two big parties: Bishara al-Khouri and Emile Edde. The people, he maintained, resented "the immorality and sterility" of the nationalist regime while in power (from 1936 to 1939) and did not conceive of independence without the continuation of French assistance and friendship. Alfred Naccache, the Lebanese President appointed by the French in 1939, was therefore confirmed in his position. A declaration of Lebanese independence was issued on 27 November 1941. It included a paragraph similar to that included in the declaration of Syrian independence regarding the indivisible unity of Lebanon. It went a step further,

[1] FO 371–27295–E3088/63/89

however, by referring to "the tutelary mission" of France and her "privileged position" as well as to the non-ratified 1936 treaty as governing French aid to Lebanon.[1]

It was clear that the Free French did not mean much by their declarations of Syrian and Lebanese independence, and that their purpose was to restore their effective control over the two states. They rejected British suggestions that they should delete all reference to the 1936 treaty, and asserted that that treaty guaranteed the predominant French position and that France needed the right to station troops for the protection of the Christian minorities.[2] They also rejected another British suggestion, that all reference to the political and territorial indivisibility of Lebanon should be deleted since it might give rise to Syrian objections. A compact Lebanon was, in the view of General Catroux, necessary for the protection of French interests. It was also "useful" to Britain and other western powers "as a bridgehead *vis-à-vis* the independent Muhammedan countries".[3] The French were therefore determined to continue their traditional policy of using Lebanon against Syria, a matter which had aroused in the past and was bound in the future to arouse Syrian apprehensions. This was not unwelcome to the French, since it was designed to throw the Lebanese more into their arms for protection against alleged Muslim domination.

The appointment of Sheikh Taj ud-Din was regarded by the Syrian nationalists as "a hollow farce". The French continued to have the whole administration under their thumb. By December 1941, General Spears reported that the high prestige which the British had formerly enjoyed in the Levant was waning. The French, Free and Vichy alike, were unpopular with the local people. He argued for the reconsideration of British policy towards the Free French who, in his view, should be brought to understand that their contribution to the war effort "must be made in accordance with British essential requirements and not General de Gaulle's aspirations".[4] Representations were made by the neighbouring Arab governments against French policy in the Levant. Iraq withheld its recognition from the Syrian and the Lebanese regimes, which were regarded as unconstitutional. Egypt withheld its recognition from the Lebanese regime, while Ibn Sa'ud made no secret of his dissatisfaction regarding the developments in the Levant. The United

---

[1] General Catroux *Dans La Bataille de la Méditerranée: Egypte, Levant, Afrique du Nord 1940–1944*, Paris 1949, pp. 217–37. It is interesting to note that General de Gaulle, in proposing a draft for a French proclamation promising independence to the Levant States late in April 1941, avoided any reference to the 1936 treaties on the grounds that in the existing state of mind of the population and as a result of the damage caused by the fall of France, these treaties became "out of date and their attractive power is no longer sufficient". Charles de Gaulle *War Memoirs*, pp. 135–6

[2] FO 371–27320–E8386/62/89

[3] F.R. of the U.S., p. 800; FO 371–27319–E8315/62/89

[4] FO 371–27320–E8545/62/89

States Government refused also to recognize the Syrian and Lebanese regimes in spite of British representations. The independence of the two states did not seem to them to be real, and they had their strong objections to the granting of a "privileged and predominant" position to France.[1]

The relations between the British and the Free French reached their most acute stage in the summer of 1942. British reverses on the Libyan front and the withdrawal of some troops from the Levant to take part in the defence of Egypt induced General de Gaulle to take a stronger line. He retracted his earlier agreement to conduct national elections in the Levant on the grounds that this was "impossible" under the threat of Axis advance into Egypt. He went around the Middle East "like a roaring lion", refused to discuss the subject of elections with the British, and asked that the Free French be given charge of the Allied High Command in the Levant. He complained to the American Consul in Beirut of British "meddling" in French affairs and threatened, if General Spears was not removed from the Levant, to make the British leave Syria and Lebanon by forcible measures if necessary.[2] The Americans, while greatly annoyed at the security hazards involved in an Anglo-Free-French open breach, were confirmed in their belief about the unwillingness of the French to forgo their effective control over the two Levant States. Churchill stuck to his guns, however, and refused either to transfer Spears or to yield to the French request with regard to their control over the High Command. He told General de Gaulle that Syria and Lebanon were part of a vital theatre of the war, and "almost every development there affects our military interests directly or indirectly". The British, he added, were committed in the eyes of the people of both states and of the whole Arab World to ensuring that their guarantee of independence "was effectively carried out".[3]

There was another aspect of the British attitude which became clear from 1942 onwards. Churchill, as will be explained later, espoused a

---

[1] F.R. of the U.S., vol. IV, 1943, p. 970

[2] FO 371–31475–5073/207/89: the American Ambassador in London was instructed by the State Department in August 1942 to inform Eden that his government could not remain unaffected by the dispute, that they felt that General Spears had intervened in the internal affairs of the Levant to an unnecessary and unjustifiable extent, and that de Gaulle's policy was at variance with Anglo-French declarations. The Foreign Office described the American intervention as "unfortunate". Some officials attributed it to the anti-British leanings of Engert, the American Consul in Beirut. This incident served, however, to increase American mistrust of de Gaulle, and Sumner Welles, the American Under-Secretary of State, was to express to Richard Law early in September 1942 his "great disquiet" about de Gaulle and his feeling that the time "will soon come" when the Allies would have to sever their association with him. The Earl of Avon *The Eden Memoirs: The Reckoning*, Cassell, London 1965, pp. 340–1

[3] Charles de Gaulle *War Memoirs: Unity 1942–1944:* Documents, translated by Joyce Murchie and Hamish Erskine, London 1959, pp. 29 and 41–2

scheme for the solution of the Palestine problem through the creation of an Arab federation. He informed the Cabinet of his scheme in 1941 and talked to Dr Weizmann about it on the eve of the latter's departure to the United States early in 1942. He also had a talk on the subject with General Spears, who seems to have agreed with him on the broad lines of his scheme.[1] French presence in the Levant and their strong objections to any Arab federation, even if Syria and Lebanon were to be excluded, had always represented a serious obstacle. The end of French control, now becoming a possibility, would have removed this obstacle and prepared the way for a satisfactory solution to the thorny Palestine problem. The British began to realize that their assurances of a "privileged and predominant" position for the French in the Levant were "unfortunately too broad".[2] The recommendations of the War Cabinet Committee on Palestine in 1943 tied a solution of the Palestine problem to the formation of a Greater Syria. General Spears, in arguing against the continuation of French effective control over the Levant States, stated in 1942 that this would be "incompatible with the Atlantic Charter and with the British conception of the future of the Arab World" as based on a federation of states.[3]

The victory of the British at Al-'Alamain in November 1942, and British regard for Free French wishes over Madagascar and French North Africa eased the situation. General de Gaulle agreed to hold elections in the Levant States in the summer of 1943. The Free French started, in the meantime, to push for the conclusion of treaties with Syria and Lebanon. In approaching the question of treaties, General Catroux defined a line of policy which did not imply any concessions or any real desire to relinquish control over the two states. In Lebanon, he proposed "to exploit the old sentimental link with France, the instinct of defence against the plans for her absorption". In Syria, he proposed to encourage the tendency among many people "to consider that the support of France, interested in preserving the territorial integrity of the country, was necessary to withstand the threat of Zionism and the Turks". He did not think it advisable to show hostility to the idea of Arab union, "which draws the Syrians towards the British". He proposed instead to try to neutralize its appeal by suggesting that the leading role should belong "by reasons of geography, history, and intellect" to Syria, and that Damascus should be the centre. He also suggested that the Syrians should be told that in view of the subservience of the other Arab countries to Britain, Syria needed the support of France and that a treaty relationship with France would not be an

---

[1] FO 371–31475–E5132/207/89

[2] F.R. of the U.S., vol. IV, 1943, pp. 953–5, from a statement by Casey, the Minister of State, during his visit to Washington in January 1943

[3] FO 371–31475–E5132/207/89

obstacle in the way of an Arab union which preserved the independence of the member states. In arguing for what he described as a "liberal" approach, General Catroux stressed that liberalism, at the present moment, "can win us moral credit".[1]

This new approach was therefore based on playing on Lebanese fears of Muslim domination and Syrian fears of Zionist and Turkish designs. There was nothing liberal in it, since the purpose was to continue French tutelage and to sow dissension between the two Levant states. The suggestion that Syria should be the leader of an Arab union which preserved independence for the component states and accepted continued French influence in the Levant was not likely to be accepted either by the British or by the other Arab states. General Catroux had, moreover, excluded the two bigger states, Egypt and Iraq, from any prospective Arab union. The exclusion of Iraq was based on the strange assumption that her "historical background, geographical position, and economic interests caused her to look towards the East". Iraq was in fact a world apart from Persia, and her relations with that country, though friendly at times, did not match her historical, cultural and economic connections with the Levant. Egypt was also excluded on the grounds that "racially and in her basic social trends, she was very much a foreign country". This statement was made at a time when Nahas Pasha, the Egyptian Prime Minister, was already engaged in the Arab unity consultations and when Egyptian involvement in Arab affairs was growing. Any connection with these two large states or with Saudi Arabia was unwelcome to the French, since this would mean their domination over any prospective federation. The French were in fact very suspicious of British protestations of sympathy with Arab aspirations for unity. They used censorship in Syria and Lebanon to withhold any reference in the press to Eden's statement in Parliament on 24 February 1943 on the subject.[2] There was nothing new, therefore, in General Catroux's suggested approach, and it meant only a change in tactics rather than in goals.

The Syrian and Lebanese nationalists were indignant at their exclusion from office, and at the reversion by the French to their repressive policies. They had got a favourable impression of British intentions from their contacts with the Iraqi, Sa'udi, and Egyptian governments. The return of the Wafd to power at British instance in Egypt in February 1942 encouraged nationalist hopes of similar developments in Syria. The announcement early in 1943 of a date for the elections enhanced these hopes. The Syrian nationalists sought and got British assurances against any possible French attempt to prevent them from participating

---

[1] General Catroux *Dans la Bataille de la Méditerranée*, pp. 336–7; George Kirk *The Middle East in the War*, pp. 272–3

[2] F.R. of the U.S., vol. IV, 1943, p. 973

in the elections. They made it known to their supporters that they had British assurances of support, which was resented by the British, and served only to intensify French suspicions of British motives.[1]

It was at that time that the American Government began to show active interest in Middle Eastern affairs in general. Their representatives in the area had stressed the strategic importance of the Levant for any assault on Hitler's Europe. They had also urged their government to compensate for the waning American influence, because of the widespread conviction about American support for Zionism, by impressing upon the French and the British the need to make the independence of the Levant states a reality. They conveyed to the British their disapproval of the retention of the mandate over Syria and Lebanon, and the grant of a privileged position to France, and their desire to see representative government established in the two states.[2]

It was then that the British began to support the Syrian nationalists in a more active manner. The Free French were told by Churchill early in July 1943 that the British were not going to quarrel with the Americans because of General de Gaulle, who was "pursuing his own interests rather than those of the Allies or even the real ones of France". The British were exasperated at the persistent refusal of the Free French to transfer any powers to the governments installed by them in Syria and Lebanon. The Syrian and Lebanese nationalists were given assurances of support. They were told, moreover, that although in the present war conditions no practical method could be found to end the mandate legally, the Free French were not in a position to conclude a treaty which would be binding upon France after the war. This, the Syrian nationalists were told, would not mean that no progress towards independence would be possible.[3] The nationalists in the Levant felt therefore that they would have solid British support in case matters came to a head with the Free French.

The elections were held in Syria in July 1943 and resulted in a sweeping victory for the leaders of the National Bloc. Shukri al-Qwatli was elected President of the Republic on 17 August. The French considered the victory of the nationalists in Syria a foregone conclusion. They concentrated their efforts in Lebanon, hoping thereby to tip the balance in favour of the pro-French candidate Emile Edde. The British exerted their efforts, however, to ensure the fairness of the elections and to neutralize whenever possible French attempts, by various means, to influence the results. A deadlock ensued between the two main candidates: Emile Edde and Bishara al-Khouri. Al-Khouri was finally elected in September 1943, following a clever manoeuvre in which the name of

---

[1] FO 371–31471–E1553/207/89
[2] F.R. of the U.S., vol. IV, pp. 964, 970
[3] FO 371–35178–E4070, 3849/27/89

Kamil Shamo'un,[1] who was suspected by the French as pro-British, was put forward as an alternative candidate. Bishara al-Khouri chose as his Prime Minister Riad al-Sulh, the pan-Arab nationalist and a life-long advocate of the unity of Syria and Lebanon.

The election of Qwatli and Khouri in Syria and Lebanon was met by jubilation in the Levant and the Arab World. The choice of Khouri was considered a defeat for the French, since he was "generally regarded as British choice". The promises of Khouri, soon after his election, of establishing close and friendly relations between Lebanon and her neighbours were regarded as "a good augury for Lebanese participation in a future Arab federation".[2] The victory of the nationalists in the Levant was in fact a triumph for the cause of Arab co-operation against parochialism and factionalism, which had sapped the strength of the Arab nationalist movement in the past. For the Syrians and Lebanese nationalists, this was only the first step towards the realization of their aspirations. They knew that their assumption of power was only made possible because of the war conditions, American support, and British opposition to French control. The Free French still controlled the police force and the Troupes Spéciales as well as the communications, the customs and the airports. They had their fears of a British change of policy and of a future Anglo-French conciliation at their own expense. They sought the support of the United States and saw in an Arab association an added guarantee of their independence.

The French, on the other hand, were much disappointed at the result of the elections, especially in Lebanon. They accused General Spears of campaigning against their candidate Edde, and of supporting the Riad al-Sulh group, which was, in their view, "notably anti-French and indeed anti-Lebanese since it was in favour of merger with Syria".[3] They started to press more for the conclusion of treaties guaranteeing their predominant position, and made the transfer of "the common interests" and the security forces conditional on the achievement of this end. This meant in effect that independence would be devoid of any real significance, with the elected governments divested of any real powers.

The nationalists realized the weakness of the French position and sought to capitalize as much as possible on the favourable circumstances then prevailing. Shukri al-Qwatli, who did not reject the idea of a treaty before his assumption of power, began to hedge, and declined to

---

[1] The name of Shamo'un was in fact suggested to Spears by the pro-French candidate Emile Edde. Bishara accepted the choice of Shamo'un since he belonged to the Constitutional Bloc of which he was the head. The French Delegate General objected strongly, however, to that choice, and Edde was to withdraw his approval of the choice of Shamo'un. Bishara Khalil al-Khouri *Haqaiq Libnaniya*, vol. I, Beirut 1960, pp. 264–7

[2] FO 371–35182–E5705/27/89

[3] FO 371–35182–E3961/27/89

make any public pronouncement on the subject, hoping that the political developments with regard to the establishment of an Arab federation would strengthen his position *vis-à-vis* the French. He pressed instead for the speedy transfer of "the common interests" still held by the French. French attempts to apply the policy proposed earlier by General Catroux did not yield any results. They were told that the issue of leadership in an Arab union was a matter to be settled between the Arab "sister" states, and that the question "would not be allowed by the Syrians to be an obstacle". Even French protestations of non-opposition to an Arab union were thought insincere. They were told that continued French control over "the common interests", including customs and communications, over the Troupes Spéciales composed of local Syrian and Lebanese levies, and over the security forces placed the two countries in a state of inferiority to the other Arab countries, and detracted from any prominent role in any prospective Arab union.[1]

In Lebanon, Riad al-Sulh, in his first policy speech before the Parliament on 7 October 1943, took a very strong nationalist line. He announced his government's intention to take several measures designed to make independence a reality. These included making Arabic the sole official language, and the deletion from the constitution of all reference to the prerogatives and powers of the mandatory state. He stated, moreover, that isolationism was out of the question for any state large or small, and that the economic and geographical position of Lebanon obliged her to place at the forefront of her preoccupations the question of relations with the sister Arab states. His government, he added, would try to place these relations on solid foundations based on the respect for the full independence and sovereignty of Lebanon within its present frontiers. The policy outlined by Al-Sulh got the backing of the Parliament and was welcomed by the Lebanese public.[2] Close contacts were established with the Syrian Government. Lebanon, for the first time in its recent history, was acting in concert with the Syrian nationalists. Lebanon had ceased to be a pawn to be played off by the French against the Syrians.

A new phase had, therefore, started in Syrio-Lebanese relations. This was supplemented by other moves on the pan-Arab plane. A Syrian delegation left for Cairo in October 1943 to participate in the Arab unity consultations with Nahas Pasha. The Lebanese Government accepted Nahas' invitation to send a similar high level delegation to Cairo for talks on Arab unity. The very warm welcome given to the

---

[1] FO 371–35182–E5601/27/89: statement of Jamil Mardam, the Syrian Foreign Minister, to General Spears relaying the contents of his interview in September 1943 with the Free French representative

[2] A. Hourani *Syria and Lebanon: A Political Essay*, London 1947, pp. 284–5. Text of the speech in: *Majmu'at al Bayanat al Wizariya al Libnaniya*, compiled by Jan Mulha, Beirut 1965, pp. 19–32

Syrians in Cairo and the messages of support and congratulations received from all over the Arab World provided an added boost, especially to the Lebanese, who were so far rather half-hearted and apprehensive of an Arab association. The position of the Syrian and Lebanese Governments was further strengthened by the unconditional recognition of their independence by the United States and later by the Soviet Union, both of whom declined specifically to concede a pre-eminent position to any other power in the Levant.

The French, rather than accept the *fait accompli* and try to salvage whatever remained of their prestige, were determined to oppose the measures proposed by Al-Sulh by force if necessary. They declared that no concessions whatever would be made until the mandate had been terminated by a treaty. A clash was bound to happen when the Lebanese Parliament decided on 8 November to approve the measures proposed by the government. The 10–22 November crisis ensued, during which M. Helleu, the French Delegate General, arrested and interned the Lebanese President, his Prime Minister, three members of the Cabinet, and a Deputy. The forceful French action engendered sharp reactions in the Arab World. The British were indignant at the French action and managed, through an ultimatum, to force the French to beat a retreat. The President and the members of his Cabinet were released and reinstated.[1] This was a turning-point in French relations with the Levant states. It was followed by the successive transfer of powers to the Syrian and the Lebanese governments, whose position was greatly enhanced in as much as French prestige had fallen.

The Free French were not to give up, however, and they clung to the Troupes Spéciales, whose transfer they made conditional on the conclusion of treaties. With the liberation of France in July and August 1944 and the assumption by General de Gaulle of power as head of the French Provisional government in Paris, the British were more in favour of conciliating the French. General de Gaulle, now well-established in Paris, was in a stronger bargaining position. Anglo-French talks in London early in September 1944 resulted in the British giving "categorical instructions" to General Spears to urge the Syrian and Lebanese governments to conclude treaties with the French. The two governments reacted sharply to the British *démarche* and reiterated their determination not to accept any preferential treaty with France, on the grounds that this would amount to a national suicide. The Syrian President would not budge in spite of General Spears' hint that the

[1] For details of this crisis see: Bishara Khalil al-Khouri *Haqaiq Libnaniya*, vol. II, pp. 34–49; Lord Casey *Personal Experience*, pp. 144–7; General Catroux *Dans la Bataille de la Méditerranée*, pp. 400–8. Catroux told the Lebanese Minister in Moscow in 1946 that he was in favour of following a conciliatory policy in Lebanon, but General de Gaulle overruled him in October 1943. Bishara Khalil al-Khouri, op. cit., p. 318

British would not be able to take a firm stand if a crisis similar to that of November 1943 arose. The two governments enlisted American help, stressing the threats involved to their national survival. All this happened less than two weeks before the meeting of the Preparatory Committee of the General Arab Congress in Alexandria, and it provided a further impetus to the desire for a closer Arab association. The Syrian and Lebanese Presidents and Foreign Ministers sent appeals for support to the British, Soviet, and American Governments. It was the United States' intervention early in October 1944 which swayed the British and staved off the crisis for the time being.[1]

The replacement in December 1944 of General Spears, who became popular in the Levant as a great supporter of Syrian and Lebanese independence, aroused fresh fears. His transfer was obviously intended to propitiate the French. The British continued, albeit in a mild way, to urge the two states to enter some form of agreement with the French, who were determined to acquire in the Levant the same position as the British in Egypt and Iraq. This led to the May–June 1945 crisis in Syria and to British intervention for the second time.[2] This marked the death knell for French presence in the Levant and was followed by the transfer of the Troupes Spéciales and later in 1946 by the withdrawal of all foreign troops from Syria and Lebanon.

Sir Edward Spears, in a final report, stated that the time when the French could have freely obtained preferential treaties with Syria and Lebanon ended in 1937, when they first declined to ratify the treaties they had signed in 1936. By allowing the cession of Alexandretta to Turkey in 1938, he added, the French showed themselves incapable of assuming the protection of the two states. Since then and particularly since November 1943, "too much water has flowed down the Orontes and Litani, and the current cannot be reversed". He did not make secret his satisfaction at the resultant enhancement of British prestige, not only in the Levant but also in the rest of the Arab World.[3]

The British, who were thinking in 1944 not only of maintaining their pre-war positions in the area, but also of acquiring additional bases and

---

[1] F.R. of the U.S., vol. V, 1944, Washington 1965, pp. 777–84. The State Department made strong representations to the British. In a memorandum to the French delegate in Washington on 5 October 1944 they emphasized their earnest hope that in their dealings with the Syrians and the Lebanese regarding the treaties issue, the French should pursue a tactful and generous policy "rather than narrow, legalistic and dictatorial methods".

[2] This was caused by intensified French pressures for the conclusion of treaties and the arrival on 7 and 17 May of fresh contingents of French troops. This was followed by riots and demonstrations in Damascus on 19 and 20 May and firing on the demonstrators by the French troops. The riots soon spread to Homs and Hama. The British finally on 30 May ordered the French army to cease fire and to remain in their barracks. George Kirk *The Middle East in the War*, pp. 296–300

[3] FO 371–40307–E7799/23/89 report dated December 1944

positions of influence, were not ready to tolerate any more French obstructionism in the Levant. George Kirk rightly deduced from General Catroux's account of Anglo-Free-French frictions that the basic cause was that the French and the pro-French minority among the Lebanese were thinking in narrow, parochial terms. The pan-Arabs and the British (both actuated no less by self-interest) were thinking "perhaps too optimistically in terms of a much larger unity". The Free French, Kirk added, were to suffer a defeat in this conflict of interests because of the interaction of their national weakness and their mental inflexibility; but their subconscious desire to evade admitting these failings led them to formulate a typical "stab in the back myth".[1] The steadfastness of the Syrian and Lebanese nationalists and their refusal, in spite of French and at times British pressure, to compromise their independence were, however, the basic factors in the situation.[2]

---

[1] George Kirk, op. cit., p. 129

[2] Bishara al-Khouri expressed his thanks to General Spears and Wadsworth, the American minister, who came to congratulate him following his release late in November 1943. Spears, in answer, stated that both the British and the American governments had assisted the Lebanese much, but if Al-Khouri had shown any weakness or willingness to compromise in any way, all this assistance would have come to naught. Bishara Khalil al-Khouri *Haqaiq Libnaniya*, vol. II, p. 49

Chapter Four

British Policy and Middle East Regionalism

The war situation imposed many strains on the British policy-makers. The whole political machinery had to be geared to the service of the war operations. Several measures were taken in the summer of 1941 to re-organize the High Command of the Middle East forces and to free the hands of the military from all extraneous responsibilities. One of these measures was the appointment of a Minister of State in Cairo. This step underlined the interrelatedness of the political and military aspects of the war operations. It was suggested both by the Commander-in-Chief in the Middle East and by Sir Miles Lampson, the Ambassador in Cairo. It was also urged by Randolph Churchill, the Prime Minister's son, following a visit to the area.

Oliver Lyttelton, the Chairman of the Board of Trade, was appointed Minister of State in the Middle East in June 1941. His task was "to ensure a successful conduct of the operations in the Middle East". This included handling relations with the Free French and the Emperor of Ethiopia as well as conducting propaganda and economic warfare. It also included providing the military with political guidance and co-ordinating "in so far as is necessary" the policy of the British representatives in the area.[1] In the assumption of his duties the Minister of State was bound to handle matters within the responsibility of the Foreign Office, the Colonial Office, the Ministry of Transport, the Ministry of Economic Warfare, the Board of Trade, as well as the three service Ministers and the Secretary of State for Defence, who was the Prime Minister himself.

A new regional structure was built around the office of the Minister of State. It included the Middle East Supply Centre, which was responsible mainly for the co-ordination of shipping facilities, and was later to be involved in the regulation of local economies. It also included the Middle East War Council, which was presided over by the Minister of State with a membership of the three Service Chiefs of Staff, the Ambassadors in Cairo and Baghdad, the High Commissioner for Palestine,

[1] Winston Churchill *The Second World War, Vol. III: The Grand Alliance*, London 1950, pp. 309–12

the Governors of Cyprus and Aden, and a representative of the Government of India. A Middle East Defence Committee was formed under the chairmanship of the Minister of State and with a membership of the three Commanders-in-Chief, the Intendent General, and the Ambassador in Cairo.[1] This new structure had wide political, economic, and military responsibilities. Apart from providing the military with a closer knowledge of the political problems in the area, it was involved in efforts to promote regional economic co-operation, effective use of local resources, and in the wider issue of Arab federation. The reports of the British representatives to their departments at home were often repeated to the Minister of State, who had a say on all issues of importance, although control of all foreign policy remained in the hands of the Foreign Secretary.[2] The views of the Minister of State, who had Cabinet rank and was more in touch with local developments, carried more weight in Whitehall.

This new development had as its main effect the consolidation of the outlook on the Middle East and on its Arab hard core, as one unit. It also underlined the central role of Egypt, whose capital was the seat of the new war-geared regional structure. The shortage of shipping and the curtailment of extra-regional trade opened the eyes of the Arab governments to the hitherto untapped potentialities of economic regional co-operation. Cairo was the meeting-place for most of the war-time technical conferences. Egyptian contacts with Arab intellectuals and nationalists increased as a result, and Egyptian prestige was further enhanced.

EDEN'S MANSION HOUSE SPEECH OF 29 MAY 1941

It was noted earlier how Nuri al-Sa'id, eager to check the growing pro-Axis trend in the Iraqi Cabinet and the army, was to suggest to the British in 1939, and again in the summer of 1940, that they should issue a declaration of sympathy with Arab aspirations. Similar requests were made by the Arab nationalists in the Levant. These requests were not responded to by the British, who realized that any declaration, to be effective, must descend from benevolent generalizations and give some assurances with regard to the future of Syria and Palestine. Any concessions on Palestine were precluded because of Cabinet opposition and possible Jewish reactions.

British reverses on the Libyan front and the worsening situation in Iraq underlined the need for some conciliatory measures. Sir Miles Lampson was to warn in April 1941 that the situation in the Arab World was getting "definitely near the danger point". He urged his government to formulate an Arab policy which would have some chance

---

[1] Lord Chandos *Memoirs*, pp. 233–4

[2] FO 371–27044–E5258/53/65

of success in countering German propaganda, "which was offering the Arabs all that they can possibly ask for". The Foreign Office were very much aware of their limitations *vis-à-vis* Axis propaganda, which could afford to be expansive and profuse in its support for the Arabs. Any British assurances or declarations had, in order to be credible, to be translated into concrete measures whether in Palestine, in Iraq, or with regard to the promotion of an Arab federation. The British recognized the political advantages of a declaration of sympathy with Arab aspirations. They were constrained by their commitments to the Jews and by their concern over the adverse reactions of Ibn Sa'ud and the Iraqis if they were to promote a specific scheme for federation. When the Foreign Office came round at last to the espousal of the idea of a declaration of sympathy with Arab aspirations, this was justified not by the wish to win over the anti-British extremists, to whom the Germans "could always offer more", but by the desire "to show our friends in the Middle East exactly what our views and intentions are".[1]

The development of an Arab policy of the type urged by Sir Miles Lampson was ruled out because of the unwillingness to make any concessions or to depart from the traditional line of policy which many considered as having paid off during the inter-war period. The story of the Newcombe Mission to Iraq in 1940, referred to earlier, was an example of this rather complacent and negative attitude. The only two attempts at the initiation of a new approach to Arab affairs at this critical juncture in the war were rather superficial, and inimical to the very ends they were designed to serve. The first was in the form of suggestions made by Churchill in a personal letter to Eden on 19 May 1941.[2] These suggestions were described by the Prime Minister as providing "the most favourable political basis for military action". The second was embodied in a memorandum on "British Arab policy" which was submitted by Eden to the War Cabinet on 27 May.[3] Both attempts are of special interest since they provide the immediate political background to Eden's Mansion House speech.

Churchill's suggestions came at a time when the British intervention in Iraq was still afoot, and when the decision to conduct operations against the Vichy French forces in the Levant was already taken. He argued that the Vichy forces should be given one more chance to rally to the side of the Allies. If they did, then Britain should refrain from raising the issue of the French mandate over the two Levant states until the end of the war. If they refused, then Britain must try to win the Syrians by proclaiming the end of the mandate and the independence of Syria "in permanent alliance with Turkey on the one side and Britain on the other". Consultation with Turkey was necessary, in his view, to

---

[1] FO 371–27043–E53/53/65
[2] FO 371–27043–E2685/53/65
[3] FO 371–27043–E2716/53/65 [W.P. (41) 116]

secure her collaboration, in return for which he mentioned the possibility of some "restoration" of territory to her in northern Syria. Churchill ignored possible Arab reactions. Any encouragement of Turkish ambitions in Syria would have caused sharp reactions in the Arab World. It would have vindicated French warnings and Axis statements that an Allied victory would mean the parcelling out of Syria between the Jews and the Turks. This would have cancelled out any favourable reaction to the proclamation of independence.

Churchill's other suggestion was that Ibn Sa'ud should be raised to a "general overlordship of Iraq and Transjordan". Ibn Sa'ud was, in his view, "the greatest living Arab", who had given "long and solid proof of fidelity" to Britain. As a custodian of the Holy Places, his authority "might well be acceptable". He would be required, in return, to negotiate with Britain a "satisfactory" settlement for the Palestine problem, possibly through the establishment of "an independent Jewish unit in the Arab Caliphate". This unit would have to have "the fullest rights of self-government, including immigration and development and the provision for expansion in the regions southwards".

Churchill's suggestion avoided any reference to the Hashimites, of whom Amir 'Abdullah was the recipient of a British promise in 1921 of assistance in his claims to the kingship of Syria. It ignored the reactions of the population in Iraq and Transjordan who, in spite of their high regard for Ibn Sa'ud, would not have relished the extension of his autocratic rule to their countries. It also ignored the fact that such an arrangement would not have been acceptable to Ibn Sa'ud, who had made it clear several times in the past that he had no ambitions outside his country. Any deal at the expense of the Palestine Arabs would have incurred the enmity of the Arab World at large, thus making his overlordship very difficult to maintain. Churchill's suggestion was in fact inspired by Dr Weizmann, to whom the idea was put forward in 1939 by Philby, Ibn Sa'ud's unofficial adviser, as will be explained later. It meant in effect the establishment of an Anglo-Turkish condominium over Syria and a Jewish state in Palestine, leaving the inland and less developed areas under Ibn Sa'ud.

It was not difficult for the Middle East experts in the Foreign Office to recognize the impracticability of the Prime Minister's approach. They considered Palestine as the main issue and that the Arabs were not expected to be won over by concessions in Syria alone. They doubted whether the Syrians would relish the idea of being guaranteed by Turkey, or of allowing Turkish or British troops to remain permanently in their country. They stressed that the Arabs would regard any territorial concessions to Turkey as "an outstanding disaster". Doubts were also cast over the readiness of the Arabs to allow a Jewish unit unrestricted immigration and development. The general overlordship of Ibn Sa'ud was not considered to be practical politics. H.M.G., they noted, should work instead for an Arab federation, "which was what the Arabs always say they want".[1]

Eden, in his memorandum on British Arab policy, admitted that the Palestine question had hitherto remained, and would in the future remain, a weighty factor in Anglo-Arab relations. He stated, however, that any decision to implement the constitutional provisions of the White Paper would not have any decisive effect in satisfying the Arabs, since the Germans could always offer more. He then suggested that if the Vichy French forces refused to rally, or the Free French refused to promise independence to Syria and Lebanon, then the British should hold themselves free to try to win the Syrians by promising them independence. He went even further than Churchill, for whom some "restoration" of territory to Turkey was considered a possibility. Eden recommended, and the Cabinet approved, that Turkey should be "urged" to seize Aleppo.[2] Possible Arab reactions were brushed aside on the grounds that in this matter British war necessities must prevail. As for Arab federation, he referred to the suggestions made by "many people" that it offered the only practical solution to the Palestine problem. He stressed that Britain had "never opposed such a federation". He stated, however, that this was a matter for the Arabs to decide, although he felt that an Arab federation was not at the moment practical politics because of the Sa'udi–Hashimite rivalries and Iraq's wish to assume the leadership. He considered it expedient at the same time, in view of the general agreement among the Arabs about its desirability, that H.M.G. should not only refrain from opposing "such vague aspirations" but should also take every opportunity of expressing support for them.

This was then the policy outlined by Eden, and later approved by the Cabinet, only two days before his Mansion House speech. The main stress was on the Syrian situation, which was natural, coming as it did ten days before the Anglo-Free-French operation in the Levant. He avoided any reference to Churchill's suggestion about the overlordship of Ibn Sa'ud over the Arabs, which was made in a personal letter about whose contents other departments were not informed. He stuck to the traditional British attitude regarding the impracticability of taking any initiative in the promotion of Arab federation. Arab aspirations for unity were described as "vague" and beset by many difficulties. This did not preclude some expressions of sympathy with these aspirations just to propitiate the Arabs. Eden did not envisage any changes in British

---

[1] FO 371–27043: minute by C. W. Baxter dated 22 May 1941, approved by Sir Horace Seymour, the Deputy Under-Secretary of State

[2] Eden justified this in a minute to Churchill on 19 May 1941. There were fears at the time of Turkey yielding to intensified German pressures to allow the passage through its territory of German troops into Syria and Iraq. The Earl of Avon *The Eden Memoirs*, pp. 246–8

policy towards Iraq or Saudi Arabia, and, with the exception of Syria, no departure from previous policy was recommended. Eden's memorandum was revealing since it was intended as a form of stock-taking about British policy in the area. The Cabinet was in agreement with him about his analysis of the situation with regard to Syria, Palestine, and Arab federation. Some ministers went even as far as to urge, after the success of the operations in the Levant, that Syria should not be treated "as a single indivisible unit" and that the divisions drawn by the French during the inter-war period should be perpetuated.[1]

In his Mansion House speech, Eden referred to his statement in the House of Commons some days earlier, expressing sympathy for Syrian aspirations for independence, and stressed that British friendship for the Arabs had been proven by deeds, not words alone. He then referred to Arab appeals for British support for their aspirations for unity. He considered it "both natural and right" that the cultural, economic, and political inter-Arab ties should be strengthened. He declared that the British Government "will give their full support to any scheme that commands general approval".[2]

Eden's statement was the first public pronouncement of its nature. It came just before the Allied operation in the Levant, and was designed, together with the promise of independence, to secure the co-operation of the Syrians with the invading forces. All British propaganda organs were therefore instructed to give it prominence and to urge local newspapers and broadcasting stations in the area to give it wide publicity and the most favourable comments. As stated earlier, it did not represent any departure from previous policy, and its contents had in fact been conveyed to the Arab governments on several occasions in the past. By the making public of British support for Arab unity, the blame for its non-achievement was therefore switched to the Arabs themselves.

Eden's speech was favourably received in the area and its positive impact was underlined by British representatives in the Arab World. The Arab nationalists in Syria, Palestine, and Iraq did not fail, however, to criticize the absence of any reference to Palestine in the speech. The Palestine issue, described by the Foreign Office officials as "the main issue" and by Eden as a "weighty factor" in Anglo-Arab relations, was swept under the rug because there was nothing to offer and no wish to arouse Jewish opposition at that stage, and because the Cabinet itself was divided on the issue. Kirk, the American Minister in Cairo, was to note that the reaction of the Egyptians consulted was one of qualified rather than of absolute approbation. The statement, to them, was "extremely vague" and savoured strongly of political expediency. They

---

[1] FO 371–27043: Cabinet conclusions 56 (41) of 2 June 1941
[2] Text included in George Kirk *The Middle East in the War*, p. 334

noted that all Arab requests since the outbreak of the war for such a pronouncement were not responded to by the British. Eden's speech, they maintained, came so late that it was difficult to follow it up with appropriate measures in time to meet the present situation in the area. They hoped that it would be followed by a more detailed declaration containing specific assurances with regard to Palestine.[1]

Nor did the speech receive any favourable reaction from the Jews. They were "puzzled and disturbed" by its containing no explicit reservation to cover the Jewish National Home. Professor Namier, conveying a message from Dr Weizmann, who was then in the United States, stated that what the Jews wanted was a sufficient area to receive great numbers of immigrants after the war and to form the basis of a sound Jewish commonwealth. The Jews, he added, were not averse to "some kind" of connection with the neighbouring Arab states provided their "full sovereignty" was safeguarded and a connection with the British Empire was maintained.[2] Lord Moyne, in answer to Professor Namier's representations, stated that Eden had shown him the draft of his speech and explained to him that the phrase postulating "general approval" was meant also to cover "Jewish rights". This meant that the Jews would have a say in the formation of an Arab federation. Viewed from the British side this was only natural, since the idea of an Arab federation began to have its appeal only as offering the best solution to the Palestine problem. The formation of a federation was in effect made contingent on the satisfaction of the Jewish claims in Palestine. This was the general import of Churchill's suggestions of May 1941.

The British policy towards Arab federation was not, however, as passive as the words of Eden might indicate. There is sufficient evidence to show that the promotion of an Arab federation in connection with Palestine became one of the determining factors for British policy in the area. The attitude towards the Free French in the Levant and towards the emancipation of Transjordan, urged at that time by Amir 'Abdullah, confirms this assumption.

Lord Moyne, the Colonial Secretary, was to evolve during the summer of 1941 a Greater Syria scheme to include Transjordan, Syria, Lebanon, and the Arab parts of Palestine. His scheme envisaged the creation of a Jewish state in part of Palestine on lines similar to those suggested by Lord Peel in 1937. He conducted several talks with some interested persons such as Sir Firoz Khan Noon, the High Commissioner for India, and Professor Reginald Coupland of the Peel Commission. He mentioned to his subordinates the possibility of suggesting to General de Gaulle that the position with regard to Syria and Lebanon should be kept fluid. His purpose was, through the inclusion

[1] F.R. of the U.S., vol. III, 1941, pp. 613–16; FO 371–27044–E4225/53/65

[2] FO 371–27044–E3101/53/65: minute of an interview between Professor Namier and Lord Moyne, the Colonial Secretary, in 1941

of these two states, to make any scheme for federation more attractive to the Arabs.[1]

The views of Lord Moyne were shared by some of his colleagues in the Cabinet. When the question of policy towards the Free French in the Levant came up for discussion late in August 1941, British support for a predominant position for the French in the Levant was described as "an embarrassing commitment" in view of General de Gaulle's "very disturbing" behaviour. It was stated that if H.M.G. could take a new view of the situation, they might be able to reach a general settlement with the Arab countries on the basis of a federation including a solution for the Palestine problem. Churchill and Eden, eager to avoid any open breach with the Free French at that stage, were, however, still in favour of Britain honouring her commitments to the French while pushing at the same time for Syrian independence. They were of the view that the Arab question in general, meaning obviously Arab federation, "raised far more difficult issues", and that it would "probably be premature to deal with it at the present time".[2] The idea was not ruled out completely, however, and General Spears was in fact influenced, in his dealings with the Free French and Arab nationalists in the Levant, by the belief that such an arrangement represented the future British line of policy. He was opposed to the retention of French effective control in the Levant, which he considered incongruous with the British conception of the Arab World as forming one unit and with the idea of Arab federation which was suggested to him by Churchill in 1941.

The emancipation of Transjordan was favoured by the Colonial Office as a reward to the Amir for his loyalty, and as a means of alleviating his disappointment over the frustration of his ambitions in Syria. They were of the view that the end of the mandate in Transjordan should be considered separately from the Arab question in general on the grounds that the only criterion for deciding the future status of that country should be the one laid down by the terms of the mandate. L. Amery, the Secretary of State for India and one of the advocates of a federal solution for the Palestine problem, was to enquire, in a letter to Eden in June 1941, whether in case Syria fell swiftly into the hands of the British it would be statesmanship "to go the whole hog" even during the war and "liberate" Palestine as a member of a new Arab federation to be formed by the Arabs themselves under British auspices. He wondered whether the Palestine Arabs would accept complete independence as part of a federation if the Jewish state envisaged by the Peel Commission was simultaneously created as part of that federation. He considered it "a good thing" if the Syrians themselves were to choose

---

[1] CO 733–444–75872/115/41

[2] Ibid.

Amir 'Abdullah as their king. He realized, however, all the difficulties involved with regard to Sa'udi and French objections. He urged in the meantime that the whole question should be discussed by the Middle East Official Committee quite early, "so that we can take a bold initiative when the situation favours it".[1]

When the Committee met to discuss the question in August 1941, the Foreign Office, so far rather sceptical about the prospects of federation, began to show some signs of a change in attitude. They did not consider the time ripe yet for a change in Transjordan, not only on account of the uncertainty about Syria, but also because the question must be regarded as one factor only in a much wider problem: the future British policy in the Arab World, including the Palestine problem and the question of Arab federation. Any change in Transjordan would also, in their view, lead to a similar demand from the Palestine Arabs and to Zionist agitation for some counter-concessions. Ibn Sa'ud's opposition and the possibility of his revival of his claims to 'Aqaba and Ma'an represented another difficulty. This view was subscribed to by the War Office, and it was agreed that the emancipation of Transjordan should be put off until the end of the war. It was also agreed that, in view of Eden's Mansion House speech, it was incumbent upon H.M.G. to take the initiative in formulating a positive policy towards the Arab states in general rather than await pressures from interested parties. The members of the Committee were of the view that if an Arab federation were ultimately to be created, "possibly under the aegis of King Ibn Sa'ud", Amir 'Abdullah would necessarily play a quite secondary part. With this possibility in view, it would be a mistaken policy to raise his status at that stage, thus causing future embarrassment and increasing the ultimate disappointment of the Amir.[2]

The views of Churchill about a Palestine settlement through the formation of an Arab federation under Ibn Sa'ud's leadership had their appeal to the other departments of the government. The Foreign Office recognized all the difficulties involved and considered the idea as not falling within the realm of practical politics. They considered, however, its realization as a possibility and formulated their policy towards the emancipation of Transjordan on this assumption.

---

[1] CO 733–444–75872/115/41: L. Amery to Eden on 11 June 1941. The Middle East Official Committee was originally a sub-committee of the Committee for Imperial Defence. When the meetings of that Committee ceased in the late thirties, the Middle East Official Committee remained and was affiliated to the Cabinet. Its meetings stopped, however, in 1944. The Middle East Official Committee was an inter-Departmental Committee chaired by the Colonial Under-Secretary of State.

[2] Cab. 95/1, 4th meeting, M.E. (0) 41, on 6 August 1941

THE QUESTION OF ARAB FEDERATION RECONSIDERED

The Foreign Office was urged by the British representatives in the Middle East, as well as by Churchill and L. Amery, to formulate an Arab policy. Eden's memorandum of May 1941 included an analysis of the situation in the area which was far from exhaustive, and no departure from previous policy was recommended. He was soon to be urged by Sheikh Hafiz Wahba, the Sa'udi Minister in London, to start working out plans for Arab federation in consultation with the Arab rulers. H.M.G., stated Sheikh Hafiz, had much experience in work of this kind, and unless they gave a lead and helped the Arabs by offering them advice and possibly putting a scheme forward, it would be hardly possible to make progress.[1] Professor Gibb, of the Royal Institute of International Affairs, was also to urge his government to initiate talks on the future of the Jewish National Home as an integral part of discussions aimed at a comprehensive settlement in Greater Syria.[2] Eden showed interest, especially with regard to Sheikh Hafiz's appeal, which as it transpired was unauthorized by his king though it was in conformity with Ibn Sa'ud's views about the central role of Britain in promoting any Arab association.

Sir Firoz Khan, one of the officials with whom Lord Moyne had conducted some exploratory talks in the summer, was to raise the subject with Churchill early in September 1941. The Prime Minister directed him to discuss it with Dr Weizmann. The solution suggested in the meeting between Sir Firoz Khan and Dr Weizmann was not very different from that proposed earlier by Churchill himself. It was based on making Ibn Sa'ud the head of an Arab federation. The kingdom of Iraq and Transjordan would, "if necessary", be abolished if the rulers of these two countries refused to accept the sovereignty of Ibn Sa'ud. The King of Yemen had also to be made to accept Ibn Sa'ud's sovereignty, thus putting the whole of Arabia, including the southern and eastern coasts of the peninsula, in addition to Greater Syria and Iraq, under Ibn Sa'ud. Ibn Sa'ud would be required, in return, to secure by a treaty an autonomous state in Palestine for the Jews. This state had to come into existence later on, "so that no Muslim ruler can blame England for having created a Jewish state in Palestine or part of Palestine".[3]

---

[1] FO 371–27044–E4761/53/65: record of an interview between Eden and Sheikh Hafiz Wahba dated 15 August 1941

[2] FO 371–27044–E3824/53/65: a Paper on Arab federation submitted by Professor Gibb to the Foreign Office on 20 June 1941

[3] A letter from Sir Firoz Khan Noon to Mr Leo Amery, the Secretary of State for India, containing details of a proposed settlement. Amery conveyed the contents to Churchill on 10 September 1941. FO 371–27045–E6190/53/65

This scheme went a little further than Churchill's scheme by its inclusion of Yemen and the Arabian coast sheikhdoms, and by mentioning specifically the possibility of the removal of the Hashimite rulers in Iraq and Transjordan. Like Churchill's scheme, it ignored possible Arab reactions and French objections. L. Amery, in conveying the proposed scheme to Churchill, doubted whether the Levantine *effendis* of Baghdad, Damascus, and Jerusalem would submit to the overlordship "of what they regard as a mere bedouin". He stated, however, that one way or another, some sort of Arab federation with "a Jewish sub-division" in Palestine as a unit in it "now seems the only possible solution, and much more feasible by the liberation of the Arabs in Syria". Churchill found the scheme suggested "full of interest and indeed the best I can think of". He instructed the Foreign, Colonial, and India Secretaries to hold a joint meeting with the Minister of State in Cairo, who was then on a visit to London, to discuss the proposed solution.

A Ministerial meeting was therefore held on 26 September 1941, with Eden in the chair. It was attended by Lord Moyne, the Colonial Secretary, L. Amery, the Secretary of State for India, Captain David Margesson, the Secretary of State for War, and Oliver Lyttelton, the Minister of State, in addition to a number of high officials from the participating departments. The whole issue of Arab federation and its contribution to a settlement in Palestine was thrashed out in the discussions. It was agreed that a scheme of federation had "considerable attractions", and if feasible seemed to offer "great advantages" with regard to a Palestine settlement. The federal scheme proposed by Sir Firoz Khan was regarded, however, as impracticable. They recognized the great difficulties involved and the fact that the Arabs could not be forced into federation. It was agreed, in the meantime, that the whole matter should be fully examined by the representatives of the departments concerned in London. They considered it undesirable at that stage to take any steps to sound the various parties concerned in the area, at least until this examination had been carried out and a decision reached as to the most promising lines on which to proceed. The Middle East Official Committee was therefore invited to examine the various forms which a scheme of Arab federation might take, and to report on their advantages and disadvantages and their practicability in offering a solution to the Palestine problem.[1] The views of the Foreign Office prevailed in the meeting and no positive decision was taken on the scheme favoured by Churchill. The whole question was left for further discussion inter-departmentally, and the views of the British representatives in the Middle East were invited.

The British representatives in Jerusalem, Jedda, Cairo, Baghdad, and

[1] FO 371–27045–E6189, 6210/53/65

Beirut were unanimous in their belief in the present impracticability of an Arab federation, and in the need for H.M.G. not to take any initiative on the matter. Sir Harold MacMichael, the High Commissioner for Palestine, considered the idea of federation "little more than a chimaera" in view of the known racial, religious, national, and dynastic antagonisms. If H.M.G. were to press for the establishment of a federation, he maintained, the two main forces operating in the area, namely internal dissension and fear of the Jews, would combine to defeat it. He doubted whether this would provide a solution to British troubles in Palestine or whether Ibn Sa'ud would agree to be the head or even to join an Arab federation. He added that it was arguable that the Arabs would be "more susceptible of control and less dangerous" if they were kept divided, and that the Jews were more likely to find it easier to extend their influence "by gradual and legitimate processes" culturally and economically, if they came to terms with each Arab state separately. He noted, however, that while political unity was difficult, closer Arab cultural and economic co-operation was more practical and worthy of encouragement. Sir Harold's views were found by the Foreign Office to be "rather discouraging" and "too negative for what we want".[1] He was right, however, in casting doubts over the willingness of Ibn Sa'ud to accept a Jewish state in return for his leadership of an Arab federation, and in stressing the disintegrative factors.

Sir Miles Lampson agreed with Sir Harold's views and recommended that the British Government should confine themselves "as in the past" to "vague expressions of good will as and when opportune". He rightly noted that if, as a practical form of good will, decisions embodied in the White Paper could be reaffirmed and their implementation expedited, this would do "far more good and be less risky" than embarking on the initiation of any scheme of federation.[2] Sir Kinahan Cornwallis, the Ambassador in Baghdad, was to go even further and to stress that in spite of the wide Arab interest in federation, there was not at present any general movement in the Arab countries in favour of raising it. He doubted whether the fundamental causes of Arab discontent with regard to Palestine and Syria would be removed merely by the creation of some form of federation. As long as these problems remained unsolved, he stated, such a federation, if political, might be used against Britain, and if cultural and economic, would not solve the political issues involved. These two problems, in his view, must be tackled directly and without reliance on any federation scheme. As for federation itself, he was in favour of making a modest start in the cultural and economic fields with the help of British experts in the area.[3] Sir Kinahan was no doubt thinking on the right lines, since a federation

---

[1] FO 371–27045–E6210, 6488/53/65
[2] FO 371–27045–E6636/53/65
[3] FO 371–27045–E6695, 6881/53/65

would have been very difficult to bring about, with the Free French determined to retain their effective control over the Levant states, and with the Jews intent on establishing a state in Palestine. These two problems had to be settled first in a way satisfactory to all parties concerned. The British Government had, however, no particular interest in an Arab federation *per se*, and it was only in relation to Palestine that the idea began to have its wider appeal.

The Foreign Office criticized the tendency of British representatives to emphasize "the impracticability of political federation". This was attributed to those representatives incorrectly understanding federation to mean political unity. It was stated that "of course" political union was impracticable at present, "but that does not necessarily mean that federation is impracticable".[1] The Foreign Office officials were therefore eager to come out with something positive in spite of their recognition of all the difficulties involved.

The whole issue came before the Middle East Official Committee on 8 October 1941. The discussions in the Committee touched on the British interests in the area. Any scheme of federation was to be acceptable only if essential British requirements in oil and communication facilities were guaranteed, and if any other power which might at any time become hostile to Britain was excluded from the area. As regards timing, it was agreed that there was something to be said for proceeding as soon as possible with any promising scheme. This was considered preferable to postponing a settlement until the peace conference. It was also agreed that complete secrecy should be maintained with regard to the Committee's discussions, so as to avoid agitation and pressures from the Arabs and the Jews which might prejudice a satisfactory settlement. The Committee then invited the Foreign Office, in consultation with the Colonial Office, to prepare a memorandum on the subject, taking into account the views of the British representatives in the area as well as those of the government of India and the joint Chiefs of Staff with regard to British strategic interests.[2] It was obvious that the emphasis here was on preparing a study of specific schemes of Arab federation rather than on an examination of the practicability or otherwise of an Arab federation.

A Report on Arab Federation was therefore prepared and submitted in the draft to the Committee in December 1941. It enumerated the arguments in favour of and against a British initiative in the matter. On the positive side, it was stated that British means of influencing political developments in the Arab World at that time were stronger than they were likely to be in future years. Britain had large military contingents in the area and Ibn Sa'ud, "the proven friend of Britain",

---

[1] FO 371–27045–E6695/53/65
[2] Cab. 95/1, 5th meeting: M.E. (0) 41, of 8 October 1941

was at the height of his power. The independence of Syria and Lebanon was considered likely to lead to Arab demands for the end of the mandate over Palestine and Transjordan. A federation, it was added, had much to recommend it if it would involve a solution for the Palestine problem.

The counter-arguments were found, however, to be more forceful. There was nothing to show that Arab opinion was yet prepared for any scheme of federation. Federation, as indicated in the reports of the British representatives in the area, had never represented "a fixed or genuine" aspiration on the part of the Arab states or the Arab peoples as a whole, and "must not be taken as one of the fundamental aims of the Arab nationalist movement". The Arab states might be willing to co-operate, when necessary, for a common purpose. None of them would, however, recognize the hegemony of any other, or subordinate local interests and aspirations to those of a larger whole. Any scheme of federation would, moreover, raise many difficulties in view of the dynastic, religious and sectarian antagonisms and French objections. Zionist interest in the idea would make it suspect in Arab eyes. The promotion of such a scheme by the British would inflame political passions throughout the Arab World, which so far had been quiet and busied with internal problems, and probably also throughout the Jewish world.

The Report did not consider as "deserving of serious consideration" the suggestion that by the granting to Ibn Sa'ud of the overlordship of the Arabs in addition to other financial inducements, he might be persuaded to give the Jews a free hand to turn Palestine into a Jewish state. Ibn Sa'ud, it was noted, with his "high spirit and honourable character" could not be "bribed or cajoled" into taking a step which every Arab would regard "as a shameful surrender of Arab interests". It was stated, however, that the Arabs might be prepared, in return for the end of the mandate and the participation in an Arab federation, to allow the Jews a greater degree of "penetration" than they would otherwise contemplate. The Jews, on the other hand, might be induced to come to terms with the Arabs within the framework of a federation. The prospects of both communities agreeing to such a solution were considered, however, "very slight".

British interests in the area were defined as communications and oil, the safeguarding of which would, the Report stated, require the maintenance of naval, military and air facilities throughout the area. These interests, it was added, would be in "real danger" if the pan-Arab movement, and hence the movement for Arab federation, were to take an extreme form. In this case such a movement might "degenerate" into an anti-British, anti-French and, "above all", an anti-Jewish movement.

On the strength of these arguments, the Report endorsed the view that this was not the time for endeavouring to formulate and carry through a scheme of political federation. It was stressed that in no case should such a scheme be imposed on the Arabs by force. It was noted, however, that H.M.G. might suitably take action in two directions. The first one was based on the conviction that Arab nationalism and the wish for closer ties were "almost certain to grow". It was considered desirable, therefore, for H.M.G. to examine carefully the question of what their future policy should be, and which form of Arab co-operation they favoured. The second would be the encouragement of more restricted measures for Arab co-operation in cultural and economic fields as a way of showing practical sympathy for the Arab cause, and willingness to assist in removing some of the barriers between the Arab states. It was recommended, therefore, that British representatives in the area should be invited to draw up a scheme for closer economic and cultural co-operation. It was also recommended that no objections should be raised to the extension of the Treaty of Arab Brotherhood between Saudi Arabia, Iraq, and Yemen to include Syria and Lebanon, if this was proposed by the Arabs themselves. The Report noted, moreover, that British post-war strategic requirements should be studied so as to find ways of reconciling them with Arab, Jewish, and French interests.

Some schemes for federation were outlined and examined in an annex to the Report. Egypt was excluded from all of them on the grounds that her willingness to limit her political independence by joining a federation was "so remote that it has not been thought necessary to pursue this suggestion in further detail". The first scheme envisaged the inclusion of all the countries of Arab Asia, with each country retaining its independence. A federal assembly would be formed and the presidency of the federation would be assumed by the Arab rulers in rotation, with an alternative of making Ibn Sa'ud president for life. It also envisaged the establishment of federal machinery for the settlement of disputes. Any external aggression against a member state would be considered as directed against the whole federation. British military guarantees would be required and could be given in return for the safeguarding of British interests and strategic needs. The advantages of the promotion of this scheme would be to show the Arabs that Britain took seriously their talk about unity. The Arabs might, if such a scheme was carried out, be induced to make concessions to the Jews. On the negative side, it was stated that such a scheme would not appeal to the Arab rulers.

The second proposed scheme excluded Saudi Arabia, and was ruled out on the grounds that it would be regarded by Ibn Sa'ud as directly opposed to his interests. The third scheme confined the federation to the four countries composing Greater Syria. Its realization would, the Report stated, be met with French objections and would necessitate the termination of the mandate over Palestine and Transjordan. Another difficulty was pointed out with regard to Amir 'Abdullah, whose kingship over such a federation would antagonize Ibn Sa'ud. These three schemes were supplemented by two alternative suggestions. The first was the encouragement of the extension of the Treaty of Arab Brotherhood. The second was the formulation of plans for closer economic and cultural co-operation between the Arab countries in the hope that this might lead to a desire for more political co-operation.[1]

The Report on Arab Federation was bound to be negative in its conclusions, since it was based mainly on the views of the British representatives in the area as well as on the previous studies on the subject, especially the one prepared by the Foreign Office in September 1939. The Report was approved by the Middle East Official Committee, whose chairman regretted the negative nature of its conclusions. He stated, however, that the logic of the circumstances was "inexorable" and that all obtainable evidence showed that political federation was not practical politics at the moment. He added that there was "small hope" in this direction of finding a solution for the Palestine problem.[2] The Report was subsequently approved by the War Cabinet.

The Report on Arab Federation was a document of great importance, since it embodied the first study of its nature to be approved interdepartmentally and by the Cabinet. It dealt with the issue from the angle of Anglo-Arab relations and British interests in the area, which was natural. It showed, however, lack of understanding of the nature and development of Arab nationalism. The statement that federation had never represented a fixed and genuine aspiration on the part of the Arabs seems rather strange. It is to be noted that the Report, in expressing this view, endorsed the analysis of Sir Kinahan Cornwallis, which was based on the state of affairs in Iraq in the aftermath of the Rashid 'Ali putsch. This was a period of stock-taking on the part of all pan-Arabs after what they considered a serious setback for their movement. The underlying causes and motives of the pan-Arab-oriented movement of Rashid 'Ali and the Iraqi nationalists were not removed by the failure of that movement.

The Arab nationalist movement had taken as its main goal, since 1919, the achievement of Arab unity. The struggle for independence whether in Palestine, Syria, or Lebanon was regarded as directly related to the efforts aimed at Arab unity. It is true that the movement towards unity suffered from many weaknesses and was beset by many difficulties, some of which were pointed out in the Report. It lacked a solid ideological basis and a political organization capable of articulating and propagating its aims and proposed methods of action on a wide scale. The movement towards unity was, however, never out of existence. Some even among the Arabs considered complete union a dream and a

---

[1] FO 371–31337–E436/46/65

[2] Cab. 95/1, M.E. (0) 41, 6th meeting, 18 December 1941

chimaera but never questioned its desirability. By 1941 there was a general consensus among Arab politicians and intellectuals that an Arab association of some sort was necessary for an Arab revival and was commendable on strategic, political, cultural, and economic grounds. Differences arose only with regard to the method of its achievement and the form it should take. It was here that dynastic rivalries and French objections had their negative impact. The main contribution of the Rashid 'Ali movement and of the Islamic movements in Egypt in particular was that they generated support for Arab unity on a much wider scale than ever before. The pursuit of pan-Arab ideals ceased to be a game played mainly by Arab rulers and old politicians whose achievements in dealing with pressing internal problems fell far short of the expectations of the masses.

To say that the Arab nationalist movement, in its pursuit of Arab unity, suffered from many weaknesses does not mean, therefore, that its ideals had lost their strong appeal to the masses. The sense of community feeling and self-identity as Arabs was stronger in the late thirties and early forties than it was ever before, due to easy communications, developed mass media, and the spread of education. The Palestine disturbances and the Syrian struggle for independence did much to articulate and crystallize that feeling. The Report on Arab Federation itself, in spite of its endorsement of the view that federation must not be taken as one of the fundamental aims of the Arab nationalist movement, was to identify Arab nationalism with the wish for closer inter-Arab ties, which it admitted was "almost certain to grow".

There was always the fear, among British policy-makers, that the development of closer Arab ties might be detrimental to British interests. In consideration of the necessity for maintaining effective British military presence and influence in the area in the post-war period, these fears were justifiable. The Arab nationalist movement had in fact developed mainly in reaction against foreign domination and influence. British professions of sympathy for the ideal of Arab unity were underlain by the belief that its achievement was almost impossible in view of the various disintegrative factors enumerated in the Report and in previous studies on the subject. They no doubt reckoned that Arab dissensions and rivalries were likely to continue for a long time to come, and that this in itself would facilitate the continuation of British influence.[1] There were still some, like Sir Harold MacMichael, who believed that the Arabs would be more susceptible of control if kept divided.

---

[1] Sir Alexander Cadogan, the Diplomatic Adviser of the Foreign Office, minuted on the Report that "our views on Arab federation were that H.M.G. must let the Arabs arrange it and that they never will". Eden margined that "never" is "a dangerous word even in Arab politics". FO 371–31337–E436/49/65

BRITISH POLICY AND ARAB ECONOMIC AND CULTURAL CO-OPERATION

The conclusions of the Arab Federation Report were not such as to stimulate great interest on the part of the Prime Minister and some of his colleagues in the Cabinet. A suggestion by Eden, that the Ministers who ordered the study should meet again to consider the action to be taken on the recommendations of the Report, was not responded to. The Foreign Office decided, however, on their own initiative, to invite the views of the British representatives in the area on possible ways for the promotion of inter-Arab economic and cultural co-operation as recommended in the Report. The question was, in the view of the Foreign Office, of "practical importance at the present time". The situation in the Arab World, they maintained, was liable "to gradual development and to sudden change". The granting of independence to Syria and Lebanon was seen as likely to lead to intensified Arab demands for the end of the mandate over Palestine and Transjordan. The Zionists' extreme demands following the Biltmore Conference of May 1942 were also mentioned. Reference was made to the possibility of Saudi Arabia "relapsing into a state of primitive lawlessness" at the death of Ibn Sa'ud. The views of the Chiefs of Staff were invited on the possible effects on British strategic interests, in view of the recent tendency of Turkey to demand territorial concessions in Syria, of Turkish control of the east–west railway through Syria in addition to the town and district of Aleppo. The Petroleum Department was asked to prepare a study on British oil interests in the Middle East.[1]

---

[1] FO 371–31337–E976, 2583/49/65. Turkey continued to entertain hopes of the annexation of parts of northern Syria, including Aleppo, in spite of her official renunciation of any further territorial claims following her annexation of Alexandretta in 1939. The outbreak of the war, and the eagerness of Britain and France to secure the support, or at least the benevolent neutrality, of the Turkish government towards the Allied cause offered a unique chance for Turkey to push her claims in Syria. Churchill, as stated earlier, did not rule out the possibility, in 1941, of making some territorial concessions to Turkey in Syria in return for her participation in the operations against the Vichy French forces in the Levant. The successful conclusion of these operations made this unnecessary. The British military were soon to press, however, for the speedy construction of a railway link between Adana and Diarbakr in southern Turkey, which they considered vital to their strategic plans and which was intentionally delayed by the Turkish government. The British, by way of inducement, were ready to concede the Duck's Bill in northern Syria to Turkey to provide for a direct railway link with Iraq. They were soon to hold back, however, when the Turks asked for Aleppo as well. Sir Hugh Knatchbull-Hugessen, the Ambassador in Angorra, was strongly against returning a categorical refusal to Turkish demands, which began to be put forward forcefully early in 1942, on the grounds that this would be "harmful" at a time when Hitler and Stalin were ready to support them. The Foreign Office were reluctant, however, to concede to Turkish pressures for fear of strong adverse reactions in the Arab World. This dilemma was soon to be solved when

These enquiries were designed mainly to assist in a re-examination of the British post-war policy in the area. There was no urgency about the question of Arab federation. No action was taken on the recommendations of the Report for more than a year. This was due in part to the worsening war situation and British reverses in the Western Desert. The victory at Al-'Alamain removed some worries and provided the chance, in the following months, for the exploration of the possibilities of economic and cultural Arab co-operation.

THE PROSPECTS OF ECONOMIC CO-OPERATION IN THE MIDDLE EAST

Enquiries on the possibilities of inter-Arab economic co-operation were initiated at the request of the Foreign Office by the Minister of State in Cairo, who was in fact the best qualified person for this purpose, in view of his supervisory role over the activities of the Middle East Supply Centre. The Centre was established in April 1941 to handle war-time problems with regard to the allocation of shipping space for military and civilian supplies. It was reorganized and expanded by Oliver Lyttelton, who chose as its head in December 1941 Commander Robert Jackson, the energetic Australian naval officer, who had much experience in supply problems during his service in Malta. The Centre as such was a British enterprise. The United States was soon to join its activities in view of the fact that she provided a great part of the military and civilian supplies. Frederick Winant, the Chief of the United States Control Office, was appointed in July 1942 Chairman of the Executive Committee of the Centre.

The Middle East Supply Centre was set up mainly to serve the Allied war effort. It did not have as its aim the achievement of economic integration of the region as a whole, in spite of the fact that its activities included devising methods for the best use of local resources and the exchange of surplus goods between the countries of the Middle East. Commander Jackson was to describe as "untrue" all that was being said at the time about regional planning through the Centre, and to deny that it was formed to serve long-term objectives. The Centre, he stated, was conceived "purely for reasons of strategy, but in carrying out that work we learnt certain lessons which it seemed could be carried forward in the future".[1]

---

the military decided that in view of the war developments in the Middle East and Hitler's attack on the Soviet Union, the construction of this railway was no longer necessary and might even be of more assistance to Germany. The British were, therefore, no longer keen on accommodating the Turks, and saw "a real danger" in Turkish appetite growing with each territorial concession and that Mosul might be second in the list. FO 371–3395–R2713, 5618/2713/44

[1] Commander R. Jackson, "Some Aspects of the War and Its Aftermath in the Middle East" in *The Royal Central Asian Society Journal*, vol. XXXII, July–October 1945, p. 259; also Keith Murray, "Feeding the Middle East in War Time", ibid., pp. 261–2

It was mainly due to the impetus given by the Foreign Office in connection with the recommendations of the Arab Federation Report that the Centre began to devote some attention to regional co-operation in matters not directly related to the war effort. This was facilitated by the Allied successes in the war from November 1942 onwards and the gradual easing of the shipping crisis. Richard Casey, the Minister of State, was to prepare early in January 1943, in response to a request from the Foreign Office, an initial study of the prospects of economic co-operation in the Middle East. He reviewed the measures taken by the Middle East Supply Centre with regard to the reduction of the area to a strict war economy through the restriction of imports, the imposition of controls on consumption, and the development of human and material resources especially in agriculture, with the object of making the area as self-supporting as possible. He recommended that a study should be made of long-term schemes of development, especially in the field of irrigation and flood control of the Tigris and Euphrates valleys, the Asswan Dam Nitrate production project, afforestation and anti-erosion measures, and transport development. He stated, however, that he did not contemplate and even deprecated any financial commitment by H.M.G. at that stage. The British role should be confined, in his view, to scientific and technical assistance. He added that this assistance could be provided on an Anglo-American basis.

The departments in London were, however, unclear in their minds about the objectives and scope of this approach. The Foreign Office were of the view that before giving Casey any guidance in the matter, it would be necessary to have a clearer idea of the shape of the postwar world. The Colonial Office doubted whether the Middle East Supply Centre should have a role in carrying out development schemes after the war. Doubts were cast over the conception of the Middle East as an economic unit after the war. It was the view of the Colonial Office that the unifying factor imposed by the war-time shipping shortage would disappear after the war. Economic relations between the Middle Eastern States would then tend to be competitive rather than complementary. They considered themselves better qualified than the Middle East Supply Centre in dealing with the affairs of the territories with which it was their responsibility to deal. They deemed it difficult for anybody established in Cairo to formulate unified proposals in respect of all the widely different countries in the area. The Middle East Official Committee which reviewed the matter decided, however, that since what Casey proposed at that stage was only to conduct enquiries rather than to carry out definite plans, it might be feasible to give him a chance to do so. It was stressed, in the meantime, that these investigations should be conducted under the direction of the Office of the Minister of State and that the Middle East Supply Centre, though its contribution might be necessary, should not be regarded as having the initiative in the enquiry.[1] The reasons given were that the governments in the area might be averse to planning carried out by an outside body such as the Middle East Supply Centre, and that there was much to be said for associating these governments with particular aspects of Casey's enquiry.[2]

The responsible departments in London were therefore unwilling to assume any financial commitments in the area even after the war. They were also unwilling to concede to the Minister of State any greater authority in formulating plans for economic development and doubted the possibilities of economic regionalism even on a limited scale confined to the Greater Syria states. Casey's proposals, even with regard to long-term development projects, did not represent a serious approach to economic regionalism, nor did they represent a comprehensive plan for economic development in each of the countries concerned. Casey felt that if these projects were suggested to the Middle Eastern governments, they might be convinced of a real British interest in their post-war welfare, and thus become more receptive to war-time economic restrictions and controls. This was obviously an attempt to relate the proposals to the Allied war effort and to increase their appeal to Whitehall. He overlooked the more important issues, in terms of economic regionalism, of inter-regional trade, industrial development and consequent structural changes in the economies of the Middle Eastern countries. What transpires from all this is that the promotion of economic regionalism in the Middle East did not represent, at least up to early 1943, a definite line of policy on the part of H.M.G.

Casey was to initiate a series of enquiries during the following three months, the results of which were embodied in a carefully prepared memorandum which he submitted in May 1943 to the Middle East War Council in Cairo. In this memorandum, he attempted an analysis of the recent trends of the Arab nationalist movement, and tried to relate them to the urge for development and co-operation in the area. Arab nationalism, in his view, combined a desire to imitate the West and to borrow the apparatus of Western civilization, with an urge for freedom from European political control. Arab nationalism in the past had been primarily a political movement following the steps of nineteenth-century European liberalism. This type of Arab nationalism guided the movement of the older Arab leaders such as Nuri al-Sa'id, and was in danger of becoming "an anachronism and a morbid one". Europe was already passing into a new phase where national sovereignty was seen to be insufficient. The war had brought a realization among the younger educated Arabs that independence of small states was by itself

[1] This was due also presumably to the fact that the Middle East Supply Centre's activities were then conducted on an Anglo-American basis. The Americans at that juncture were not informed of British intentions in this regard.

[2] Cab. 95/1, M.E. (0) 43, 1st meeting of the Middle East Official Committee, 19 January 1943

worth very little. The war was also beginning to show that the older group of Arab nationalist leaders, closely identified as they were with the landowning classes and with vested interests, were, at least potentially, an actual obstacle to "modernistic" national development. This Casey took as evincing signs of a new and more realistic trend in Arab nationalism, which would only remain healthy if encouraged and led.

Casey's sound analysis overlooked one important fact. The situation in the Arab countries at that time was dissimilar to that of Europe, which had enjoyed real independence for a long time, and which had reached a high degree of maturity in its political development. The horrors of two world wars seemed to discredit the national-state system, with its attributes of sovereignty and territorial integrity. This was not the case with the Arab countries which were under foreign domination and influence of one sort or the other, and which were struggling for their independence. History has shown that newly independent states always tend to be keen on preserving their independence with all that goes with it in enhancement of status, prestige, promise of economic development, and freedom of action. Casey was rather too optimistic in expecting the Arab countries to realize the limitations of the independence which they had not yet achieved in a real sense. He was right, however, in sensing the urge for westernization among the young educated elements, and in relating it to the wish to get rid of foreign influence. This was in fact a central theme in the Arab nationalist movement.

Casey then attempted an evaluation of the experience of the Middle East Supply Centre and its affiliated agencies. The Allied distribution and supply regulations represented, in his view, the first constructive attempt at regional organization, and at educating the various governments to think in Middle Eastern terms. He argued for the introduction of an increasing element of consultation and consent into the operation of the Allied supply controls to avoid nationalist resentment. Various methods were suggested, including the holding of technical conferences participated in by local experts; the recruitment of local staff to take part in the operations of the supply and general economic controls; and the convening of economic conferences to discuss selected current problems such as inflation and price-control.

He then proposed the establishment of a Middle East Economic Council. Its natural nucleus would comprise the countries of Arab Asia. The addition of Egypt, Sudan, and Persia was envisaged only for war-time purposes and the inclusion of Turkey after the war was contemplated. The proposed Council would also include British, American, and possibly Free French and Soviet representatives. It would be a consultative body which would act as a kind of parliament for the discussion of supply, economic, and financial matters of common concern to its members. The British and American members would endeavour to exercise a guiding influence over its debates and resolutions. If the Council developed satisfactorily, its functions could then be extended in the transitional period from war to peace to cover the broad lines of post-war economic reconstruction, the co-ordination of Middle Eastern demands on Anglo-American exports in repayment of accumulated war-time debts, the allocation of the intake to the most productive purposes, and the sponsoring of large-scale development schemes. It could also examine and sponsor schemes for removing economic barriers between particular groups of countries in the region, including the establishment of customs and currency unions. The Council in this way would be, in the view of Casey, a constructive lead in the direction of closer economic association between the Middle Eastern countries and would therefore have a political value. It would also, in the long run, provide a framework for a regional economic group under United Nations' guidance on a peace-time basis. This would contribute towards satisfying the urge for economic and social progress in the area. The establishment of the Council would, moreover, realize British short-term war-time objectives as well as the long-term objective of establishing a regional grouping in the area "under Anglo-American leadership". Casey stressed, however, that the success of this initiative would depend, among other things, on the settlement of the Palestine and Syrian problems "in such a way that we and other external powers could not be accused of imperialism and exploitation at the Arab expense". He stated also that his proposals were based on the necessity for a joint Anglo-American initiative in view of the Anglo-American nature of the Middle East Supply Centre, the increasing American share in responsibility for civilian supplies, and the benefits of continued Anglo-American co-operation on a long-term basis.[1]

Casey's proposals were based on the current belief among the advocates of functionalism on a regional and an international basis, that by bringing the representatives and experts in the region together, habits of co-operation could be created and the chances of closer political relations enhanced. The chief snag about his main proposal regarding the formation of a Middle East Economic Council was his assumption of Anglo-American leadership and guidance. This contradicted Casey's analysis of the Arab nationalist movement as guided by the wish to get rid of all foreign influence. The establishment of a regional Council under foreign guidance would have naturally been viewed in the area as a pretext for the continuation of foreign domination in another form. His stipulation that a settlement satisfactory to the Arabs in Syria and Palestine was necessary for the success of this initiative was no doubt on the right lines. By removing all sources of antagonism towards the West, he hoped that a new and closer relationship would develop

[1] Cab. 95/1, M.E.W.C. (43) 3, Annex II: memorandum dated 2 April 1943

between the Arab nationalists and Britain. This was easier said than done. This stipulation, in view of the strong pro-Zionist elements in the War Cabinet, was enough to prejudice his scheme.

Sir Miles Lampson, by way of comment on Casey's proposals, thought it unfortunate that a Middle East Economic Council had to be the offspring of the Middle East Supply Centre, whose restrictive controls were disliked by the countries of the area. Such a Council, he maintained, would be viewed with suspicion, and the widely divergent interests of the member countries would make it unlikely for it to achieve enough consensus, or to take final decisions. It would, therefore, remain essentially consultative, and might degenerate, as was the case with some war-time regional gatherings, into inconclusive debate. He believed, however, that the scheme was worth a try. Action, in his view, could be taken in the direction of the establishment of customs and currency unions. A customs union linking Syria and Lebanon with Palestine and Transjordan would satisfy the Jewish industrialists' dream of finding markets in the neighbouring countries for the goods manufactured in Palestine. This would not be possible, in his view, without a prior settlement of the Palestine problem, and a change of attitude on the part of the Arabs towards the Jewish question. A currency union, on the other hand, could be established regardless of political problems, since it was desired in Palestine and Syria. Currency would have to be controlled by London, and a general sterling currency would not affect French and Zionist political interests.[1]

The Middle East War Council, to which Casey presented his proposals, approved most of them. The Council expressed the view that the economic stability, and consequent social and political contentment of the Middle East, were "a major strategic interest of H.M.G. and thus of the United Nations". To achieve this purpose, it was deemed necessary to consider the Middle East as a regional unit. The proposal regarding the formation of a Middle East Economic Council was endorsed. It was suggested that this Council could have an executive and a planning agency developed out of the existing Middle East Supply Council, adapted and liberalized to meet the changing circumstances. The Council, it was agreed, had to be established by stages, making it possible for it to take shape before the end of the war. A starting-point was suggested in the form of bringing the local governments, both collectively and individually, into consultation by means of technical and economic conferences. The evolution of a regional economic secretariat linked at the beginning to the Middle East Supply Centre was also suggested. Reference was made to the possibility of establishing a currency union as a natural corollary to any form of

[1] Cab. 95/1, M.E.W.C. (43) 16, Annex III: memorandum prepared for the Middle East War Council, dated 7 May 1943

economic union between Palestine, Transjordan, Syria, and Lebanon. The War Council favoured an early initiative in that direction by Britain, preferably in association with the United States. This was considered necessary in view of the widespread desire for closer co-operation in the region, and the desirability of guiding this drive into healthy channels, thus preventing it from developing into a form of acute nationalism hostile to British influence. It was stressed that the success of this scheme would depend on the solution of the problems of Syria and Palestine.[1]

The proposals of Casey and the resolutions of the Middle East War Council came up for discussion early in July in the Middle East Official Committee in London. There were still doubts and hesitations. The Colonial Office doubted the extent to which these proposals could successfully be put into practice. They felt that the Middle East as a geographical unit was the creation of the war conditions, and would not survive the war. They considered a currency union for Palestine and Syria "difficult or impossible to achieve" and disadvantageous to Palestine. This view was also held by the Treasury Department, which maintained that Palestine and Syria followed policies which led to widely divergent prices and wage levels. There was a general agreement, however, about the desirability of testing this approach in its initial stages through the proposed technical and economic conferences. The Ministry of Food favoured Casey's proposals, which they found in line with their current thought regarding post-war needs, with world developments, and with the resolutions of the Hot Springs Conference on Food and Agriculture. It was agreed therefore to proceed on an experimental basis, and not to make any public statement about the subject until it was known whether the proposed conferences on specific subjects were successful or not.[2]

The whole question came up before the War Cabinet on 12 July 1943. Casey, who was then in London, did much lobbying for his scheme. He induced Eden to prepare a supporting memorandum. He clarified to the departments concerned some points about his scheme. Reference to the Cabinet was in fact thought necessary by the Middle East Official Committee and by the Foreign Office in relation to the suggested participation of the United States Government in the proposed initiative. The discussion in the Cabinet centred mainly on the American role in the Middle East. Eden explained the increasing American interest in the area with regard to oil in particular. He referred to American prejudices against what they considered as British "exploiting and imperialist" policies. The Americans, he stated, wanted to have their say in Middle Eastern affairs. H.M.G., he maintained, could not expect anything else if American help was desired, and any indication of a move away from

---

[1] Cab. 95/1, M.E.W.C. (43)–25: meeting of 19 May 1943
[2] Cab. 95/1, M.E. (0) 43: 2nd meeting, 2 July 1943

isolationism was to be welcomed. He noted, however, that H.M.G. must somehow ensure that the United States influence was not used against the British in an area of vital interest to their Empire. He therefore proposed a frank exchange of views with the Americans, and suggested that British policy in the area should be explained to them. He also proposed that the Americans should be informed of the possibility of setting up an economic organization in the Middle East to fulfil a unifying role among the Arab countries.

The War Cabinet agreed in principle that the Middle East Supply Centre should be developed by stages into a Middle East Economic Council, which would include representatives from Britain, the United States, and the governments of the main countries in the region. The Minister of State was authorized to conduct enquiries, and to report any progress to the War Cabinet, seeking its approval before taking any steps towards the formal establishment of the Council. It was also agreed that an endeavour should be made to reach an understanding with the American Government as to general policy in the Middle East, and to inform them of the proposed initiative.[1]

The discussions in the War Cabinet did not evince any great interest in economic regionalism in the Middle East. The qualified approval of Casey's scheme was mainly due to his efforts in pushing it through and arguing forcefully for its acceptance. Casey was to stress once and again in London that, in the post-war period, British influence and guidance could only be exerted through economic matters. The need for a prior solution for the Palestine and Syrian problems was brushed aside, since what was proposed at that stage was a mere exploration of the possibilities of co-operation through regional conferences. The transfer of Casey from his post in Cairo late in 1943 deprived the scheme of its initiator and most active promoter.

The first stage in Casey's scheme was, however, carried out, and several technical and economic conferences were held at British initiative, and with the participation of the Middle Eastern governments. These conferences were:

---

[1] Cab. 66/39, W.P. (43) 301; Cab. 66/35: Cabinet conclusions: W.M. (43) 99th and 101st conclusions of 14 and 19 July. The State Department was invited in October 1943 to send a representative to London for a frank exchange of views on policy in the area. It was also informed of the proposed initiative on the lines suggested by Eden. These talks, after much procrastination on the part of the State Department, took place in April 1944 during the visit of the Stettinius Mission to London. It was then agreed that both governments should collaborate in making a joint effort in the direction of setting up a system of economic co-operation between the Middle Eastern countries which should eventually be autonomous and self-supporting. It was also agreed to provide assistance, technical and general guidance to these countries in dealing with their common social and economic problems. F.R. of the U.S., vol. IV, 1943, pp. 6–18; Cab. 21/858–File 9/12/2, Part I

1 The Middle East Conference on Rationing and Control of Distribution: August 1943

This was the first war-time regional meeting in which an attempt was made to bring the officials and experts of all the Middle Eastern governments together in conference with the officials of the Middle East Supply Centre, to discuss a current problem of common concern. A useful exchange of information took place. The Middle East Supply Centre was asked to act as a clearing house for the periodical circulation of information on rationing throughout the area and abroad. Periodical digests of information on the subject were subsequently circulated by the Centre.

2 The Middle East Statistical Conference: November 1943

It was attended by representatives from Egypt, Iraq, Lebanon, Syria, Sudan, Palestine, and Transjordan, as well as by American, British, and Free French representatives. A standing committee was formed with the purpose of drawing up a scheme for a permanent Middle Eastern Statistical Bureau and of advising the countries in the area on statistical matters until such a Bureau was formed. The Conference drew up also a constitution for the proposed Bureau. Financial contributions were made or promised later by the governments of Egypt, Sudan, Syria, Lebanon, Palestine, the UK, and the United States. Progress was slow, however, due to the shortage of trained personnel, and no one was found to act as head of the proposed Bureau.

3 The Middle East Agricultural Development Conference: February 1944

It was preceded by two agricultural conferences convened by the Supply Centre in 1942 and 1943, which were participated in by British officials and experts, and were confined to the discussion of the more immediate problems of maintaining and increasing local food supplies. The third conference was of a different nature. It was concerned with long-term problems of agricultural development, and was confined to experts from "the hard core" Middle Eastern countries, meaning the Arab states and Cyprus, "in order that maximum attention could be focused on the similarity of problems".

The major outcome of the Conference was the decision to establish a permanent Middle East Council of Agriculture. A sub-committee was formed to draft a constitution for the proposed Council. Political difficulties slowed down progress in this regard. There was first the difficulty of finding a formula, acceptable to the British, allowing for the inclusion of the colonial and mandated territories. The Colonial Office were still doubtful about the prospects of success of the whole enterprise, and were reluctant to grant any greater authority to the local authorities in Aden, Cyprus, Palestine, and Transjordan. The Egyptian Government were eager to stress the Arab nature of the Council, and insisted that the Arabic text of its constitution should prevail in cases of difference in interpretation. The Arab countries were anxious to run the proposed Council without foreign advice. The discussions in the Conference were significant, however, from a purely technical point of view. Papers were presented on the regional control of water resources, the improvement of standards of nutrition, and the common wealth of the Middle East. The results of the Conference were described by its British sponsors as "very encouraging". The Middle East, it was noted, was the first region of the world to follow the lead given at the Hot Springs Conference of June 1943 and to begin to tackle, on a regional basis, the practical problems of agricultural and rural development.

4 The Middle East Financial Conference: 1944

It was convened at the invitation of the Minister of State to review war-time inflationary trends in the area and to discuss the various measures that had been, or could be, taken to counteract these trends. It was attended by ministers, bankers, and technical experts from Egypt, Palestine, Syria, Lebanon, Iraq, Transjordan, Saudi Arabia, Cyprus, Iran, and Ethiopia. It was also attended by representatives of the government of India, the American and French Treasury Departments, and the Economic and Financial Department of the League of Nations.

It was by then that the inflationary tendencies in the area had reached alarming proportions. This was caused mainly by the increase in purchasing power arising from increased military expenditure unmatched by an increase in the supply of goods. Civilian imports decreased from 5·25 to 1·5 million tons per year, while the allied expenditure in local currencies in payment for goods and services for the maintenance of troops rose from £6 millions in 1939 to £195 millions in 1943.[1] The wholesale prices rose from 100 for the base year 1939 to 329·1 in Egypt, 328 in Palestine, 1088 in Syria, 521 in Iraq, and 228 in the Sudan by 1944. This was accompanied by a commensurate rise in the cost of living.[2] Many jobs were provided for the local population during the war, and private contractors and profiteers found the chance to make money. The majority suffered, however, from soaring prices and low income. This was a latent cause for social unrest, which the British were eager to contain in order to maintain the stability of the area for the duration of the war.

The Conference recommended that all possible measures such as taxation, loans, control of prices, and the development of production

---

[1] George Kirk *The Middle East in the War*, p. 186

[2] Cab. 21/859–File 9/12/2, Part 2

should be taken to bring price levels in the Middle Eastern countries into better equilibrium with one another, and with those of other regions of the world. No proposal was made for the creation of a permanent organization to deal with financial matters. It was recommended, however, that the heads of the participating delegations or their deputies should meet as occasion arose to discuss these matters. By 1945 no request had been made for any further meeting of the delegates, though some of the measures recommended were carried out by the participating governments.

5 The Middle East Anti-Locust Conferences

The expected severe outbreak of desert locust, with its implied threat to agriculture and food supplies in the area, became a matter of urgency in 1942. A Middle East Anti-Locust Unit was set up early in 1942 by the British, and a series of conferences were held in 1943 to discuss the problem. An extensive anti-locust campaign was conducted in Arabia and Persia, using British military facilities and personnel, during the winter and spring of 1944/45. The anti-locust campaign was described as "a remarkable example of co-operative effort" participated in by all the countries in the region with technical expertise, equipment, and qualified personnel from Britain and the Soviet Union. No permanent body was set up, however, to deal with future locust threats.[1]

The war-time conferences were all held at British instance, and organized by the Minister of State and the Middle East Supply Centre. They dealt with matters related either directly or indirectly to the abnormal war-time conditions. The guiding and leading role of Britain and the United States was maintained in each of these conferences. This was enough in itself to prejudice the proceedings of these regional meetings. The Middle Eastern countries were much in need of foreign assistance, but they wanted that assistance to be extended on an advisory basis. They were not ready to grant a leading role to any foreign power, and were determined to be the sole arbiters in their own affairs. They were hoping after the war to free themselves from all vestiges of foreign influence. It was natural therefore that they should object to having British representatives in the governing body of the proposed Council of Agriculture. It should be noted that this was a time when the Arab unity consultations in Cairo in 1943 and in 1944 had resulted in the evolution of the Arab League scheme. This scheme provided for inter-Arab economic, social, and cultural co-operation. Having formed their

[1] Cab. 21/859–File 9/12/2, Part 2. For material about the war-time conferences, also *The Middle East Supply Centre:* Agricultural Report No. 5, "Proceedings of the Conference on Middle East Agricultural Development, Cairo, February 7th to 10th 1944", Cairo 1944; Martin Wilmington *The Middle East Supply Centre*, Albany, New York 1971, pp. 150, 159

own machinery for regional co-operation, the Arab states were naturally averse from associating themselves with any organization inspired and led by foreigners.

The departments in London were also far from enthusiastic towards this whole enterprise. They had serious doubts, which were expressed in July 1943 and again in 1944, about the prospects of economic regionalism in the Middle East. The Foreign Office doubted any desire on the part of the Arab countries for a Middle East Economic Council. They objected even to the establishment of a co-ordinating committee in London to study and re-examine the scheme. The case for the formation of this Council, they maintained, was not as strong in 1944 as it had been a year earlier. It was considered impracticable at that stage to decide on British post-war economic policy towards the Middle East. The proposal regarding the establishment of a Middle East Economic Council was therefore allowed to die a slow death. There was an agreement, however, that some co-operation in "limited technical fields" between the Middle Eastern countries, "possibly with some slight assistance from H.M.G.", was possible and desirable.[1]

There was therefore no definite policy with regard to the promotion of economic regionalism in the Middle East. The endorsement by the War Cabinet of the conclusions of the Arab Federation Report and of Casey's proposals was not in itself sufficient. There were serious problems regarding finance and the provision of technical experts. There were also difficulties in securing American co-operation. This was a period of Anglo-American rivalry over oil in Saudi Arabia in particular. Many American officials suspected British motives and were resentful of British efforts to establish their influence and "guidance" in the area, especially in economic matters.

It is true that the war situation contributed towards the evolution of an outlook on the Middle East as one unit. This was not reflected, however, on the organizational level in Whitehall. There was no machinery in London responsible for co-ordinating and relating British economic and political interests in the Middle East. The Middle East Official Committee, which had for years handled such affairs on an inter-departmental basis, stopped its meetings in 1944. The Foreign Office were reluctant to revive it. The chairmanship of the Colonial Office representative over its meetings was always irksome to them. The Colonial Office were also opposed to Foreign Office chairmanship over any inter-departmental committee concerned with Middle Eastern affairs.[2] This was the case in spite of persistent appeals from the British representatives in the area that a central body similar to the Office of the Minister of State should be established in London to formulate policies

[1] Cab. 21/859–File 9/12/2, Part 1
[2] Cab. 21/859–File 9/12/2, Part 1

towards the area, which they stressed should be dealt with as one unit.[1] By 1945, Middle Eastern affairs were still being handled in London by several departments, including the Foreign, the Colonial, and the India Offices, with the minimum of inter-departmental co-ordination. The British representatives and officials were still arguing in April 1945, during the meetings of the Economic Conference in Cairo, about the merits of regionalism in the area, a month after the establishment of the League of Arab States. The Middle East Supply Centre and the Office of the Minister of State were established for war-time purposes. They played a great role in dealing effectively with the problems arising from the shipping crisis. Once the war was over, they lost their relevance and had to be liquidated. The war-time technical conferences had their beneficial impact in bringing Middle Eastern experts together for the discussion of common problems. They made these experts more conscious of thc similarity of technical problems in the area and provided them with a wider outlook and a regional orientation. The Arab League provided more acceptable and useful machinery for guiding and enhancing this new drive for regional co-operation.

THE PROSPECTS OF ARAB CULTURAL CO-OPERATION

It has been noted earlier that while there were differences among the Arabs with regard to the political and economic aspects of any possible union, there was a consensus about the necessity for closer inter-Arab cultural relations. It was in this field in particular that most politicians and intellectuals in Egypt saw that a promising start could be made. It was also in this field that Egypt was at the very centre of the movement for closer Arab ties. Egypt's leading role was enhanced throughout the years through its flourishing press, and by the pioneering efforts of its intellectuals in developing a simple form of written Arabic which could be easily understood in the other Arab countries.[2] Many issues related to Egypt's orientation and cultural identity were discussed and settled by the mid-thirties. These included the attitude towards western cultural influences and the relevance of the ancient cultural heritage. By the mid-thirties there was general agreement about the central role of Arab culture in Egypt's life and future development.

The pan-Arab effervescence in Arab Asia during the late thirties and the early forties was dominated by the political issues of Palestine, Syria, and Arab federation. This was one of its main weaknesses, since it meant a neglect of the no less important economic and cultural aspects of Arab unity. Egypt, herself excluded from all schemes of Arab

---

[1] Commander R. Jackson, in *The Royal Central Asian Society Journal*, pp. 261–2; also Cab. 21/859–File 9/12/2, Part 1

[2] A census conducted in 1943 showed that about 70 per cent of the books published in Egypt find their way to Arab readers in Palestine, Sudan, Syria, Lebanon, and Iraq. *Al Musawar*, 21 May 1943

federation and with no wish to join an Arab union, was to play a significant role in the movement towards Arab cultural revival. An Arab Cultural Bureau was established in Cairo in 1943, with the initial membership of Egypt and Iraq, to discuss the harmonization of educational curricula and teaching methods, and to formulate an Arab cultural pact. The Arab Medical Congresses and the cultural exchanges and contacts between Egypt and the Arab countries were a manifestation of this drive towards closer cultural co-operation with the rest of the Arab countries.

The movement towards Arab cultural revival had three distinct aims. It aimed first at raising the cultural level of the more backward Arab regions to that of the more advanced, thus removing one of the main obstacles to political union. It strove secondly towards making the Arabs more fully aware of the common elements in their cultural heritage, and thus counteracting the particularist spirit which was one of the weaknesses of Arab life. Its third aim was the introduction of a certain, although not a complete, uniformity into the chaos of the educational systems which had grown up in the Arab countries: public and private schools, national and foreign, Anglo-Saxon and French, religious and lay.[1] The movement in this way was directly related to the Arab drive for independence and progress.

The Arab Federation Report rightly noted the positive impact of closer Arab cultural co-operation and saw this as one of the fields in which a British initiative could be made with some chance of success. The main objective was to encourage the secular trends in Arab culture, and to exercise some influence on the moulding and the direction of the Arab cultural revival. Richard Casey was authorized by the Foreign Office in 1942 to conduct enquiries and to report on the most suitable action to be taken in this regard. This was one of the main subjects discussed by the Middle East War Council in its meetings in May 1943, in which various aspects of British policy in the area were reviewed. The main document submitted by Casey was a memorandum prepared by Albert Hourani, of Chatham House,[2] in April 1943, following a tour of six months in the area. Casey, who agreed with Hourani's recommendations, suggested that the memorandum be taken as a focus for discussion in the Council.

In his memorandum, Hourani concentrated on the role Britain could

---

[1] Cab. 95/1–M.E.W.C. (43) 4–Appendix II. From a memorandum on Arab cultural co-operation by A. Hourani. The third aim was emphasized by Ahmad Amin, "Unity and Diversity" in *Majallat al-Risalh*, 1st year, issue No. 25, 20 June 1939; by Muhammad Hussein Haykal, "Cultural Union Between the Arab Nations" in *Majallat al-Hilal*, issue No. 5, April 1939; and by Dr Taha Hussein: *Mustaqbal Al Thaqafa*, pp. 386–90

[2] Hourani was a member of a war-time body set up at the request of the Foreign Office by the Royal Institute of International Affairs, which developed later into the Research Department of the Foreign Office.

play in promoting cultural co-operation in the Arab world. This was a time, he noted, when the very nature of Arab culture was being remoulded and the deepest problems were revealing themselves. He stressed that in approaching this task the only criterion should be the intellectual and spiritual welfare of the Arabs, and not some immediate political advantage. The aim, in his view, should be to help the Arab nation to achieve full understanding both of the present state of Arab culture, and of the general nature of European culture. His recommendations for British action in this field were:

1. To help in the creation of an educated public through the expansion of the educational system in Palestine, the development of British institutes and high schools on an Anglo-Arab basis, and inducing Arab intellectuals to publish an *Everyman's Library* in Arabic acquainting the public with western works. He also suggested that financial and intellectual assistance should be provided in this regard by the British Council.
2. To help in the creation of an intellectual élite through the appointment of a number of first-class English scholars and thinkers to positions in the cultural centres around the Egyptian University, the American University of Beirut, and among Christian Arab thinkers. Their role would be to act as consultants to the Arab cultural movement. The most important contribution, in his view, would be made through the establishment of an academy or institute of higher studies, where Englishmen, Europeans, and Arabs would work together on the basic problems of the Arab World. This would help in directing and canalizing the Arab cultural movement, and in bringing the Arabs into the community of western civilization. He suggested also the development of Arab studies in England on a basis of partnership between Arab and English scholars.
3. To help towards Arab cultural union, especially with regard to the unification of the educational system. There was an urgent need, in his view, for a centre for educational research where problems of Arab education could be studied scientifically, and where educational officials could be trained. Such a centre, he added, could be attached to the proposed academy or to one of the universities in the area.
4. The creation of a central body for planning British cultural policy in the area. This body could be supplemented by "a centre of ideas and studies" attached to the British Council or directly to H.M.G. for this purpose.[1]

The proposals of Hourani were based in fact on a general assessment of the development of the Arab nationalist movement in the aftermath

[1] Cab. 95/1–M.E.W.C. (43) 4–Appendix II

of the Rashid 'Ali *putsch*. He saw the movement at that time as characterized by a desire for change, a feeling of humiliation and frustration, a widening gap between generations, a suspicion of the western powers, and a tendency towards westernization among a section of the youth. He favoured British encouragement of the constructive trend espoused by the educated youth, which aimed at the construction of a modern westernized state and society. The negative trend characterized by violent resistance to the West was, in his view, distinct among old nationalists who had been embittered throughout the years against Anglo-French domination, and little could be hoped of them.[1] The stress on the role of the younger elements explains his emphasis on the need for guidance and influence in the cultural sphere, since it was in the schools and universities that attitudes and views were shaped and could be influenced with a greater chance of success. Hourani's proposals answered a widely felt need among Arab intellectuals for the secularization of the educational programmes, and for a greater understanding of, and opening on, western culture.[2]

Hourani's proposals were viewed favourably both by the Middle East War Council and by the Middle East Official Committee. The Foreign Office representative in the Committee underlined their significance as the first proposals of their kind to be received from the Middle East. He noted that Hourani's recommendations with regard to the encouragement of Arab cultural union were in line with the conclusions of the Arab Federation Report. He added that the Foreign Office attached great importance to the work of the British Council, and would favour increasing its financial and personnel capacity. The representative of the British Council stated that if these proposals could be put into effect, it would be possible in a few years "to swing Arab opinion completely in our favour". The Committee expressed the view that the organization and development of British enterprises in the cultural field should be regarded as an important part of British policy in the Middle East. The Minister of State in Cairo was authorized to study the proposals, especially with regard to the establishment of an academy of higher studies and an agricultural college. It was also agreed that the British Council should be strengthened as soon as possible, to enable it to conduct its activities to cover this field.[3]

The recommendations of the Middle East War Council based on

---

[1] FO 371–34958–E2549/506/65. From a report on "Great Britain and Arab Nationalism"

[2] Dr Taha Hussein argued for an open contact with Europe and for adopting European methods and techniques: *Mustaqbal Al Thaqafa*, pp. 34, 36, 44. Dr Muhammad Hussein Haykal stressed also the need for the Arab cultural movement not to isolate itself from the main intellectual currents in the world and to apply European research methods: *Al-Hilal*, April 1939. This need for an opening on the west was also stressed by Qustantin Zuraiq *Al-wa'y Al-Qawmi*, pp. 31–7

[3] Cab. 95/1–M.E. (0) 43–3rd meeting, 9 July 1943

Hourani's proposals drew the attention of the policy-makers in London to the political significance of a British initiative in the cultural field. The conclusions of the Arab Federation Report did not envisage any active British role in promoting inter-Arab cultural co-operation. They pointed only to the advisability of encouraging any movement among the Arabs in that direction. There were some weak points, however, in Hourani's proposals. There was first the possibility of French opposition to any British initiative, especially among the Christian elements in Syria and Lebanon. There was secondly the aversion of the Arab governments from accepting such an ambitious scheme, especially with regard to the establishment of purely English educational institutions. This was a time when many Arab intellectuals were calling for the inclusion in the curricula of the foreign schools of a study of Arabic language and religion as well as national history.[1] There was finally the fact that foreign schools drew their students mainly from the privileged classes and the foreign communities in the Arab countries. Their impact on shaping the mentality of the youth in these countries was therefore bound to be very limited. The main outcome of Hourani's proposals was the decision to strengthen the British Council, and to conduct further enquiries in this field.[2]

---

[1] Dr Taha Hussein: *Mustaqbal Al Thaqafa*, p. 385
[2] FO 371–34958–E2549/506/65

Chapter Five

Wartime Schemes for a Palestine Settlement within an Arab Federation

An uneasy truce prevailed in Palestine for the duration of the war. The militant Arab leaders were excluded from the country and somewhat discredited because of their role in the Rashid 'Ali movement and collaboration with the Axis. The moderate elements were divided among themselves, with no single body to represent their interests *vis-à-vis* the British and the Jews. The initiative passed from their hands to those of the neighbouring Arab governments, which continued to press the British for the modification, or at least the full implementation, of the terms of the White Paper. Events in Palestine were overshadowed by developments in Syria and Lebanon.

The Zionist leaders, on the other hand, appreciated correctly that the pursuit by H.M.G. of the White Paper policy was no more than a temporary expedient. All the Labour members of the War Cabinet and most of the Conservative members including Churchill had put themselves publicly on record in 1939 in opposition to that policy.[1] Within the Zionist movement the extreme elements gained the ascendency. Their programme for the reconstitution of Palestine as a Jewish commonwealth was endorsed by the Biltmore Conference of May 1942, and later by the executive of the Jewish Agency in Palestine. Their efforts were directed, from the outbreak of the war, at the extension of Jewish settlements to the frontier areas of Palestine in order to be able to lay claim to the whole country at the appropriate time. They were also aimed at the formation of a Jewish fighting force to be the nucleus of the army of their future state. With news about the extermination of the Jews seeping out of Europe from 1942 onwards, pressures were intensified on the British to admit a greater number of immigrants than provided for in the White Paper.

The Zionist leaders decided in 1941 to concentrate their efforts in the United States, "where the greatest number of Jews, as well as the most

---

[1] Parl. Deb., H. of C., 5th ser., vol. 347: Debate on the White Paper policy on 22, 23 May 1939 [coll. 2167–2179 for the views of Churchill; 2011–2015 for those of L. Amery; 2130 for the views of Herbert Morrison; 2157 for the views of Sir Archibald Sinclair; and the voting pattern in Division 149 on 23 May]

influential, were to be found". They appreciated that the United States was likely to play a dominant role in world affairs after the war. American support for their programme might, therefore, be the key to its success.[1] The fact that the Biltmore resolutions[2] were adopted by a conference of American Zionists was significant in itself in spite of the fact that these resolutions were formulated by David Ben Gurion, the head executive of the Jewish Agency. Zionist propaganda activities in the United States reached their height in 1944 before the Presidential elections, and they managed to get the support of some members of the administration for their aspirations.

THE INITIATIVES OF DR CHAIM WEIZMANN AND WINSTON CHURCHILL

The idea of a Palestine settlement through the creation of an Arab federation had its attraction for prominent Zionists such as David Ben Gurion[3] and Dr Chaim Weizmann. Dr Weizmann responded favourably to a suggestion made to him and Moshe Shertok in September 1939 by H. Philby, who had strong connections with Ibn Sa'ud. It was based on securing the overlordship of Ibn Sa'ud over the Arab countries, and raising a loan of £20 millions to help him to re-settle displaced Palestine Arabs elsewhere. The British and American Governments would provide this sum and try to persuade the king, in return, to reach a settlement with the Jews. Philby undertook to endeavour to secure Ibn Sa'ud's goodwill towards this plan in anticipation of a combined Anglo-American *démarche* to be made to him in due course. Dr Weizmann undertook, on his part, to use all Zionist influence in London and Washington to secure the acceptance of this plan.[4]

Philby had advised Ben Gurion as far back as 1937 to try to reach an agreement with Ibn Sa'ud, which idea was also suggested to Ben Gurion in 1938 by Lord Lloyd, the then head of the British Council, and by Malcolm MacDonald, the Colonial Secretary.[5] Philby recounted that

---

[1] Michael Bar-Zohar *The Armed Prophet: A Biography of Ben Gurion*, translated from the French by Len Ortzer, London 1967, p. 67; Cab. 66/36 [W.P. 43 (200)]—annex to a memorandum by Eden citing as his source intercepted letters of the leading personalities of the Jewish Agency

[2] These resolutions called for the establishment of Palestine as a Jewish commonwealth, the formation of a Jewish national army, and the control by the Jewish Agency of immigration and land development in Palestine.

[3] Ben Gurion suggested the idea to Musa al 'Alami as far back as 1933 and put it forward to the Arab delegates during an informal meeting presided over by the Colonial Secretary in London in February 1939. Geoffrey Furlonge *Palestine is My Country: The Story of Musa Alami*, London 1969, pp. 102–5; Michael Bar-Zohar, op. cit., p. 64

[4] H. St. J. B. Philby *Arabian Jubilee*, New York 1953, pp. 213–14

[5] David Ben-Gurion *Letters to Paula*, pp. 172–3, 204

when he put the idea to Ibn Sa'ud in 1939, his initial reaction was not completely negative, but when no approach was made to him in the following months by the British and American Governments, he had naturally adopted an unresponsive and rather enigmatic attitude.

Dr Weizmann, on the other hand, assured Philby in May 1940 of his confidence in securing British and American acceptance of the plan. It was at that time that he started to call for the establishment of a Jewish state in Palestine after the war, and to voice his support for the creation of an Arab federation provided the Zionist programme was carried through. He expressed his readiness to conduct talks with any of the Arab leaders under the aegis of H.M.G. on this basis.[1] He had presumably discussed the said plan with Churchill some time in 1940, and got his support for it. He tried also to mobilize support for it during his visit to the United States early in 1941. He returned from that visit "in an optimistic mood" and expressed to Lord Moyne, the Colonial Secretary, in August 1941 his hope for a Palestine settlement through the creation of an Arab federation under Ibn Sa'ud's leadership. He talked also of a loan of £15 to £20 millions to be raised in the United States and used for the development of Saudi Arabia. Ibn Sa'ud would be asked, in return, to persuade his fellow Arabs to accept a Jewish enclave, which should be more than a token state, in Palestine. Displaced Arabs would be re-settled with Jewish money in Iraq or elsewhere.[2]

Reference had been made earlier to Churchill's letter to Eden of May 1941 in which he suggested a similar solution which he said represented his own thinking "for some time past".[3] The Foreign Office had their serious objections to the Prime Minister's suggestion. Churchill remained, however, in his conviction that it offered the best solution for the Palestine problem. He conveyed his views on the subject to Dr Weizmann in March 1942, just before his departure to the United States, and suggested that he should talk it over with President Roosevelt, since there was "nothing he and I can't do if we set our minds to it".[4] Dr Weizmann broached the subject a week later with Viscount Cranborne, the Colonial Secretary. He said that he had been "immensely attracted" by a plan which had been proposed by certain quarters, including Philby, for the creation of a Jewish state within an Arab federation under Ibn Sa'ud's leadership. The implementation of this plan, he added, would cost a lot of money. This could certainly be made available by world

---

[1] CO 733–444–75872/115/41. In an interview with Churchill in the Admiralty in December 1939, Weizmann spoke of the establishment of a state of three to four million Jews. In an interview with Lord Moyne in September 1941, he called for the admission into Palestine of one and a half million more immigrants over a period of ten years. David Ben Gurion insisted, however, on the admission of three millions over the same period. Chaim Weizmann *Trial and Error*, London 1949, pp. 525–6

[2] CO 733–444–75872/115/41

[3] FO 371–27043–E2685/53/65

[4] Chaim Weizmann, op. cit., pp. 525–6

Jewry if H.M.G. showed willingness to adopt this scheme. He then expressed the hope that this idea would be continually explored, so that at the end of the war a definite effort could be made to set up such a federation. In the meantime, he himself proposed to say nothing about it publicly lest it would be part of the Zionist propaganda, and thus become anathema to the Arabs.[1]

The chance to explore Ibn Sa'ud's views on the whole issue of Arab federation offered itself during two visits which Lord Moyne, the Deputy Minister of State, paid to Saudi Arabia in December 1941 on his way to and back from Ethiopia. Arab union, the King stressed more than once, was both "impracticable and undesirable". The Arabs wanted to achieve and preserve their independence. Uniting them under one of the present ruling dynasties would mean throwing off French or British tutelage only to fall under that of the Hashimites or the Egyptians. As for himself, he only wanted to be secure within his country and did not have any territorial ambitions.[2]

Dr Weizmann tried during his visit to the United States in 1942 to secure the sponsorship of the plan by the American Government. He explained it to Sumner Welles, the Under-Secretary of State, and showed him a telegram which he had received from Churchill on the 25th anniversary of the Balfour Declaration, in which the Prime Minister stated that Dr Weizmann's plan would win in the end. He told Welles that Churchill had informed him that President Roosevelt was in accord with him on the subject. Welles, in recording this interview, stated that the President had never mentioned the matter to him.[3] Lord Halifax, the British Ambassador in Washington, reported early in 1943 that Weizmann was "making play" with Churchill's name as the sponsor of a scheme for turning Palestine into a Jewish state in agreement with Ibn Sa'ud. He added that the said scheme was welcomed by the American officials. When Churchill was asked by Eden about the subject, he evaded the issue, stating "in one of his more defiant minutes" that Dr Weizmann had no authority to speak for him. It was noted in the Foreign Office, however, that it was "sufficiently well known" that the views of Dr Weizmann were in fact "substantially those of Mr Churchill".[4]

The next stage in the pursuit of the plan came in 1943. The Zionist leaders saw in the Allied successes in North Africa a sign that the end of the war was drawing near, and that they should hurry up with the formulation and propagation of their platform in order to be in time for the peace conference. Colonel Hoskins, following an exploratory visit to the Middle East late in 1942 and early in 1943, found them "uncom-

[1] CO 733–444–75872/115/41
[2] FO 371–35147–E469/69/25
[3] F.R. of the U.S., vol. IV, 1942, p. 550
[4] FO 371–24955–E1196/506/65

promisingly outspoken" in their determination that Palestine should become a Jewish state at the end of the war in spite of any opposition from the Arabs. He attributed their "enormously increased assurance" to their feeling that they had the greater public support in Britain and the United States, and to their confidence in their increased numbers and supply of arms, which made them feel that they could hold their own in actual fighting with the Arabs in Palestine. He, as well as Sir Harold MacMichael, the British High Commissioner for Palestine, felt that the Zionists would welcome some manifestation of Arab resentment which they could exploit for publicity purposes outside Palestine.[1] Their intention seems to have been to bring the situation in Palestine to a boiling-point, and thus to impress upon the United States and Britain the need for an urgent solution on the lines advocated by Weizmann.

The State Department shared the Foreign Office scepticism about the practicability of Dr Weizmann's plan. They doubted whether Ibn Sa'ud would accept such a scheme, and whether his writ would run in the other Arab countries unless the intention was to impose him on the Arab World. These views were conveyed to Dr Weizmann and Moshe Shertok, the head of the Political Department of the Jewish Agency. Shertok suggested, however, that a British or an American representative should discuss the matter confidentially with the King. He thought that Ibn Sa'ud's reaction would be negative, but his interviewer would no doubt be able to interpret the degree of his negative reaction. Dr Weizmann then urged the American Government "to grasp the nettle" at once, since it would be easier to set up a Jewish state then than later. He stressed that the Jews would not let the United States disclaim her moral responsibility in this matter, and that Palestine "will never again be an Arab country".[2]

Dr Weizmann spoke on the same lines during his meeting with President Roosevelt on 11 June 1943. The President said that he had had a talk with Churchill on the subject[3] and got him to agree to the idea of calling the Jews and the Arabs together in a conference in which he and Churchill would participate. He agreed to a suggestion made by Welles, who was present at the interview, that someone should be sent to explore the views of Ibn Sa'ud on the subject. Colonel Hoskins, a specialist in Arab affairs then attached to the State Department, was chosen for this mission. Dr Weizmann expressed his readiness to take part in the proposed conference. He stressed, however, that it was necessary, in order to avoid its failure, that the Arabs should be told beforehand that the Democracies meant to affirm Jewish "rights to Palestine", and that they (the Arabs) had got much out of the two world wars owing to the blood and treasure spent by the Democracies, "who

[1] F.R. of the U.S., vol. IV, 1943, pp. 747–9
[2] F.R. of the U.S., vol. IV, 1943, pp. 553–6
[3] This was presumably during their meetings in Casablanca in January 1943.

therefore have the right to determine what sort of settlement they consider fair".[1]

The Foreign Office were rather sceptical about the chances of success of the American initiative. They raised no objections, however, to the visit of Hoskins as long as he refrained from making any suggestions involving territorial alterations in the other Arab countries. Hoskins was in fact instructed to confine himself to an enquiry into the readiness of the King to enter into discussions on Palestine with Weizmann or any other representative of the Jewish Agency.[2]

Hoskins arrived in Saudi Arabia late in July 1943, and had several interviews with Ibn Sa'ud. The King refused to meet Weizmann or to send someone to meet him elsewhere. He accused Weizmann of trying to bribe him by £20 millions whose payment would be guaranteed by President Roosevelt. He said that he was so incensed by the offer, made through Philby, and by the inclusion of the President in such "a shameful matter", that "he had never mentioned it again". Hoskins thought that the King's silence had been completely misinterpreted in certain quarters as implying his willingness to consider the proposal. He returned from Saudi Arabia with the conviction that there was never any possibility of the King's acceptance of the idea, and that "there is none today". President Roosevelt, when informed by Hoskins of the results of his visit, expressed "surprise and irritation" at the implication of his name as the guarantor of payment, since there was no basis in fact for doing so. He instructed Hoskins to go to London and inform the British of the results of his mission, in order to clarify the situation to them.[3]

Hoskins told Weizmann that Ibn Sa'ud spoke of him in "the angriest and most contemptuous manner" for attempting to bribe him. Weizmann remonstrated that the idea was not his but Philby's.[4] Philby had in fact given Weizmann the incorrect impression in May 1940 and again in April 1941 that Ibn Sa'ud's reaction was far from negative. He took the King's "enigmatic" response as a sign of readiness to consider the plan if a serious offer was made to him.[5] He no doubt thought that the execution of the plan would solve the King's financial difficulties, and secure the end of Hashimite control in Iraq and Transjordan. Ibn Sa'ud was, however, far from being the Machiavellian ruler that Philby and Weizmann thought he was. The reactions of the Arabs in Palestine would have made the implementation of the plan very difficult without an overwhelming coercive power, a thing which Ibn Sa'ud

---

[1] F.R. of the U.S., vol. IV, 1943, pp. 792–4

[2] Ibid., pp. 795–6

[3] Ibid., p. 812; FO 371–34963–E6823/506/65. Also: Al-Zurkally, *Shibh al-Jazira fi 'Ahd al-Malik 'Abdul 'Aziz*, pp. 1134–43

[4] Chaim Weizmann *Trial and Error*, p. 532

[5] Ibid., p. 532; H. St. J. B. Philby *Arabian Jubilee*, pp. 214–15

lacked, and which the British would have been far from ready to provide. The idea of making the offer to him rather than to any other Arab ruler, such as Amir 'Abdullah, who might have been more co-operative, was based in fact on the mistaken belief that, with his prestige in the Arab World, he would be able to sway Arab opinion in favour of the plan. This ignored also the strength of Ibn Sa'ud's feelings with regard to Palestine, which had impressed all his British and American interlocutors, and which derived mainly from his religious convictions and his leading role as an Arab and Muslim ruler.

Churchill, in espousing the plan, overruled all his foreign affairs experts in his eagerness to bring about a settlement favourable to the Jews. He was obviously guided by his past experience in dealing with the Arabs, when, as Colonial Secretary in 1921, he was able in very few sessions to appoint rulers and to carve out a Kingdom in Iraq and an Emirate in Transjordan. He no doubt felt that Ibn Sa'ud's indebtedness to the British for financial assistance, and for checking Hashimite intrigues against him, would make him ready to carry out whatever they thought fit in the area.[1]

President Roosevelt was also eager to assist in the settlement of the Palestine problem. He was coming under increasing pressure on the issue from the American Zionists and their supporters in the Congress. He was, however, far from being the avowed Zionist that Churchill was. He had to make some expressions of sympathy for Jewish aspirations, and to embody in his party's election platform a pledge to assist in turning Palestine into a Jewish commonwealth. His own thinking leaned, however, towards a wider use of the idea of trusteeship in Palestine by making it a real holy land for all three religions, with a Jew, a Christian, and a Muslim as the three responsible trustees. This, he argued, would provide a solution larger and more inclusive than the establishment of an Arab or a Jewish state in Palestine.[2]

THE PROCEEDINGS AND RECOMMENDATIONS OF THE WAR CABINET COMMITTEE ON PALESTINE

In a note to the members of the War Cabinet, dated 28 April 1943, Churchill urged that a careful examination should be made by the departments concerned of the possibility of turning Eritrea and Tripolitania into Jewish colonies, affiliated, if desired, to the National Home in Palestine. This, he argued, would broaden the whole issue "perhaps

---

[1] Churchill, in his meeting with Ibn Sa'ud in Fayoum in February 1945, stated that the British had always supported and subsidized him in the past and would expect him to help in the settlement of the Palestine problem. He got nowhere, however, with the King. F.R. of the U.S., vol. VIII, 1945, pp. 689–90

[2] F.R. of the U.S., vol. IV, 1943, p. 813

making general agreement possible between the Arabs and the Jews". H.M.G., he said, had certainly treated the Arabs very well by installing and maintaining King Faisal and Amir 'Abdullah in Iraq and Transjordan, and by supporting the rights of self-government for the Syrians. The Arabs, on the other hand, with the exception of Ibn Sa'ud and Amir 'Abdullah, had been "virtually of no use to us in the present war". They, therefore, had created no new claims upon the Allies in the event of an Allied victory.[1] Churchill was in fact using the same argument which Dr Weizmann had been using for the last two years in Britain and the United States. He ignored the hardships caused by the war, and the supply and communication facilities provided by the Arab countries for the Allied troops. He also ignored the fact that Iraqi offers to send troops for service on the Libyan front (1940), and in Syria (1943), were turned down in order not to give justification to any Arab claims after the war.

The whole question was discussed by the War Cabinet on 2 July 1943. It was decided that the five-year period stipulated for in the White Paper, for Jewish immigration up to 75,000, should be extended beyond March 1944. It was also decided that a Cabinet Committee should be formed to consider long-term policy on Palestine.[2]

The Committee was formed under the chairmanship of Herbert Morrison, the Home Secretary, with the membership of Viscount Cranborne, the Lord Privy Seal; Leopold Amery, the Secretary of State for India; Colonel Oliver Stanley, the Colonial Secretary; Sir Archibald Sinclair, the Secretary of State for Air; and Richard Law, the Minister of State in the Foreign Office. Lord Moyne, the Deputy Minister of State in Cairo, joined the Committee later on. The Committee was asked to start by examining the Peel Commission's Report, and to consider whether the partition scheme which it proposed, or some variant of it, could be adopted. It was also asked to consider the possibilities of development in Negeb, and the suggestion that satellite Jewish settlements should be established in other areas such as Cyrenaica, Tripolitania, or Eritrea.[3] The deliberations of the Committee are of special importance to any study on Arab federation, since the idea of a Palestine settlement through the creation of a united Arab state in the Levant was a central theme in its discussions.

In its first meeting, on 4 August 1943, the Committee was urged by Amery to re-examine partition from the start. A new factor had arisen with the strong Arab desire for some form of federation as manifested by the recent proposals of Nuri Pasha al-Sa'id. He thought that H.M.G. could find some means of showing sympathy for the ideal of Arab unity on the basis of a new Jewish state forming a co-operative unit in

[1] Cab. 66/36, [W.P. (43) 178 dated 28 April 1943]
[2] Ibid. [W.P. (43) 187, 192 and 200]
[3] Cab. 66/44 [W.P. (43)–563]

any prospective federation. He added that once the Jewish National Home had been securely established, the Jews whom Palestine could not absorb could be settled in colonies of the National Home in North Africa or Eritrea.[1] Lord Cranborne suggested that it should be the Arabs of Palestine who should be compensated by the grant of additional territory in Cyrenaica or elsewhere. To create a Jewish state complete with colonies was, he thought, going further than the Jews themselves wanted. Herbert Morrison stated that Palestine was already a small country. To partition it as it stood would create two states even smaller. He therefore suggested that the Committee should consider readjustments over a larger area including Transjordan. It was agreed that Colonel Stanley should prepare, in consultation with the Palestine Government, a plan for partition for consideration by the Committee.

The scheme proposed by Colonel Stanley, which was subsequently approved by the Committee, was based on the one put forward by the Peel Commission in 1937. It excluded, however, Galilee with its Arab majority of ninety-eight percent from the Jewish state, adding to that state instead a valuable area lying to the east of the River Jordan at the southern end of Lake Tiberias, as well as the town of Jaffa with the fertile land to the east and the south. The area allotted to the Jewish state was less by 410 square miles than that proposed by Lord Peel. Colonel Stanley pointed out, however, that most of the land omitted was barren hillside, and that the Jewish state contained all the Jewish industries except the potash works on the Dead Sea, as well as most of the taxable capacity of Palestine as a whole. The Negeb was left temporarily under British control. In terms of population, the proposed Jewish state included eighty percent of the existing Jewish population, with an Arab population of 300,000, allowing for a Jewish majority of 80,000.

The significant thing was the decision of the Committee to tie the execution of this scheme with the union of the Arab parts of Palestine, Transjordan, Syria, and Southern Lebanon in a Greater Syria state. This idea was put forward, and persuasively argued for, by Lord Moyne. He stated that his discussions in the area revealed a unanimous opinion in favour of a settlement on these lines. The Palestine Arab residue would otherwise be too weak an economic unit to stand alone. The fusion with a stronger unit would give confidence to the Palestine Arabs

[1] This idea was also suggested by Colonel Hoskins in a report transmitted by Cordell Hull to President Roosevelt on 7 May 1943, in which he also suggested the establishment of a Jewish state in part of Palestine together with an Arab federation in the Levant. These proposals were not seriously considered by the President, who told Hoskins in March 1945, following the Yalta Conference, that he had found Churchill "as strongly pro-Zionist as ever and, among other ideas, Mr Churchill wanted to put the Jews into Libya". He added that when he mentioned the idea to Ibn Sa'ud during their meeting in February, the King objected "violently" to it. F.R. of the U.S., vol. IV, 1943, pp. 784–5; vol. VIII, 1945, pp. 690–1

against further encroachments by force or diplomacy. The Galilee area, if left out of the Jewish state, would be an awkward island isolated from the other Arab parts unless it was added to Syria. The restoration of Greater Syria, he added, would be a return to a political arrangement which had lasted for many centuries.

The Report of the Committee, in espousing Lord Moyne's argument, stated, moreover, that the creation of Greater Syria would give the Arab parts of Palestine political and economic viability, since the property tax assessment of these parts represented only one eighth of the total property tax assessment for the whole of Palestine. Fusion with Syria in particular would make partition "infinitely easier", since it was to Syria, rather than to Lebanon or to the more backward state of Transjordan, that the Palestine Arabs looked. The reconstitution of Greater Syria would also "greatly enhance" British prestige in the area, and would be "eagerly welcomed" by the Arabs as a necessary first step towards the realization of their cherished ideal of federation. Britain would then be able to take an active interest in the promotion of the welfare and the development of Greater Syria, since the technical backwardness and the low standard of life of the Palestine Arabs were among the underlying causes of Arab-Jewish differences.

The Committee decided also to adopt Lord Moyne's suggestion that a small international state should be created which would consist of the Jerusalem area and Bethlehem. This meant the formation of four states in the Levant: Greater Syria; Lebanon stripped of its southern parts; the Jewish state; and the Jerusalem state. Lord Moyne did not rule out the possibility of Greater Syria, or even of all these four states, joining a federation with the other Arab states, and with Iraq in particular. The practical arrangements adopted by the Committee for the new proposed states included Anglo-French, and possibly Anglo-American–French treaty guarantees for their territorial integrity and for Anglo-French strategic interests in the Levant. They also included joint administration for the common services; and the establishment of an international body with a British chairman and British, French, and American members, to administer the Jerusalem state, to supervise the observance of treaty obligations, and to arbitrate on differences referred to it. Immigration would be a matter for state control, and the Jews would have the sole responsibility for immigration into their state.

The scheme evolved by the Committee contained many snags, which some of its members were well aware of but tended to brush aside. It was based on the mistaken belief that the creation of Greater Syria, and the prospect of inclusion in a wider federation, would of itself be sufficient to secure Arab acceptance of the creation of a Jewish state in the coastal and most fertile parts of Palestine. Richard Law warned the Committee that any attempt to link a Palestine solution to an Arab federation would merely be to hang a new kind of millstone around the neck of the Palestine controversy. He considered it a fallacy to suppose that the present Arab rulers passionately wanted some kind of federation, and that British assistance was all that was needed to make their dreams come true. Even were a federation to materialize, he added, there would be little credit to be drawn from it when the Arabs realized that it would not involve the removal of foreign military control. It was "infinitely preferable", in his view, to avoid partition altogether. If the creation of a Jewish state was deemed necessary, then the best way to minimize Arab reactions would be to make it a token state, much less extensive than that proposed by Lord Peel, and supplemented by Jewish settlements elsewhere.[1]

The second difficulty was the French presence in Syria and Lebanon, and their strong objections to the inclusion of these two states in an Arab federation. Lord Moyne was very much alive to this problem. The advantage of partition, he argued, would be lost unless Greater Syria were to be free, since it would be of no advantage to the Arabs to exchange British mandate for a similar status under France in Syria. He thought, however, that the French could have a sphere of interest in the northern part of Greater Syria corresponding to a British sphere of interest in the south. He felt that the French, once they managed to conclude treaties with Syria and Lebanon, would be most unwilling to disturb their treaty obligations in favour of the creation of Greater Syria, which would make such a scheme impossible to achieve. The Report of the Committee referred to possible French obstructionism. It doubted, however, the willingness of Syria and Lebanon to grant special privileges to the French. It added that it could be argued with the French, therefore, that it was better for them to safeguard their strategic interests within this new arrangement. The Report considered it most important that the close connection between a Palestine settlement and the future of Syria and Lebanon should be borne in mind in any future negotiations with the French. It added, however, that the scheme should go through even without French acquiescence, since they would be powerless to prevent the union of Greater Syria if the British were to make it clear that they would place no obstacle to it. This was obviously a misreading of the attitude of the Free French and of General de Gaulle in particular.

The third difficulty was the certain Lebanese opposition to the truncation of their state by the addition of its southern parts to Greater Syria. The preservation of the independence and sovereignty of Lebanon within its present frontiers was the cornerstone of the National Pact, and of the policy of the new constitutional regime. The French proclamation of Lebanese independence of 1941 stressed, in spite of British objections, the territorial inviolability of Lebanon as one indivisible unit. This

[1] Cab. 95/14. [P. (M) (43) 16: statement made in the Committee meeting on 1 November 1943]

difficulty was brushed aside by the Report on the grounds that there were indications that no strong objections would be raised by the Lebanese in this regard. The addition of southern Lebanon was considered necessary for providing a physical connection between Galilee and Greater Syria. It was later, when both Richard Casey and Sir Edward Spears stressed that the Lebanese would not accept such an arrangement, that it was suggested in a supplement to the Report that a strip of 735 square miles should be detached from the proposed Jewish state as a corridor connecting Galilee through the Huleh Salient with Syria.[1]

The fourth difficulty was related to the question of leadership over Greater Syria. Very little thought was given during the discussions to the position of Amir 'Abdullah in Greater Syria, and the possible objections of Ibn Sa'ud to the future union of Greater Syria with Iraq or the assumption by the Amir of the leadership of the new united state. Lord Moyne and the other members of the Committee were of the view that the personal animosities of Ibn Sa'ud should not be allowed to interfere with the implementation of what, even were partition not in question, would be "the most statesmanlike redistribution of the territories of the Levant".

The fifth difficulty was the stipulation that Anglo-French strategic interests should be safeguarded within the new arrangement. It should be noted that this was a time during which the nationalist movement in Syria and Lebanon was riding high, and had as its main objective the end of all vestiges of foreign influence and presence. The Arabs were expected, in return for the creation of Greater Syria, to accept the establishment of a Jewish state in Palestine, an international state in Jerusalem, the arbitration authority of a foreign body, and continued Anglo-French military presence and influence in the Levant.

The Report of the Committee stated in its conclusions that, should H.M.G. decide on partition, they should carry it through whatever the opposition. Should the Arabs accept and the Jews refuse, then H.M.G. should administer the new Jewish state. Should both refuse, partition should nevertheless be carried through with the Arab parts of Palestine annexed to Lebanon and Transjordan. The creation of Greater Syria would minimize the risks involved in the "unlikely case" of the Jews accepting and the Arabs refusing the new scheme. As for timing, it was agreed that the matter should be proceeded with in three stages. The first would be to get Cabinet approval for partition and the creation of Greater Syria. The second would be to prepare the necessary details of the scheme. This would be followed by its announcement at the psychological moment when the Arabs and Jews could be consulted. It was also agreed that strict secrecy should be maintained as to the

---

[1] Cab. 66/45–W.P. (44) 50

Committee's discussions and the proposals. The Chiefs of Staff were invited to state their views on the said proposals and their requirements in the area.

In a Note of Dissent annexed to the Report, Richard Law expressed agreement with the other members that a practical scheme for partition could be devised, and that it offered the best, and possibly the only, solution for the Palestine problem. He also agreed that partition would be more acceptable to the Arabs if it could be linked with the union of Greater Syria. He argued, however, for the exclusion of Jaffa, the Huleh Salient, and the area Beisan–Nazareth–Tiberias, which contained an Arab majority, from the proposed Jewish state. This, he stated, would make the scheme at least tolerable to the Arabs without wrecking or even weakening the Jewish state.[1]

Two other reservations were made by Richard Casey and by the Chiefs of Staff Committee on the recommendations of the Report, which was forwarded to the War Cabinet for consideration on 20 December 1943. Casey expressed the view that the proposed settlement must be preceded by the formal termination of the mandate over Palestine, Transjordan, Syria, and Lebanon by the League of Nations or whatever international organization inherited its authority. To proceed with partition without such an approval would invite constant unrest and agitation by the Arabs and the Jews in an attempt to prove it unworkable. This would be all the more dangerous in view of the fact that the Americans were not expected to support partition. This would mean that H.M.G. would have to carry out the scheme in the face of American, French, Jewish, and Arab opposition.[2]

The Chiefs of Staff defined British strategic needs in the area as requiring: the control of the eastern exit of the Mediterranean; security of the sources of oil and their supply lines; safe use of airfields and other communication facilities; and a base for imperial strategic reserves. They stated that the records of Iraq and Egypt, since their independence, were a warning against placing too much reliance on the proposed new independent states in the Levant as pillars of British security in time of crisis. The proposed settlement might not continue to

---

[1] Cab. 66/44–W.P. (43) 563: for the Report and the dissenting Note

[2] The American government were not given any intimation by the British about the proposals of the Committee. The State Department received many reports, however, late in 1943 and early in 1944 to the effect that partition was being revived by the British. Colonel Hoskins told Casey in 1943 that H.M.G. would have no chance of securing American support for partition. In a memorandum prepared for the Stettinius Mission in March 1944 just before its visit to London, it was stated that if the British were to raise the issue of partition, the American delegation should avoid any commitment on this point at present. The British did not in fact raise the issue, though a passing remark was made by Sir Maurice Peterson, the Ambassador then attached to the Foreign Office, to the effect that there was a strong feeling for partition in British "official circles". F.R. of the U.S., vol. V, 1944, p. 602

satisfy Jewish ambitions, which would make it likely that the Jewish question would continue as a disturbing element in the area. The partition of a small country such as Palestine into three separate entities[1] was bound to complicate military control because of the multiplicity of treaties and arrangements. The proposed demarcation of frontiers would also have certain military disadvantages. They anticipated widespread disorder and trouble as a result of any premature announcement of any decision on partition. They recommended, therefore, that every effort should be made to avoid any leakage of the fact that such a scheme had been under consideration, since the effect on operations in Europe and the Far East of finding the necessary troops to meet any trouble would be great.[2]

The Report was discussed by the War Cabinet on 25 January 1944. Richard Law reiterated his views, stressing that his difference with his colleagues was one of degree rather than of principle. Anthony Eden reserved his final view pending the result of a private reference he had made to the Ambassadors in Cairo and Baghdad. Churchill referred to the views of the Chief of Staff and noted that he certainly did not contemplate forcing on Palestine a scheme which the Jews, and possibly the Arabs, would resist with violence. The general view of the Cabinet was, however, that the scheme proposed was "probably as good as any" that could be devised, and was fair to all parties concerned. The Report was, therefore, approved in principle on the understanding that any particular details of the scheme could, if necessary, be further examined before a final decision was taken. It was also decided that strict secrecy should be observed as to the existence and nature of the Committee's proposals, which should not be disclosed or acted upon until the defeat of Germany. No intimation was to be given either to President Roosevelt or to Dr Weizmann on the subject.[3] The Colonial Secretary was instructed, in the meantime, to ensure that action proceeded without delay in working out details of the preliminary steps.[4]

The views of Lord Killearn and Sir Kinahan Cornwallis were received in February 1944. Both were in agreement with the opinion expressed by Richard Law in his dissenting Note, and anticipated great trouble in the area if the scheme proposed was to be carried through. Sir Kinahan stressed that the underlying motive of Arab nationalism was in essence

---

[1] According to the scheme proposed, these were: the Jewish State; the Jerusalem State; Greater Syria, incorporating the Arab parts of Palestine with Syria, Transjordan, and Southern Lebanon.

[2] Cab. 66/45 [W.P. (44) 46–22 January 1944]

[3] Dr Weizmann recounted, however, Churchill informing him as far back as September 1943 of the Committee's proposals with regard to partition and the formation of a Jewish state in which he (Churchill) favoured the inclusion of the Negeb. Chaim Weizmann *Trial and Error*, p. 436; J. C. Hurewitz *The Struggle for Palestine*, New York 1950, p. 204

[4] Cab. 65/45 [W.M. (44) 11th Conclusions, Confidential Annex, 25 January 1944]

anti-foreign. The Arabs wanted to form a bloc strong enough to strengthen their independence, to secure the achievement of their goals in Palestine and Syria, and to present a united front to all foreign powers, especially Britain and France. The execution of partition would draw these countries together, and political federation, which in normal conditions might be of such slow growth, would be rapidly developed in a way detrimental to British interests. The formation of Greater Syria would not soften the blow for the Arabs, since an offer of this sort would not be considered a new development at a time when their leaders had been consulting for some months on the assumption that something of the sort would come about. He doubted the readiness of the Syrians to sign a treaty with France or Britain on the basis of recognizing the establishment of a Jewish state in Palestine. He stressed that any departure from the White Paper policy should have the open support of the Allies, and particularly the Americans, the Russians, and the French. If this was not secured, the influence of these powers, and particularly of the United States, would rise in the Middle East in proportion as British stock fell.[1]

Other reports were received from the area which cast doubts over the advisability of implementing the scheme proposed by the Committee. The Foreign Office, so far subscribing to the argument that partition represented the best solution, began to have second thoughts, and were veering towards outright opposition to partition in principle. The Colonial Secretary, rather than let his scheme die a slow death, brought the whole issue to the fore again in September 1944. He argued strongly against any further deferment of a decision on partition. He proposed some modifications to the original scheme. The Greater Syria project, he argued, should continue to have the cordial support of H.M.G. without making its execution part of their immediate policy. He suggested, as an alternative, the union of the Arab parts of Palestine with Transjordan, with the exception of Galilee, which could be merged into Syria. This, he stated, was favoured by British representatives in the area on the grounds that British obligations to Amir 'Abdullah would preclude them from merging his country into Syria against his will. The Amir would never consent to such a step unless he was accepted as the ruler of Greater Syria, a position which the Syrians were unlikely to concede. The union of Greater Syria could be postponed, unless the Arabs themselves took steps to secure it, until the death of the Amir, who was "already an elderly man and whose health was by no means good".

The second consideration justifying this modification was that if French influence remained strong in Syria, the union of Transjordan with Syria would mean an extension of that influence half-way to the Suez Canal. It was therefore advisable to defer action in this regard until

[1] Cab. 95/14–Annex I to P (M) (44) 11: Report of Sir Kinahan dated 24 February 1944

a clearer appreciation could be made of the French future position in the Levant. The third consideration was that the union of Greater Syria would depend on factors outside the control of H.M.G., and would necessitate lengthy negotiations with all the interests concerned, whereas what was needed was a policy which could be put into effect at short notice should circumstances so require.

Colonel Stanley therefore suggested an approach of two stages. The first and immediate one would be the creation of a southern Syrian state comprising Transjordan and the Arab parts of Palestine, excluding the Negeb. The union of Greater Syria would be an integral part of British policy in the area. This approach, he argued, might be favoured by the Palestine Arabs, who would stand much higher in the counsels of the smaller Southern Syria than they would do in a larger state. From their position in this state, they would be able to ensure their interests in the eventual fusion into Greater Syria more effectively than they could do at present. The union of Greater Syria would therefore be left to the Arabs themselves to negotiate, which would remove a number of serious obstacles from the path of partition.

Eden, arguing against partition, distinguished four main errors in the Committee's approach. The first was its grave underestimation of the upheaval which would be caused throughout the Middle East as a result of the creation of a Jewish state in any part of Palestine. Partition would alienate the Arabs and endanger British interests, which were likely to increase in importance after the war. The second was its placing too much emphasis on American opinion at a time when that opinion could not properly, nor finally, be assessed. He had a "tolerably strong conviction", in the light of numerous indications that had reached him, that after the elections American opinion, influenced by oil and other strategic considerations, would incline rather to the Arab than to the Jewish side of the argument. The third error was the undue weight given, on the Jewish side, to the extremists, whose views might well not be endorsed by the bulk of their less vocal co-religionists in America, Britain, and elsewhere. The fourth error was the tendency to assume that the creation of a Jewish state in part of Palestine would achieve finality. It would not deter the Jews from filling their small state with immigrants beyond its capacity. They would think of it as a stepping-stone towards the realization of their wider hopes for a larger Jewish state covering the whole of Palestine and Transjordan.[1] The Arabs would always be

[1] This is a correct appreciation of the attitude and intentions of the Zionists in Palestine. David Ben Gurion, in favouring partition, in 1937 stated that he worked on the assumption that a Jewish state in part of Palestine "will not be the end, but the beginning", and "will constitute a powerful lever in our historic effort to redeem the country in its entirety". He spoke of bringing into Palestine "all the Jews we can possibly hold", and of forming a first-class army. He hinted at the possible use of other means if the Arabs could not be prevailed upon by persuasion. David Ben Gurion: *Letters to Paula*, pp. 154–6

kept in a state of continual tension and there would always be disorders and bloodshed.

He did not consider it practical, however, to continue the White Paper policy after the war. He felt, in the meantime, that whatever settlement might be decided upon must have the backing of the United Nations and of the United States in particular. His own alternative solution for the Palestine problem was not very different from that favoured by the State Department and President Roosevelt.[1] It was based on devolving sovereignty over Palestine on the United Nations, who would in turn devolve it on a British High Commissioner or Governor-General, assisted by an advisory committee representing the three religions. Jewish immigration would be allowed until the Jews came within 100,000 of the Arabs. A great measure of local autonomy would be granted to the predominantly Jewish and Arab districts. This solution, he stated, would not satisfy the politically-minded among the Zionist leaders, but then no plan that H.M.G. could offer would satisfy them. To the Arabs, this solution would be less objectionable than partition, the pursuit of which would involve the serious risk of losing, to America, British pre-eminence in such a vital part of the world.[2]

The Cabinet Committee was reconvened on 19 September 1944 to review the whole issue. It was urged by Colonel Stanley that a final decision be taken in favour of partition. The whole situation was very similar to that of 1938, when the Foreign Office came into an open clash with the Colonial Secretary, Ormsby-Gore, over the same issue. Eden told the Committee that the original scheme outlined in the Report had been radically modified as a result of dropping the Greater Syria plan. The other members argued that Lord Moyne had been in 1943 the sole supporter of the union of Greater Syria as a primary feature of a Palestine settlement, and that this was favoured by the Committee as an ultimate objective. Eden suggested, however, that his views should be put to the War Cabinet when the Report came up again for discussion.[3]

The Committee meetings came to naught in the face of the strong Foreign Office opposition to partition. It was reconvened in September 1945 under the new Labour Government to reconsider the situation. Churchill, who took an active interest in its proceedings at the beginning, was soon to realize the difficulty of evolving a scheme satisfactory

---

[1] Wallace Murray, the head of the Near Eastern Section of the State Department, explained to the British during the Stettinius Mission's visit in April a scheme devised by the State Department on the lines suggested by President Roosevelt: the appointment of three trustees representing the three world religions to administer Palestine. Sir Maurice Peterson, speaking on an unofficial basis, favoured a scheme on these lines. F.R. of the U.S., vol. V, 1944, pp. 594, 600–2

[2] Cab. 95/14 [P. (M) (44) 11: Eden's memorandum dated 15 September 1944 and his alternative scheme in Annex II]

[3] Cab. 95/14 [P. (M) 44: 2nd meeting on 26 September 1944]

to the Jews. He complained to Weizmann late in 1944 of the opposition to Zionism within the Cabinet. He stressed the need for American participation in the efforts designed to bring about a Palestine settlement, adding that he could carry the day with the support of President Roosevelt.[1] This was an obvious attempt to exonerate himself, partially at least, from the failure of his Cabinet to satisfy Zionist demands.

This was the end of the second serious attempt during the war at a Palestine settlement through the creation of an Arab federation. This attempt, like the earlier one, had to fail because it was based on a misconception with regard both to Zionist ambitions, and to the nature of Arab nationalism. The Arab advocates of a federal solution, such as Nuri Pasha, used the same argument in support of their schemes. Inclusion in an Arab union would remove the Palestine Arab fears of Jewish domination, and would make them more accommodating to the Jews. They differed from the British and Zionist advocates of such a solution on some basic points. Their schemes did not envisage either the establishment of a Jewish state or the grant of unlimited immigration and settlement rights to the Jews. For them an Arab federation was supplementary to, and not an alternative to, the White Paper policy. Arab unity, for them, was an end in itself, and they were ready to give the Jews a great degree of local autonomy within an Arab federation.

For the British, federation was a means to an end, and had its appeal mainly as offering what was thought to be the best solution for the Palestine problem. The main issue for most of the members of the Cabinet Committee was the establishment of a Jewish state with sufficient room for the settlement of an additional number of immigrants. The inclusion of the Arab parts of Palestine in a Greater Syria, or in a more limited Southern Syria, was therefore unavoidable, both on economic and on political grounds. The scheme evolved was not in fact a partition scheme involving the creation of two or more entities. The Arab parts were not such as to form a separate entity, with the Negeb placed temporarily under British control, Jerusalem and Bethlehem under the authority of an international body, and Galilee separated from the rest of Arab Palestine. The partition scheme was devised first, and the Greater Syria plan was endorsed later, to make it more acceptable to the Arabs. Once it had become obvious that the union of Greater Syria would encounter many obstacles, it was dropped, and the Committee had to fall back on the original idea suggested by Lord Peel in 1937 with regard to the merger of the Arab parts of Palestine into Transjordan.

---

[1] F.R. of the U.S., vol. V, 1944, pp. 642–3

PART THREE

The Formulation of the Alexandria Protocol and the Pact of the Arab League

Chapter Six

The Arab Unity Consultations July 1943 to February 1944

Eden's Mansion House speech came at a very critical juncture of the war. The British as well as the Arabs were preoccupied with the immediate Axis threat, and the more pressing economic problems caused by the curtailment of shipping facilities. British reverses in the war cast doubts over an eventual Allied victory. Some Arab leaders such as Rashid 'Ali and 'Ali Maher were in favour of keeping lines of contact open with the Axis in order to reinsure and guard against all eventualities. Others, like Nuri al-Sa'id, saw that the only hope for the Arabs was to be federated at once. They felt that even if Britain was defeated in North Africa, there would be a stalemate in Europe. A united Arab World would, therefore, be in a relatively stronger position *vis-à-vis* Britain and the Axis powers.[1] The failure of the Rashid 'Ali movement dashed the hopes of the Iraqi extremists. A pro-British government was established in Egypt following the ousting of 'Ali Maher from office in June 1940. A foothold was gained by the British in Syria and Lebanon after the defeat of the Vichy French forces in July 1941. The British were, therefore, and in spite of their military weakness *vis-à-vis* the Axis powers, in full control of the area.

The instalment of the Wafd in power in Egypt at British instance encouraged hopes among the Syrian and Lebanese nationalists of a similar development in the Levant. Nahas Pasha was very outspoken, when out of office, in support of the Arab cause in Syria and Palestine. The pursuit of an active Arab policy became a main item in the Wafd's programme. Nahas was to start his exploratory talks with the Arab leaders right after his assumption of office in February 1942. He invited both Jamil Mardam and Bishara al-Khouri, who were then out of office, to consult with him in Cairo on future Arab relations. Their visit to Egypt took place in June 1942 and was of great significance both in terms of future Arab co-operation and of subsequent developments in Lebanon. General Catroux was kept informed about these

[1] FO 371–24548: Nuri expressed these views to Amir 'Abdullah as far back as August 1940; also: *Mudhakkirat Taha al-Hashimi: 1919–1943*, ed. by Sati' al-Husri, Beirut 1968, p. 347

preliminary talks by Nahas and Jamil Mardam. Bishara al-Khouri explained to Nahas and his senior foreign affairs advisers that his country wanted its full independence within its existing boundaries, and that it would seek co-operation with the other Arab states on this basis. He added that there were some among the Lebanese Christians who believed in the necessity for some form of foreign protection, and who were opposed to closer relations with the neighbouring Arabs. He stressed that he and his supporters did not hold this view, and were ready to co-operate with the other Arab states. Jamil Mardam, who was present, stated that they, in Syria, had confidence in Al-Khouri's statements, and were ready, once this line had been officially adopted by Lebanon, to renounce any territorial claims in that country.[1] This understanding strengthened the position of Al-Khouri, and was to form the basis of the National Pact, as will be explained later. It also secured for the Constitutional Bloc, led by Al-Khouri, full Egyptian support in their struggle for full independence and the restoration of constitutional rule in Lebanon.[2] Nahas was also to exchange views with Nuri Pasha al-Sa'id, the Iraqi Premier, during his visit to Egypt in December 1942. It was during this visit that Nuri explained his ideas about Arab federation and the Palestine problem to Richard Casey, who asked him to put them down on paper.[3]

By February 1943, the tide of the war appeared to be turning at last against the Axis powers, following the battles of Al-'Alamain, Stalingrad, and the American landings in North Africa. The Allies became more confident of a successful conclusion of the war, and started to give serious thought to post-war world organization. It was at that time, and in answer to a parliamentary question on 24 February 1943, that Eden made his second public statement of support for Arab unity. He stressed, however, that the initiative must come from the Arabs

---

[1] Bishara Khalil al-Khouri *Haqaiq Libnaniya*, vol. I, pp. 243–6. Al-Khouri stated that Nahas put down some notes during the meeting and that Muhammad Salah ud-Din, the Under-Secretary of State in the Ministry of Foreign Affairs, who was to play a great role in the subsequent formal consultations, recorded the statements of Al-Khouri and Mardam. Nahas subsequently arranged a meeting between Al-Khouri and General Catroux, who was then in Cairo. The Nahas–Khouri meeting was later to be used by the French and their supporters in their campaign against the Constitutional Bloc before the elections in August 1943. Documents described by Al-Khouri as "false from A to Z" were published about an alleged agreement reached in Cairo between Al-Khouri, Mardam, Nahas, and Nuri al-Sa'id for an economic union between Egypt, Lebanon, Syria, Transjordan, and Iraq. Dr Yusuf Muzhir *Tarikh Libnan al'Am*, vol. II, Beirut (n.d.), pp. 1076–81

[2] Nahas Pasha, on being asked by Catroux in March 1942 for the reasons behind Egyptian refusal to recognize the regime installed by the French in Lebanon, hinted that it did not represent the wishes of the people, and that Bishara al-Khouri would be the most true representative of the Lebanese public. General Catroux *Dans la Bataille de la Méditerranée*, p. 259

[3] Lord Casey *Personal Experience*, p. 141

themselves, and that so far no scheme commanding general approval had yet been worked out. Cocks, M.P., enquired whether the Foreign Secretary would consider sending to the Middle East "the very best men that the Foreign Office can command" for the purpose of getting the Arab states together in view of the importance of the issue with regard to the future of Palestine. Eden replied that H.M.G. were "very well represented" in these countries and that the whole question was "a complicated one of individual national views".[1] In suggesting this answer, Eyres, of the Eastern Department of the Foreign Office, recommended that nothing should be revealed about Nuri's Note on Arab Independence and Unity, sent to Casey some weeks earlier, or about Casey's intention to make special enquiries into the possibility of the removal of the existing economic barriers between the Arab countries.[2] Eden's answer followed the lines of his earlier statement of May 1941.

Eden's statement was well received in the Arab World. Press comments underlined his stipulation that the initiative should be made by the Arabs themselves. The Arab governments were, therefore, urged to take active steps towards closer inter-Arab co-operation. In Egypt both 'Abdul Rahman 'Azzam and Muhammad 'Ali 'Allouba,[3] who had their affiliations with the Palace, called for immediate consultations between the leaders and the popular organizations in the Arab World. Eden, 'Azzam stressed, had laid the responsibility on the Arabs for the evolution of acceptable schemes for Arab unity. He added that the pan-Arabs everywhere now blamed their governments for their laxity in this regard. An Arab Union Club was formed in Cairo in May 1942 under the presidency of Fu'ad Abaza Pasha. It managed to establish close ties with the Palace, and with the Iraqi Government through Tahsin al-Askari, the Iraqi Minister in Cairo and the brother-in-law of Nuri al-Sa'id, who was to be appointed in October 1943 Minister of the Interior in Nuri's Cabinet. It also called for contacts and consultations between the popular Arab organizations on the issue.[4]

The first move was made by Nuri Pasha al-Sa'id in two directions. He sent Jamil al-Madfa'i, a former Iraqi Prime Minister, on a special mission to the Arab capitals to conduct unofficial consultations on

[1] Parl. Deb., H. of C., vol. 387, 5th ser., col. 139

[2] FO 371–34955: minute by Eyres on 11 February 1943. The parliamentary question was put by Price.

[3] *Al Ahram*, 28 February and 1 March 1943; *Al-Muqattam*, 26 February 1943

[4] The Arab Union Club Nadi al-Ittihad al-'Arabi was active up to 1945 in organizing meetings and in sending petitions to the Arab leaders in support of the Arab cause in Syria and Palestine. A branch of the Club was opened in Baghdad in 1943 which gave rise to British complaints. The attitude of the founders of the Club towards Arab unity was rather dubious, with its president favouring at one time a Nile Union between Egypt, Sudan, and Ethiopia. It was consistently against closer political associations between the Arab countries. *Al Ittihad al-Arabi fi al Qahira*, Cairo, 1946; Jalal al Orfali *Al Diplomasiya al Iraqiya wal Ittihad al-'Arabi*, Baghdad 1944, pp. 311–17

Arab unity. He called at the same time for the meeting of an Arab conference as soon as possible to discuss future action. The British, in spite of their professed support for Arab unity, felt that Nuri was trying to force the pace of the movement. They had their doubts about the chances of success of Nuri's initiative in view of the adverse reactions it was bound to engender from the other Arab leaders. They were apprehensive of Jamil's visit to Syria and Lebanon at a time of internal tension prior to the general elections which the Free French had finally agreed to hold. They thought that the visit might "give rise to anxiety locally" and would "greatly disturb" Ibn Sa'ud. Nuri was asked to impress upon Jamil the need for the greatest discretion in any official contacts with the local political leaders in the Levant. He was also told that H.M.G. were strongly averse to any propaganda in support of the candidature of the Regent of Iraq for the Syrian throne.[1] It should be noted that this was a time when Amir 'Abdullah was intensifying his own propaganda for the creation of Greater Syria under his leadership, for which purpose he issued his famous manifesto to the people of the Levant in April 1943, which was not well received either in Syria or in Egypt.[2] The British were eager as long as the war lasted to avoid inter-Arab frictions and disputes which were likely to endanger the stability of the area.

Nuri, in giving the necessary assurances to the British, stated that the idea of the visit was inspired by Eden's statement, and that its object was not to consider the form of government in any of the countries concerned, or the claims of individuals to leadership. He stressed at the same time that, in England and elsewhere, much thought was being given to post-war planning, and that the British could not prevent the same thing happening in the Middle East. He referred to Churchill's speech on 21 March 1943[3] about regionalism as a basis for future world organization, and noted that small nations could no longer remain separated. With the lead given in Eden's statement, and with so much Zionist activity going on, consultations among the Arab leaders were inevitable. The Arabs, he added, should endeavour with the help of H.M.G. to evolve a plan which would fit into the world scheme envisaged by Churchill.[4]

Nothing came out, however, of Jamil al-Madfa'i's exploratory mission. In Jedda, he assured King Ibn Sa'ud that Iraq had no national

---

[1] FO 371–34955: Eden to Sir Kinahan Cornwallis, 5 March 1945

[2] *Al Kitab al Urduni al Abiad*, pp. 75–7

[3] In a broadcast speech on 21 March 1943, Churchill envisaged the establishment, within a world organization, of a Council of Europe, a Council for Asia, and a Council of the Western Hemisphere, each composed of a group or confederations of states. His views were not, however, favourably received by the Americans. Ruth Russell and Jeannette Muther *A History of the United Nations Charter*, Washington D.C. 1958, pp. 103–7

[4] FO 371–34956: Sir Kinahan to Eden, 21 March 1943

or dynastic ambitions in Syria. Ibn Sa'ud, who viewed the Iraqi initiative as part of the current Hashimite propaganda for the creation of Greater Syria, was completely negative in his attitude. He stated that Iraq had not yet set her own house in order, and was therefore in no position to say what should be done in Syria. He added that the Iraqis "have no shame", and that they had treated the Syrians abominably in the past and wanted only to annex Syria. He stressed that the Arab states were keen on maintaining a certain equilibrium among themselves and anything that disturbed this equilibrium would not be to their good. He did not even respond favourably to Al-Madfa'i's suggestion of making a joint Arab *démarche* to the American Government with regard to Palestine. He considered the idea a bad one, since Palestine was within the responsibility of Britain.[1]

In Amman, the Amir told Jamil Pasha that it was not the business of the Iraqis to speak for the Syrian states while there were "others with better qualifications and claims".[2] In Cairo, Jamil was not impressed by his meeting with Nahas Pasha who, he said, had monopolized the conversation almost entirely.[3]

As for the idea of an Arab conference, Nuri indicated that it had been put to him by some Palestinian Arabs, who suggested that it should be held in Cairo or in Baghdad. Baghdad was ruled out by Nuri in order not to create any complications with the British. He therefore sent a letter to Nahas in March 1943 inviting his views on the meeting of the proposed conference in Cairo, and enquiring whether Nahas would prefer it to be official under his presidency, or semi-official under the chairmanship of a distinguished Egyptian to be nominated by him. The idea was not well received by Nahas Pasha. He gathered from his talks with Jamil al-Madfa'i that the Iraqis were in favour of a meeting in which unofficial organizations would participate. This was the idea being favoured at the time by the pro-Palace elements in Egypt.[4] He suspected that Nuri must have had some contacts with King Farouq in this regard. He was determined to have the field all to himself, and to short-circuit any Palace moves in that direction. He used the press censorship to put an end to any debates on Arab unity, and advised Fu'ad Abaza not to accept an Iraqi invitation to visit Baghdad to open a branch of the Arab Union Club. He made it clear to all concerned that he intended to conduct all discussions on Arab unity. This, he argued,

[1] FO 371–34956: message from Ibn Sa'ud to the British Minister in Jedda relayed to the Foreign Office on 2 March

[2] FO 371–34956: Sir Harold MacMichael conveying the Amir's account of his talks with Jamil, 22 March 1943

[3] FO 371–35231–J1615/2/16: the meeting took place on 17 March 1943

[4] 'Allouba Pasha called for the convocation of "a permanent conference of the Arab peoples". 'Azzam stressed that any practical scheme for federation should be preceded by full consultations "between governments and political organisations" in the Arab countries. *Al Ahram*, 28 February and 1 March 1943

would not give irresponsible elements any chance to raise contentious issues, or to make colourful statements.[1] His mind was all set against the convocation of an Arab conference at that stage. He insisted that if there were to be any discussions on Arab unity, they should be conducted between the Arab governments and not between unofficial bodies.[2]

Amir 'Abdullah was greatly annoyed at Nuri's moves. He had called in his manifesto for the meeting in Amman of the prominent personalities in the Levant to discuss ways to achieve the unity of the component parts of Greater Syria. Sir Harold MacMichael found him in a very nervous, restless condition, obsessed with the question of his own personal leadership in the Arab World. He resented the attempt by Nuri and Nahas to take the lead in the Arab unity discussions. Nuri was in fact the first to raise serious objections to the Amir's activities. He thought that most of the countries concerned would refuse the Amir's invitation, and that raising the question of the Syrian throne would be most damaging to the Arab cause, since all energies should centre on the greater ideal of Arab unity. The Amir was discouraged by the British from any further pursuit of the idea. He was told that his prestige would suffer severely if he attempted to hold any formal meeting, or if he was left out in the end, either with a collection of nonentities as a result of the refusal of the more important personalities to attend, or if those who attended were to differ widely in their views, particularly in respect of the Amir's own future. The Amir admitted that his moves were prompted by jealousy of Nuri and Nahas.[3]

Ibn Sa'ud was not informed of Nuri's suggestion. He was to warn the British, however, against "the dissentient Arab leaders" who were agitating for an Arab conference. He stated that he did not trust any one of them as they were all playing their own hands in order to strengthen their own position in their countries. He added that he trusted only the British and would act in concert only with them. If H.M.G. considered it advisable in the genuine interests of all concerned that he should participate, then he would be ready to do so, provided he was assured that this would not be contrary to his interests. If he took part, he would consult with H.M.G. at every step, and would continue to advise the Arabs that their interests lay in co-operating with the British, and in avoiding all matters which might embarrass them during the war.[4]

The British were not in favour of the meeting of an Arab conference at that stage. The situation in Palestine was approaching a boiling-point because of Zionist propaganda activities and Arab unrest. They

[1] FO 371–35530: Weekly Appreciation Summary, Cairo Embassy, 6 March 1943
[2] FO 371–34956: Sir Miles Lampson, April 1943
[3] FO 371–34956: the Acting High Commissioner on 21 April 1943
[4] FO 371–34956: Wikeley (Jedda) on 26 April 1943

were still not clear in their minds about their post-war policy in the area. It was only in September 1943 that serious discussions were started in London on Palestine, as explained earlier. Sir Kinahan Cornwallis raised objections to any Arab conference in Baghdad. He argued that, in spite of the set-back of the Iraqi pan-Arabs in May 1941, feelings about the future of Palestine were as strong as ever, and passions were easily aroused.[1] Sir Miles Lampson warned that the meeting of such a conference in Cairo would only strengthen Egypt's claim to leadership in the Arab World. He stressed that while it would be unwise for H.M.G. to oppose such a claim, they would appear to have no interest in encouraging it.[2] Richard Casey thought that the conference was unlikely to produce constructive results, and might end up by passing resolutions on Palestine and Syria which would be embarrassing to the British at that stage of the war.[3]

The Arab leaders were informed that H.M.G. had no objections to any inter-Arab discussions designed to formulate a plan for Arab unity. Doubts were cast, however, as to whether a conference was the most suitable method of approaching this question, either from the point of view of the Arabs themselves, or from that of the Allied war requirements. Much spade-work was needed which could best be done through confidential discussions conducted by diplomatic or specially accredited representatives. Ibn Sa'ud was told that H.M.G. would not wish to dissuade him from such part as he might think fit in any discussions that might take place confidentially between the Arab leaders. His participation would be as much in the interests of H.M.G. as of the Arabs themselves.[4] Amir 'Abdullah was informed that H.M.G. were not encouraging Nuri or Nahas to make any premature announcements, or to arrange any conferences before the necessary spade-work had been carried out without publicity. He was told, moreover, that the cause was greater than individual states or persons, and that Arab jealousies which endangered it were to be deplored.[5]

The main purpose of these representations was to check the pace of the movement towards Arab unity, and to induce the Arab leaders to isolate the more thorny questions of Palestine and Syria from the general question of Arab federation. The British had, in fact, through these representations, outlined for the Arab leaders their future course of action. Their communications to Ibn Sa'ud were highly significant, since they were designed to alleviate the King's suspicions of the activities of Nuri and Nahas. Amir 'Abdullah was also brought into

---

[1] FO 371–34956: Sir Kinahan on 18 March 1943

[2] FO 371–34956: Sir Miles on 18 March 1943

[3] FO 371–34956: Sir Miles conveying Casey's views on 27 March 1943

[4] FO 371–34957: Wikeley relaying a message from Ibn Sa'ud on 26 April and the Foreign Office telegram of instruction on 3 May 1943

[5] FO 371–34957: the Acting High Commissioner on 21 April 1943

line by making it clear to him that H.M.G. were strongly opposed to his agitation for the Syrian throne, and to his petty intrigues and jealousies.

Nuri, when informed of the British views, stressed that the proposed conference was most certainly intended to make a serious approach to the question of Arab unity. He added that confidential inter-Arab discussions favoured by H.M.G. could be said to have already started through the talks of Jamil al-Madfa'i in the Arab capitals. He stated that he had no intention of exploiting the conference for propaganda purposes, or of going behind the back of the Egyptian Government by dealing with elements of whom they did not approve.[1]

Nuri wanted obviously to move as fast as possible in the most favourable world circumstances then prevailing. He hoped, through the meeting of an Arab conference, that a practical scheme for Arab unity could be evolved before the end of the war. This, he felt, would strengthen the bargaining position of the Arabs in the Peace Conference, and ensure a satisfactory settlement of the issues of Palestine and Syria. The new thing was his acceptance of a central role for Egypt in the matter. His argument, put forward to Amir 'Abdullah, who had his fears of Egyptian domination, was that Egypt only wanted popular prestige and had no political pretensions in Syria. The Egyptian influence, he maintained, was merely being used for what it was worth to further the cause of Arab federation with the French, who had stakes in Egypt, and with the Lebanese, who had ties with the Egyptians.[2]

Nuri realized no doubt that if his efforts were to be confined to Arab Asia, they would be sabotaged by Ibn Sa'ud and resented by Amir 'Abdullah. He wanted to break the vicious circle in which the Arab nationalists had found themselves in the past in their efforts to bring about some form of Arab union. He realized the weight of Egypt in the area and the increased interest of its leaders in Arab affairs. He also realized the desire of Nahas Pasha to make up for the Palace antagonism and his internal difficulties following the "Black Book" incident, by posing as the leader of the Arab World. He recognized the strong streak of vanity in the character of Nahas. By playing on this weakness, stressing on many occasions that Egypt was the "eldest sister", and could be the leader of the Arab states if she wanted to,[3] he hoped to

---

[1] FO 371–34956: Sir Kinahan, 18 March 1943

[2] FO 371–34960: record of the meeting relayed by the Amir to the British Resident, 24 July 1943. It should be noted that the Hashimite agitation for the formation of Greater Syria at that time antagonized both the Lebanese, who had no wish to enter a close Arab association, and the French who suspected British instigation behind the moves of 'Abdullah and Nuri. Egypt was therefore in a better position *vis-à-vis* the French and the Lebanese, and her efforts were less likely to be resented.

[3] *Majallat al Musawar*, 30 July 1943. Nuri used to say "flatter an Egyptian and you fuddle his brain". For an example of Nuri's playing on Nahas' vanity see account given by an Iraqi official in: Patrick Seale *The Struggle for Syria: A Study of Post-War Arab Politics: 1945–1958*, London 1965, pp. 22–3 (footnote)

win Nahas to his ideas, and to marshal Egyptian influence and prestige to the support of Arab aspirations for unity. The Egyptian central role, while very beneficial, was not thought likely to compromise the leading role envisaged by Nuri for Iraq and for himself within an Arab federation.

Nahas Pasha responded faster than Nuri had anticipated. In his meeting with Jamil al-Madfa'i, he seemed to have his own ideas about the most suitable course of action. He was soon to make a public statement in the Senate on 30 March 1943 in answer to a question put forward by Dr Muhammad Hussein Haykal. He indicated his long interest, in and out of office, in Arab affairs. He stated that he felt, after Eden's statement in the House of Commons, that the best way to achieve a satisfactory result would be through official inter-governmental consultations. He had decided therefore to ascertain the views and wishes of each of the Arab governments, and to try, in so far as was possible, to reconcile them. These governments would then be invited to send representatives to a preliminary meeting in Egypt, which, if successful, would be followed by the convocation of an Arab Congress whose purpose would be to take all the necessary decisions. He stated that he had discussed his plan with Jamil al-Madfa'i, the Iraqi envoy, on 17 March, and had started carrying it out by extending an invitation to Nuri Pasha al-Sa'id to consult with him. If Nuri approved this approach, discussions would be conducted with him on the whole issue with its economic, social, and political aspects. The other Arab governments would then be invited to send representatives to consult with him (Nahas) on the subject.[1]

By coming out into the open by expressing his views on the subject, Nahas was in fact responding to increasing public pressure from the opposition and the Palace elements. His statement was given wide publicity and was commended in the Egyptian press. By defining his role as that of exploring different views and of reconciling them, he conceived of himself as the arbiter in the Arab arena. The fact that it was he, rather than any other Arab leader, who was wooed by Nuri Pasha, gave him the leading role he had aspired for. This did not leave much room for the anti-Wafdi elements to criticize him on that count, and it justified his plan to deal with the whole issue in his own way.

His public statement laid the responsibility on the other Arab governments, in front of their own peoples, for making the next move. It removed the whole issue from the confidential plane, infested with intrigues and jealousies. Nahas was the only Arab leader suited for this role, since, especially with his well-known antagonism to the Palace, he could neither be accused nor suspected of attempting to further any dynastic ambitions. By taking this step, Nahas had in fact taken the reins out of the hands of Nuri Pasha. As the leader of the largest Arab

---

[1] *Madabit Majlis al Shiukh, 1943* [the 20th session on 30 March 1943], Cairo 1943, p. 346

state in population, wealth, economic and cultural development, and prestige, he assumed that his central role would be accepted by the other Arab governments.[1] He approached the subject with an open mind, making it clear to all concerned that he did not favour any particular scheme, and that he would be guided by the consensus of the other Arab governments.

It is doubtful whether Nahas Pasha, in taking this line, was in any way instigated by the British. It is true, however, that his proposed approach was the one favoured and suggested by the British and by Richard Casey in particular.[2] He was in full agreement with them about the need for much spade-work and for official consultations conducted on a confidential basis. This had been, however, his view since he started his exploratory contacts with Al-Khouri and Jamil Mardam in June 1942. He reckoned, therefore, that any initiative on his part would not be unwelcome to the British. No objections were raised to his statement in the Senate, and to his subsequent contacts with the Arab governments. Nuri's activities in the past had always been a source of embarrassment to the British in their relations with Ibn Sa'ud, Amir 'Abdullah, and the French. His schemes were often described as fantastic, and no serious consideration was given to his Note to Casey referred to earlier. Nahas must have seemed to the British to be the more moderate leader, whose efforts were less likely to entangle the issue in the deeply rooted rivalries and antagonisms in the area. Nuri was, moreover, possessed with the idea of a regional grouping in which Iraq and its army would assume the leadership. British experience in Iraq had shown the hazards of allowing a central role to that country in the area in view of its strong pan-Arab orientation, and the rather violent nature of the reactions of its people to developments in the neighbouring Arab countries. Egypt, with her traditional aloofness from Arab affairs and her preoccupation with internal problems, was better qualified for this role, which was, moreover, her due in view of her large population, wealth, and prestige.

The only negative reaction to Nahas' initiative was to come from Ibn Sa'ud. He felt that he should have been consulted before and not after Nahas' statement in the Senate. By the priority given to consultations with Iraq as indicated in Nahas' statement, Ibn Sa'ud argued that he was placed in the same category as the President of the Lebanese Republic, which he resented very much. He added that he did not see any reason why he should co-operate with Nuri on such an important issue while trivial matters were still outstanding in Sa'udi–Iraq relations. He feared that if a conference was held, the questions of Palestine and Syria were bound to be raised, with his representatives being placed in the most embarrassing position of having either to listen in silence,

[1] Ahmed Tarbin *Al Wihda al'Arabiya Bain 1916–1945*, Cairo 1959, pp. 279–80
[2] FO 371–34956: Sir Miles Lampson to Eden on 27 March 1943

which would be difficult, or to agree with what was said, which he would never do, or to dispute and argue, which would be even more harmful. He proposed, therefore, to tell Nuri and Nahas that he was not interested in their schemes. He stated at the same time that he wished to do what H.M.G. would think best since he "places his trust in God and H.M.G.".[1]

Ibn Sa'ud's reaction was based on his strong suspicions of Nuri's motives, and his resentment at this attempt to take the lead, which he thought belonged to himself, in Arab affairs. Nuri had in fact conveyed to the King his views on Arab unity,[2] and sent his special emissary Jamil al-Madfa'i to consult with him on the issue. Ibn Sa'ud himself was to suggest to Nuri following the visit of Al-Madfa'i that there should be a meeting of persons known for their integrity, good sense, disinterestedness, and friendliness towards H.M.G., to study the best means of approaching the question of Arab unity. He stressed at the same time that the outstanding questions between Iraq and his country should be settled, and that he attached special importance to the independence of Syria and Palestine. Nuri, in reply, agreed with the King about the importance of a settlement of the questions of Syria and Palestine, stating at the same time that he wished to see these two countries united into one strong and independent state, to which end all Arab leaders should exert their efforts. He conveyed to the King the gist of his contacts with Nahas, adding that Nahas had agreed to his suggestion that there should be a meeting between the two of them to discuss the subject, after which Ibn Sa'ud would be invited to join. Nuri then expressed his hope that the King would accept this invitation.[3] The King was not justified therefore in his claim that he was not consulted on the issue. The Foreign Office were in fact very much aware of the King's susceptibilities and impressed upon Nuri the need not to antagonize him, and to keep him informed on all developments. They did not see any justification for the King's complaint, and urged him to adopt a more constructive attitude by at least making his views known to Nuri and Nahas.[4]

Nuri accepted Nahas' invitation to meet him in Cairo for talks on Arab unity. He agreed with Nahas' proposed approach with regard to the confidential and official nature of the consultations. He paid, on his way to Cairo in July 1943, a visit to Amman, Damascus, and Beirut to

---

[1] FO 371–34956–E3388/605/65: Wikeley (Jedda) to FO, 10 June 1943

[2] Al-Zurkally *Shibh al-Jazira fi 'Ahd al-Malik 'Abdul 'Aziz*, pp. 1147–50. Nuri's suggestion for the concentration of all efforts on the achievement of the unity of Greater Syria was turned down by Ibn Sa'ud, who referred to Nuri's "hidden motives" in the matter.

[3] FO 371–34958–E2821/506/65: Wikeley to FO on 27 April 1943, relaying content of Ibn Sa'ud's message and Nuri's answer

[4] FO 371–34958–E3117/506/65: Wikeley to FO, 27 May 1943, and FO to Wikeley on 2 June 1943

explore the views of the other Arab leaders on the issue. In Beirut, he saw almost everybody of importance. He struck Lascelles, of the British Legation there, as being "unduly optimistic" about the prospects of Arab federation in relation to the Levant states and Lebanon in particular.[1] In Amman, Nuri urged the Amir to abstain from premature disputes with regard to the Syrian throne, since Arab energies should be concentrated first on the reunion of Greater Syria. He told the Amir that the British were not prepared to quarrel with the French over Syria at that stage, and that he (the Amir) would be well advised to concentrate on the Palestine end rather than on Syria. The Amir noted, in reply, that life was short and that he had been in the background for twenty-five years and wanted something done. He added that he would in no event tolerate Egyptian domination of Syria. Nuri assured him that the Egyptians wanted merely prestige, and were not interested in dominating Syria.

Tawfiq Pasha Abul Huda, the Prime Minister of Transjordan, told Kirkbride, the British Resident in Amman, that Nuri was fooling the Amir by raising false hopes, and that his real intention was to further the claims of the Iraqi Regent to the Syrian throne. He added that the Amir seemed pleased with Nuri's attitude of deference, and appeared convinced that Nahas was working only for personal prestige. The Amir had therefore re-drafted a letter which he had intended to send to Nahas, disputing his right to take the leadership. In his new letter, the Amir urged Nahas to continue his efforts for the Arab cause on the basis of the principles laid down by the late Sherif Hussein. It was the view of Sir Harold MacMichael and Kirkbride that the main object of Nuri's manoeuvres in Amman was to neutralize the Amir until his own plans were ripe, and that he seemed to have been reasonably successful in his mission. Nuri did not in fact have any illusions about the Amir's chances in Syria. He told Kirkbride that the Amir had few supporters in Syria and Lebanon but that there was no point in telling him so. He noted at the same time that the Syrians wanted a kingdom and had a leaning towards the Hashimite family, which had two outstanding candidates: namely Amir 'Abdullah, and the Iraqi Regent.[2] Having ruled out any possibility of the Amir's assumption of the Syrian throne, Nuri was therefore tipping the balance in favour of the Iraqi Regent, in spite of his protestations that the Regent had no desire to increase his responsibilities.

Nuri was optimistic as a result of his contacts in the Levant. He thought that things were moving not unfavourably from the Arab point of view in Syria. The French were losing grip, and the Americans appeared to be ready to go to greater lengths to remove French influence

---

[1] FO 371–34959–E4227/506/65: Lascelles to FO, 18 July 1943

[2] FO 371–34960–E4391/506/65: Sir Harold MacMichael to CO, 24 July 1943

than were the British, who tended to conciliate the Free French. The Maronites in Lebanon were opposed to inclusion in an Arab federation, but other sects were more inclined to accept it. He tried, in association with the Lebanese Muslim leaders, to form a society composed of Sunnis, Shi'as, and Orthodox Christians to work for Arab federation. He told the Maronites that if they persisted in their opposition, it would be necessary to reduce Lebanon to its pre-1920 boundaries while giving them the chance to co-operate with the other Arab states to whatever extent they liked. In Palestine, Nuri found all Arab leaders prepared to accept the White Paper policy.[1] In Cairo, he was further encouraged following an interview with Lord Moyne, the Deputy Minister of State, who commended his approach to the question of Arab federation through confidential consultations. Nuri suggested that he should pay a visit to Algiers to explain to the Free French the lines on which he and the other Arab leaders were thinking. His purpose was, through a friendly exchange of views, to clear the air, and to remove French suspicions in order "to facilitate the final objective". Lord Moyne did not discourage the idea and saw the benefit of a greater frankness with the French on the future of the Arab World.[2] Nuri felt, therefore, that he had achieved a fair degree of success in his visits, and was able to explore the views of all the parties concerned.

THE CONSULTATIONS BETWEEN NAHAS AND NURI

Nahas Pasha prepared a detailed questionnaire covering all the issues related to the subject of his prospective consultations with the Arab leaders. Views were invited on the definition of the Arabs, and whether Egypt and Sudan formed part of the Arab nation; the advisability of the participation of the non-independent Arab countries; the form and system of government of any future federation; the Greater Syria scheme and the status of the Jewish and Christian minorities; the question of representation within a League or a common Council and whether it should be equal or weighted; the readiness of each state to renounce part of her sovereignty; the question of Jewish expansion within a federation; and the readiness to assign part of Palestine for Jewish settlement and how the terms of the White Paper could be reconciled with Nuri's proposals accepting the Jewish National Home with semi-autonomy for the Jewish areas within a Greater Syria and an Arab federation.

In preparing his questionnaire, Nahas obviously wanted to maintain some detachment until the various views of the participants were received. He left it to the other Arab states to decide whether Egypt should be included in an Arab union or not, and avoided identifying

---

[1] Ibid.

[2] FO 371: Sir Miles Lampson to Eden conveying the record of an interview between Lord Moyne and Nuri, 26 July 1943

himself with one scheme in particular.[1] Many issues were raised, however, which indicated that Nuri's ideas were not altogether acceptable to him. Nuri had conveyed his Note on Arab Independence and Unity to Nahas before the consultations. His enquiry into the form of government in a prospective union, the wish of Syria and Lebanon to be united, the status of the Jews and the Maronites, the acceptability of a semi-autonomous Jewish National Home, and the leadership in a unified Greater Syria, all touched on the main weaknesses in Nuri's scheme. The ideas and proposals embodied in Nuri's Note were very helpful to Nahas, however, at least as providing a focus for discussion.

The Nahas–Nuri talks started on 31 July 1943. It was decided in the first meeting that a union with a central government should be excluded, owing to external difficulties and internal differences and disagreements between the Arab countries. Nuri then defined two alternative forms which Arab co-operation could take:

> A union vested with executive authority, with an assembly in which the member states would be represented proportionately to their population and budgets. This union would have a president elected or nominated and an executive committee composed of representative elements to supervise the various forms of co-operation in political, economic, cultural, and social affairs. This committee would be responsible to the assembly and its decisions would be obligatory.
>
> A union whose decisions would not be obligatory, with the same form as described above. The member states would be represented on an equal basis.

Nahas Pasha compared the second form with that embodied in the Pan-American Union,[2] and remarked that this form excluded entirely political co-operation. Nuri noted that he personally was in favour of the first form, but he left it to Nashas Pasha to ascertain the views of the other Arab states on this question.

It was then agreed to limit the current consultations to the independent Arab countries which had participated in the London Round Table Conference of 1939, in addition to the Palestine Arab repre-

---

[1] FO 371–34961: Lord Killearn to Eden, 19 August 1943, enclosing text of the minutes of the Nahas–Nuri talks

[2] The Union of American Republics was founded in 1890 and was represented in Washington by a Commercial Bureau. In 1910 this Commercial Bureau was renamed the Pan-American Union. Its activities were confined to the promotion of economic co-operation between the South American states, and between them and the United States. With the formation of the Organization of American States in 1948, the Pan-American Union in Washington became the headquarters of its permanent Secretariat. Nahas Pasha had obviously studied the inter-American system, which appealed to him since it retained for the component states their sovereignty and freedom of action while providing for closer co-operation. He conceived of Egypt's role as similar to that of the US in the western hemisphere.

sentatives. It was also agreed that the door should be left open to every Arab state to join any prospective form of association, and that if Syria, Lebanon, Palestine, and Transjordan wished to unite in a single state, this should not prevent a more extensive form of Arab co-operation. It was left to Nahas Pasha to sound the various shades of opinion in Lebanon on the matter. As for the minorities, it was agreed that they should continue to enjoy their existing rights. Nuri thought that in a Greater Syria state a special status could be granted to the Maronites in Lebanon and to the Jews in Palestine. An Egyptian guarantee for the privileges accorded to these two communities, he maintained, would make the union of the Greater Syria states more easily acceptable, since the Maronites and the Jews would regard Egypt's guarantee as "safer and more weighty". He added that the Palestine Arabs would accept the White Paper provided they were sure of their merger into Greater Syria, and that the Jews would have only a semi-autonomous status in the areas in which they formed a majority at present, excluding Jerusalem, which could not be included in these areas. The question of allowing the Jews to spread into the other parts of Greater Syria would depend on the opinion of the inhabitants of these parts. Nuri maintained that his plan was to preserve the *status quo* in Palestine in conformity with the provisions of the White Paper. This would mean that the number of the Jews would not exceed that specified in the White Paper, and that their areas of concentration would remain as they were. They would remain therefore a minority in Palestine, and a still smaller minority in Greater Syria. Local autonomy for the Jews would mean local administration in matters such as public health, education, municipalities, and other local services. In conclusion, Nahas asked Nuri about the statement attributed to him in the press regarding the desire of Iraq to have a port on the Mediterranean. Nuri explained that he meant the construction of a railway line connecting Iraq with the Mediterranean in agreement with the Levant states.[1]

Nuri tried to win Nahas to his idea about the formation of Greater Syria as a first step towards the formation of a more extensive Arab federation. Nahas was rather reserved in his attitude, leaving the matter to the countries concerned to decide. His reference to Nuri's statements to the press, about Iraq's wish to establish a link through the Levant with the Mediterranean, could only indicate his realization that Nuri's motives were far from altruistic. The Foreign Office got the false impression that Nahas seemed interested in the formation of Greater Syria on the grounds that he might like to win the credit for securing the

[1] Text of the minutes in: *Mulakhas Mahadhir Mushawarat al Wihda al 'Arabiya Ma': al 'Iraq, Sharq al Ardun, al Mamlaka al 'Arabiya Al So'udiya, Lebnan, al Yaman*, Arab League publication, 1949, pp. 1–3; also FO 371–34961–E5376/506/65: Lord Killearn to Eden, 19 August 1943

independence of Palestine, Syria, and Lebanon as a result.[1] Shone, the British Minister in Cairo, reported being informed by a reliable source, however, that Nahas was very suspicious of Nuri Pasha, and strongly opposed to the idea of any union between Iraq and Syria, since such a united state might take the place of Egypt as the predominant local power in the area.[2]

Nuri, on the other hand, told the Minister of State in Cairo that his talks with Nahas were satisfactory, and that he was surprised at the readiness of Nahas to play this role in the Arab unity consultations. He noted, however, that the countries chiefly concerned were those of the Fertile Crescent (Iraq and the Greater Syria states). He indicated that he would not mind much if, for the present, any scheme of federation was confined to these states. As regards Ibn Sa'ud, he noted that he wished he could remove from his mind the illusion that Nuri was scheming to place a Hashimite on the throne of Syria. He added that this was a matter in which Iraq had no *locus standi*, since it was for the Syrians themselves to decide upon their own form of government.[3] In limiting the union to the Fertile Crescent states, of which Iraq was the largest in population, size, and wealth, Nuri obviously envisaged the leadership of Iraq over the proposed union. He did not make any secret of his wish to see a Hashimite as king of Syria. Iraqi ambitions in Syria were not therefore a mere "illusion" entertained by Ibn Sa'ud, as stated by Nuri.

Nuri, while in Cairo, expressed his wish to visit Algiers to confer with the Free French on the matter. The idea was welcomed by the British but was put off because of French resentment of Nuri's activities, which were viewed as inspired mainly by the wish to extend Iraqi, and hence British, influence to Syria. Nuri proposed also to pay a visit to Turkey to inform its government of the results of his talks in Cairo and his contacts in the Levant. His purpose was to explain to the Turks that an Arab federation, if achieved, could form part of a regional grouping of Middle Eastern states including Turkey, Persia, and Egypt. The idea was not welcomed by the British and the Turks, and the visit did not take place.[4] It was obvious that Nuri was determined to go his own way even if it meant conducting contacts behind the back of Nahas Pasha. His aim was to bring about the union of Iraq and the Greater Syria states, and it was on the theme of Syrian unity that he harped for most of the time during his talks with Nahas Pasha. It was also for this purpose that he proposed to contact the Free French and the Turkish

[1] FO 371–34961: minute by Eyres on 15 September 1943

[2] FO 371–34961: Shone to Eden, 5 September 1943

[3] FO 371–34960: Lord Killearn conveying report of Casey to Eden, 10 August 1943; Thompson (Baghdad) to Eden, 12 August 1943

[4] FO 371–34960: Lord Killearn to Eden, 10 August 1943; Thompson (Baghdad) to Eden, 19 August 1943

Government. Nuri then wanted to secure Egypt's support for his schemes, and to neutralize Sa'udi opposition through the acceptance of Nahas' leading role in the consultations. He was to declare to the press following the first round of his talks in Egypt that all attention must be centred for the moment on the basis, rather than on the form, of unity. Co-operation was, in his view, the best word to use until the Arab Congress met. He stressed that the formation of Greater Syria should be an essential first step, and that such a state, when formed, could be represented in the future Congress.[1] He therefore envisaged the creation of a Greater Syria state before the meeting of the Arab Congress, to the convening of which the Cairo consultations were aimed.

The Iraqi Regent was to throw further light on the real motives of his country with regard to the Arab unity consultations. He told his uncle, Amir 'Abdullah, during a visit to Amman late in October 1943, that he was dissatisfied with the Egyptian attitude, and the tendency of Nahas Pasha to arrogate the leadership to himself. Amir 'Abdullah stated, in reply, that serious efforts must be made to assert the leadership of the House of Hashim.[2] The Syrians, he added, apparently wanted to remain republican, and the Egyptians were encouraging them, since they were only concerned about increasing their own prestige. He noted that he had neither the funds nor the men to make an effective impression, and could only ask the Regent, who had both, to take action.[3] The Regent told Lord Moyne in London shortly afterwards that he agreed with Nuri's views that Greater Syria had to come about before the formation of a wider Arab federation. He added that he agreed with Amir 'Abdullah that in no circumstances would they compete with each other but would abide by the decision of the Syrians themselves.[4] It was obvious that the Hashimites in Iraq and Transjordan did not pin much hope on the Cairo consultations for the realization of their dreams, and found Nahas far from ready to back their schemes.

In Egypt, King Farouq was very sceptical about the whole issue. He considered the matter a mere competition between Nahas and Nuri, neither of whom seemed, in his view, to realize the dominant role of Ibn Sa'ud, "who will fight if he thinks necessary". He added that he was purposely keeping aloof from these talks, "which had no substantiality", though he was in favour of cultural or economic co-operation.[5] The opposition leaders in Egypt adopted also a sceptical and rather hostile

---

[1] FO 371–34960: Lord Killearn to Eden, 31 July 1943

[2] Amir 'Abdullah, in a note prepared for the perusal of the Iraqi Regent, stressed the need for Baghdad and Amman to follow "a unified Hashimite policy" and referred to "a dangerous Saudi–Lebanese–Syrian understanding" to deviate from the path of the Great Arab Revolt. *Mudhakkirat al Malik 'Abdullah*, pp. 317–30

[3] FO 371–34963: Sir Harold MacMichael to CO, 3 November 1943

[4] FO 371–34963: record of interview in London between Lord Moyne and the Iraqi Regent on 28 November 1943

[5] FO 371–34961: Lord Killearn to Eden, 31 August 1943

attitude towards the Arab unity consultations. This was a time of internal tension following the "Black Book" incident. They were infuriated at the attempt by the Wafd to compensate for the loss of prestige caused by this incident, by giving prominence to Nahas' role in the Arab unity talks, and by presenting him as the leader of the Arabs. They thought of addressing a letter to the Arab leaders suggesting that the British, through their agent Nahas Pasha, were trying to put something undesirable across to the Arabs, and that it would be advisable to postpone any negotiations on the subject until the end of the war, when things would generally be much clearer.[1]

Lord Killearn, by way of comment, stated that the Nuri–Nahas talks gave the impression that they were fairly methodical, and that an endeavour had been made to keep them within the sphere of practicabilities. He added, however, that the problems were so complex, the external and internal obstacles so great, that an early attainment of Arab union as a result of these and further discussions was extremely unlikely. He pointed to the difficulties which were likely to arise with the British and the French as a result of Nahas' intention to sound the views of the Lebanese, the Palestine Arabs, the native governments in North Africa, and the Sanussis in Libya. Nahas, in the meantime, sent one of his senior advisers to Palestine, Syria, and Lebanon to ascertain the views of the leaders of these countries on the subject.[2] He was determined to pursue his talks to their natural conclusion in spite of all the difficulties involved.

THE TALKS BETWEEN NAHAS AND TAWFIQ ABUL HUDA

Amir 'Abdullah, as stated earlier, was very resentful of the attempt by Nahas to take the lead in Arab affairs. He was urged by Nuri Pasha to adopt a more co-operative attitude on the assumption that Nahas was after personal prestige rather than concrete political gains for Egypt. In his instructions to Abul Huda Pasha before his departure for Cairo late in August 1943 to take part in the Arab unity consultations with Nahas, the Amir reiterated his views regarding the necessity for the creation of Greater Syria before a wider federation including Iraq and Egypt could be formed.[3]

The talks between Nahas and Abul Huda started on 28 August 1943. Abul Huda gave a detailed account of the developments in the four countries comprising Greater Syria. He stated that Syria and Lebanon were still subject to the mandate in practice in spite of the fact that their independence had been proclaimed and recognized by various states. He stressed that these two states must enjoy real independence before they could associate themselves with any form of Arab co-operation.

[1] FO 371–34961: Lord Killearn to Eden, 19 August 1943
[2] FO 371–34961–E5376/506/65
[3] *Mudhakkirat al Malik 'Abdullah*, pp. 335–9

Transjordan was, on the other hand, free, by virtue of its agreement of 1928 with Britain, to conclude agreements with the other Arab states on economic, cultural, and social matters. Transjordan, he maintained, had always been treated differently from Palestine. This was an obvious attempt to refute the argument that Transjordan, in view of her obligations to the British, was not free in handling her own affairs, and could not be expected to play any role outside her borders.

Abul Huda then stated that the four Syrian states wanted to be united once they had been released from their bonds. He added that Nuri was aware of this wish and had made the creation of Greater Syria the cornerstone of the scheme which he had put forward to Richard Casey. He then asked Nahas Pasha, "in view of his prestige as the leader of Egypt and of the Arab nation", to help these four Syrian states to achieve their unity. He stressed that the Palestinian Arabs sought unity to eliminate the Jewish threat. The Syrians wanted it to strengthen their country, while the Transjordanians wanted it to make their small and poor country viable. As for the Lebanese, he did not think that they wanted unity, because of their special conditions.

He added that his impression from his conversations with certain British officials was that if the four Syrian states were to agree on union, they would encounter no obstacle provided a suitable status was maintained for the Jews in Palestine and for the Maronites in Lebanon. He added that, in any case, there would be no obstacle in the way of an immediate union between Transjordan and Syria, after which Palestine and Lebanon could be invited to join in a tripartite federation. The difficulty over the participation of Lebanon could be surmounted, in his view, by detaching the territories added to that country in 1920 and reincorporating them into Syria. He favoured a monarchical regime for the united Syria–Transjordan state. He said that he knew that many Syrians would favour a monarchy, and would not let the question of the form of government hinder the achievement of their cherished ideal of unity. When Nahas asked whether Transjordan would accept a king chosen from among the Syrians if Syria were to opt for a monarchy, Abul Huda replied that only descendants of kings could aspire to the Syrian throne. He added that his country was ready to co-operate with the other Arab states in political, defence, economic, cultural, and social affairs, and that even if the present mandated status of Transjordan was to continue, this would not prevent her from concluding whatever agreements might be deemed necessary in this regard. He noted that he, like Nuri Pasha, ruled out the idea of a central government, and would favour the first form of co-operation outlined by Nuri. He indicated, however, that his country would accept the second form if necessary.[1]

---

[1] *Mulakhas Mahadhir Mushawarat*, pp. 5–8; FO 371–34962–E6891/506/65; Lord Killearn to FO, 28 August 1943

The views of Abul Huda were therefore not very different from those of Nuri. The only exception was his proposed union of Syria and Transjordan as an alternative first step towards the formation of a Greater Syrian federation. This union would obviously bypass the usual obstacles represented by Maronite objections and Jewish ambitions. It would strengthen the Amir's position, and act as a magnet for Lebanon and Palestine. Abul Huda, like Nuri, tried to enlist Egypt's support for the Amir's ambitions in Syria.[1] There was nothing new in his long statements about his country's championship, over the years, of the cause of Syrian unity, and her efforts, since 1941 in particular, to promote and marshal support for this idea: the inference being that the Amir, through his long interest in the affairs of Syria, had established a right, so to speak, to have a voice in its future. All this was a reflection of the Amir's restless mood at a time when the situation in Syria was still fluid because of the refusal of the Free French to transfer any real powers to the duly elected national government. The victory of the National Bloc in the Syrian elections of August 1943 was, however, a blow to the Amir's hopes. The new Syrian leaders were strongly resentful of the Amir's activities, and committed to the preservation of their republican regime.

IBN SA'UD AND THE CONSULTATIONS

Nahas' contacts with Ibn Sa'ud continued over a period of four months, during which the King was at the beginning strongly opposed to the precedence given to Nuri in the Cairo consultations, and to the leading role of Nahas in these talks. This was to prove the most difficult part of the whole consultations. Ibn Sa'ud's participation was made possible in the end as a result of British intervention.

Nahas communicated to the King in July the results of his talks with Nuri, and urged him to send a representative to Egypt to consult with him on the issue. Ibn Sa'ud, in reply, stated that there were four points to be borne in mind about Nuri. The first was that he wished to exploit the situation for his own ends. The second was that he planned to annex Syria and Palestine to Iraq. The third was his attempt to cause a rift between Egypt and Saudi Arabia. The fourth was that he was

---

[1] Abul Huda told Kirkbride later that Nahas raised with him, off the record, the question of the Syrian throne, stating that some, presumably with Nuri's knowledge, had suggested that King Faisal II of Iraq should assume it by virtue of his being the grandson of the first proclaimed King of Syria, Faisal I. Abul Huda, in reply, said that the Syrian Congress of 1920 which had proclaimed Faisal I as King of Syria had also proclaimed Amir 'Abdullah King over Iraq. He added that if the one was binding so was the other. Abul Huda and Nahas agreed, however, that discussion of personalities was premature and that it was up to the Syrians to decide on the issue. Nahas then referred to the likely objections of Ibn Sa'ud and Imam Yehya, adding that he did not propose to trouble them since they could fall into line later if they wished. FO 371–34962: Sir Harold MacMichael, 16 September 1943

scheming to strengthen the Hashimites at the expense of Ibn Sa'ud. He added that the situation in Palestine and Syria was not yet sufficiently clear, which made it difficult for these two countries to preoccupy themselves with the wider question of Arab unity. The Axis menace still hung over the Arab World. An Allied victory was necessary before the Arabs could get together and, provided they were sincere and disinterested, there would be no reason why they should not reach agreement and establish a union. He stated, moreover, that it was unthinkable for himself to yield to Nuri's pressure, and be dragged along "as a compliant follower in Nuri's train". He noted, in conclusion, that he had already conveyed these views to H.M.G.[1]

Ibn Sa'ud was also to convey his views on the subject to Harold Hoskins, the special representative of President Roosevelt, late in August 1943. He stated that he could not suggest a plan for Arab unity because he could not foresee what the situation in the Arab countries would be after the war. He added, however, that he was aware of the fundamental unity of culture, language, and religion among the Arab states, and realized the necessity for economic and political unity. He would be ready to assist in achieving this object provided his country was allowed to play its proper part in the negotiations leading to this unity, and the Hashimites had no finger in the government of Syria and Palestine. The first step, in his view, could take the form of grouping all the independent Arab states on the lines of the Pan-American Union. This could be followed by a closer association.[2]

Nahas, in reply, thanked Ibn Sa'ud for his message, and noted that the subject had many ramifications and involved many details. He referred to the King's suggestion in an earlier telegram that he could, if he wanted additional information, send a representative of his to meet him. Nahas noted, however, that circumstances did not permit him to send an envoy, and that he would let the King's letter suffice for the present while proceeding with his consultations with the other Arab leaders.[3]

Nahas seemed therefore to have given up hope of Sa'udi participation in the consultations, following his failure, through several communications in July and August, to induce the King to take part. He was soon to change his attitude, however, and to realize the necessity for the participation of Ibn Sa'ud. He had probably felt that, if Ibn Sa'ud was to refuse to take part, and with Egypt still undecided about full participation in any prospective federation, the result of his efforts would only further Hashimite ambitions, and might lead to the establishment of a Fertile Crescent union under Iraqi domination. He was resentful of Nuri's intrigues and activities with regard to the creation of Greater

[1] FO 371–34960: Wikeley to Eden, 28 July 1943
[2] FO 371–34961: Wikeley to Eden, 30 August 1943
[3] FO 371–34961: Wikeley to Eden, 12 September 1943

Syria. The idea of an Arab union under Iraqi leadership in the Levant was naturally distasteful to him, since such a union would most probably take the lead in Arab affairs and be a dominant power in the area. This would lead to the isolation both of Egypt and Saudi Arabia. The participation of Ibn Sa'ud came to be viewed by Nahas, therefore, as an essential balancing factor, in view of the King's strong opposition to Hashimite domination of Syria, and his success in the past in foiling Nuri's intrigues. Nahas realized, moreover, that the participation of Ibn Sa'ud would lend more weight to any future structure in view of the King's great prestige in the Arab and Muslim World. He reckoned also that any success in securing Ibn Sa'ud's participation in any association in which the Hashimites, his arch enemies, took part, would testify to his own abilities as a statesman and a skilful negotiator. It would also be in harmony with the role which he had envisaged for himself as the arbiter and the conciliator of different views. This explains the eagerness of Nahas to give the impression that the King was responding to his initiative, by publishing the positive parts of his message to him while withholding the negative parts. This action enraged the King, who thought of publishing the texts of all his messages to Nahas. He thought also of publishing an article connecting Nuri's scheme of Arab unity with that proposed by some Zionists such as Dr Magnes of the Hebrew University in Jerusalem. He referred to Dr Weizmann's offer of £20 millions to him to keep out of the Palestine question, and hinted that if the bribe had been offered to him, it might just as probably have been offered to other Arab leaders. The King was deterred from publishing only by British advice.[1]

Nahas decided, in view of all these complications, to send a special envoy to meet the King and to explain the situation to him. He sent at the same time a letter to him on 7 September in which he tried to assure him that this stage would be confined to a mere exchange of views, and that no decisions had been or would be taken at present on the issue. The ideal of Arab unity, Nahas added, though aspired to by all, remained a general idea whose features had to be defined. In an oral message entrusted to his envoy Kamel Hubeisha who arrived in Riyadh on 21 September, Nahas urged the King once again to send a representative to consult with him in Egypt. He told the King that he attached great importance to his participation in these consultations. He added that he knew well what the King thought about the part

[1] FO 371–34962: Jordan to Eden, 11 September 1943. Dr Judah Magnes had always been an advocate of the creation of a bi-national state in Palestine within an Arab federation. He expounded his views in an article entitled "Toward Peace in Palestine" in *Foreign Affairs*, 21 January 1943. He belonged to the Ilhud group of moderate Zionists which included also Professor Norman Bentwich. They were, however, in the minority, and were sharply criticized by the leading figures of the Jewish Agency like Ben Gurion, who called for the establishment of a Jewish state in Palestine.

played by "certain quarters" in this matter, and felt that the King's participation would help in removing his doubts.

Ibn Sa'ud sought the views of Jordan, the British Minister who was then on a visit to Riyadh, before meeting the envoy or committing himself to any line of action. Jordan advised the King to send a representative to Cairo to consult with Nahas. He stressed that H.M.G. were not opposed to Arab unity, but were in favour of a "go slow" policy and deprecated any hasty action while the war was still in progress which would be harmful to them. The King was prevailed upon at last and decided to send an envoy to Egypt to discuss the matter with Nahas. He insisted, as a pre-condition, that Nahas should accept his views on the matter, and that a preparatory committee should meet in Mecca or Jedda during that year's pilgrimage to evolve an agenda for a plenary conference. Ibn Sa'ud was, however, to drop his conditions when urged by Jordan to do so, on the grounds that the King would be busy during the pilgrimage, and the presence of large Arab delegations at that time would lead to lobbying. In his letter to Nahas of 24 September, which was handed to Kamel Hubeisha, the King stated that he did not have "the slightest doubt" as to the genuineness of purpose and the sincerity of Nahas' intentions. The uniting of the Arabs under one central government was, in his view, an impracticable and an unworkable idea. He had therefore always refrained from speculation about it since it would be a waste of time leading to nothing except dissensions. Similarly, any discussion about political unity would cause difficulties with the Allies. It would, moreover, be difficult to find a solution for the problems of Syria and Palestine in any conference held under the present war circumstances. He noted, however, that he would welcome any steps in the direction of economic and cultural co-operation. He added that since Nahas Pasha had taken the initiative in trying to arrange a meeting of Arab representatives, and since he (Ibn Sa'ud) considered that any meeting was a good thing and that an action initiated by Nahas should command his support, he would be prepared to send an envoy to Egypt to explain his views regarding a preparatory committee "so that people may know that we are in harmony and agreement". The meeting of this committee, the King stated, would have to confine itself to working for the welfare of the Arab nation as a whole rather than towards the benefit of any single country at the expense of the others. It had to be based on equal participation of the Arab states without precedence of one over the others. It had also to avoid anything likely to cause trouble between the Arabs and the Allies in the present war circumstances.[1]

The British were, throughout the contacts between Nahas and the

[1] FO 371–34962: record of several interviews between Jordan, the British Minister, and the King and his advisers in Riyadh in September 1943; Jordan to FO, 2 October 1943

King, rather concerned about Ibn Sa'ud's negative attitude. They were very much in favour of his participation, since he represented a useful moderating influence. His participation would, moreover, provide an additional guarantee that the consultations and the proposed preparatory meeting would not take any line unacceptable to H.M.G. They considered it "very tactless" of Ibn Sa'ud to make the accusations, included in his first letter to Nahas, against Nuri, and thought that he was not justified in his claim that he had not been consulted by Nuri and Nahas about the whole matter. They feared lest the King's negative response might discourage Nuri and Nahas from continuing to consult him. They impressed, in the meantime, upon Nuri and Nahas the need for keeping the King informed on all developments, and for paying due regard to his susceptibilities. Ibn Sa'ud was urged also to adopt a more co-operative attitude. He was told that it was in H.M.G.'s, as well as in his own, interest to do so, since it was important for the Arabs to present at least the semblance of a united front, and that he would not be committing himself in any way by sending a representative to Cairo, or receiving one at Riyadh.

Some confusion was caused, however, as a result of unauthorized statements by Jordan and his second-in-command, Wikeley. Wikeley was to advise the King, for instance, to reply to Nahas' letter, since his silence might be taken to give tacit consent to the leadership of Nahas. He made a suggestion, which he said would be distasteful to H.M.G., that the King should try to rob Nahas of the leadership by taking the lead himself by calling a conference of Arab representatives. Jordan was also to point out to the King, in September, the advantage of forming a united front with Yemen and Syria, thus ensuring a good number of votes at the discussions on Arab unity. The King welcomed the idea and said that he proposed to contact the Imam of Yemen and Shukri al-Qwatli, the Syrian President, for this purpose. He suggested at the same time that the British Minister in Beirut should suggest to Qwatli that H.M.G. would favour a greater co-operation between Syria and Saudi Arabia on the subject. The Foreign Office thought that Jordan's suggestion was unwise, since they did not want to appear to favour a Sa'udi–Syrian combination against Egypt and Iraq.[1]

The talks between Nahas and Sheikh Yusuf Yassin, Ibn Sa'ud's envoy, started on 11 October 1943. Sheikh Yusuf reiterated the views expressed earlier by the King. He suggested that a preparatory committee should meet in Mecca to discuss the preliminaries of the future Arab conference. Nahas agreed in principle to the idea of forming a preparatory committee, but objected to its meeting in Mecca on the grounds that this might cause difficulties with Iraq and with the Christian elements which might take part in the discussions. He preferred

---

[1] FO 371–34962: minute by Eyres, 27 October 1943

that the committee should sit in Cairo. He did not agree with Ibn Sa'ud's views about the need to avoid any political discussions until the end of the war. He maintained that the committee should not limit itself to the discussion of cultural and economic questions, and should discuss the political problems of Palestine and Syria, as well as the general issue of inter-Arab political co-operation. He agreed, however, with Ibn Sa'ud's views about the impracticability of a union with a central government. There was, therefore, a basic divergence of views between Nahas and the Sa'udi delegate. The talks were suspended temporarily for a short period during which Sheikh Yusuf proposed to refer the whole matter back to his King.

During the interval, various pressures were exerted on the King to adopt a more flexible attitude. The whole matter was discussed by Lord Killearn and Richard Casey. Both agreed that any approval by H.M.G. of the King's attitude would amount to encouraging him to insist on a line displeasing to Nahas and Nuri. Sir Walter Smart, the Oriental Counsellor in the British Embassy in Cairo, impressed upon Sheikh Yusuf the advisability of tactful handling of Nahas and, if possible, of avoiding any sort of unpleasantness in ending his talks with the Egyptian Prime Minister. The British were still opposed to the meeting of an Arab conference at that stage. Anthony Eden, who passed through Cairo in October, noted, however, that H.M.G. could not, overtly at least, discourage the idea. No intimation was given to Nahas, therefore, of any British objection to the meeting of such a conference.[1]

In the meantime, Sheikh Yusuf approached the American Minister in Cairo, seeking his views on the matter. The Minister told him, on instructions from the State Department, that the United States had complete sympathy with Arab aspirations for full independence. His government, the Minister added, would sympathize with any wish of the Arab countries to unite of their own free will provided this was in accordance with the principles of the Atlantic Charter, and the declarations of Secretary of State Hull regarding the equality of all states, and their entitlement to freedom from outside interference in their internal affairs. The same views were conveyed to Amir Faisal, the Sa'udi Minister for Foreign Affairs, during his visit to the United States early in November 1943, in reply to his complaints about Hashimite intrigues and efforts to unite Iraq and Transjordan with Syria and Palestine, and thus to surround and strangle Saudi Arabia.[2]

---

[1] FO 371–34963–E6706/506/65: Shone to Eden, 26 October 1943

[2] F.R. of the U.S., vol. IV, 1943: record of an interview between Amir Faisal, Ibn Sa'ud's son, and E. Stettinius, the then Acting Secretary of State, in Washington on 1 November 1943: pp. 845–7; telegrams of instructions to Minister Kirk in Cairo: pp. 852–4. It should be noted that the American views on Arab unity were similar to those of Britain. Kirk recognized the weaknesses of the pan-Arab movement but urged his government to express sympathy with the ideal of Arab unity in view of its wide appeal, and the tendency of some of its proponents to look to the United States

The greatest and most effective pressure on the King was, however, to come from the Syrians, who accepted Nahas' invitation, and whose delegation arrived in Cairo on 21 October. Ibn Sa'ud had singled out Syria as the only Arab country in whose affairs he was particularly interested. He had long and close relations with its new president, Shukri al-Qwatli, and was keen on maintaining this relation if only to foil any Hashimite manoeuvres and overtures to the new nationalist regime. The King had so far stuck to his guns and refused to be prevailed upon by Nahas' argument concerning the advisability of holding the preparatory conference in Egypt, and of not excluding political matters from the discussion. Sheikh Yusuf, himself a Syrian, decided to postpone communicating Ibn Sa'ud's negative reply to Nahas until he saw how the Syrio-Egyptian talks were evolving, and until he had a chance to explore the views of the Syrian delegates. He found the Syrians in complete agreement with Nahas Pasha. They stressed, moreover, that the exclusion of any talks on the political problems of Syria and Palestine would do them more harm than good. They stated that they saw in political co-operation a guarantee against French victimization if British support were to weaken in the future. They felt at the same time that the issue of the union of Palestine and Syria should be left over until the Palestine problem was settled.

Sheikh Yusuf reported the results of his talks with the Syrian delegates to Ibn Sa'ud, whose efforts to win the Syrians to his side of the argument had obviously failed. The King did not wish to antagonize the Syrians, or to appear obstructive with regard to a cause which had the support of the general Arab public. He therefore instructed his delegate to adopt a more flexible attitude. Sheikh Yusuf therefore conveyed to Nahas at their last meeting on 2 November 1943 a reply, which was shown to the British, who did not raise any objections, while stating that this was a matter for the Arabs themselves to thrash out. In his reply, Sheikh Yusuf stated that Ibn Sa'ud approved of the meeting of a preparatory committee to discuss cultural, economic, and any other form of co-operation which might prove possible. He added that the King still thought that political issues should be postponed until the time was more appropriate. He suggested that the time and place of this meeting should be subject to consultation between the Arab states at the proper time. The union of Syria and Palestine, he argued, should be postponed until the removal of the Jewish threat from Palestine. If this was achieved, the two countries could then take whatever steps they saw fit to achieve unity provided no other party's rights were infringed upon, and the resulting form of union was neither to their

---

for support. The State Department were not ready in 1941 to go as far as to issue a public declaration of support for Arab aspirations to unity, in order not to cause Zionist reactions and because they were unwilling to appear more pro-Arab than the British, who had more stake in the area. Ibid., vol. III, 1941, pp. 613–16

own, nor to anyone else's, disadvantage. The King, added Sheikh Yusuf, supported the republican regime in Syria, and would approve any steps designed to draw Syria and Lebanon into closer co-operation.

This was an improvement on the earlier negative attitude. The issues of the meeting-place of the conference, and the inclusion in the discussions of political issues were, however, left unsolved. Sheikh Yusuf, in accordance with the King's instructions, refused to sign the written minutes of his talks with Nahas in spite of the latter's expressed desire that he should do so. He reported, however, that Nahas seemed "very pleased" with his statement.[1] The persistent efforts of Nahas to bring about Sa'udi participation in the consultations had therefore borne fruit. Ibn Sa'ud's delegate was able to ascertain facts and to explore various views. He was able to discover for himself that Nahas, rather than being a mere figure-head for Nuri's manoeuvres, had his own ideas on the subject.

THE TALKS BETWEEN NAHAS AND THE SYRIAN DELEGATION

The Syrian delegation to the Arab unity consultations led by Sa'adallah al-Jabri, the Prime Minister, and Jamil Mardam, his Minister for Foreign Affairs, arrived in Cairo on 21 October 1943. This was the first visit by a Syrian high-level delegation to an Arab country since independence was proclaimed. King Farouq insisted that a very showy welcome should be accorded to the delegation, in view of the warm welcome given earlier by the Syrians to his envoy, Omar Fathi Pasha, who carried his message of congratulations to the Syrian President on his election. The Syrian delegates were received, soon after their arrival, by the King and by Nahas. The news of the visit was highlighted by the press with many articles stressing the historical ties between Egypt and Syria. The period of the visit was named "The Syrian Week", and much space in the newspapers and magazines was given to Syrian affairs, with several receptions held by the different Arab and Islamic societies for the delegation.[2]

The talks between Nahas and the Syrian delegates started in Alexandria on 26 October 1943. Nahas did not confine himself, as he did in the previous talks, to an exploration of the other side's views. He summarized the previous consultations especially with regard to the creation of Greater Syria. He raised doubts as to the possibility of the realization of the Greater Syria project on the basis of complete fusion, since each of the component states had its identity, distinct national development, and regime. He referred to the difficulties represented by the Maronites in Lebanon, and by the Jews in Palestine. He then

---

[1] FO 371–34963: Shone to Eden, 9 November 1943, reporting on an interview with Sheikh Yusuf; Shone to Eden, 26 October 1943, reporting on the first round of talks between Sheikh Yusuf and Nahas; also: *Mulakhas Mahadhir*, pp. 14–15

[2] *Al Musawar*, 29 October 1943; FO 371–34963–E6706/506/65

explained the suggestion put forward by the Prime Minister of Transjordan about the initial unity of his country with Syria to be followed by a federation with Palestine and Lebanon. This, in his view, raised the difficult issue of the differences in the forms of government in existence in Syria and Transjordan.[1] Nahas then invited the views of the Syrian delegation on this issue. He enquired about their attitude towards Iraq, which wanted to have closer ties with Syria and to obtain an outlet on the Mediterranean. He also enquired about their attitude towards Saudi Arabia and whether co-operation should, in their view, include political as well as cultural and economic matters. Nahas then expressed his long interest, in and out of office, in Arab unity, and pointed to the advantage of himself conducting these consultations. He stressed that he was eager that the talks should be between official representatives in a confidential manner, in order to guarantee a suitable and calm atmosphere, and to avoid misrepresentation and coloured statements which might result from public unofficial debates on the subject. He stressed that Egypt had no ulterior motives, and that he was guided only by what he considered to be to the benefit of all the Arabs.

Sa'adallah al-Jabri, in reply, gave a historical review of the Arab question, in the course of which he explained how the regions composing Greater Syria had been divided up regardless of natural, geographical, and political configurations. The Syrians, he stated, wanted unity, but they realized the difficulties involved especially with regard to Zionist designs in Palestine, and to the attitude of the Maronites in Lebanon. As for Palestine, the Arabs, under the pressure of the *fait accompli*, had tended to accept the White Paper of 1939, the main lines of which were reasonable, though there were difficulties regarding details. There was another serious question, in his view, which should be evaluated and discussed. It concerned the possibility of Jewish expansion from Palestine into the other Arab countries if these countries opted for union with Palestine. This expansion, he stated, would be strongly opposed by the Syrians. He then suggested that the Palestine Arab delegates who took part in the London Conference of 1939 should be invited to come to Cairo to state their views on the Palestine problem and on Arab unity. Nahas Pasha agreed with Al-Jabri, and stressed that the Jews should not be allowed to spread into the other Arab countries in the event of the formation of Greater Syria.

In the interval between the meetings, the Syrian delegation prepared a statement, which was read by Al-Jabri, embodying their views on the issues raised by Nahas. He noted that they had always wished that

[1] Nahas Pasha refrained from expressing these views to Abul Huda Pasha, who got the incorrect impression that Nahas would favour the creation of Greater Syria, though Nahas stated clearly that, as far as he was concerned, the Syrians could preserve their republican regime if they wished. FO 371–34962: Sir Harold MacMichael to CO, 16 September 1943

Syrio-Lebanese relations should have a unitary basis, in the absence of which Syria should regain the parts detached from it in 1920. This was the wish of the Syrian people as well as that of the population of these parts. He added, however, that a new chapter had been opened with the efforts of both Syria and Lebanon to get rid of foreign influence and to consolidate their independence and sovereignty. Syria, he stated, had encouraged the new policy adopted by Lebanon, which would remove Syrian fears of the possibility of the pursuit by Lebanon of an attitude subservient to the French. The recognition by Syria of the independence of Lebanon and the renunciation of any territorial claims in that country was, he said, made conditional on the retention by Lebanon of her independence, Arab orientation, and the establishment of closer economic relations between her and Syria. He referred to an agreement recently concluded between Syria and Lebanon about matters of common concern such as customs and freedom of passage without passports or restrictions. He also referred to the pledge made by the new Lebanese President and his Prime Minister not to allow any foreign power to dominate Lebanon, or to make her a bridgehead for the domination of Syria.[1]

Sa'adallah al-Jabri stated, moreover, that his country was keen on the formation of Greater Syria in order to put an end to the artificial foreign-imposed division of the area. He noted, however, that twenty years of division had made each of the component parts of Greater Syria accustomed to its own mode of life and national identity. There was much in common between Syria and Lebanon which made easier the evolution of a closer form of co-operation. He wondered whether a similar arrangement would be possible between Palestine and Transjordan in view of the fact that Britain, the mandatory power, had put herself on record in support for Arab unity. If a Greater Syrian state was to be formed, he stressed, Damascus should be its centre, since it had always championed the cause of Arab unity. It could not, therefore, be replaced by Amman, Jerusalem, or Aleppo. Syria would, in the meantime, preserve her republican regime, and would refuse to change her form of government if incorporated in a united Greater Syria.

Al-Jabri then expressed his country's readiness to join a federation

---

[1] This pledge was embodied in Al-Sulh's first Cabinet statement before the Lebanese Chamber of Deputies on 25 September 1943: *Majmu'at al Bayanat al Wizariya al Libnaniya*, p. 23. The Lebanese–Syrian agreement referred to here is the Shutura agreement concluded on 1 October 1943, less than a week after the assumption by Riad al-Sulh of the Premiership. The agreement was criticized by the opposition in the Chamber, especially with regard to its stipulated establishment of a common council to arbitrate in all matters related to the agreement. This was criticized as involving an infringement on Lebanese sovereignty. This clause was modified by a subsequent exchange of letters between the Syrian and the Lebanese governments. The agreement was finally ratified by the Chamber on 3 February 1944. Bishara Khalil al-Khouri *Haqaiq Libnaniya*, vol. II, pp. 20, 77–8

vested with executive authority and comprising all the independent Arab states. It would also be ready to participate in any form of political, cultural, social, and economic co-operation. It realized, however, all the difficulties involved in achieving this strong form of association, and would be ready to accept any other alternative. Syria, he stated, had her internal reasons for wishing to ally herself with the other Arab countries in order to avert the threat to her traditions, language, and identity which would occur if she was to pursue an isolationist policy. This explained her eagerness to strengthen her relations with all the Arab countries, and to avoid antagonizing any one of them.

Al-Jabri stressed that any form of union must include Egypt, the four Levant states, Iraq, Saudi Arabia, and Yemen. Syria, he added, recognized the leadership of Egypt, which was the most developed and populous of the Arab countries, and which had prominent public figures capable of assuming the leadership of the Arabs. He urged Nahas to extend his efforts to the wider Arab sphere, where he could exercise the statesmanship he had shown in dealing with Egyptian affairs.

The Syrian Premier then proposed that a committee should be formed after the conclusion of the current consultations. The said committee would meet periodically in one of the Arab capitals to discuss some of the issues which had been raised in the consultations. The Syrians, he stated, wanted unity but would not wish to force the hand of any other Arab state. They had no wish to exercise hegemony of any sort in the Levant. They knew that there were matters related to Arab unity which would require objective assessment, and others which would require that due regard should be given to subjective susceptibilities. Some Arab countries would have to be induced by various means to associate themselves with any form of Arab co-operation. In all this, Syria would be ready to accept any scheme which Nahas Pasha might have in mind. He would himself be quite ready to help in smoothing matters, and in trying to persuade the other Arab countries to join it. He concluded by stating that, if a practical scheme could be evolved at the end of the consultations, the name of Nahas would be inscribed in the annals of all the Arab countries.

Nahas, in reply, stated that he would not spare any effort in serving the Arabs, and in helping them to realize their aspirations in spite of his heavy responsibilities at home. He thanked the Syrian delegates for their positive and co-operative attitude. He stated that he had previously raised objections to the idea of a peripatetic committee. The proposal was, however, worthy of consideration if the purpose of such a committee would be to register points of agreement, as suggested by the Syrian Premier.[1]

---

[1] *Mulakhas Mahadhir*, pp. 23–9; FO 371–34963: Lord Killearn to Eden, 8 December 1943, conveying the text of the minutes

The consultations between Nahas and the Syrian delegates were the most successful so far. The Syrians stressed their determination to retain their republican regime, and their eagerness not to antagonize any Arab leader or country. They obviously disapproved of Amir 'Abdullah's schemes, but were reluctant to engage in polemics against him. They had their strong connections with Ibn Sa'ud, and were keen on securing the support of Egypt for their aspirations. For them, an Arab association was vital to the continued independence of their country. They hoped that it would provide an additional guarante against any aggressive French policy in the future. They had managed to consolidate their relations with Lebanon, and thus to remove one of the dangers inherent in a pro-French Lebanese line of policy. They conceived of a central role for Egypt, and were ready to concede to her a leading role within an Arab association. Arab unity, for them, was a matter of national interest. A wider association including the more internationally prestigious states, Egypt and Saudi Arabia, was to be preferred to a smaller one confined to Greater Syria, or to the Fertile Crescent states. Nahas was greatly flattered by the Syrians, who, unlike the Sa'udis, did not dispute his leading role. He was, therefore, more frank with them than with any of the other Arab delegations.[1] The whole atmosphere of the talks was different. The Syrians, like the Egyptians, had no dynastic ambitions, and were keen on preserving their independence. They had old and strong ties with Egypt which had been, since the late nineteenth century, the refuge for their persecuted politicians and intellectuals. Their participation in the consultations with Nahas was the first positive foreign policy step taken after the independence of their country.

THE CONSULTATIONS BETWEEN THE LEBANESE DELEGATION AND NAHAS

Reference has been made earlier to the exploratory talks between Jamil Mardam, Bishara al-Khouri, and Nahas in June 1942. In these talks Al-Khouri stressed that, while keen on preserving the full independence of Lebanon, he was in favour of taking big steps towards closer co-operation with Syria and the other Arab countries. Jamil Mardam promised, if this was adopted as the official line of policy of the future constitutional government in Lebanon, to pledge his country's respect for the independence within its present frontiers of Lebanon, and thus to renounce any claim to the Syrian parts annexed by the French to that country in 1920. Having got these firm assurances from the Syrians,

[1] Sheikh Yusuf Yassin was to report, following his talks with Nahas, that he tried in vain to ascertain the views of Nahas on the issues raised in the discussions. He wondered whether Nahas had some special idea in mind, or wanted simply to make use of the ideas expressed by the other delegates. In his talks with the Syrian delegation, Nahas did not refrain from expressing his views on the Greater Syria scheme and on Nuri's suggestions. FO 371–34963–E7797/506/65

Bishara al-Khouri tried to rally forces with the traditionally pan-Arab elements such as Riad al-Sulh. In a secret meeting with Al-Sulh on 19 September 1943, two days before his election as President of Lebanon, Bishara al-Khouri secured Al-Sulh's support in return for a pledge to follow an Arab oriented policy, and to appoint him as his first Prime Minister.[1] It was in this meeting that the bases of what came to be known as the National Pact were laid down. They embodied a compromise between the isolationist line favoured by the Maronites and the pro-French elements, and the Arab-oriented line favoured by the Muslims and part of the Christian community. It was, as explained later by Al-Khouri, "a contract between all Lebanese of different classes and inclinations: true independence; national sovereignty; preservation of the constitution of the country; disallowing of any infringement of whatever nature (on that independence and sovereignty); and cordiality and close co-operation with the other Arab countries for the good of all on a basis of equality, justice, and fairness".[2] The main basis of the Pact was therefore the preservation of the full independence of Lebanon "without any resort to protection from the West, or unity or union with the East".[3]

It was on the basis of this pact that the Al-Sulh–Al-Khouri coalition was formed. The pact had provided henceforward the guiding line for the foreign policy of Lebanon, which explains the eagerness of the Lebanese Government to establish closer co-operation with Syria, and to participate in the Arab unity consultations. Bishara al-Khouri tried to win the Maronites to this line of policy, stressing the determination not to allow of any infringement on Lebanese sovereignty and independence. Riad al-Sulh pledged not only to try to win the Lebanese Muslims, but also to gain recognition from the neighbouring Arab countries for the independence of Lebanon within her existing frontiers.[4] He stressed in his speeches the necessity for co-operation, as distinct from union, with the Arab countries. Lebanon, he argued, could no longer live in isolation from its neighbours, since, in the modern world, no country, however large, can live in isolation. This policy did not fail to encounter some opposition from among the Maronites. The question

[1] Bishara Khalil al-Khouri *Haqaiq Libnaniya*, vol. I, p. 264

[2] Ibid., vol. II, p. 290

[3] Ibid., vol. II, p. 21. For material on the National Pact: Kamal Yusuf al-Haj *Falsafat al Mithaq al Watani*, Beirut 1961, pp. 171–4; Pierre al Jumail *Libnan Waqi' wa Murtaja*, vol. I, Beirut 1970, pp. 45–7

[4] Bishara al-Khouri asked Al-Sulh during their secret meeting in September 1943 whether all the Muslims would accept the National Pact and the independence of Lebanon as final without working for its eventual unity with Syria. Riad al-Sulh, who was himself a strong advocate of Syrio-Lebanese unity, replied that he undertook not only to secure the endorsement by the Lebanese Muslims of the Pact, but also to persuade the Syrian and Arab leaders to recognize the independence of Lebanon within its present frontiers. Kamal Yusuf al-Haj *Falsafat al Mithaq al Watani*, p. 143

of Lebanese–Arab relations was one of the main issues in the election campaign. Several forged documents were circulated by the National Bloc of Emile Edde about an alleged agreement between Al-Khouri and the other Arab leaders for the formation of an economic Arab union, and an agreement between Nuri al-Sa'id and Jamil Mardam for the unity of Greater Syria under a Hashimite ruler. Bishara al-Khouri denied all these reports, which were designed to influence the electors against him.[1]

For the neighbouring Arab countries, an independent and Arab-oriented policy for Lebanon was to be welcomed and encouraged. This was particularly so in Syria, where there were still some apprehensions about the possibility of the retention of some form of association between Lebanon and France. The Lebanese crisis of November 1943[2] was, however, a turning-point in this regard. The strong support given to Lebanon by the Arab countries was one of the main factors weighing on the British in deciding to intervene in the situation. It underlined the advantage of consolidating relations with the rest of the Arab World. The forceful French action did much to undermine French prestige, and to discredit the pro-French elements who formed the main opposition groups to the constitutional regime of Bishara al-Khouri. Al-Sulh declared on more than one occasion that his government would never allow Lebanon to be used as a bridgehead for French designs against Syria. The wish not to antagonize the Maronites, who had their fears of Muslim domination within an Arab association, was, however, a limiting factor of which the Lebanese leaders were well aware.

The Lebanese delegation, after some delay as a result of the November crisis, arrived in Egypt in January 1944. It was led by Riad al-Sulh accompanied by Selim Taqla, the Minister for Foreign Affairs, and Musa Mubarak, the head of the president's office. It was given a very warm welcome by the King, the government, and the various Arab organizations in Egypt.[3] Press comments stressed the historical ties between Egypt and Lebanon, and commended the Arab-oriented policy of the Lebanese Government. The fact that the initiative in this round of consultations was taken by Egypt accounted for the prompt response of the Lebanese Government, since Egypt, in addition to her great prestige in the area, was not involved in the current Hashimite propaganda calling for the unity of Greater Syria, which was strongly resented in Lebanon. Lebanese intellectuals and writers had always been very active in Egypt, especially in the press and the arts. The Egyptian–Lebanese connection was therefore of a special nature, which

---

[1] Dr Yusuf Muzhir *Tarikh Libnan al 'Am*, vol. II, pp. 1076–83

[2] See p. 95

[3] Bishara Khalil al-Khouri *Haqaiq Libnaniya*, vol. II, pp. 71–2. Al-Khouri described the warm reception given to the Lebanese delegation in Egypt as "unprecedented".

was demonstrated by the reactions of its people and leaders during the November crisis.

Nahas Pasha, in his first meeting with the Lebanese delegation, submitted a written questionnaire covering all the issues involved. Riad al-Sulh prepared a written answer which stressed the eagerness of his country to co-operate with the other Arab states to the mutual benefit of all of them. The new Arab-oriented policy of Lebanon, he explained, was made possible through the interaction of three factors. The first was the weakening of the foreign influence which had dominated the country for the past twenty-five years. The second was the recognition by the other Arab countries of the independence of Lebanon within her present frontiers, and their understanding of the reserved attitude of that country with regard to Arab unity. The third was the realization by Lebanon of the need for co-operating with the other Arab countries in the interest of the political and economic well-being of Lebanon herself. The Arab countries were eager in the first place to insure against the use of Lebanon by any foreign power in a way detrimental to their interests, and they got the necessary assurances from the Lebanese Government to that effect.

The Lebanese written answer referred to the Shutura agreement with Syria, signed on 1 October 1943, regarding the administration of the common interests between both countries. This agreement was described as the first practical step taken in the field of inter-Arab co-operation. Lebanon, while reserving her full rights in matters of defence and foreign affairs, was ready to consolidate economic, cultural, and social relations with Syria. Its attitude towards general Arab affairs was similar to that of Egypt. It favoured inter-Arab co-operation on the basis of mutual respect for each country's sovereignty. Lebanon was eager at the same time to see that all possible assistance should be extended to the non-independent Arab countries, and that no foreign power should be enabled to use any Arab association for her own advantage at the expense of these countries.[1]

Selim Taqla stated later that the Lebanese delegates found "to their great satisfaction" that the Egyptians were in full agreement with them regarding Arab co-operation. The Egyptians, he said, were determined not to be drawn into the orbit of a pan-Arab consortium of Asiatic states, probably under Iraqi leadership, and thought that Egypt should have towards these states the same position as the United States towards the Latin American Republics. Egypt, Taqla had gathered, would be ready to participate in an annual Arab conference similar to the Pan-American Conference to exchange views on subjects of mutual interest, but would not join any Arab federation or confederation. He added that he had found that the Egyptians, unlike the Syrians and the

[1] *Mulakhas Mahadhir*, p. 33; FO 371–39987: Lord Killearn, 21 February 1944

Iraqis, were uninterested in the Palestine problem. He added that Riad al-Sulh had a brief conversation on Arab federation with King Farouq and found that his views were even more moderate than those of Nahas Pasha. The Lebanese delegates were told that the Egyptian Government had ascertained the views of Turkey on the subject, and that the Turkish Government would raise no objection to any Arab association provided it was secular in nature, and no attempt was made to revive the Caliphate.

The Lebanese delegates, on their way back, visited Nuri Pasha, who was in hospital in Haifa. They described his ideas on the future of the Arab states as "vague and inchoate". He explained to them his scheme about the unity of Greater Syria but was taken aback when Selim Taqla suggested that this meant that the Jewish citizens of Greater Syria would have the right to circulate or to reside in any part of that united state.[1]

The understanding and sympathetic attitude of Nahas Pasha managed to win the Lebanese as it did the Syrians. The participation of a high level Lebanese delegation in the consultations was of great significance. The readiness of Lebanon to co-operate fully in non-political spheres with the other Arab countries was a major departure from the traditional Lebanese isolationism from Arab affairs.

THE CONSULTATIONS WITH YEMEN

Yemen was the most backward and inward-looking of all the Arab states. The Imam, with his extreme caution and ingrained suspicions, managed to preserve his country's independence, and to keep aloof from the pan-Arab activities of the more sophisticated politicians of Iraq and the Levant. He adopted an attitude of deference to Ibn Sa'ud in Arab and foreign affairs in general. This was the result of his realization that Saudi Arabia was the stronger power in the Arabian Peninsula, a fact which was confirmed during the seven weeks' Sa'udi–Yemen war of 1934. Ibn Sa'ud, for his part, kept the Imam informed of his views on Arab issues such as those of Palestine, Syria, and Arab federation. The two monarchs had, in fact, more in common with each other than with the other Arab rulers. They tended to co-ordinate their policies towards the outside world. Ibn Sa'ud understood very well the Imam's suspicions and susceptibilities. He was therefore careful in all his contacts with him to stress that his purpose was only to keep him informed of his views, and that he did not wish to influence his independent judgement on any of the issues involved.

Nahas Pasha was eager to ensure the participation of all the independent Arab states in the consultations. He sent a letter to the Imam, following his consultations with Nuri, informing him of his plans and inviting him to send a representative to Egypt to consult with him. The Imam received a letter soon afterwards from Ibn Sa'ud explaining the

[1] FO 371–39987: Consul General Furlonge (Beirut) relaying a conversation with Taqla, 21 January 1944

reasons behind his objection to Nahas' initiative. The Imam's reply to Nahas was very similar to that of Ibn Sa'ud. He stated that Arab unity was very desirable but impracticable in the present circumstances. He stressed the importance of the Palestine problem, adding that a conference which included Palestinian Arab delegates, at a time when they were threatened by Jewish domination, would be damaging to their cause, and "sickening" to the participants. Their exclusion would, on the other hand, be "vexatious and humiliating for Arab feelings". Any useful action would be very difficult in the present war circumstances. The Imam therefore expressed the view that the Arab leaders should try first to clear the ground from all obstacles so that they could be in the best position to serve the Arab cause as soon as the war ended. He favoured economic and cultural inter-Arab co-operation provided this was preceded by sufficient preparations, and no advantage was given to any state over the others.

The Imam was reluctant to send a representative to Cairo to consult with Nahas. He decided, however, after some procrastination, and after Ibn Sa'ud had changed his negative attitude, to send Hussein al-Kabsy to Egypt for this purpose. In his talks with Nahas, which took place in February 1944, Al-Kabsy reiterated the views expressed in the Imam's letter. He added that he would, however, refer to the Imam the idea of forming an organization to promote commercial, industrial, agricultural, social, and cultural co-operation between the Arab countries. This organization would be of an advisory nature, and would not involve any infringement on the sovereignty of each state. It would also attempt to co-ordinate action in cases of aggression against a member state, and would extend assistance to the non-independent Arab countries such as Palestine. Nahas commended the idea and thought that it would be acceptable to the other Arab states, although the details would have to be studied.[1]

THE PARTICIPATION OF THE NON-INDEPENDENT ARAB COUNTRIES

In his statement in the Senate in March 1943, Nahas indicated that he would conduct consultations with the representatives of the Arab governments in succession. This ruled out the participation of the representatives of the non-independent Arab countries such as Palestine. Some Arab delegates expressed the view that these countries should be allowed to participate in these exploratory talks. Nahas was also urged by the various Arab and Muslim societies in Egypt to include representatives from Palestine and North Africa in his consultations. He raised the matter with Anthony Eden during his visit to Cairo early in November 1943. He stated that it had emerged from the talks conducted so far that there was a general feeling that some exploration of

---

[1] *Mulakhas Mahadhir*, p. 34; FO 371–39987: Lord Killearn, 16 March 1944

the views of the Palestine Arabs in particular was necessary. If they were left out, this would create bad feeling. He promised, if they were allowed to take part, to direct them in the right way. He had in mind asking the Palestine Arab delegates who participated in the London Conference of 1939 to consult with him. Eden was non-committal. He replied that the matter had to be discussed and decided upon by the responsible departments in London. Both the Foreign and the Colonial Offices were strongly against the participation of the Palestine Arabs "at least until the way to a Palestine settlement is clearer".[1] The main concern of the British at the time was "to maintain the *status quo* and to keep the Jewish–Arab pot off the boil". It was felt that a general eruption in Palestine was being averted at the time because of the exclusion and internment of the militant Palestine Arab leaders.[2] Any attempt to secure the release of these leaders in order to allow them to take part in the Arab unity consultations, which would have further enhanced their prestige in Palestine itself, was to be avoided.

The British were also against the participation in the consultations of any representatives from Tunisia, Morocco, and Algeria, since this was likely to antagonize the Free French. They were opposed to the participation of the Libyan leader Muhammad Idris al-Sanussi, whose country was then under British occupation following the eviction of the Axis forces. Libya, they maintained, was an occupied enemy territory, whose future had to be decided only by the Allied powers at the Peace Conference.[3] Al-Sanussi was then in Egypt and was very active in trying to secure the support of the Palace and the Arab organizations for his country's independence after the war. The British refused, however, either to recognize him as the temporal chief of Libya, or to respond favourably to his persistent efforts to assert his country's national identity and right to independence. The whole issue of the participation of the non-independent Arab countries was raised in the Egyptian Senate late in February 1944.[4] Nahas was accused by the opposition of laxity in providing for the participation of the representatives of these countries. In a secret session held on 29 February, Nahas explained his position and the difficulties involved. The opposition and the Palace elements continued, however, to press for the inclusion of representa-

---

[1] FO 371–34963: record of Nahas–Eden talks on 7 November 1943 and the Foreign Office minutes

[2] Lord Casey *Personal Experience*, pp. 139–40

[3] FO 371–34963: Lord Killearn conveying a message from Casey, whom Al-Sanussi had approached on the matter on 29 November 1943, and the Foreign Office minutes approving of Casey's suggestion that Al-Sanussi should not be allowed to participate

[4] *Al Ittihad al 'Arabi fil Qahira: Nasha'th, Nizamh, Wa a'amalh Munz Ta'sish fi 25 May 1942*, Lighayet 1945, Cairo 1946, pp. 82–3. The question was put in the Senate by 'Abdul Majid Pasha Saleh, who was a prominent member of the Arab Union Club, of which Al-Sanussi was also a member.

tives from Palestine and the North African Arab countries. Nahas' efforts in this regard came to naught because of British opposition, and the whole issue was shelved for the time being.

By the end of February 1944, the Arab unity consultations, conducted over a period of little over six months, had been completed. Many developments took place during this period which were to have their impact on the development of the subsequent inter-Arab talks. There was first of all the intensification of Zionist activities in the United States in particular, and the growing Arab unrest in Palestine. This provided a new urge for co-ordinating policies in order to counter the Zionist threat. The Syrians and the Lebanese were very apprehensive at that time of the possible extension of Jewish settlement to their countries.[1] This was one of the reasons behind the refusal of the two states to support Nuri's scheme for Greater Syrian unity. It was also a period during which the new regimes in Syria and Lebanon were able to consolidate their position, following the November crisis and the gradual transfer of powers from the French to the two states. The war had receded from the area, and the Allies were discussing plans for future world organization. The indications were that regional bodies would be recognized and encouraged.

The successful conclusion of the Arab unity consultations was a great step forward in the road towards closer Arab co-operation. The leaders who participated in these talks had their feet well and truly on the ground. They realized all the difficulties involved. Arab unity was commended by all as an ideal, but its achievement at that time was not considered to fall within the realm of practical politics. The emphasis from then onwards was on co-operation rather than on integration within any form of union. They found in Nahas a seasoned negotiator and a statesman of great experience. In him Egypt provided "as no other country could have done, a catalyst to fuse together the elements of the Arab World".[2]

---

[1] It was reported late in 1943 that rumours were afloat throughout Syria and Lebanon about schemes for extending Jewish influence northwards. Robert Montagne, who was a member of General Catroux's staff, stated in December 1943 that the Jews had their eyes on Lebanon in particular, and were trying to enlist the support of the Christians against the Muslims and to establish a Jewish–Christian Bloc for mutual defence. Sir Harold MacMichael, while recognizing French motives, stated that these reports were not without substance, and that some Lebanese Christians might welcome the idea out of fear of Muslim domination. FO 371–39987–E742/41/65. David Ben Gurion stated in July 1937 that one of the advantages of the Partition scheme then proposed by the Royal Commission was its inclusion of the Galilee in the Jewish state, thus giving it common borders with Lebanon. This, he said, "has a tremendous political value as both Lebanon and the Jews are interested in being neighbours. The Christians in Lebanon could scarcely exist at all without a Jewish state next door, and we are also interested in an alliance with Christian Lebanon." David Ben Gurion *Letters to Paula*, p. 132

[2] *The Times*, 28 January 1944

Chapter Seven

The Enunciation of the Alexandria Protocol 1944

In his statement before the Senate on 30 March 1943, Nahas Pasha had suggested the idea of a preparatory meeting following the completion of the Arab unity consultations. This was approved by the Iraqi, Sa'udi, and Syrian delegates during the consultations. The Sa'udi delegate suggested, however, that such a meeting should be held in Mecca or Jedda to discuss the agenda for a future Arab Congress. The Syrians, on the other hand, favoured the formation of a peripatetic committee which would meet in each of the Arab capitals in rotation. This, they maintained, would draw some of the rather reluctant Arab states such as the Lebanon and Saudi Arabia into the movement, and would generate more public interest in its proceedings. Nahas Pasha was, however, more in favour of a preparatory meeting to be held in Egypt. He was aware of the difficulties which a meeting in Mecca would create for the Christian delegates from Lebanon in particular. He was also aware of the difficulties which might arise as a result of the Sa'udi aversion from a meeting in Baghdad or Amman and the Hashimite resentment of a meeting in Mecca or Jedda. He wanted, moreover, to avoid the protracted nature of the proceedings of a peripatetic committee which, if held outside Egypt, would be likely to fall under the influence of the Sa'udis or the Hashimites, making any common agreement rather difficult to bring about. The whole idea of a preparatory meeting at that stage of the war was not welcomed by the British, who exerted all their efforts to bring about the postponement rather than the cancellation of the proposed meeting, as will be explained later.

Nuri Pasha, rather than let Nahas handle the whole matter in his own way, was determined to remain at the forefront of the movement. He stressed in his talks with Nahas the necessity for the creation of Greater Syria as a first step towards any wider Arab association. His main purpose was to secure the support of Egypt for the idea. Nahas, as indicated earlier, did not express disagreement with Nuri's views.

The Iraqi and the Transjordanian delegates came out from the consultations with the impression that the formation of a Greater Syria state would not be unwelcome to Nahas. An understanding was reached at the same time between the Iraqi Regent and his uncle Amir 'Abdullah to unite their efforts in that direction, and to avoid competing with each other over the issue of the Syrian throne. Nuri was soon to find an opening for further action in the eagerness of the Syrians to see an Arab association brought about as soon as possible. They had their difficulties with the French and were unsure about continued British support. They had pressed for an early meeting of a preparatory conference which Nahas, out of deference to British objections and Sa'udi reservations, was not likely to succeed in arranging as soon as desired. Nuri was informed of the gist of the Syrian and Lebanese statements during the consultations about their determination to preserve their republican regimes.

Nuri paid a long visit to Syria, Lebanon, Palestine, and Transjordan, late in January and early in February 1944. In Amman he told the Amir that he was attempting to reorganize the Arab leaders of Palestine so that they could resume their political activities. He proposed to prepare a memorandum for submission to H.M.G. This memorandum would carry the signature of the leaders of the Palestine Arabs, the Syrians, and the Iraqis, and would call for the early formation of Greater Syria. The Amir asked what had happened to Egypt, which had taken the lead in the talks on Arab unity. Nuri said that as the memorandum would deal only with the union of Greater Syria, Egypt was not directly concerned at the moment and could join a wider Arab union later. The Amir expressed the opinion that, having regard to the past talks in Cairo, H.M.G. would be surprised to receive a memorandum on the subject which Egypt had not signed, and Nahas Pasha would be furious. The Amir then enquired about his own claims to the Syrian throne. Nuri replied that the position was difficult because the Syrian delegation in the consultations with Nahas had demanded a republican regime for Greater Syria, and copies of the minutes of these consultations had already been sent to the British and American Governments. Nuri then tried to quiet the Amir, who was very angry, by saying that when the reunion of the Syrian states was complete, a plebiscite would be held to ascertain the desires of their peoples regarding their future form of regime. In reply to further reproaches, Nuri stated that the Syrians had been so emphatic regarding a republic because Abul Huda Pasha, in his talks with Nahas, had expressed the opinion that Greater Syria should be a monarchy. The Amir later told Kirkbride, the British Resident, that Nuri was betraying both himself (the Amir) and Nahas, and that between them the Arab politicians had killed Arab unity. He added that it was now for H.M.G. to take charge and form a Greater Syria on their own design. He hinted that it might be necessary to work more closely with Nahas in order to check Nuri's trickery.[1]

In Baghdad Nuri informed Sir Kinahan Cornwallis of his contacts in the Levant. He spoke appreciatively of the kindness shown to him by a number of "non-political Jews", and said that he had a not unfriendly talk with Shertok, the head of the Political Department of the Jewish Agency. He had found the Palestine Arabs very strongly opposed to any idea of partition or unlimited Jewish immigration, about which rumours were current. He was feted in both Beirut and Damascus. In Damascus he said that he had reached agreement with the Syrian Government that Iraq and Syria should federate no matter what the other Arab states did. These states could join in gradually if they wished. It was also agreed, he added, that Nahas Pasha should be asked to form, before March 1944, a small committee consisting of one or two representatives from each country to draw up an agenda for the main conference, which should take place in Cairo in April. The conference would be attended only by official representatives. It would decide on the nature of the federation, and the extent to which each country would be prepared to conform.[2]

Nuri's manoeuvres in the Levant had serious repercussions all around. Amir 'Abdullah, who was some months earlier strongly resentful of the leading role of Nahas Pasha in the Arab unity consultations, began to realize the threat to his own position in Transjordan, and to his ambitions for the Syrian throne, if Nuri's scheme were to succeed. He was quick to send a letter to the Iraqi Regent in which he complained of Nuri's activities and noted that it would be a great mistake to break with him on the issue. He concluded by stating that it was possible that he had misunderstood Nuri Pasha. This was an obvious attempt to give Nuri the chance to desist from the pursuit of his scheme. The Amir expressed to Abul Huda Pasha his belief that the change of attitude on Nuri's part was on instructions from H.M.G. with the object of preventing the Cairo consultations from achieving any practical results. He stressed that in view of these developments Transjordan must look to its own interests and press the British for its emancipation from the mandate.[3] The Iraqi Regent informed Sir Kinahan at the same time that the Amir was under "the mistaken impression" that Nuri Pasha wished to exclude Egypt from the talks between the Arab countries about unity. This, he noted, was far from

---

[1] FO 371–39987: Sir Harold MacMichael to the Colonial Secretary, 31 January 1944. An account given by the Amir to Kirkbride, which Sir Harold described as "a remarkable volte-face".

[2] FO 371–39987: Sir Kinahan Cornwallis to Eden on 8 February 1944 reporting on an interview with Nuri Pasha

[3] FO 371–39987: Sir Harold MacMichael to Colonial Secretary, 9 February 1944, conveying a statement by the Transjordan Prime Minister to Kirkbride

being the case. Nuri had actually seen the Egyptian Minister with a view to persuading Nahas Pasha to form a committee immediately for the purpose of proposing an agenda for the main conference. The Regent confirmed that Iraq and Syria intended to federate whatever the other countries did. He added that the Amir had told him in December 1943 that he was anxious to join an Arab federation, and that he wondered at the time how this would square with the Amir's obligations towards H.M.G. in such matters as foreign policy and defence.[1]

Sir Edward Spears, the British Minister in the Levant, was to conduct his own enquiries into the matter. He stated after careful soundings that it was almost certain that Nuri Pasha had not reached with the Syrians any such concrete agreement, though he might well have made some progress with regard to the general plans for an Arab conference. Such an agreement, he noted, would be out of keeping with the firm personal attachment of the Syrian resident, "who was the real power in Damascus", to Ibn Sa'ud. Shukri al-Qwatli, when sounded on the subject, noted that the question of Arab federation was one in which several Arab states were concerned, and it would be "treacherous" to conclude a separate agreement with Iraq. The Syrian President added that Syria would abide by whatever decision might be taken by the Arab Congress, which would meet shortly.

Sir Edward Spears stated, moreover, that reports from secret sources suggested that Nuri's talks in Damascus were embarrassing to the Syrian Government and disappointing to himself. He considered it possible that Nuri had derived a misleading impression of the Syrian attitude from Jamil Mardam, the Syrian Minister for Foreign Affairs, "whose loyalty to the President is not above suspicion and who is a great intriguer". Jamil Mardam was on a visit to Baghdad late in December 1943, and had the intention of passing through Baghdad again in February 1944 on his way to Saudi Arabia.[2]

The sharpest reaction to Nuri's moves was to come from H.M.G. Sir Kinahan Cornwallis was instructed in February 1944 to warn Nuri to go slow with regard to the idea of an Arab conference and any federal schemes. Nuri was to be told, moreover, that H.M.G., in view of their obligations as regards the defence of Iraq under the Anglo-Iraqi treaty of alliance, would wish to be formally consulted in accordance with Article 1 of that treaty,[3] before any attempt was made to put such a project into effect. The Ambassador was also instructed to

---

[1] FO 371–39987: Sir Kinahan to Eden, 12 February 1944

[2] FO 371–39987: Sir Edward Spears to Eden, 22 February 1944

[3] Article 1 referred to provides for "full and frank consultation" in "all matters of foreign policy" which may affect the common interests of the contracting parties. It also includes an undertaking "not to adopt in foreign countries an attitude which is inconsistent with the alliance or might create difficulties for the other party thereto". Text in: J. C. Hurewitz *Diplomacy in the Near and Middle East*, p. 178

inform Nuri that at first sight it would appear that such a federal scheme had better be postponed until the end of the war, when the French position in the Levant could be regularized. Lord Killearn was also instructed to seek information as to whether the idea of an Arab conference was in Nahas' mind, and to ask that H.M.G. should be consulted on the matter beforehand.[1]

The British warning was delivered to Nuri on 25 February 1944. He stated, in reply, that he fully realized the necessity of prior consultations with H.M.G. in accordance with the treaty provisions. He added that, quite apart from any treaty obligations, both he and other Arab leaders realized that they could not attain their aims without British help, and were most anxious to do nothing which might be misunderstood. As regards the agreement with the Syrian Government about the federation of Syria and Iraq, he noted that there was no occasion for formal consultation with H.M.G. at present. The agreement was a verbal one with the Syrian President, his Prime Minister, and his Minister for Foreign Affairs. It was to the effect that if the proposed conference produced no effective results, Iraq and Syria would then enter into negotiations with each other. There would be no idea of double-crossing the other Arab countries in this matter, which would be discussed at the Cairo meeting which both the Syrians and the Iraqis had suggested should be held in March. Nuri did not think that King Ibn Sa'ud, who would have an opportunity of co-operating, could reasonably object. When Sir Kinahan suggested that it would be better to postpone the whole matter until the French position could be regularized after the end of the war, Nuri replied that he had understood from the Syrian leaders that they did not recognize the mandate, and had no intention of concluding a treaty with the French. He added that he could not predict with certainty what would be done at the proposed Cairo meeting. The delegates might only prepare an agenda for a later meeting in April or May. They might find so many points of common agreement that they could prepare a definite scheme for further consideration. Nuri added that the proceedings would be secret, but H.M.G. would be kept informed. Sir Kinahan, by way of comment on Nuri's statements, noted that Nuri had deceived himself regarding the intentions of the Syrians, and that his ideas about the two conferences were possibly his own. He added, however, that Nuri certainly appeared confident in his own mind.[2]

Nuri had therefore drawn upon himself the wrath of the Amir and the British. As the most experienced and intriguing of the Iraqi and probably of the Arab politicians, Nuri could not possibly have initiated this move without knowing the adverse reactions it was bound to engender. He was eager to inform both the Amir and the British of his

[1] FO 371–39987: Sir Kinahan to Eden, 8 February 1944
[2] FO 371–39987: Sir Kinahan to Eden, 25 February 1944

so-called agreement with the Syrians. His purpose was probably to use it as a test balloon to gauge the reactions of the parties directly concerned. He spoke first of an agreement, which he watered down later to a verbal understanding, to be carried out only in case the Cairo talks failed to yield any tangible results. It is also possible that he had some encouragement from Jamil Mardam, and wanted to secure British support before proceeding any further with his scheme.

Amir 'Abdullah provided a sound explanation of Nuri's motives. He stated that Nuri, having failed to gain ascendancy over Nahas in the Arab unity talks, was endeavouring to bypass the Egyptian Premier by attempting himself to take the lead in a limited scheme embracing Greater Syria and Iraq. The Amir was also of the view that Nuri, in an attempt to outbid Nahas, had accepted the suggestion of the Syrians that Greater Syria should be a republic.[1] He paid a visit to Baghdad in April, during which he pressed his claims to the Syrian throne, reminding Nuri and the Regent of British promises to him in 1921. He seemed to have got satisfactory assurances from the Iraqis, and started once again to speak disparagingly of Nahas' efforts to bring about an Arab federation. He maintained that the time had not yet come for such developments.[2]

Lord Killearn, as stated earlier, was instructed to express his government's reservations with regard to the meeting of an Arab conference. He informed the Foreign Office that Nahas was careful to keep the British closely informed about his consultations with the various Arab delegations, by conveying to the Embassy all the texts of the minutes of these talks. He added that no objections were raised to these consultations. He "gravely doubted" in view of this, and of Mr Eden's statements of support for Arab unity, the wisdom of any attempt now to prevent the proposed conference, for the meeting of which Nuri Pasha was pressing. Eden minuted on this communication from Lord Killearn, "Why do we want to prevent it?" The attitude of H.M.G. was explained in more detail to the Ambassador. He was informed in March 1944 that he had mistaken the Foreign Office intention, and that they agreed that it would be undesirable to oppose the meeting of the proposed conference, and thus to draw upon H.M.G. the blame for any failure to achieve Arab unity. This was the more so, in their opinion, in view of British declarations on the subject, and especially as the serious efforts which Nuri and Nahas had been making "did not seem to threaten British interests in any way". Lord Killearn was told, moreover, that the main concern of H.M.G. was that the conference should not degenerate into a demonstration against their policy in Palestine. H.M.G. also considered that it would be very difficult for such a conference to achieve any concrete agreement. The delegates might well be tempted to seek an easy way out by blaming others for their

---

[1] FO 371–39987: Sir Harold MacMichael to Colonial Secretary, 10 April 1944
[2] FO 371–39987: Sir Kinahan to Eden, 11 April 1944

failure. It therefore seemed essential, both in the British interest and that of the Arabs, that a concrete agenda should be prepared in advance, so that the delegates would have some idea of what they were likely to agree about. H.M.G. would, therefore, like Nahas Pasha to inform them about the points he thought there was common agreement about. In the absence of such points the conference would be foredoomed to failure, and would only harm the cause of Arab unity. H.M.G., the Ambassador was informed, would also want to know that Nahas would make serious efforts to keep the conference from taking a turn which would increase tension in the area, either among the Arabs or among the Jews, and thus harm the Allied war effort. From this point of view, it would be essential that no unsuitable publicity should be given, and that its public sessions, if any, should be carefully prepared in advance.[1]

Nahas Pasha was determined to consult the Palestine Arab representatives about the whole issue. His persistent efforts to persuade the British to allow such consultations came to naught. He therefore informed Sheikh Yusuf Yassin and Hafiz Wahba, during a private visit they had paid to Egypt in March, that no advantage would be gained by holding the conference at that time, in view of British refusal to allow Jamal al-Husseini and Amin al-Tamimi, the two Palestine leaders then interned in Rhodesia,[2] to consult with him. He added that without much preliminary committee work, the plenary congress would have little prospect of success, and might embarrass the Allied war effort. He added that he was being pressed by Nuri Pasha and Sa'adallah al-Jabri to call the conference immediately. He urged Sheikh Yusuf and Hafiz Wahba to ask King Ibn Sa'ud to use his influence to dissuade the Syrians from pressing him on the issue. Sheikh Hafiz, in reply, stated that the King entirely agreed with this view.[3]

Nahas Pasha might have known of Nuri's activities in Syria and tried to counter them by enlisting the assistance of Ibn Sa'ud, with his known close relations with the Syrian leaders. He was pressed during the consultations to seek the Palestine Arab views on all the issues involved. The Palace and the anti-Wafdi elements in Egypt were also calling for the participation of the Palestine Arab representatives in the consultations. Such participation, if achieved, would have meant a personal victory for Nahas, especially since it would have entailed the release of the two interned Palestine Arab leaders. Nahas was in effect applying some form of pressure on the British by making the whole question of Arab unity, which had their support, hinge on the issue of Palestine Arab representation. Lord Killearn was annoyed at Nahas'

---

[1] FO 371–39987: Sir Kinahan to Eden, 8 February 1944

[2] He considered these two leaders truly representative of the Palestine Arabs, since they were also among the Palestine Arab representatives in the London Conference of 1939.

[3] FO 371–39987: Lord Killearn to Eden, 16 March 1944

attempt to saddle the British with the responsibility for the delay by their refusal to allow Husseini and Tamimi to confer with him. He talked to Sheikh Hafiz on these lines, and indicated that Nahas might have other reasons, which the Ambassador did not specify, for the postponement of the conference.[1] The British, as stated earlier, were not opposed to the meeting of an Arab conference, and were mainly concerned about its implications with regard to the Palestine situation, which was approaching a critical stage as a result of Jewish agitation and propaganda both inside and outside Palestine.

Jamil Mardam paid a visit to Ibn Sa'ud in March 1944. He tried to persuade the King to use his influence to bring about an early meeting of the Arab conference, stating that this was the time to press Arab demands. The Allies, and especially Britain, were preoccupied with the prosecution of the war, and the Arabs would be able to get more out of them then than later. This was in fact the argument which Nuri had been using since 1940. A united Arab front, in his view, would place the Arabs in a better position *vis-à-vis* the Allies, and would ensure for them a better deal in the peace conference.

King Ibn Sa'ud snubbed Jamil Mardam, telling him that he frankly disliked his attitude, which he believed was wrong. He did not consider the time appropriate for pressing Arab claims. If a conference was to be held at that time, it would yield no results in view of the conflicting claims of the various Arab states, and the absence of a representative Palestine Arab delegation. The conference, the King asserted, had to be postponed until the end of the war. He added that H.M.G. meant well for the Arabs, and that as far as he was concerned, he always put his trust in God and then in H.M.G. The best course for Syria, in his view, was to put her own house in order first, and to desist from the clamour for Arab unity. Syria, he thought, had best follow his advice, which was to go slow and be patient. He added that the Syrians had only got as far as they had thanks to the British. Jamil then asked the King about his enmity towards Nuri Pasha. The King replied that he personally cherished no feelings of enmity towards Nuri, and that on the contrary he had helped him financially when he fled from Iraq during the Rashid 'Ali *coup*.[2] Jamil enquired about the King's views on

---

[1] FO 371–39987: Lord Killearn to Eden, 26 March 1944

[2] Ibn Sa'ud stated that he gave Nuri two thousand gold sovereigns and a car, and arranged accommodation for him in Egypt. The King, in spite of his deeply rooted hatred for Nuri and his financial difficulties at that time, found it expedient to provide financial assistance to Nuri in an attempt to buy his friendship. He no doubt recognized Nuri's influence in Iraq and his nuisance-value as the promoter of the Hashimite designs on Syria. It is not clear, however, whether this assistance was given in response to a request from Nuri, or was an offer from the King which Nuri had accepted. It only shows how shrewd and somehow devious Ibn Sa'ud's methods were. Nuri did not obviously change much in his championship of the Greater Syrian scheme as a result of the King's act of generosity.

the current situation in Lebanon, and criticized Riad al-Sulh as "hasty and impotent". Ibn Sa'ud replied that this was not so, and that Al-Sulh was an old friend of his. He added that he had invited the Lebanese Prime Minister to visit him, and would counsel him to maintain continued patience and moderation. He thought that the ideal solution would be a union between Syria and Lebanon, but if this was not possible, then each of them should retain its independence while maintaining good neighbourly relations towards the other.[1]

Jamil Mardam did not get much out of Ibn Sa'ud, who described him later as "an unreliable and headstrong fellow". Jamil told Nuri, however, that the King had agreed to be represented at the preliminary meeting, and at the full Congress on Arab Unity. It transpired that Nuri Pasha was behind the efforts of the Syrians and the Lebanese to urge Ibn Sa'ud to give his approval for an early meeting of an Arab conference. Riad al-Sulh, during his visit to Saudi Arabia in April, stated that Nuri had asked him and Jamil Mardam to try to speak to the King in this sense. Ibn Sa'ud replied that he did not know whether Nuri Pasha was sincere in his activities, or whether he was merely working for his own ends. He reiterated his views regarding the inadvisability of holding a conference before the end of the war. Riad al-Sulh suggested, as an alternative, that a preparatory committee should meet to deal with financial and cultural relations. Ibn Sa'ud replied that he himself had originally proposed the formation of such a committee, but that he was unable to agree to it definitely until he had studied the idea further. He added that if the proposal was adopted, the committee should avoid discussing any controversial political issues such as those of Palestine and Syria. He suggested that Nuri should write to Nahas Pasha proposing the formation of this committee, leaving it to him to issue the invitations to the countries concerned. He explained that he did not like to interfere in the matter himself as this would appear discourteous to Nahas. The King, in a message to the British representative in Jedda containing the record of his meeting with Riad al-Sulh, explained that, by making this suggestion, he hoped to postpone "indefinitely" the meeting of the preparatory committee, as he felt sure that the relations between Nuri and Nahas were such as to prevent the latter from accepting any proposals from Nuri.[2]

Ibn Sa'ud was determined, therefore, to sabotage Nuri's activities. He was under the incorrect impression that H.M.G. were opposed to the meeting of an Arab conference during the war period. He was encouraged by the statements of Nahas Pasha to Hafiz Wahba and Yusuf Yassin. Sir Edward Spears was to note that the King's attitude had evidently fortified the Lebanese Christian elements, including the President, who feared an Arab federation but could not afford to say

[1] FO 371–39987: Jordan to Eden, 1 April 1944
[2] FO 317–39987: Sir Kinahan to Eden, 22 March 1944

so. He added that Jamil Mardam was a professional schemer, and was quite capable of playing Nuri's game. He felt strongly that, with so many purely Arab factors operating in the form desired by H.M.G., it would be most inadvisable for the British to come out too openly against the conference, thus laying themselves open to the charge of inconsistency, and of having killed the Arab seedling after ostentatiously watering it for months.[1]

Nahas Pasha was placed in the most awkward position regarding an issue about which almost everything was subject to disagreement. Nuri Pasha had told the British that he did not think that the participation of the interned Palestine leaders was essential, though it was desirable. He, as well as the Syrians, was pressing for an early meeting, whereas Ibn Sa'ud was strongly against any conference until the end of the war. The British were opposed to any consultations with the interned Palestine Arabs. The Palace elements were pressing not only for the participation of the Palestine Arab representatives, but also for the participation of Idris al-Sanussi, the Libyan leader who was then in Egypt, as well as of the non-independent North African Arab countries. Nahas had to yield to their pressure by making a statement in the Senate expressing sympathy for Arab aspirations in North Africa, and by addressing in April a note to the allied powers in which he called for the independence of the North African countries so that they could join in the movement towards Arab unity. This incurred upon him the wrath of the French and the British. It should be remembered that it was in April 1944 that King Farouq made his second attempt to dismiss him from office, and was prevented from doing so as a result of British intervention. The Foreign Office appreciated that Nahas' tendency to balance his internal instability by "pan-Arab stunts" seemed liable to become embarrassing to the British, "who keep him in power". It was noted, moreover, that he presumably thought that the Arab conference was hanging fire, and as he could not get the Palestinian delegation he wanted, he had better try something else to keep himself in the limelight as the pan-Arabist *par excellence*. A Foreign Office official noted that H.M.G. "want a friendly Arab leadership for Egypt, more like Ibn Sa'ud and more of his dignity and reserve too".[2]

This was not to be all for Nahas Pasha. Lord Killearn was to deliver to him, early in June, a strong warning against the immediate convocation of an Arab conference. The Ambassador stated that he did not see how the vexed question of Palestine could be avoided. He added that H.M.G. were not at all anxious that it should appear, through their action or inaction, that the proposed conference was

[1] FO 371–39988: Sir Edward Spears to Eden, 23 April 1944

[2] FO 371–39988: Lord Killearn to Eden, 22 April 1944, and a minute by Hankey in comment on the Egyptian note handed by the Egyptian Ambassador to Eden on 5 May 1944

being held up, "nor was it in accordance with Nahas Pasha's own policy or to his personal interest that it should seem so". Nahas Pasha, Lord Killearn stated in his warning message delivered through Amin Osman Pasha, had much better let the idea "quietly peter out". This, he said, would be easier now since Nahas' competition for leadership with Nuri, who had just left office, was no longer a factor in the situation. Nahas was reminded of the wise attitude adopted by King Ibn Sa'ud in this regard.[1]

This was probably the most forceful representation, amounting to an admonishment, that Nahas Pasha had received so far as a result of his labours in the field of Arab unity. It was delivered by an Ambassador who, less than two months earlier, had intervened with a veiled threat to resort to force, to compel the King to keep him in office. Lord Killearn's attitude was that of someone who wanted the repayment of a debt, and in the most open and unequivocal way. His warning was phrased in a way that implied British opposition to the whole idea of a conference. This did certainly go beyond the Foreign Office instructions referred to earlier. Nahas was in effect asked to bear the sole responsibility for the failure of the whole movement which he had initiated through his consultations with the Arab delegates. Nahas, on the other hand, was well aware of his precarious position at home and, rather than let the whole enterprise end in failure, for which he would be blamed, or leave the task unfinished for others to accomplish and get the credit for, he was more determined than ever to continue his efforts in this regard. He reckoned that the British would not try openly to oppose the meeting of the Arab conference, because of their eagerness not to appear obstructive towards a movement which had their declared sympathy and support. The Ambassador, in waving the big stick at him, and in asking him to do for the British their odious job without exposing them to the Arab World, did confirm his appreciation of the British attitude.

Lord Killearn's representations produced results opposite to his intentions. Nahas Pasha was to forward to him nine days later (on 14 June) the draft of a letter which he proposed to address to the Arab governments. In this draft Nahas stated that he still considered it important that he should consult with a truly representative Palestine delegation, and that the next stage should not be started before this had been accomplished. He added that available information showed that, without the release of Jamal al-Husseini and Amin al-Tamimi, it

---

[1] FO 371–39988: Lord Killearn to Eden, 5 June 1944. Nuri Pasha left office for reasons pertaining to Iraqi internal politics on 3 June 1944 and was succeeded by Hamdi al-Pachachi. Nuri remained, however, very active in the Arab arena. He paid a visit to the Levant and Egypt shortly afterwards, and continued to press for an early Arab meeting. He was chosen as a member of the Iraqi delegation to the Alexandria preparatory meeting of September 1944.

would be impossible to form a body suitably representative and satisfactory to Palestine Arab public opinion. He referred to his efforts to secure the release of these two leaders, with no results so far. He noted, however, that public interest necessitated the acceleration of the Arab unity scheme so that events should not outstrip the Arab leaders. He therefore suggested that a preparatory committee should meet in Cairo at the end of July or early in August. If consultations with a truly representative Palestine Arab delegation proved possible before that meeting, so much the better. If not, then the committee should meet all the same. Nahas, in conclusion, invited the views of the various Arab governments, asking them, if they agreed with his suggestion, to notify him of the names of their delegates.

Sir Walter Smart, to whom this draft was conveyed, was annoyed at its contents and asked Amin Osman, Nahas' liaison officer with the Embassy, to urge Nahas Pasha to go slow, and to do nothing more before consulting them. Lord Killearn, in the meantime, asked for instructions from London, noting that H.M.G. should act quickly as Nahas was under pressure from Nuri Pasha, who was then in Cairo, and others, and might go ahead without waiting further for British views. The Foreign Office, in reply, thought it undesirable for Nahas to send the proposed letter at the present juncture. Lord Killearn was therefore instructed to point out to Nahas that the summoning of an Arab conference was inopportune in view of the existing war conditions, and that it was likely to provoke adverse reactions by raising the Palestine question with no good done to anybody. The Foreign Office considered Nahas' specific reference to the two interned Palestinian leaders "unfortunate", since he had already been informed of the final British decision refusing their release.

Lord Killearn conveyed the Foreign Office views on 23 June only to be informed that Nahas had already sent copies of his letter to the Arab governments. Amin Osman stated that, on being informed of the British refusal to release Tamimi and Husseini, Nahas had decided to go ahead all the same, since he could not have postponed the matter any longer in view of the pressures that were being exerted on him. Nahas thought that if H.M.G. were concerned about the Palestine aspect, he could see to it that the discussions about Palestine were kept within the proper limits. Lord Killearn attributed Nahas' action to Iraqi and Syrian pressures, and recommended that British representatives in Damascus and Baghdad should be instructed to make similar representations to the leaders of these two countries.[1]

The British were therefore faced with a *fait accompli.* In their instructions to the British representatives in the area, the Foreign Office stated that since the invitations to the Arab governments had already

[1] FO 371–39988: Lord Killearn to Eden, 14 June 1944, and Eden to Lord Killearn, Sir Edward Spears, and Sir Harold MacMichael, 4 July 1944

been sent out, it was "clearly undesirable" that H.M.G. should attempt actively to obstruct the meeting of the preparatory committee. It was noted, however, that if the recipients of the invitation appeared reluctant to send representatives, or doubtful about the utility of such a meeting, H.M.G., if consulted, should encourage any tendency towards postponement. Nahas Pasha was to be told that H.M.G. appreciated his unwillingness to allow the Arab unity discussions to fade out after the trouble he had taken to ascertain the separate views of each of the Arab governments concerned. He was also to be asked whether in view of the absence of sufficient points of agreement on the political side, the intention was to concentrate mainly on the economic and cultural aspects of Arab co-operation. H.M.G., Nahas was to be told, wanted the preparatory committee to try to discover a substantial measure of common agreement, especially on non-political forms of co-operation, and to draw up actual resolutions for subsequent approval by the General Congress. Otherwise, it would be useless and even harmful to the cause of Arab unity to hold a formal congress at all.

The Foreign Office circular telegram of instructions stated, moreover, that H.M.G. should take note of Nahas' assurances that the discussions about Palestine would be kept within the proper limits. H.M.G., it was added, must also request that these assurances should be extended to cover the past and the future of the French in the Levant states. Publicity at this stage had to be curtailed, with no unsuitable resolutions taken or tendentious public speeches made on either of these points. It was stated in conclusion that the course of the discussions could not be foreseen at present, and a failure of the delegates to achieve a substantial measure of agreement would be all the more harmful if the meeting had previously been loudly publicized.

In addition to these general instructions, a special telegram was sent to Jedda stating that if Ibn Sa'ud seemed reluctant to participate he should be encouraged to suggest further postponement of the proposed meeting, and to make his views known to the Syrian leaders. In case he thought of sending a delegate and sought British advice, he should be informed of the gist of the general instructions referred to earlier.[1]

The Foreign Office were eager, therefore, if a preparatory meeting were to be held, that it should not end in complete failure, thus providing a fresh cause for inter-Arab friction and acrimony. They appreciated that no agreement would be possible on political union in view of the divergence of opinions among the Arab states. They were anxious, however, that the meeting should come out with something tangible, at least in the economic and cultural fields. They were not ready at the same time to give any positive advice to any reluctant Arab leader. This was to prove a major obstacle in the way of an early meeting of

---

[1] FO 371–39988–E3686/4/65

the committee, as will be noted later. The rather ambiguous line taken by the Foreign Office in its approach to the issue was mainly responsible for the subsequent complications as far as Ibn Sa'ud was concerned.

Lord Killearn felt somewhat embarrassed at Nahas' action, which outmanoeuvred him on the issue. He told the Iraqi Regent, who was on a visit to Egypt late in June, that Nahas was summoning a pan-Arab meeting without British concurrence, and that his action was likely to be embarrassing and harmful both for the British and for the Arab states, since it would be very difficult to avoid raising the Palestine problem in some form or the other. This would be unwise, and would also give reason for renewed Jewish agitation in America and elsewhere. The Iraqi Regent, Lord Killearn reported, was in full agreement with him, stating, moreover, that in Iraq there had been from the outset considerable feeling against Nuri Pasha for pressing for Arab union at this stage. The Regent also agreed with the Ambassador that the most that was likely to come for a long time was some form of cultural or economic collaboration. He believed that the Palestine problem was insoluble along the existing lines, and should be kept asleep for as long as possible. Lord Killearn then suggested to the Regent that he might feel disposed to pour cold water upon Nahas' invitation. He got the impression that this suggestion had fallen upon receptive ground.[1]

The reaction of the Iraqi Government to Nahas' invitation did not, however, confirm Lord Killearn's impression. The new Iraqi Premier, Hamdi al-Pachachi, felt that the preparatory meeting was the natural culmination of the previous consultations. He considered it important for the Arab states to lose no time in coming to an agreement ensuring the pursuit of a common foreign policy should any one of them be subjected to any threat, and the strengthening of their economic, cultural, and other ties. He felt that it would be difficult to postpone the proposed meeting, but he saw no reason why a resolution should not be passed by the committee postponing any discussions on the Palestine question until the end of the war. He thought that the cause of Arab co-operation depended on the strengthening of Anglo-Arab relations. He therefore intended to propose that, as part of their common policy, the Arabs should enter into an alliance with H.M.G. for an initial period of thirty years. He added that he did not himself intend to be present at the meeting of the committee and the conference, but thought that the cabinet would appoint Nuri Pasha as the Iraqi representative.[2]

Amir 'Abdullah was also prompt in accepting the invitation, and in asking his Prime Minister, Abul Huda Pasha, to attend the proposed meeting.[3] The invitation was accepted by the Syrians, who promised, in response to Sir Edward Spears' representations, not to raise the Pales-

[1] FO 371–39988: Lord Killearn to Eden, 26 June 1944
[2] FO 371–39988: Sir Kinahan to Eden, 6 July 1944
[3] FO 371–39988: Sir Harold MacMichael to Colonial Secretary, 7 July 1944

tine question themselves, and to do their best to prevent its being raised by others.[1]

There remained the main problem concerning the participation of King Ibn Sa'ud. The King was pleased when he was informed by Sheikh Yusuf Yassin in March that Nahas Pasha was in agreement with him on the inadvisability of holding an Arab conference at that time. He was soon to send a letter to Nahas expressing his suspicions of the motives of some persons like Nuri Pasha, and pointing out the necessity for postponing the conference. He suggested to Nahas that they should consult on the action to be taken in case of any new development. Ibn Sa'ud's envoy who carried his letter to Nahas informed the King that Nahas expressed agreement with his views and proposed that Egypt, Yemen, and Saudi Arabia should come to an agreement with each other "to the exclusion of Iraq and the other states". The King was flattered by what he considered to be his strong influence over Nahas. In reply to a remark made by Jordan, who met him late in March, that it was thanks to him that Nahas had agreed to the postponement of the conference, the King stated that even if Nahas had thought differently, he would have obliged him to change his mind. He added that he had considerable influence with Nahas thanks to a group of Nahas' followers, headed by Sabri Abu 'Alam Pasha, who were the King's close friends. He stated that he was working on Nahas through the Sa'udi Counsellor in Cairo, Khair ud-Din al-Zurkally, and would continue to advise patience. He noted that Nahas had only fallen in with his views regarding the conference to secure his support against Nuri.[2]

Ibn Sa'ud was therefore deeply offended when he heard of Nahas' action in sending invitations to the Arab governments without prior consultations with him, and without sending any written reply to his letter of March 1944. He was also offended when he knew that the invitations had been received by the other Arab states a few weeks before a similar invitation had reached him.[3] This was probably due to the communication difficulties with Saudi Arabia. The King was encouraged in his attitude when British views favouring the postponement of the meeting were conveyed to him. He stated that he had sent a frankly worded telegram to Shukri al-Qwatli urging him to take no action prejudicial to Britain's war effort, as British support and goodwill were the surest guarantees for the interests of the Arabs in general and the Syrians in particular. The acceptance by the other Arab states of Nahas' invitation placed him in a most awkward position, however, and he sought definite British advice on whether he should accept or refuse. He also asked, in case the advice was in favour of refusal, that

[1] FO 371–39988: Sir Edward Spears to Eden, 13 July 1944
[2] FO 371–39987: Jordan to Eden, 1 April 1944
[3] FO 371–39988: Ellison (Jedda) to Eden, 6 July 1944

H.M.G. should suggest some way of refusal which would not appear too abrupt.[1]

The attitude of Ibn Sa'ud was rather embarrassing to the British. They were eager not to come into the open against the proposed meeting, but were at the same time in favour of its postponement. They were told by Nahas Pasha that if one or two Arab governments refused the invitation, or suggested the postponement of the meeting, he would not go ahead with his plans. Their only chance, if they wanted to sabotage or to postpone the meeting, was to advise Ibn Sa'ud in that direction. They had before them the views of Lord Moyne, the Minister of State in Cairo, who considered it "unwise" for H.M.G. to advise the King to refuse, since if the meeting were to take place, it would be better to have a Sa'udi representative exercising a moderating influence on its proceedings.[2] The problem would have solved itself for them if Ibn Sa'ud had made up his own mind one way or the other. They did not wish to advise the King to refuse and so to be later blamed by him if the meeting took place without his participation, or to be saddled with the responsibility of sabotaging the meeting if it were to be called off because of the King's refusal.

The British advice to the King was delivered in a carefully worded *aide mémoire* prepared by Jordan out of the Foreign Office telegrams on the subject. It stated that the present time was not propitious for holding the committee meeting, and that it was likely that such a meeting, if allowed to get out of hand, might do more harm than good to the Arab cause. H.M.G. had reason to believe that if one or more of the Arab states were to inform Nahas Pasha that the present time was not suitable for such a meeting, he would drop the idea. Should, however, a sufficient number of Arab states signify their willingness to participate, it would be advisable for the King to send a representative to make his views known, and in order that the committee might enjoy the benefit of his moderating influence. In this case, H.M.G. would request that discussions about Palestine and the past or the future of the French in the Levant states should be kept within proper limits. The discussions would have to be confidential, and a decision to hold a formal congress should only be taken by a unanimous vote of the delegates.[3]

Ibn Sa'ud had, on the receipt of British views, prepared a draft letter to Nahas proposing that the meeting of the preparatory committee

---

[1] FO 371–39988: Ellison to Eden and Eden to Ellison, 13 July 1944, instructing him to reply to Ibn Sa'ud's request for advice, that H.M.G. "do not advise him to refuse Nahas's invitation", while stating British reasons for favouring postponement in view of the war situation.

[2] FO 371–39988: Lord Killearn conveying telegram from Lord Moyne to Eden, 11 May 1944

[3] FO 371–39989: Jordan to Eden conveying a copy of his *Aide Memoire*, 3 August 1944

should be postponed until an understanding had been reached with the Allies over Palestine and Syria. He sent, in the meantime, a letter to Shukri al-Qwatli referring to Syrian acceptance of Nahas' invitation, and noting that, by taking this action, Al-Qwatli had faced him with a *fait accompli.* He added that Nahas' invitation was a surprise which took him very much aback, since he was not consulted beforehand. He was unaware of the reasons for calling such a meeting as well as of its basis, and whether it would endeavour to unite the Arabs. He was also unaware of its attitude with regard to the Palestine problem. There was, moreover, the question of precedence and of who should preside over the meetings. He stressed, in conclusion, that he could not agree to any action prejudicial to H.M.G., nor could he tolerate the domination by one party over the others. He therefore would refrain from participating in the proposed meeting. He sent a similar letter to the Lebanese Prime Minister, and three telegrams on the same lines to the Imam of Yemen. He expressed to the British representative his confidence that the Imam at least would follow his lead.[1]

It was at this time that the American election campaign was in full progress. The ruling Democratic Party had just published its programme which called for the establishment of a Jewish Commonwealth in Palestine. This caused sharp reactions all over the Arab World, and several telegrams of protest were sent to the American Government. Jordan advised Yusuf Yassin immediately that perhaps, in view of the agitation which this programme would surely produce in the Arab countries, the King might wish to consider withholding his reply to Nahas for some days until the situation became clearer. The King was in fact perturbed by the contents of the programme, and decided not to send his letter to Nahas. He also decided to send Yusuf Yassin to Egypt early in August to discuss the matter with Nahas. This, Jordan maintained, did not imply any change in the King's attitude towards the proposed meeting. It was aimed rather at gauging general Arab reaction to the pro-Zionist election campaign in the United States, and at avoiding an outright refusal to Nahas' invitation in such a situation.[2]

In Cairo, Sheikh Yusuf found Nahas determined to hold the preparatory meeting. He had postponed it from early August to 25 September because of the non-receipt of the Sa'udi and Yemeni replies. He felt that events made it impossible to postpone it any further, and gave Sheikh Yusuf a letter to Ibn Sa'ud to that effect. In the meantime, Shukri al-Qwatli asked Sheikh Yusuf to go to Syria to discuss the matter with him. Sheikh Yusuf, in seeking the views of H.M.G., thought

---

[1] FO 371–39989: Ellison to Eden, 16 July 1944. Mr Eden minuted on Ibn Sa'ud's action, "all very Arab", while Mr Baxter, the head of the Eastern Department of the Foreign Office, minuted that the King had obviously decided to refuse Nahas' invitation, "but not at our instigation!"

[2] FO 371–39989: Jordan to Eden, 3 August 1944

that the King would stick to his refusal unless he received an intimation from the British to the contrary. Lord Moyne, with whom Sheikh Yusuf discussed the matter, felt that perhaps the King was under the impression that H.M.G. would like him not to be represented, and asked the Foreign Office to instruct Jordan to remove any misunderstanding in this regard. Jordan, in answer, stressed that neither the King nor his advisers had been left in any doubt that H.M.G. would prefer Ibn Sa'ud to be represented if a meeting took place. It is true, however, that Jordan's *aide mémoire* laid more stress on the advisability of the postponement of the meeting, and inserted the statement of Nahas that such an end could be achieved through the refusal of one or more states to take part in the conference. Jordan had in fact described the King's decision to withhold sending his letter to Nahas, and to send Sheikh Yusuf to Cairo, as "unfortunate".

The King's letters to Qwatli and Riad al-Sulh caused some confusion, and gave the impression that H.M.G. were opposed to the meeting of the preparatory committee. Nuri Pasha, in concert with the Syrian and Lebanese Prime Ministers, sought the views of the British Consul in Beirut early in August. He stated that he, as well as the Syrians and the Lebanese, was ready to delay the meeting, or to abstain altogether from holding it, should this be the desire of H.M.G. This was a clever move by Nuri, which would have switched the responsibility for any delay or failure to hold the meeting to the British, a thing which he knew very well that they would be reluctant to accept. He was in fact using the same tactic as Ibn Sa'ud, though in the case of the King there was no desire to see a meeting held at all, and a wish at the same time to avoid being blamed by the Arabs for obstructing their efforts towards unity. Nuri was told that H.M.G. were in favour of postponement at the present time, and that if the meeting intended to discuss the Palestine issue, then they would advise all concerned strongly against holding it.[1]

Sheikh Yusuf Yassin conducted several talks in Cairo, Damascus, and Beirut. He told Lord Moyne on 2 September 1944 that Ibn Sa'ud was at present resolved not to be represented, and more than hinted that his attitude was due to the fact that he believed that this course of action was the one desired by the British. He stated, however, that all the Arab leaders with whom he had recently been in contact in Syria appeared resolved to hold the conference, and that it seemed likely that they would go ahead with their plans despite the King's attitude. He thought that, unless the King received definite advice to attend, he might well stick to his refusal. Lord Moyne, whose views were all along

---

[1] FO 371–39989: Consul Mackereth (Beirut) to FO, 9 August 1944, reported being approached by Nuri Pasha acting for himself and on behalf of the Prime Ministers of Syria and Lebanon and enquiring about the views of H.M.G. on the meeting of an Arab conference in Cairo. Mackereth affirmed the fact that Nuri was truly authorized by the Syrians and the Lebanese to make these enquiries.

not in favour of British outright opposition to such a meeting, told Sheikh Yusuf that though the present time was not suitable, H.M.G. would leave it to the King himself to decide on whether to attend or not.

On his return to Jedda on 3 September, Sheikh Yusuf raised the matter again with Jordan. He felt that if a meeting was held without the participation of the King, it would be unfortunate and would place him (the King) in an equivocal position. Ibn Sa'ud, he added, had committed himself so far to non-participation by his communications to the Arab governments, and now he found himself in an impasse from which only H.M.G. could extricate him. He felt certain that if the British were to intimate to the Iraqi, Syrian, Lebanese, and Egyptian leaders that they considered the present time unsuitable for this meeting, it would be abandoned. The Foreign Office, in a reply conveyed to the King, expressed their unwillingness to oppose the meeting of the committee if the Arab countries really wished to hold it. They recognized that, if the committee were to meet, it would be embarrassing for Ibn Sa'ud not to be represented. In this case the King might consider being represented by an observer to enable him to be kept informed, and to convey his views without committing himself in any way.[1]

The British had come round then to accepting the idea of an early meeting of the preparatory committee. Lord Moyne was of the view that H.M.G. had already gone "as far as is wise" in discouraging the holding of the conference, and that any further pressure was likely to arouse suspicions. He was against any representations to the Syrians and the Lebanese on the issue, since he was not sure that they would fall in with British wishes. If they did, the responsibility for stopping the meeting would fall on the British, "which is what Ibn Sa'ud would like". If they refused, H.M.G. would have incurred a rebuff.[2] The attitude of Ibn Sa'ud was obviously exasperating to the Foreign Office.

Nahas Pasha made a final attempt to secure the participation of Ibn Sa'ud in the meeting. In a letter to the King on 9 August, he explained in great detail that he had never expressed to his envoys his wish to see the meeting postponed until the end of the war. He added that the misunderstanding was probably caused by his statement to Sheikh Yusuf and Hafiz Wahba that, without the release of the interned Palestine leaders, it would be difficult to have a truly representative Palestinian Arab delegation, and that the movement towards Arab union might not succeed if the Palestine Arabs did not participate. He stressed that his argument concerned only the case of the Palestine representation, and that the King's envoys must have raised the question from the level of the particular to the general, thus causing a

---

[1] FO 371–39990: Jordan to Eden, 3 September 1944, and Eden to Jordan, 12 September 1944

[2] FO 371–39990: Lord Killearn conveying message of Lord Moyne to Eden on 7 September 1944

misunderstanding of his intentions. He then apologized for not being able to answer the King's letter of March, since he was awaiting the results of his efforts with the British for the release of Husseini and Tamimi.

Nahas stated, moreover, that he was in agreement with the King on the whole principle, and was also keenly solicitous for good understanding with the Allies, and particularly Britain. He noted, however, that nothing of this would conflict with the efforts designed to strengthen inter-Arab co-operation. Events were hastening fast and he feared that if the Arabs missed the opportunity, they might miss the train or lose their chance. He added that the King was among the first who had suggested the idea of the meeting of a preparatory committee.

Nahas then assured the King that his fears of lack of agreement, or the appearance of dispute, could be easily removed since the agenda of the preparatory meeting would be kept entirely secret. He added that there were already common grounds of agreement in matters of practical importance such as economic and cultural co-operation, the unity of the Arab countries, and their welfare. A meeting was therefore necessary to arrange the procedure for the execution of these matters. He therefore entreated the King to send a representative to participate in the proposed meeting.

Nahas' clarifications did not satisfy Ibn Sa'ud, however, and he prepared a long reply which he insisted on sending in spite of British reservations with regard to its contents. He stated in his reply that he was the first to call for Arab unity following his war with Yemen in 1934, and that he had ever since continued his efforts in that direction without any ulterior motives, seeking only the good of the Arabs. He added that those who were then conducting pan-Arab propaganda fell into two groups: the first included those who were using the issue as a screen to hide their ambitions in Syria and Palestine; while the second included some well-meaning Arabs who were sometimes lured by hopes for the achievement of Arab unity and wanted to rescue their countries from the dangers of colonialism and Zionism. He, on the other hand, had no ambitions and did not make a show in order to strengthen his position in his own country "as do some politicians and leaders". He then criticized Nahas' handling of the whole matter since his statement in the Senate in March 1943, about which the King was not consulted. He added that the non-answering by Nahas of his letter of March was "a blow" to him, and that he took Nahas' failure to reply as signifying agreement with his views. He stated that he was surprised when he heard that an invitation had been sent to the Syrians, which invitation reached him three weeks later. He then added that besides the error which had been committed by continually ignoring him and failing to give him his due, he still did not see any advantage in holding the meeting under the war circumstances, and until his conditions for such a meeting were satisfied. These conditions were that there should be a prior definition of the subjects to be discussed as well as of the purpose of the meeting. There also should be an understanding with the Allies securing the rights of the Palestine Arabs and future Arab relations with them.

The King's letter amounted, therefore, to a virulent attack on Nahas for continually ignoring him. It was not devoid of some scathing remarks about Arab politicians who sought, through their pan-Arab activities, to strengthen their position at home, by which he obviously meant Nahas and Nuri. It was, moreover, completely negative as far as the issue of his participation in the proposed meeting was concerned. Ibn Sa'ud was not swayed from sending his letter by the strong arguments made by Jordan, who was of the view that Nahas would have to provide an explanation for the non-participation of the King. If he chose to publish the letter, it might be "very prejudicial" to the King's prestige in the Arab World, since at least four-fifths of its contents represented a personal attack on Nahas and, in certain parts, on Nuri too. It might therefore lead the Arabs to think that the King had based his refusal on his personal squabble with Nahas and his extreme dislike for Nuri, rather than on his conviction that the moment was not propitious for such a meeting to be held.[1]

The King was soon to change his attitude, however, after all the delegates, with the exception of his and the Yemeni representatives, assembled in Egypt on 25 September 1944. Nahas, in a telegram to him, expressed his apologies for offending him, and the wish of all the delegates that he should be represented and should advise Imam Yehya to do the same. The King realized that he had failed to make his views regarding the postponement of the meeting prevail. It was the sense of the British advice to him that his participation would be favoured if the meeting were to take place. He therefore instructed Sheikh Yusuf to proceed immediately to Egypt, and communicated his decision to the Imam of Yemen. Sheikh Yusuf arrived in Egypt early in October. He told Lord Moyne that Ibn Sa'ud had only finally sent him because he believed that H.M.G. wished him to do so. He assured the Minister of State that he would do his utmost to keep the discussions on a reasonable level and to make sure that the Palestine problem, if discussed, would be dealt with in a general way with all violent resolutions on the issue avoided.[2]

There remained the question of the representation of the Palestine

---

[1] FO 371–39990: for copies of the exchanged letters between Nahas and Ibn Sa'ud handed to the British Legation on instructions from Ibn Sa'ud on 14 September 1944; and E5683/41/65 for Mr Jordan's advice to Sheikh Yusuf Yassin conveyed on 14 September 1944

[2] FO 371–39990: Lord Killearn conveying telegram from Lord Moyne to Eden on 2 October 1944

Arabs. The British had by now come round to accepting their participation, which was thought essential by the Arab governments. They were opposed, however, to the participation of any of the interned leaders, and were anxious to ensure that their policy in Palestine would not come under attack during the meetings. The Palestine Arab politicians of various parties were, on the other hand, eager to express their views, and to draw support for their cause from the Arab delegates. They chose as their representative Musa al-'Alami, a brother-in-law of the interned Jamal al-Husseini, who was a lawyer by profession and a member of the Palestine Arab delegation to the London Conference of 1939. Musa al-'Alami proceeded to Egypt without an invitation from Nahas Pasha, who seemed to have given up hope of the participation of the Palestine Arabs, in view of British objections. The presence of Musa placed Nahas and the other Arab delegates in an awkward position. Nahas evaded at first Musa's request that he be admitted as a delegate, arguing that Palestine needed no representation since all the delegates in a sense represented her. When Musa insisted on taking part in the discussions, Nahas intimated to him that to let him sit as a delegate would annoy the British. Musa then found an unexpected ally in King Farouq, who was at loggerheads with Nahas, and who sought to use the issue of the Palestine representation to embarrass his Prime Minister. The King caused Musa to be sent a series of invitations to functions held in connection with the conference, some of which were addressed to "The Prime Minister of Palestine", and others to "The Chief of the Palestine Delegation".[1] This was rather embarrassing to Nahas, who was eager not to let the meeting fail on that count.

Nahas sought British views on the participation of Musa al-'Alami. He stated that there was no question of his admission as a delegate of the Palestine Government in any way. He also sought the views of Brigadier Clayton, who was attached to the Office of the Minister of State in Cairo, and with whom Al-'Alami had been in touch. Brigadier Clayton thought that Nahas should avoid according the status of a delegate to Al-'Alami, and should consider him merely as a representative of the Palestine Arabs, since he was clearly not quite on the same footing as the others. Amin Osman, for Nahas, assured Clayton that Musa would not take part in any discussions or sign any resolutions. He would be ruled out of order by Nahas at any time if he spoke on subjects which did not, in the chairman's view, affect the Palestine

---

[1] Geoffrey Furlonge *Palestine is my Country: The Story of Musa Alami*, London 1969, pp. 132–3. The Palestine Arab leaders were divided among themselves. They were dismayed, however, when no invitation was extended to them to take part in the Alexandria meeting, which was bound to discuss their affairs in their absence. They achieved the "unprecedented feat" of agreeing on sending Musa al-'Alami as their delegate. They felt that he was the only leader of the requisite calibre who belonged to no party and could therefore represent all of them.

Arabs. In no way would he be considered as representing, or committing, Palestine as a whole. Brigadier Clayton stated that he personally could not see any objection to the participation of Musa within the limits indicated by Amin Osman.[1] Nahas, in the meantime, suggested to Musa that he should be present only at the final session after the delegates had passed all their resolutions, so that he could present the Palestine Arab case. Musa enquired "icily" if Nahas had received British permission for this concession, to which Nahas answered in the positive. Musa then contacted Clayton and asked that British objections to his participation should be withdrawn, or else he would feel compelled to return to Palestine and to publicize the reasons for his exclusion, which could hardly redound to British credit. Clayton, on being assured by Musa that he was there only to represent the Palestine Arabs, handed him, after consultation with the Minister of State, a note addressed to Nahas stating that Lord Moyne had no objection to the participation of Musa as a representative of the Palestine Arabs. Musa was admitted to the meeting of the Committee on this basis.[2]

There was another minor snag, with regard to the intention of the Iraqi Government to appoint Nuri Pasha, who was then out of office, as their delegate. After leaving office early in June 1944, Nuri visited Syria, Lebanon, Palestine, and Egypt. He was very active in Syria, where he had talks with the Syrian leaders, who were pressing for an early meeting of the preparatory committee, for which purpose he contacted the British, and urged the Syrian and Lebanese Governments to try to induce Ibn Sa'ud to accept the idea. His activities gave rise to many rumours, which were the subject of some articles in the Iraqi, Egyptian, and British press about a scheme allegedly agreed upon between him and Shukri al-Qwatli for the union of Greater Syria and Iraq in an Arab League which the other Arab states could later join if they wished.[3] This was the scheme proposed by Nuri in his Note to Mr Casey, which had probably leaked to the press. This was possibly done on purpose by Nuri, who was eager to give his Note the largest possible circulation. Nahas Pasha was rather resentful of Nuri's efforts, which betrayed an attempt to wrest the leadership from him on the issue of Arab unity. He complained to the British of Nuri's attempt to arrange with the Syrians and the Lebanese the formation of a united front

---

[1] FO 371–39990. Mr Shone to Eden, 6 October 1944

[2] Geoffrey Furlonge, op. cit., pp. 134–5. Musa, after being allowed to join the meetings, berated the other delegates for their "tergiversations over his admission, and in particular for their lack of courage *vis-à-vis* the British in this purely Arab matter". Nahas ordered his remarks to be stricken from the record. Muhammad Ali al-Taher, a militant Palestinian living in Egypt, noted that Al-'Alami failed in his mission and absented himself from some sessions and showed impatience and dissatisfaction with the proceedings. Muhammad Ali al-Taher *Zalam al-Sijn, Mudhakkirat wa Mufakkirat Sajin Harib*, Cairo 1951, p. 572

[3] *Majallat al Rabita al- 'Arabiya*, 12 and 19 August 1944

against him. He indicated that he had received information from Syria to that effect. The purpose was, he added, to enable the Iraqi, Syrian, and Lebanese delegates to come to Egypt with a concerted policy designed to produce some academic ending of the talks, and themselves to get busy later on with a conference among themselves which would exclude Nahas.[1]

Nuri's activities were also to cause sharp reactions in the Levant. The Maronites in Lebanon were furious. Stormy meetings were held by "Al Kataib", whose leader, Pierre al-Jumail, made strong representations to the Lebanese President and Prime Minister.[2] Riad al-Sulh authorized Al-Jumail to publish a statement to the effect that his government were determined to base Lebanese relations with the other Arab states on full respect for the independence of each state.[3] He referred, in a speech in August, to the rumours that Iraq and Syria had agreed to incorporate Lebanon. He declared that this could and would never happen, and that he preferred the union of the Christians and the Muslims within Lebanon to the establishment of "large non-independent empires".[4] He obviously meant that a Greater Syria, united with Iraq, would subject Lebanon and the whole federation to British influence, then dominant in Iraq, Transjordan, and Palestine. He was also to state early in September, in the presence of Hamdi al-Pachachi, the Iraqi Prime Minister, who was then on a visit to Lebanon, that he, as well as Al-Pachachi, considered that the main aim of any conference on Arab unity should be to safeguard the full independence of each Arab country. The Iraqi Prime Minister concurred with Al-Sulh's statement, and renewed Iraqi respect for Lebanese independence.[5] Riad al-Sulh assured the parliament, just before his departure to Egypt, that he would not accept any infringement upon Lebanese independence. Abdul Hamid Karami, another life-long pan-Arabist, was also to declare that he used in the past to call for Syrian unity and the creation of an Arab Empire. He added, however, that he had now changed his views, and would favour continued Lebanese independence "not out of fear or deference to anyone but out of national convictions".[6]

---

[1] FO 371–39989: Lord Killearn to Eden, 26 July 1944

[2] Al Kataib was founded by Pierre al-Jumail in 1936 with a predominantly Maronite membership. It started as a youth organization of a social and cultural nature. Its leader supported the National Pact while stressing the necessity for Lebanese independence from Arab and European influences, and was strongly against the inclusion of Lebanon in any Arab association. Pierre al-Jumail *Libnan Waqi' wa Murtaja*, pp. 96–7, and Anis Sayigh *Libnan al Taifi*, Beirut 1955, pp. 150–1

[3] *Majallat al Rabita Al-Arabiya*, 19 August 1944

[4] *Al Ahram*, 11 August 1944; also on the same subject article in *Al Ahram*, 14 August 1944

[5] *Majallat Akher Sa'a*, 3 September 1944

[6] *Al Misri*, 24 September 1944. This was the line to which all prominent Lebanese politicians were committed in accordance with the terms of the National Pact referred to earlier.

Amir 'Abdullah was also resentful of Nuri's activities. He felt greatly offended early in August, when he was asked, at the last moment, by the Syrian Government to postpone a visit which he intended to make to Damascus, on the grounds that the Amir's arrival at that time, when rumours about an Iraqi–Syrian agreement for the creation of Greater Syria were circulating, might cause political complications.[1] He was more offended when his consul in Damascus reported early in September, the Syrian Prime Minister telling him of his country's support for the formation of Greater Syria provided the republican regime in Syria was preserved. The Syrian Prime Minister, Sa'adallah al-Jabri, stated, moreover, that Transjordan was an integral part of Syria, and that while Syria was ready to enter a federation with other Arab countries, it would not be ready to fall under the influence of anyone else. Syria, Al-Jabri stated, was also desirous of complete reunion with the Lebanon, or else the Lebanon should be reduced to its pre-1920 frontiers. He added that some people thought that they had the monopoly of Arab nationalism, and could claim the whole credit for the Arab revolt against the Turks.[2] This was an obvious hit at the Amir, who had based his claims to Syria on his family's contribution to, and leadership of, the Great Arab Revolt.

Sir Edward Spears, by way of comment on this report, thought that it might be slightly exaggerated, since it would be "sheer folly" for Jabri to speak in this sense officially with the representative of a ruler "notoriously hostile" to the Syrian Government.[3] The statement of Al-Jabri was, however, in line with his statements during his consultations with Nahas referred to earlier. Amir 'Abdullah was not to give up, however, and he was to circulate a lengthy memorandum to the Arab leaders expected to participate in the preparatory meeting, with the exception of the Sa'udi representative. It recapitulated the part played by the Hashimites in the Arab awakening, and included some criticism of the present regimes in Syria and Saudi Arabia. It was clearly designed to draw attention to his own claims to leadership as the senior surviving Hashimite ruler.[4]

Nahas Pasha, as stated earlier, was annoyed at Nuri's activities in Syria. The Egyptian Chargé d'Affaires in Baghdad, presumably on instructions from Nahas, was to put to the Iraqi Minister for Foreign Affairs on 13 September 1944 the "personal" suggestion that Nuri should not be appointed a member of the Iraqi delegation. The Iraqi

---

[1] FO 371–39990: Lord Killearn to Eden, 16 August 1944, reporting a statement to him by the Transjordan Consul in Cairo

[2] FO 371–39990: the Acting High Commissioner for Palestine and Transjordan to the Colonial Secretary, 8 September 1944

[3] FO 371–39990: Sir Edward Spears to Eden, 22 September 1944

[4] FO 371–39990: the Acting High Commissioner to the Colonial Secretary, 8 September 1944

Minister, in conveying this information to the British, stated that he knew that this suggestion came straight from Nahas. He added that King Ibn Sa'ud had also expressed his opposition to the participation of Nuri. The Iraqi Cabinet, with the full support of the Regent, decided, however, that they could take no account of the "advice" from Cairo and Jedda which, if accepted, would be "grievously insulting" to Nuri Pasha. It was decided, therefore, that the Iraqi delegation should be headed by the Prime Minister, assisted by the Minister for Foreign Affairs and Nuri Pasha.

Nuri Pasha was in fact no less influential out of office. His strong connections with the Iraqi Regent and his forceful personality made the new Iraqi Prime Minister eager to placate him. The change of government in Iraq had aroused the apprehensions of the Iraqi pan-Arabs. Hamdi al-Pachachi was eager to declare publicly that this change did not mean any cooling in the pan-Arab stand of Iraq, and that any other Iraqi leader would be no less keen on Arab union than Nuri Pasha.[1] The Iraqi Government suspected the hand of Nahas in the publicity given in the Egyptian press to the rumours about a Syrio–Iraqi agreement for the union of the two countries. The Iraqi Minister for Foreign Affairs, who was himself sceptical and cynical about the prospects of Arab union,[2] was to declare that Iraq had never thought of forming a large Arab state. He described these rumours as devoid of any grain of truth, adding that his country worked for Arab unity through political, economic, and cultural co-operation, and without infringement on the freedom and independence of any state.[3] The Iraqi Government were dismayed at the implication in the Egyptian press that the aim of Iraq was to exploit Syria and the Lebanon, and to secure a direct access route to the Mediterranean. They thought that this was probably instigated by Nahas, presumably because of his anger at the decision to appoint Nuri as a member in their delegation to the Alexandria meetings.[4]

This shows how highly charged were inter-Arab relations on the eve of the preparatory meeting. It is to the credit of Nahas Pasha that a meeting was possible in spite of all the difficulties and rivalries involved. Nuri's activities made Nahas more eager to secure the participation of Ibn Sa'ud, and to attempt to draw the Syrians and the Lebanese into Egypt's orbit.

---

[1] FO 371–39989: Statement by the Iraqi Prime Minister to the Reuters representative in Baghdad, published in the *Sawt al Ahali* newspaper of 14 July 1944

[2] FO 371–39990: Thompson (Baghdad) to Eden, 13 September 1944

[3] *Majallat al Rabita al-'Arabiya*, 19 August 1944: this statement was made to the correspondent of Reuters in Baghdad and was published by the Iraqi Embassy in Cairo in denial of the reports in the Egyptian press about the subject.

[4] FO 371–39989: Thompson to Eden, 10 August 1944 conveying a statement made to him by the Iraqi Minister for Foreign Affairs

THE PROCEEDINGS OF THE PREPARATORY COMMITTEE

The meetings of the Preparatory Committee started in Alexandria on 25 September 1944 under the chairmanship of Nahas Pasha. The opening session was attended by the Prime Ministers of Iraq, Transjordan, Syria, and Lebanon. The purpose of the meeting was defined earlier by Nahas as: to register the various points of view; to record points of agreement; and to discuss the date, the venue, and the agenda of the future Arab congress.

Nahas Pasha suggested in the first meeting that the delegates should circulate the minutes or a summary of their earlier talks with him, if they wished to suppress some parts. This was to cause the first tussle in the opening session. The Lebanese and the Iraqi delegates declared that they had nothing to hide and produced the minutes of their consultations with Nahas. Sa'adallah al-Jabri was apparently embarrassed in view of his remarks about the Maronites, and the need for closer co-operation with Lebanon in the absence of which Syria should regain the parts ceded to Lebanon in 1920. He finally said that he was a frank man, and would not conceal anything he had said. He then circulated the minutes of his talks with Nahas. Musa Mubarek, the head of the cabinet of the Lebanese President, said that, as the representative of the Lebanese President, who was a Maronite, he must protest against Al-Jabri's remarks. A reconciliation was finally patched up thanks to the intervention of Riad al-Sulh, and the clarifications of Al-Jabri.[1]

Riad al-Sulh then enquired whether the Egyptian delegation would also wish to state their views on the issues raised during the consultations. Nahas was still eager to maintain his role as a conciliator of the various points of view without compromising his position at that stage by committing himself to one side of the argument or to a new viewpoint. He stated, in reply, that he would confine himself, for the time being, to recording the views of the other Arab governments.

It was agreed in the first meeting that telegrams should be sent to Ibn Sa'ud and Imam Yehya entreating them to send delegates to participate

[1] FO 371–39991: Shone to the Foreign Office on 10 October 1944. Palace sources voiced to the British their criticism of Nahas' clumsy suggestion, which was embarrassing to the Syrians. King Farouq had subsequently met with the heads of the Syrian, Lebanese, and Transjordanian delegations in an attempt to ease the situation. Nahas Pasha, on his part, strongly objected, on constitutional grounds, to the King receiving and discussing political matters with the Arab delegates without the presence of the Egyptian Minister for Foreign Affairs. He was very much against any involvement by the anti-Wafdist Palace elements in the proceedings of the Committee. The King did, however, take every opportunity to show interest in the proceedings and several receptions were arranged by the Palace elements for the delegates. Riad al-Sulh stated later that King Farouq showed great sympathy for the Arab cause and brotherly inter-Arab co-operation, and great interest in Arab affairs. *Al Ahram*, 12 October 1944

in the subsequent meetings of the Committee. The Imam responded by sending a representative, who participated as an observer in the second meeting, held on 28 September, and who was later authorized by the Imam to take part as a full delegate in the final meeting. The Saudi delegate arrived in time to attend the third meeting, held on 1 October, to which the Palestine Arab representative was admitted for the first time.

Riad al-Sulh was eager right from the start to explain the attitude of his country. He was very much alive to the apprehensions of the Maronites with regard to any closer political union with the other Arab countries. He referred during the third meeting to the statement of the Maronite Patriarch to the effect that a central Arab union was logical, but not practical.[1] He then suggested that the Committee should start by discussing the issue of the independence of the Arab countries, since it was closely related to that of their union. He stressed that if the delegates were to agree to base their efforts on respect for the sovereignty and the independence of each state, the question of inter-Arab co-operation would be much easier to tackle.

Ahmed al-Hilali Pasha, the Egyptian Minister for Education, expressed disagreement with Al-Sulh. He thought that the Committee, rather than agreeing on independence as the basis and then discussing the details, should concentrate on the details, which would in itself define the basis of any future association. Sa'adallah al-Jabri agreed with Al-Hilali. He expressed the readiness of Syria to give up its sovereignty, and the wish that the other Arab states would do the same. He stated that there was nothing to prevent the Arab states from adopting similar policies and establishing a collective security system against aggression, of the sort embodied in the Treaty of Arab Brotherhood between Iraq, Saudi Arabia, and Yemen. He added that in view of the apprehensions of some states, it could be affirmed that the independence of each state would be respected and defended.

Riad al-Sulh, in reply, referred to the special position of Lebanon and stated that his country considered herself an Arab state, and had refused to conclude any agreement with France which would have meant the return of the mandate in another form. He added that the matter should be treated objectively, and that it should not be said that the attitude of Lebanon represented the only obstacle to Arab unity, since delegates of countries more deeply Arab than the Lebanon had stated that they would not favour political co-operation at present because of "certain circumstances". Al-Sulh was obviously referring

---

[1] The Maronite Patriarch was the first to protest against the Shutura agreement of 1 October 1943 for co-operation in economic and customs affairs with Syria. His protest, published in the press, caused much embarrassment to the newly elected Lebanese president and his Prime Minister. Bishara Khalil al-Khouri *Haqaiq Libnaniya*, vol. II, p. 98

to the attitude of Saudi Arabia in particular. Sheikh Yusuf Yassin, the Sa'udi delegate, saw no reason why a statement should not be issued affirming the independence of each of the participating states.[1]

In the fourth meeting, held on 2 October, Nahas defined the fields in which there was common agreement. These included all the non-political matters such as finance, agriculture, industry, communications, culture, passports, social and health affairs. It was decided to refer all these matters to subsidiary committees of experts, with a co-ordinating committee formed to formulate draft agreements in these fields for consideration by the Arab governments.

The discussion then turned to the more difficult question of political co-operation. All the delegates present ruled out the idea of a union with a central government. It was agreed, however, that an organization of Arab states should be established. A long discussion ensued on whether the decisions of this organization should be binding on the member states or not. This issue was of vital importance to the participant states, and especially Lebanon and Saudi Arabia. Most of the delegates were not in favour of any surrender of their countries' sovereignty in full or in part for the sake of evolving a stronger regional association. The idea of an organization with executive authority favoured during the consultations by Iraq, Transjordan, and Syria was therefore dropped. The idea of weighted representation of the member states in any future body, which would have given an advantage to Egypt and Iraq, was also rejected. The alternative was an organization whose decisions would be binding only on the states accepting them. Such an organization would be based on equal representation of the participant states. This form was found acceptable to all the delegates present with the exception of Sheikh Yusuf Yassin, who insisted that any discussion of political co-operation should be postponed until the circumstances changed.

Nahas then suggested a formula for an organization without an executive authority. This organization would be called the League of Arab States, and would be participated in by the independent Arab states which would wish to join. It would have a council in which the member states would be represented on an equal footing. The Council would supervise the implementation of agreements concluded between the member states. It would hold periodical meetings to discuss in general terms the affairs of the Arab countries, and would endeavour to strengthen inter-Arab ties and to co-ordinate the policies of the member states. The decisions of the Council would be binding on those who had accepted them except when a dispute occurred between two member states, in which case the decision of the Council would be binding.

---

[1] *Mahadhir Jalasat al Lajna al Tahdiriya Lil Mu'tamar al 'Arabi al 'Am*, Arab League publication, Cairo 1949, pp. 24–28

Nahas also suggested the formation of a subsidiary committee to prepare a draft of the statutes of the proposed organization, and to discuss relevant political questions.

The Syrian delegation preferred the use of the word "alliance", on the grounds that an alliance denotes a more comprehensive approach.[1] Nahas noted, however, that the word "League" was in fact stronger and more comprehensive. It was agreed, therefore, to adopt the name suggested by Nahas. Nuri Pasha then suggested that the decisions of the Council should be binding on those who accepted them except in issues related to the non-resort to force to settle inter-Arab disputes, the non-adoption of a policy detrimental to that of the other member states, and respect for the obligations aimed at the general good which were already binding most of the Arab states. It was decided to refer such matters to a political subsidiary committee composed of Iraqi, Syrian, and Lebanese representatives.

The subsidiary committee suggested a new addition to Nahas' formula. It proposed a provision to the effect that "in no case will the adoption of a foreign policy prejudicial to the policy of the League or of an individual member state be allowed". The Council of the League would intervene in every dispute which might lead to war between a member state of the League and any other member state or other power, so as to reconcile them. This provision was accepted by all the delegates with the exception of the Sa'udi and the Yemeni representatives, who withheld approval pending the receipt of the views of their governments.

Riad al-Sulh, while approving the proposed text, stated for the record that Lebanon was not at present, and would not be in the future, ready to enter into any treaty relations with any Great Power. He enquired whether her abstention from concluding a treaty with a foreign power with which most of the member states had contractual arrangements would mean that she followed a policy detrimental to that of the League. Nahas answered in the negative, on which Al-Sulh said that he was satisfied and wanted only to register this point. Al-Sulh was eager to counter the arguments of the Maronites and the French to the effect that the Arab unity talks were inspired by the British, and aimed at establishing a union under British domination. His assertion of his country's intention not to conclude treaties either with Britain or with France was in line with his warning during the

[1] Sa'adallah al-Jabri noted that the word "league" refers to some associations of countries very different from each other, like the members of the Pan-American union. Al-Hilali Pasha stated, however, that the word "alliance" has certain legal connotations and would cause misunderstanding which he was eager that the Committee should avoid, since some difficulties had already been caused by the use of the term "Arab unity" in the consultations, which idea was later ruled out because it was "impossible to achieve and because it infringes on the sovereignty and independence of each state". *Mahadhir* (5th session), op. cit., pp. 36–38

consultations about the necessity to guard against the use of an Arab association by any foreign power to secure her own ends in the area.[1]

As for Greater Syria, Nuri stated that he still believed that a union could be brought about if the peoples concerned desired it. He added that since all the delegates present had recognized the independence of Lebanon, that country could be excluded. He thought, however, that the issue could be left out for the present in view of the difficulties involved, including that of Palestine. He stated that if the peoples of the Syrian states desired to unite, or to have a central government, this would be their own business.[2] In this Nuri was obviously trying to isolate the issue of Greater Syria from that of a wider Arab association. An association of the sort envisaged by Nahas Pasha and approved by the other delegates would, therefore, not preclude a closer Syrian union, to the creation of which Nuri was to dedicate his efforts in the following months.

Jamil Mardam, the Syrian Minister for Foreign Affairs, stated that Syria hoped for the unity of all the Arab countries, and would welcome the creation of Greater Syria. He noted, however, that there was the case of Lebanon with her special circumstances, and that of Palestine and Transjordan, over which the mandate was still in existence. He was of the view that any discussion about Syrian unity would be premature until the mandate had been terminated and a settlement of the Palestine problem had been achieved. Abul Huda Pasha, the Prime Minister of Transjordan, noted that there was nothing to prevent Syria and Transjordan from uniting. Palestine could join them later if this proved possible. He suggested that contacts should start between his country and Syria with the purpose of discussing and agreeing on a form of union to be carried out at the appropriate time. Jamil Mardam replied that there were technical difficulties involved, since Transjordan was still under the mandate, which gave Britain a say in its foreign policy.

The suggestion made by Abul Huda Pasha was to encounter sharp opposition from the Sa'udi delegate. Sheikh Yusuf Yassin enquired whether the contacts suggested would aim at the establishment of a central government for Syria and Transjordan. Abul Huda replied that the aim would be to prepare for unity or co-operation. An awkward situation developed, with Sheikh Yusuf insisting that his question should be answered, since his country had recognized Syria as an independent

---

[1] Al-Sulh was obviously referring to Nuri's suggestion about the binding nature of the Council's resolution in relation to the respect of the international obligations of most of the member states "based on the general good". The acceptance of this suggestion would have meant a recognition of British treaties with Iraq, Egypt, Transjordan, and an admission that they were for the general good of the Arabs, thus implying some kind of commitment of the members of the League to a close and friendly relation with Britain.

[2] *Mahadhir*, p. 48

republic and would be interested to know of any possible future change in her constitution. Nuri stressed that this was a matter of concern only to the peoples of Syria and Transjordan. This was hardly satisfying to Sheikh Yusuf. Nahas Pasha supported Sheikh Yusuf in his argument. He argued that any future union between Transjordan and Syria was a matter of interest to the other Arab countries. Some clarification was therefore needed in view of the fact that a union with a central government had been ruled out by the Committee. Jamil Mardam stressed, to the satisfaction of Sheikh Yusuf, that the Syrians favoured the retention of their republican regime.

Jamil Mardam then expressed the readiness of Syria to end the old dispute over the annexation of some Syrian parts to Lebanon in 1920. He suggested a provision stating that the Arab countries represented in the Committee affirmed their respect for the independence and sovereignty of Lebanon within her present boundaries. This was approved by all the delegates present.[1] It was welcomed by Riad al-Sulh, who had committed himself earlier to the preservation of the full independence of Lebanon, and who asserted more than once during the discussions that this should be the basis of any future co-operation between his country and the other Arab states. The other delegates showed understanding for the special circumstances of Lebanon and the pressures being exerted by the Maronites against Al-Sulh's Arab policy. They were eager to strengthen his position *vis-à-vis* the opposition, and to remove the old Christian fears of Muslim domination. This eagerness to accommodate the Lebanese was in fact a limiting factor. A Lebanese delegate was chosen to participate in the Drafting Political Sub-Committee to ensure that any scheme evolved would have a fair chance of acceptance by the majority of the Lebanese public.

When the Committee resumed its meetings on 4 October, they had before them an Iraqi proposal calling for the establishment of two Arab propaganda offices, in England and the United States. Nuri Pasha was, of all the Arab leaders, much concerned about the implications of Zionist propaganda, in the United States in particular. He realized that American interest in the area and her role in world politics were likely to increase after the war. He had urged the Iraqi Cabinet as far back as 1940 to establish high level diplomatic representation in the United States, and urged the other Arab countries to do the same. Ibn Sa'ud did not respond at that time to Nuri's initiative, on the grounds that the Middle East was primarily the responsibility of Britain. He was against the encouragement of an active American role in the area at that stage. The British supported Nuri's moves in their eagerness to ensure that due regard was given in the United States to the Arab

[1] *Mahadhir*, p. 51

side of the argument, and to the difficulties facing them in the area.[1] The Iraqi proposal was approved by the committee in principle, and was referred to a special sub-committee to study its immediate implementation.

There remained the thorny question of Palestine, which the delegates were anxious to avoid discussing in their earlier meetings. Musa al-'Alami was invited to explain the situation, and to state the views of the Palestine Arabs. His speech, delivered in a tone of quiet melancholy and suppressed passion, moved all the delegates deeply.[2] He stated that the White Paper policy was being neglected by H.M.G. Jewish immigration had been extended beyond the deadline date of March 1944. Land sale regulations were not being carried out. The Jews controlled most of the fertile lands and it would not be long before Arab Palestine was virtually wiped out. He added that negotiations were going on between the British and the Jews for the partition or the cantonization of Palestine, on the basis of numerical equality, with the possibility of a Jewish majority in the future. There was also an alternative of keeping Palestine as it was, provided that unlimited Jewish immigration were allowed until the Arabs had only a nominal majority of several thousands. The intention, he stated, was to impose one of these solutions at the end of the war. He then suggested the establishment by the Arab countries of a general Arab national fund to assist in keeping the lands then owned by the Arabs from Jewish hands. He also suggested that the Committee should send an Arab delegation to London, Washington, and Moscow to explain the dangers of the new British policy and to remove all misconceptions about the laxity of the Arab countries with regard to the Palestine problem.[3]

The second suggestion was not found acceptable to the Committee. It was decided to include the views of the participant states in an annex[4] on Palestine. The annex stated that Palestine constituted an important part of the Arab nation. Any infringement on the rights of the Palestine Arabs would prejudice peace and stability in the Arab

---

[1] Mahmud al Durra *Al Harb al Iraqiya al Biritaniya*, p. 168; and FO 371–40283, the Annual Report on Saudi Arabia for 1943: Jordan to Eden, 15 February 1944

[2] The Syrian Prime Minister wept three times, and even the Egyptians, who until then had shown some coolness towards Al-'Alami, were moved to enthusiasm. The choice of Al-'Alami as the representative of the Palestine Arabs helped to ease the difficulty of dealing with the Palestine problem within the Committee, since, in spite of his persuasive arguments and zeal, he was the most moderate of the Palestine Arab leaders. He accepted the moderate resolution taken on the Palestine issue and did not sign the Protocol since he was not a full delegate like the others. FO 371–39991: from an account by an unofficial observer included in Weekly Appreciation Summary: Shone to Eden, 24 October 1944

[3] *Mahadhir Jalasat*, pp. 58–66

[4] This was embodied in the Protocol of Alexandria as a special resolution concerning Palestine. The text was proposed by Nahas Pasha and was approved by the Committee.

World. It expressed the view of the Committee that the Arabs had every right to demand the prompt implementation of British pledges regarding the stopping of Jewish immigration and land purchases. This, if realized, would ensure peace and stability in the area. It registered the approval of the Committee for the proposed establishment of an Arab National Fund. The proposal was referred to the sub-committee for financial and economic affairs for further study. Nahas was authorized to continue his efforts for the release of Jamal al-Husseini, Amin al-Tamimi, and the other interned Palestine Arab leaders.

At their last meeting, on 7 October, the delegates had before them what came to be known as the Protocol of Alexandria. It was drafted by the Drafting Political Sub-Committee, in the light of the previous discussions. It included two special resolutions, regarding Palestine and the respect for the independence of Lebanon within her present boundaries. The Sa'udi delegate suggested that the Protocol should not be made public until his government and the Yemeni Government had been informed of its contents. He feared lest the refusal of Saudi Arabia would, if the Protocol was published, give the impression of disagreement between the Arab states, thus giving rise to rumours which might have an adverse effect in Saudi Arabia. He was of the view that the Committee was of a preparatory nature and was convened to conduct confidential discussions whose results would have to be submitted to the General Arab Congress. He stressed that his country had only agreed to participate in its meetings on this basis.

The Sa'udi representative was in fact placed in a most awkward position. Neither he nor King Ibn Sa'ud had anticipated that the discussions of the Committee would evolve any tangible scheme for Arab co-operation. He was authorized by the King to attend, but his hands were tied and he did not make any significant contribution to the discussions within the Committee. He kept the King informed of the proceedings and the suggested formation of an Arab League. Ibn Sa'ud, in his instructions to his delegate, insisted that the establishment of such a League was premature, and could only be considered after the end of the war. He strongly admonished Sheikh Yusuf for appearing in his telegrams to favour co-operation in non-political matters, attributing this to his being influenced by his contacts with the other delegates. He reminded him that the other participants were ministers whose stay in office would depend on the success of the Committee. He refused to be bound even by any agreement regarding economic and cultural co-operation because "other people have economic aims and intentions". In his last telegram, Ibn Sa'ud instructed his delegate not to bind him to anything "even by one word", and not to sign anything. He insisted that everything should be referred back to him. He stressed that he did not wish to be drawn into participation with the other Arab states, and wanted always to be "far from them". Sheikh Yusuf did not find any guidance from the British, who stressed that this was a matter for the Arabs themselves to tackle. The British representatives in Egypt had in fact absented themselves from Alexandria for fear that it might be rumoured that they had interfered in the deliberations of the Committee. Ibn Sa'ud remained adamant, in spite of Sheikh Yusuf's statements that the proposed formation of the Arab League had been approved by all the other Arab delegates, who had also favoured economic and cultural inter-Arab co-operation.[1]

The Yemeni delegate was authorized by the Imam to participate as a full delegate only in the final meeting. He did not make any contribution to the discussions, and was instructed not to bind the Imam to anything until the whole matter had been referred back to him. The proposed statement accompanying the Protocol was therefore modified to indicate that the Protocol was signed and approved by the heads of the Syrian, Transjordanian, Iraqi, Lebanese, and Egyptian delegations, and that the Yemeni and Sa'udi delegates had deferred approval pending reference to their respective sovereigns.

Nahas Pasha, on the other hand, was eager to see his efforts, conducted over the last fourteen months, come to fruition. His relations with the Palace were as tense as ever. The removal of the Axis threat from the Middle East was followed by Allied successes on all fronts. The end of the war was finally in sight. British reasons for ensuring his stay in office on account of the war were not as strong as they had been before. He realized that, if the Committee meetings were to end without any tangible results, the Arab governments might have second thoughts about the whole issue. The failure of his initiative would be a blow to his prestige, both in Egypt and in the Arab World. This would give the chance to Nuri Pasha to push forward his own scheme for the union of Greater Syria with Iraq, which would be disadvantageous to Egypt's leading role in the area.

He was therefore anxious to see the meetings come out with something concrete which would commit the Arab leaders in front of their own peoples. In order to overcome last minute qualms and hesitations, he ordered open contact with the Egyptian broadcasting station from the conference hall at the end of the last meeting. He started reading the Protocol and the accompanying statement, modifying or omitting some words as suggested by the delegates as he went on. He noted later that he wanted to put the Protocol on record officially, and thus to make it a *fait accompli* for the other Arab states.[2]

The Protocol was a mere statement of intentions which left the details to be studied later by a subsidiary committee. It was rightly

---

[1] FO 371–39991: for the text of the telegrams exchanged between Ibn Sa'ud and Sheikh Yusuf. Jordan to FO, 12 October 1944

[2] Muhamad al-Tahir *Zalam al Sijn*, p. 573 recounts a statement made to him by Nahas after his ousting from office.

described as "a strongly popular document", which appealed constantly, especially in its preamble, to Arab public opinion, the Arab peoples, and the Arab nation.[1] The main purpose of the League was defined as: to consolidate inter-Arab ties, and to direct the Arab countries towards the welfare of their peoples and the realization of their aspirations. The membership was confined to the independent Arab states which would wish to join. The object of the League was to co-ordinate political plans, to protect the independence and sovereignty of the member states by suitable means against any aggression, and to supervise, in a general way, the affairs and interests of the Arab countries. It was stipulated, moreover, that in no case would the adoption of a foreign policy which might be prejudicial to the policy of the League, or to an individual member state, be allowed. The decisions of the Council of the League were to be made binding on those who had accepted them, except in cases where a dispute between two member states was referred by the disputants to the Council. In this case, the two states concerned would have given their prior agreement to the intervention of the Council on the understanding that they would be bound by its decision. If one of the two states chose not to refer the dispute to the Council, no decision would be taken on the issue, or if taken, would not be binding. It was stipulated, moreover, that in no case would resort to force to settle a dispute between any two member states be allowed. The role of the Council was therefore that of arbitration when a dispute was referred to it by the parties, and of conciliation in other cases.

The Protocol expressed the wish of the signatory states to co-operate closely in all non-political fields. It provided for the formation of a sub-committee of experts to devise draft regulations for co-operation in these fields. A Political Sub-Committee was also to be formed to prepare a draft of the statutes of the Council of the League. A significant clause was added expressing the hope that the Arab states would be able in the future to consolidate this step by other steps, "especially if post-war events should result in institutions which bind various powers more closely together".[2]

The scheme embodied in the Protocol fell far short of union or federation. No mention of Arab unity was made in the Protocol. The emphasis throughout was on Arab co-operation, and no surrender of sovereignty was envisaged. By expressing the hope that further steps

---

[1] Cecil Hourani "The Arab League in Perspective" in *The Middle East Journal* vol. I, no. 2, April 1947, p. 131

[2] Nuri Pasha told Lord Killearn later that this section, which was proposed by himself, envisaged the possibility of the accession of other states such as Turkey, Persia, and Afghanistan, and the eventual integration of all the Middle Eastern States in a regional bloc forming part of any future world organization. FO 371–45236–E840/3/65: Lord Killearn to FO, 23 January 1945

should be taken in the future in the direction of closer inter-Arab ties,[1] it was implied that the scheme embodied in the Protocol represented only the first step. It was left to the Arab governments, if they so wished, to evolve stronger forms of association in the future. This was to be the subject of prolonged discussions later on within the Sub-Committee. The Iraqi and the Transjordanian delegates who were behind the inclusion of this provision did not want the formation of the League to preclude them from further pursuit of their schemes of Greater Syria and Fertile Crescent unity.

The Protocol included two special resolutions, on Palestine and Lebanon. Reference had been made earlier to the provisions of the resolution on Palestine, which avoided any denunciation of British policy and confined itself to the support of the rights of the Palestine Arabs.[2] The resolution on Lebanon followed the same lines as the text proposed by Jamil Mardam. It stressed the respect of the participant states for the independence and the sovereignty of Lebanon within her existing frontiers, "which the governments of the above states have already recognized in consequence of Lebanon's adoption of an independent policy, which the government of that country announced in its programme of 7 October 1943, unanimously approved by the Lebanese Chamber of Deputies". The implicitly conditional nature of this assertion was subject to some controversy in Lebanon. Some Lebanese newspapers concluded from the wording of the resolution that this guarantee would be made subject to nullification if a subsequent Lebanese government came to adopt a policy at variance with that embodied in the programme to which the Protocol referred. Riad al-Sulh was to explain to the Lebanese parliament that the phrase "in consequence of" was essentially chronological in import, registering the fact that the recognition by the Arab governments of Lebanese independence had come after the adoption by the parliament of an Arab-oriented policy for Lebanon. He added that this should not detract from the acknowledgement by the Arab states of the attainment by Lebanon of internal harmony and of triumph over her former internal bipolarity as a result of her adoption of an independent and Arab-oriented policy.[3] The conditional nature of this resolution went

---

[1] The inclusion of this provision in the Protocol was in fact suggested by Nuri Pasha who wanted to leave the door open for closer and stronger bonds in the future.

[2] The Correspondent of *The Jerusalem Post* noted that the striking thing about the Palestine resolution was its support for the White Paper policy. He added, however, that, confronted with numerous difficulties, the talks were shifted to the Palestine issue, on which complete agreement could be achieved more easily. *The Jerusalem Post*, 10 October 1944

[3] Fayez A. Sayegh *Arab unity: Hope and Fulfilment*, New York 1958, p. 128 (footnote) referring to an article in the Lebanese newspaper *Al Amal* of 16 October 1944, and the statement of Al-Sulh in Parliament on 15 October 1944 included in *Ad-Diar* newspaper of 16 October. The word used in the Arabic text was "ba'd", literally

unnoticed during the discussions inside the Committee. It was the sense of the Syrian statements, both in their earlier consultations with Nahas and in the preparatory Committee, that they would only recognize and respect the independence of Lebanon within her present frontiers if the Lebanese Government would continue to uphold its independent and Arab-oriented line of policy. The text of the resolution, as devised by Jamil Mardam, implicitly embodied this stipulation. No objections were raised by Riad al-Sulh, who was rather impressed and expressed his thanks to Jamil and the other delegates.

The Protocol of Alexandria was a document of great significance. It was brought about mainly as a result of the strong desire of the Syrians and the Lebanese for an Arab association to consolidate their independence against French designs. This was accompanied by the eagerness of Nahas to ensure the success of his initiative in order to compensate for the slump in the Wafd's popularity following the "Black Book" incident. It was an exercise in the art of the possible. The discussions were confined to the realm of the practical, and avoided rhetoric, recriminations, and wishful thinking. Minor frictions over Greater Syria and Lebanese independence were smoothed out in a spirit of mutual understanding and co-operation. The fact that the Protocol was formulated and approved in the course of eight meetings, over a period of less than two weeks, was of great significance. This was in itself to the credit of the Arab leaders present, and of Nahas Pasha in particular, who assumed an air of detachment and objectivity, and who was able to devise a scheme acceptable to most of the participant states. Of all the Arab leaders, Nahas was the one most fitted for that role, in spite of the fact that at times he was subjected to criticism by the Sa'udis, the Iraqis, and the Transjordanians. With the Syrian delegates declaring their readiness to go all the way in favour of closer Arab unity, there was not much room for bickering about the rather modest scheme proposed in the Protocol. The concentration on general principles, leaving the details for further study by specialized sub-committees, avoided any prolongation of the meetings over issues approved in principle. The Protocol devised the structural basis of the future League. Most of the principles it embodied were similar to those included in the Covenant of the League of Nations. The positive addition was the provision disallowing the adoption, by any state, of a policy which might be prejudicial to that of the League or of an individual member state.[1]

---

meaning "after", translated here as "in consequence of". As such it had a chronological connotation as explained by Al-Sulh, but it also carried an implicit conditional meaning.

[1] Bishara al-Khouri, the Lebanese President, expressed his objections to this provision of the Protocol. He noted that although it did not infringe on sovereignty and independence and was included in many contractual agreements between other states,

The successful conclusion of the Alexandria meetings and the decision to establish an Arab League came as a surprise to the British, who had doubted the ability of the Arab states to evolve any practical scheme for political co-operation. Robin Hankey, of the Foreign Office, was to state that the scheme approved in the Protocol went "very much further than anything we have hitherto been led to expect as likely to emerge from the Arab unity conference". He admitted that the scheme was still very vague, but noted that H.M.G. would have to reckon with periodical meetings of the Arab states, which would be able to voice authoritative views on questions of interest to the Arabs. He was sceptical, however, about the chances of agreement over the details of the scheme. The resolution on Palestine was, in his view, "pretty mildly worded" compared with what might have been expected. He stated, however, that it was "firm", and he described the reference to the pledges embodied in the White Paper as constituting acquired rights for the Arabs as "awkward". He thought that if Ibn Sa'ud sought the views of H.M.G. he should be advised to sign the Protocol, since the British would not derive any advantage from "minor wrecking tactics at this stage", and since there was nothing the King need fear from these developments.[1]

Lord Moyne, the Minister of State in Cairo, considered the results of the Alexandria meeting as marking a "considerable advance in

---

it was liable in Lebanon, because of its special circumstances, to give rise to "real or imagined suspicions". He therefore agreed with Al-Sulh and Taqla, his Foreign Minister, that it should be deleted from the final text of the Pact. Bishara Khalil al-Khouri *Haqaiq Libnaniya*, Vol II, pp. 109–10

[1] FO 371–39990: minute by Robin Hankey, 10 October 1944. *The Times*' correspondent in Alexandria stated that "a far greater measure of agreement than expected" had come out of the preparatory meeting. This was also the view of the correspondent of the *Jerusalem Post*. His remark that the Palestine issue had proved a useful subject on which all could agree without cost or danger to themselves was not altogether correct, since the issue was shelved for a while and discussed only after all the other provisions of the Protocol had been worked out. The participation of Musa al-'Alami, and the discussion of the Palestine problem were, as explained in this chapter, subject to serious disagreement between the Arab leaders, and between them and the British. The Zionists were in fact very apprehensive of the creation of the Arab League, and thought that it was a British scheme executed by Sir Walter Smart and Brigadier Clayton, who was then attached to the Office of the Minister of State in Cairo, with the object of provoking a holy war against the Jews in Palestine. These allegations were far from true, and the agreement to establish the League came as a surprise to the British. Christopher Sykes noted that Smart's role was "quite the opposite of what Zionist propaganda maintains". Smart told him that he was opposed to Mr Eden making a public statement of sympathy for Arab aspirations in unity in 1941 and had continuously advised against it, as he believed that it might give encouragement to extremists. Clayton, Sykes noted, was no T. E. Lawrence, and the formation of a warlike alliance of Arab states would have been quite beyond him. *The Times*, 9 October 1944; *The Jerusalem Post*, 10 October, 1944. *Walter Smart: by some of his Friends*, Sussex (mid.) (St Antony's Private Papers)

constructive political thinking" on the part of the Arab states. The Protocol, he noted, looked to the future, not to the past. Regionalism was "in the air" and it was noteworthy that it should be the newly developed Arab states who had taken the lead in attempting to work out a practical scheme of regional co-operation. He added that the Arab states were willing to co-operate with Britain on the basis of independence and free association. He warned at the same time that the pursuit by H.M.G. of any policies unacceptable to the majority of these states would involve the risk of the whole orientation, which was now friendly towards Britain, being changed to some other direction. He singled out the Palestine problem as a case in point in this regard.[1]

Terence Shone, the British Minister in Egypt, considered it "imprudent" to ignore the fact that the results of the Alexandria meeting constituted a step forward towards the political solidarity of what he called the "Egypto-Arab world" against European encroachments. He considered it possible, however, for the Arab solidarity movement to be conciliatory towards British interests in communications and oil provided H.M.G. were able to adapt themselves to the new conditions quickly enough.[2]

Sir Kinahan Cornwallis was also highly appreciative of the results of the Alexandria meetings. He endorsed Lord Moyne's view that the aim of the meeting seemed to have been to unite the Arab World in co-operation with Britain. This was stressed to him by Nuri Pasha and the Iraqi Minister for Foreign Affairs. This, in his view, meant that the Arabs had responded "wholeheartedly and practically" to Mr Eden's statements of support for Arab unity. He warned that any divergence from the White Paper policy would confront H.M.G. with the hostility, not only of the Palestine Arabs, but also of all the signatories of the Alexandria Protocol. He added that the Arab states considered a solution to the Palestine problem on the basis of strictly limited Jewish immigration, like the guarantee of Syrian and Lebanese independence, as "an integral part of their scheme for Arab unity". Any threat to Palestine, Syria, or Lebanon would unite "even those to whom the ideal of Arab unity means little or nothing at all".

Sir Kinahan stated, moreover, that the results of the Alexandria meeting, certainly so far as Iraq was concerned, presented H.M.G. with a crisis. If the British were ready to support the scheme proposed, fully and openly, and "to respond to the invitation which has been given to us to act as the guide and mentor of the Arab World", their interests would be safeguarded more surely than ever before, and a period of stability and prosperity would start. If, on the other hand, H.M.G. were not willing or able to do so, then, whatever the advantages the

---

[1] FO 371–39991: Lord Moyne to Eden, 1 November 1944
[2] FO 371–39991: Shone to Eden, 10 October 1944

British might reap elsewhere, they would suffer in the Middle East "a blow resulting in unrest, violence and confusion".[1]

Mr A. Kirkbride, the British Resident in Amman, drew attention to the difficulties involved in the participation by Transjordan in the proposed Arab League, in view of that country's obligations under the mandate and the 1928 agreement with Britain. He thought, however, that it would be "unwise" to try to prevent Transjordan from joining the League as long as her government respected her obligations towards H.M.G. This was endorsed by the Foreign and the Colonial Offices. The Colonial Office, in their instructions to the British Resident, stated, however, that the Transjordanian Government should be careful not to accept any resolutions of the Council of the League which might run counter to British policies "whether with regard to Palestine or elsewhere". The Transjordanian Government was also to be requested not to submit disputes to the League's Council without the approval of H.M.G.[2] This vindicated the remarks made by Jamil Mardam during the discussion of the issue of Greater Syria referred to earlier.

THE ALEXANDRIA PROTOCOL: A SEQUEL

Nahas Pasha was dismissed from office on 8 October 1944, one day after the conclusion of the Alexandria meetings. This was followed on 14 October by a change of government in Transjordan and Syria. These changes were due to considerations of internal politics, and had been withheld for some time pending the conclusion of the Preparatory Committee meetings. Coming in rapid succession following the signature of the Protocol, they gave rise to apprehensions in the Arab World. German propaganda accused the British of engineering them to sabotage the Arab unity movement.[3] Of all of them, the ousting of

---

[1] FO 371–39991: Sir Kinahan Cornwallis to Eden, 5 November 1944. The Special Correspondent of *The Times*, in two articles entitled "Rebuilding the Middle East", called for a fresh examination of the bases of British policy in the area in response to the new situation. He considered the Middle East as "the nodal point" in any international security system and the main testing ground for the new world order. He noted the most disastrous failure of the Western powers during the inter-war period to assume moral leadership of the area, and considered any attempt to restore the pre-war system as the surest way to a breakdown whose international effects would be incalculable. He stressed the necessity of building a stable political society in the Middle East which would co-operate in maintaining British interests "because they are its own interests also". The Middle Eastern peoples, he stated, should not be thwarted by the divisive pressures of foreign political and economic interests which should co-operate in assisting these peoples to develop their society and economy until it had been fully integrated with the outside world. *The Times* of 30 November and 1 December 1944

[2] FO 371–39991: Kirkbride to Colonial Office, 11 November 1944

[3] FO 371–39991: Lord Moyne to Eden, 1 November 1944

Nahas Pasha from office in such an abrupt manner, and at a time when most of the Arab delegates were still in Egypt, was the most sensational. The fact of the matter was that relations between King Farouq and his Prime Minister had reached the point of no return some time before. The King found his chance at last to dismiss him. This was offered by the absence of Lord Killearn, who was then in South Africa, and by the favourable turn in the war developments which made the British less insistent on the retention of Nahas in office.

The Palace and opposition elements in Egypt were incensed at Nahas' attempt to compensate for his loss of popularity, as a result of the charges of corruption made against his government, by intensifying his pan-Arab activities. Nahas' exclusion of the non-Wafdist experts on Arab affairs, such as 'Azzam and 'Allouba, and insistence on having the field all to himself, increased their antagonism. They decided, therefore, and in spite of their earlier advocacy of close Arab co-operation, to adopt a rather cynical and sceptical attitude towards the Arab unity consultations. They were to change this attitude as soon as they were installed in office. Dr Ahmed Maher, Nahas' successor to the Premiership, embodied in his letter of acceptance a pledge to put the policy adopted in Alexandria above any other considerations, and to raise Arab policy from the local to the national non-partisan level. This was demonstrated by his retention in office of Dr Muhammad Salah ul-Din, the Wafdist Under-Secretary of State for Foreign Affairs, whose efforts during the consultations and the Alexandria meetings were commended by the Arab delegates.[1] Makram 'Ubaid, the author of the "Black Book", who was released from internment and appointed Minister of Finance in the new Cabinet, declared that he was for Arab co-operation, and that what had been achieved so far was only "a short and a small step towards the greater ideal".[2]

The publication of the Protocol made it extremely difficult in fact for any new government, whether in Egypt or in the other Arab countries, to retract their approval for a scheme which, modest as it was, commanded the wide support of the Arab public. Both Faris al-Khouri and Samir al-Rifai', the new Premiers in Syria and Transjordan, made strong public statements affirming their determination to follow up the steps taken in Alexandria.[3]

There remained the major problems of securing the signature of Saudi Arabia and Yemen, for which purpose the meeting of the

---

[1] FO 371–39991: Nuri's statement to Shone on 8 November 1944

[2] *Al-Muqattam*, 10 October 1944. Makram stated also that Nahas used to laugh at him when he used to call in 1930 for Arab co-operation, and that he had only started to play an active role in Arab affairs to make the Egyptians forget their internal problems.

[3] *Al-Ahram*, 17 October 1944

Political Subsidiary Committee was put off for some months. Ibn Sa'ud had failed in his attempts either to secure the postponement of the Alexandria meeting, or to exclude all political matters from its discussions. The decision of the other Arab delegates, including his old friends in Syria, to establish an Arab League faced him with a *fait accompli*. His completely negative and blunt instructions to his delegate reflected his dismay at the turn of events.

The new Egyptian Government were eager to secure the King's signature of the Protocol, a task which was entrusted to 'Abdul Rahman 'Azzam,[1] the newly appointed Minister Plenipotentiary in charge of Arab affairs in the Foreign Ministry. 'Azzam was appointed Amir al-Haj for that year to enable him to visit Saudi Arabia and to meet Ibn Sa'ud. In the meantime, King Farouq sought a meeting with Ibn Sa'ud, who agreed to meet him at some place on the Red Sea coast of Saudi Arabia.

Ibn Sa'ud's first reaction to the news of the visit of 'Azzam was completely negative. He conveyed to the British his refusal to take part in any discussions on Arab unity. He argued that some provisions of the Protocol were not suitable for application in Saudi Arabia, whose system of government was based on Islamic law. There were, moreover, "interests at play behind the scene secretly working for their own ambitions and aims". He was not ready to assume obligations which he could not fulfil. He was aware, at the same time, of the fact that his refusal would place him in a delicate position and subject him to hostile propaganda. He therefore proposed to suggest to 'Azzam an alternative plan for Arab co-operation which included the conclusion of an alliance and a multi-lateral treaty of friendship and good-neighbourliness between the Arab countries. If a dispute arose, or a state failed to honour her obligations, the other Arab states would endeavour to advise the offending party to fulfil these obligations. If it refused, it should be treated as an enemy by all these states.[2]

The British were rather perturbed at Ibn Sa'ud's attitude, which they attributed to his distrust of Nuri and of Amir 'Abdullah, and to his fears of the formation of a northern Arab bloc directed against him. His alternative scheme was found "altogether unsuitable". His reference to the possibility of treating any Arab state as an enemy contrasted unfavourably, in their view, with the provision in the Protocol disallowing any use of force for the settlement of inter-Arab disputes. Jordan was of the view that the King's proposals contained a "veiled threat" to any country imposing an unacceptable settlement in Palestine, and could be used to further the claims of any Arab country to greater autonomy. These proposals were seen as unlikely to induce the

---

[1] 'Azzam was son-in-law of Khalid al-Qarqani, the Libyan nationalist who was then an adviser to Ibn Sa'ud.

[2] FO 371–39991: Jordan to Eden, 30 November 1944

other Arab countries to abandon the Protocol. The choice before Ibn Sa'ud was seen as one between participation in the Cairo talks, which was favoured by the Foreign Office, and refusal to take part, in which case the discussions would proceed without his participation. He was therefore told that, while H.M.G. considered him the best judge of the way in which his interests would be affected by the Protocol, they would only observe that, according to their information, the Protocol had been well received in the Arab World, and there was a widespread desire for proceeding with the more detailed discussions in this regard. If these discussions were to take place, H.M.G. would "greatly hope" that he would be able to participate, in order that he could guide them on the right lines. He could in the forthcoming discussions with 'Azzam and Farouq find a satisfactory solution for some of the points causing his apprehensions. The difficulty regarding Islamic law in application in his country could be surmounted by a reservation. He was told, moreover, that the prohibition of any use of force embodied in the Protocol was more appropriate for inclusion in a document whose object was to stress the feelings of unity and brotherhood between the Arab states.[1]

This positive British advice did much to mitigate the King's opposition to the Protocol. The ground was therefore prepared when 'Azzam arrived in Saudi Arabia in December 1944, during the pilgrimage season. He carried with him three letters to Ibn Sa'ud, from King Farouq, his Prime Minister, and the Minister for Foreign Affairs, all entreating him to sign the Protocol. He was given the necessary assurances by 'Azzam, who had several meetings with him late in December and early in January. The King was finally prevailed upon, and authorized Sheikh Yusuf Yassin to sign the Protocol on 7 January 1945. He also informed the Imam of Yemen of his decision. The signature of the Imam was secured on 5 February 1945. 'Azzam was to express his thanks to Jordan for the part played by H.M.G. in persuading the King to sign the protocol and to co-operate with the other Arab states in the matter. He added that it was doubtful whether he would have succeeded in his mission had it not been for the positive British advice, of which he had learnt from Ibn Sa'ud. The King's main preoccupation at present, 'Azzam noted, was to enter into close alliance with Egypt to counter Hashimite designs.[2]

---

[1] FO 371–39991–E7636/41/65
[2] FO 371–45235: Statement by 'Azzam to Jordan on 5 January 1945

Chapter Eight

The Formulation of the Pact of the Arab League 1945

The signature of the Alexandria Protocol was followed, two days later, by the enunciation of the Dumbarton Oaks Proposals, which provided for the existence, side by side with the future world organization, of regional agencies and arrangements. Like the Proposals, the Protocol was a statement of general principles which left the details for further study by the representatives of the countries concerned. The Proposals were conveyed to the Arab delegates assembled in Cairo in February 1945 to formulate the Pact of the League. They were taken into account during the discussions and helped to familiarize the delegates with the main trends of world thought on international organization. The establishment of the League was, in this sense, a move with the times, and a step in the right direction.

More than four months elapsed between the conclusion of the Alexandria talks and the start of the meetings of the Political Subsidiary Committee. The most significant development during this short period was the emergence of a Sa'udi-Egyptian bloc, to which Syria and Lebanon were attracted. This marked the beginning of a serious polarization of the Arab World. Egypt, whose involvement in Arab affairs was a relatively recent phenomenon, began to be drawn into inter-Arab feuds and rivalries.

Ibn Sa'ud was very much upset at that time by Nuri's activities in Syria, and he had his fears of a British attempt to settle the Palestine problem through the union of Greater Syria, an idea which was then being mooted in the British press. He realized that Egypt would not relish the prospect of Hashimite hegemony over the Levant, a situation which would undermine her leading role in the area. He also realized that Egypt, with her larger population, wealth, development, and historical connections with Syria and Lebanon, would stand a better chance of attracting these two states into her orbit. He therefore decided to try to join forces with Egypt, and to draw her to his side in his old conflict with the Hashimites. He promptly responded to King Farouq's suggestion that they should meet somewhere on the Red Sea coast of Saudi Arabia. The meeting took place in Radwi on 24 January

1945. The visit of King Farouq, as it was emphasized in the official statements, was a personal one, in which no government official except 'Azzam accompanied the King. The visit was described by King Farouq as "a great success from all points of view". The two monarchs agreed that they should consult with each other freely and frankly on all questions of interest to the Arabs.[1]

This was followed in February by a visit paid by Shukri al-Qwatli to Saudi Arabia and Egypt, and by the meeting of the three Arab rulers in Fayoum on 16 February 1945. The official communiqué issued by the Palace in Egypt stated that the three rulers had consulted on matters related to Arab unity, and that their discussions were expected to have a great impact on the history of the Arab World. Shukri al-Qwatli made a very important speech soon after his return from Egypt, in which he reiterated his country's determination to preserve her independence. He added that his government would welcome the union of Greater Syria only if the new united state had a republican regime with Damascus as its capital, and if no Zionist infiltration was allowed into its territory.[2]

The Hashimite rulers of Iraq and Transjordan were annoyed at these developments. Amir 'Abdullah spoke "in rather bitter terms" about "the growing confraternity" between Egypt and Saudi Arabia. He expressed his fears that this might lead, on the demise of Ibn Sa'ud, to Egyptian domination of Saudi Arabia. He asked the Iraqi Regent to visit him without delay. The Regent, accompanied by Nuri Pasha, visited Transjordan, where they had talks with the Amir in Al-Shawna on 5 February 1945. This led to press reports which described the meeting as a "Hashimite conference" designed to concert policies on Arab affairs.[3] Nuri, on the other hand, attributed Ibn Sa'ud's moves

---

[1] Ahmed Maher Pasha, the Egyptian Prime Minister, was opposed to the visit, but King Farouq insisted on going to Saudi Arabia. This was in fact the first visit by an Egyptian monarch to that country. Farouq said that he had been "immensely impressed" by Ibn Sa'ud, who was also impressed by Farouq. Ibn Sa'ud stated later that he had advised Farouq to put his trust in God and then in H.M.G., and not to place great reliance on his ministers and advisers, many of whom, like Nahas, had their own particular axe to grind. Farouq had therefore got some encouragement for his autocratic tendencies from another absolute ruler, and hence was his admiration for Ibn Sa'ud. FO 371–45552: Lord Killearn to Eden, 8 February 1945, and Jordan to Eden, 2 February 1945

[2] It is no wonder then that when Al-Qwatli visited Iraq on 10 March 1945 his reception there was lukewarm, with Nuri absenting himself from any function connected with the visit. FO 371–45542–Weekly Appreciation Summary, 28 February 1945 and 45553–E278/5/89

[3] Samir al-Rifai', the Transjordanian Prime Minister, tried to deny these press reports, which had aroused some apprehensions in Syria, while the Iraqis were incensed at comments in the Egyptian press on the matter, which they suspected were instigated by the Egyptian Government. Al-Rifai's statement that the visit of the Iraqi Regent was only a family visit does not tally, however, with Nuri's statement to Sir Kinahan that it was at the urgent request of the Amir and was related to the

to his desire to secure Syrian and Egyptian support, and thus to have a predominant voice in the proposed Arab League. As a result, the Iraqi attitude of all-out support for closer Arab co-operation during the Arab unity consultations underwent a radical change. The Iraqi delegates in the Subsidiary Committee resisted all Egyptian and Sa'udi attempts to give the Council of the League any greater mediatory and arbitration powers. There was always the fear of isolation within the League and of being confronted by a combination of all the other Arab states led by Egypt and Saudi Arabia.

Ibn Sa'ud was to go a step further and to suggest the conclusion of a treaty of alliance between his country, Egypt, and Syria. The idea was discouraged by the British, who were annoyed at the developing rift between Egypt and Iraq. Some Foreign Office officials argued, however, that once Egypt was persuaded to join the Arab unity movement, her wealth and advanced civilization "naturally gave her the leadership", and it would be "ridiculous" for Iraq to compete for this position. The Hashimites, they added, had not been relegated to the background, they had merely been put in their proper place.[1]

The second significant development was the worsening of the Palestine situation as a result of intensified Zionist propaganda abroad and campaign of terror inside Palestine. Nuri began to have second thoughts about his original scheme of Arab federation with a semi-autonomous status for the Jews. He seemed to favour partition and the confinement of "the Zionist danger within permanent boundaries". He called also for the union of Iraq with Transjordan and the Arab parts of Palestine. Amir 'Abdullah welcomed the idea and pointed to the necessity of consolidating the position of the House of Hashim by himself assuming the Regency of Iraq, together with the Emirate of Transjordan, until such time as the infant Iraqi king attained his majority, when he would relinquish the leadership to the young monarch. This was not what Nuri had in mind, and his reaction to the Amir's suggestion was not at all favourable. The Amir, on the other hand, thought that Nuri's purpose was to distract his attention from Syria, and that a union, in the form suggested by Nuri, would only mean the expansion of Iraq and the disappearance of Transjordan.[2]

Nuri had obviously realized that it would be difficult for Iraq to assume a leading role within the Arab League. A limited union of this type under Iraqi leadership would strengthen Iraq's position, and act as a magnet for the Syrians. This would, moreover, realize Iraq's desire to secure an outlet to the Mediterranean. Nuri's suggestions did

---

latter's bitterness at the Sa'udi-Egyptian confraternity. *Al-Muqattam*, 3 March 1945, and FO 371–45542: Sir Kinahan to Eden, 31 January 1945

[1] FO 371–45237: minutes by Holt, Hankey, and Coverley Price, March 1945

[2] FO 371–39991: Lord Gort, the High Commissioner for Palestine, conveying the Amir's account of his talks with Nuri given to Kirkbride, 14 December 1944

not find any positive response either from the Amir or from the British, and nothing came out of them.

The third development was the growing "uncertainty and anxiety" in the Levant over French insistence on the conclusion of treaties, and fears lest they should take forceful action to compel Syria and Lebanon to accept their demands. The British conciliatory attitude was criticized by the British representatives in the area and especially by Lord Killearn. H.M.G., he said, "seems to have been pursuing two diametrically opposing policies at the same time." On the one hand, they had been encouraging Arab union, and on the other hand, they had been "promoting Zionism in Palestine and French predominance in Syria". A conflict was bound to happen, he argued, with the worst possible consequence for British prestige and influence in the area.[1] Strong representations were made to the British by the Arab governments. Nuri stressed that no Arab League could be formed if the British were to insist on France having a predominant position in Syria. The British would then be responsible for the collapse of the pan-Arab movement, which would force the Arabs to wait another twenty-five years in "disorganization and wretchedness". He expressed the readiness of Iraq to offer Syria all possible military assistance, in the form of training facilities and a volunteer force recruited from among the Iraqis of Syrian origin.[2] The British were greatly annoyed at Nuri's suggestion, and became more aware of the serious consequences of their conciliatory policy towards the French.

The fourth development was the resignation of Riad al-Sulh on 7 January 1945. His successor, Abdul Hamid Karami, was also in favour of closer co-operation with the other Arab countries. He did not have, however, the strength of character and the wider appeal of Riad al-Sulh. Some provisions in the Alexandria Protocol were not well

---

[1] FO 371–40307: Lord Killearn to Eden, 25 December 1944, Sir Kinahan to Eden, 27 December, and Jordan to Eden, 29 December 1944. The Foreign Office, in reply, stated that their advice to the Syrians and Lebanese to reach agreement with the French did not mean that the two states "must accede everything, or indeed any specific thing" which the French might ask for, and that H.M.G. did not intend to sit back and leave the French to dispose of the situation in whatever manner they thought fit. They argued, however, that they believed that an agreement with France need not involve any real derogation from the independence of the two Levant states, and would not prevent them from joining the Arab League (Eden to Killearn, 5 January 1945). The statement of Richard Law in the House of Commons on 7 February 1945, in which he expressed the hope that the two Levant states would conclude agreements of some sort with France, together with the British press articles suggesting that British friendship with France was more important than their friendship with the Arabs, aroused fears and were sharply critized in Syria and Lebanon (407 H.C. Deb. 55, Col. 2046; and *The Economist*, 27 January 1945, article entitled "Middle East Dilemmas")

[2] FO 371–39991: Sir Kinahan to Eden, 1 November 1944; and 45610: Sir Kinahan to Eden, 13 February 1945

received by the Maronites, whose fears of Muslim domination were as intense as ever. Karami was in a much weaker position *vis-à-vis* the Maronites, and had to contend at the same time with criticism from the constitutional bloc of Al-Sulh, who were strongly in favour of closer ties with the other Arab countries. The task of the Lebanese delegation to the meetings of the Subsidiary Committee in Cairo was, therefore, one of extreme delicacy. It was led by the Lebanese Foreign Minister, Henry Phara'oun, a former wealthy banker and a Greek Catholic, who was very much alive to the interplay of local forces in Lebanon, and who was determined not to allow any infringement upon the full sovereignty and independence of his country.[1]

These four developments had their impact on the evolution of the Pact of the League. The League developed as a means for the formation of a united Arab front against French designs in Syria and Lebanon, and against Zionist ambitions in Palestine. It also developed as a means for the consolidation of the *status quo*.

THE EVOLUTION OF THE PACT OF THE ARAB LEAGUE

The meetings of the Political Subsidiary Committee started on 14 February 1945 and were concluded on 3 March after sixteen sessions during which a draft Pact was agreed upon. The Preparatory Committee was reconvened on 17 March to review the said draft, following which a General Arab Congress was held on 22 March 1945. The final text of the Pact was approved and made public on the same day. The Pact was duly ratified by four out of the original six participant states. The League came officially into existence on 10 May 1945.

In the first meeting of the Subsidiary Committee,[2] which was presided

---

[1] Henry Phara'oun, before leaving for Cairo to attend the Subsidiary Committee meeting, was reported to have given assurances to the Maronite Patriarch to the effect that his policy was to ensure that Lebanon would gradually drop out of the Arab orbit (FO 371–45553–Weekly Appreciation Summary, 21 February 1945). The weakness of the position of Karami made him more eager to appease Phara'oun, who was known for his subservience to the Maronites in spite of the fact that their relations were far from good and that President al-Khouri had to intervene several times to reconcile them. Bishara Khalil al-Khouri *Haqaiq Libnaniya*, Vol. II, pp. 110 and 135. The principles of the National Pact have continued to determine Lebanese foreign policy. Each faction tended, however, to lay more stress on some rather than the others, with the Muslims underlining the need for Arab co-operation, and the Maronites insisting that Lebanese sovereignty should not be compromised in any way.

[2] The meetings were attended by delegates from Egypt, Iraq, Syria, Lebanon, Saudi Arabia, and Transjordan. Yemen did not send a delegate to the meetings of the Subsidiary Committee, and those of the Preparatory Committee and the General Arab Congress. Yemen was considered, however, a founding state. The delegates in the Subsidiary Committee received a telegram from the Imam informing them that any agreed-upon document sent to him would be under his consideration. The Pact was sent to him and was signed on 10 May 1945

over by Noqrashi Pasha, the Egyptian Foreign Minister, a long discussion ensued about the participation of Musa al-'Alami. Henry Phara'oun argued that this would weaken the legal basis of the discussions, which were supposed to be conducted between the representatives of independent states. Al-'Alami, he added, did not represent an independent country, and could not commit Palestine to any course of action. It was decided, however, to brush aside the legal considerations, and to treat Palestine as a special case in view of the general Arab sympathy for the plight of its Arab people, and of the fact that a precedent had already been established by the participation of Al-'Alami in the Preparatory Committee meetings in Alexandria. It was therefore agreed that he should take part in any discussions related to Palestine "on an advisory basis" without any voting rights, since he was not in a position to assume or fulfil any of the obligations involved.[1]

Three important documents provided a focus for discussion within the Subsidiary Committee. The first was a letter sent by Sheikh Yusuf Yassin to the Egyptian Prime Minister, who was *ex officio* Chairman of the Preparatory Committee, on 7 January 1945, signifying his government's approval of the Protocol (Appendix II). It suggested several principles on the basis of which future Arab co-operation could be achieved. These included collective security provided for in a multilateral treaty of alliance; the right of each country to conclude treaties provided they were not detrimental to the interests of any other Arab state; the prohibition of war; respect for the independence and the existing regimes in Syria and Lebanon; and economic co-operation without any infringement on the freedom of each country to administer her economy according to her special circumstances and interests. The second document was a draft Pact proposed by the Iraqi Government (Appendix III). The third document was a Lebanese draft (Appendix IV) in which an attempt was made to harmonize the Iraqi, Sa'udi, and Lebanese views.[2]

The main features of the Pact of the League as evolved during the meetings of the Subsidiary Committee, the Preparatory Committee, and the General Arab Congress, were as follows.

---

[1] *Mahadhir Jalasat al-Lajna al Fari'ya al Siasiya Liwada' Mashru' Mithaq Jami'at al Dowal al'Arabiya* (Minutes of the Meeting of the Political Subsidiary Committee for Drafting a Pact for the League of Arab States, hereafter contracted as M.M.P.S.C.) Arab League Publication, Cairo 1949, pp. 4–11

[2] Henry Phara'oun, the Lebanese Foreign Minister and delegate in the Committee, suggested that the Lebanese draft should provide the basis for the discussion. Samir al-Rifai', the Transjordanian Prime Minister, was of the view that the Lebanese and the Iraqi drafts as well as the Sa'udi principles should all be considered as mere proposals to be made use of in the discussion. This was accepted by the other delegates. M.M.P.S.C., p. 31

THE CONSTITUTION AND GENERAL PURPOSES OF THE LEAGUE

1 *The General Purposes*

The Aims of the League were defined both in the Preamble and in Article 2 of the final text. The Preamble was copied from that of the Protocol, with a significant addition specifying that the achievement of these objectives would be "on the basis of respect for the independence and sovereignty of these states". This principle was embodied in both the Iraqi and the Lebanese drafts, and was endorsed by the Sa'udi delegate. The Iraqi text stipulated, however, that each member state should guarantee the sovereignty and independence of the other states. This was objected to by Phara'oun, who argued that the word "guarantee" implied protection, which of itself was an encroachment on national sovereignty. He suggested that the cases to be excluded from consideration by the League, as falling within the limits of sovereignty, should be specified in a separate article. The Committee agreed, however, to a suggestion made by 'Azzam, the Egyptian delegate, that it would be sufficient to incorporate this principle in the Preamble.

The Preamble of the Pact followed the same lines as the Protocol concerning the general Arab nature of the activities and interests of the League. It stated that the League had been formed in response to the wishes of Arab public opinion "in all the Arab lands". Its purpose was to concert efforts "towards the common good of all the Arab countries, the improvement of their status; the security of their future, the realization of their aspirations and hopes".

Article 2 of the Pact (Appendix VIII) defined the objectives of the League in the political and non-political spheres. The Sa'udi delegate stated that the special circumstances of his country, the home of the holy shrines of Islam, precluded her from applying any principle in education or legislation which might contravene Islamic law. An addition was made, therefore, to the said article, specifying that, in attempting to promote closer co-operation in the non-political fields, due regard should be given "to the organization and circumstances of each state".[1]

2 *Membership*

The Iraqi draft considered it an established right of any independent Arab state to be a member of the League. The only condition was that such a state should express her desire to join by depositing a statement to that effect with the Secretariat. Nuri Pasha argued that to give the Council the right to decide on whether a state was independent, and thus qualified for admission or not, would create problems in the future. Some Arab countries were still under different forms of foreign

---

[1] M.M.P.S.C., p. 58

domination, and it might be deemed expedient to provide for their participation.

The Lebanese view was that admission of new states should be made contingent upon the approval by the Council of an application submitted to it by the state concerned. This was also the view of the Sa'udi delegate, who did not wish to see a new state force herself on the League, which might dispute the fact of her independence. 'Azzam, while expressing agreement with Nuri's views, feared lest a foreign power might in the future instigate a state under her tutelage to join the League in order to achieve some ends thereby. The majority were therefore in favour of adopting the Lebanese suggestion. 'Azzam stressed, in the meantime, that the two criteria for admission should strictly be those of independence, and of being an Arab state. No other political considerations should prejudice the judgement of the member states in this regard.[1]

The text approved by the Subsidiary Committee was, however, slightly modified by the Preparatory Committee in an attempt to approximate it to the Iraqi draft. It was stated that any independent Arab state should have the right to join the League if it wanted to. The procedure for admission proposed in the Lebanese draft was accepted. No definition was made as to what constituted an Arab state, and whether full or partial independence was required. Transjordan, which was one of the founding states, was not yet independent, while Egypt and Iraq were bound by treaties of alliance with Britain providing for consultation on foreign affairs, and for the stationing of British troops in their territories. Syria and Lebanon, though declared independent, were still unsure about the possibility of the liquidation of French presence and influence.

Another limitation on the admission of new states was implied in the voting procedure adopted by the Committee. It was not specified whether a decision on admission should require unanimity or just a simple majority. Article 16 of the Pact seemed to indicate that unanimity was the rule unless otherwise specified. This would mean that any member state could veto the admission of a new state.

3 *The Council*

The Council was to be the principal organ of the League. Article 3 of the Pact stipulated that it should be composed of the representatives of the member states, each of which should have one vote irrespective of the number of her representatives. Its functions were defined as to achieve the realization of the purposes of the League, to supervise the execution of agreements concluded between the member states, and to decide upon the means of co-operation with future world organizations (Article 3). It was empowered to mediate in any dispute which

[1] M.M.P.S.C., pp. 33–4

might lead to war, and to arbitrate in any disagreement referred to it by the parties concerned (Article 5). It was also authorized to decide upon the action to be taken to repel any aggression against a member state (Article 6). It was to appoint the Secretary-General, his assistants, and the main officials in the Secretariat. It was to approve the annual budget (Article 13), and decide on the cases in which representatives from the non-member states could participate in the activities of the specialized committees (Article 4).

The exercise by the Council of these functions was limited, however, by the stipulation of unanimity in all important matters. This was an issue which touched on the very nature and status of the League. The choice was one between a supra-national organization vested with wide powers involving a partial surrender of sovereignty, and a loose one which preserved for each state her full rights in sovereignty and independence. The decision was for the second form. This was bound to reflect on the voting procedure in particular. Article 7 stipulated that unanimous decisions would bind all the member states, whereas majority decisions would bind only those who had accepted them. The binding nature of unanimous decisions was further qualified by stipulating that these decisions should be implemented in each state in accordance with her basic laws. This qualification was suggested by the Sa'udi delegate and supported by Henry Phara'oun, who stressed that reference to the respective legislative bodies in the member states would be necessary. Otherwise the League would be turned into a union, which form of association had been ruled out by all the participants.[1]

The idea of making majority decisions binding only on those who had accepted them was an innovation in the law of international institutions.[2] It provided for some flexibility in the voting procedure. The possibility of the development of a stalemate whenever unanimity was found impossible to achieve was therefore avoided. This provision enshrined at the same time the principle of consent as a basis for the assumption by any state of any obligations.

4 *The Secretariat*

All the delegates were in agreement that there should be a permanent secretariat for the League, and that the Secretary-General, as well as his assistants and the main officials of the Secretariat, should be appointed by the Council. Nuri Pasha suggested, however, that the Secretary-General should have an assistant from among the nationals of each member state, whose name would be proposed by his government and approved by the Council. Jamil Mardam, the Syrian delegate, felt that this would not be practical, and might obstruct the work of the Secretariat. 'Azzam, while expressing his objections to the Iraqi

---

[1] M.M.P.S.C., p. 29

[2] Dr Hafez Ghanem *Muhadarat 'an Jami'at al Dowal al 'Arabiya,* Cairo 1966, p. 59

suggestion, proposed, and the Committee agreed, that it should be stated in the minutes that the delegates were in favour of including officials from the member states in the Secretariat. He stressed at the same time that the post of the Secretary-General was administrative in nature. The person chosen by the Council for this post would cease to represent any particular member state.

Nuri's attitude was indicative of the rather cautious and reserved line which the Iraqi Government began to adopt towards the Cairo talks in general. He had stated some months earlier that the post of the Secretary-General would be "the most important element in the whole organization". He told Sir Walter Smart, the Oriental Counsellor in Cairo, that it was essential that the man chosen for this post should be "entirely in British confidence" in order that he might discuss confidentially with them all sorts of matters before they became subject to official handling within the League. He should also be a man of real character who enjoyed the general confidence of the Arab states. Nuri was eager to see a non-Egyptian chosen for this post, since the appointment of an Egyptian as Secretary-General would certainly enhance Egypt's leadership in the area, and might in the long run, in view of the consolidation of Sa'udi–Egyptian relations, be detrimental to the interests of Iraq. He said that he did not see any suitable man for the post in Egypt, and thought that 'Azzam was "too volatile" to occupy such a position. He felt that Faris al-Khouri, the Syrian Prime Minister, would be a good candidate. He added that he intended to keep up his sleeve the offer of the first presidency of the Council to Egypt as a sop for having a Secretary-General from outside Egypt.[1]

The attitude of the other Arab delegates in the Subsidiary, and later in the Preparatory Committee upset Nuri's calculations. Most of the delegates were in favour of granting Egypt the prominent role she had aspired to. Cairo was chosen as the centre of the League "in recognition of the great services of Egypt to the Arab cause".[2] The first presidency of the Council was accorded to the Egyptian Prime Minister. In proposing this appointment, Henry Phara'oun referred to the precedent established when the League of Nations was founded. President Wilson was given the honour of calling the first meeting in recognition of his services as the sponsor of the idea of the League.[3] Most of the delegates favoured the choice of 'Azzam as the first Secretary-General of the League. His appointment was left to the Preparatory Committee and the General Arab Congress. The choice had, however, been rumoured in Cairo since the conclusion of the

---

[1] FO 371–45237: Lord Killearn to Eden, 9 March 1945; and 39991: Lord Killearn to Eden, 1 November 1944

[2] M.M.P.S.C., p. 38: statement by Henry Phara'oun in support of his suggestion, which was accepted by the other delegates

[3] Ibid., p. 39

meetings of the Subsidiary Committee on 3 March.[1] The Iraqis had to accept his appointment, since their refusal would have made no difference in view of the stipulation in the Pact that the appointment of the Secretary-General would require only a two-thirds majority decision. 'Azzam had been, since the twenties, the most enthusiastic of all the Egyptian advocates of closer ties with the Arab countries. He went so far as to call for the restoration of the Arab Empire, and never ceased to stress the economic, political, and strategic advantages to Egypt from associating herself with Arab Asia. He seemed to have established close relations with the Palace, and was the only government official to accompany the King on his visit to Saudi Arabia in January 1945. He had obviously got the ear of King Farouq in Arab affairs, and secured his support both for establishing closer ties with Saudi Arabia and Syria, and for championing the Arab cause in North Africa in general and in Libya in particular. He was not the man whom the British would have liked to assume such a key post, and he was often described by Lord Killearn as full of fantastic ideas and not at all practical.[2] His earlier strong connections with 'Ali Maher Pasha could not have endeared him to the British Ambassador, though he was the only one in Maher's close circle to escape internment for security reasons. He was described by his British friends in 1935 as an "attractive young fanatic" who had all the Bedouin qualities: courage, indifference to discomfort, an acute sense of honour, "together with a sense of humour and a high measure of sportsmanship and idealism".[3]

THE STATUS OF THE LEAGUE VIS-À-VIS ITS MEMBERS AND INTERNATIONAL ORGANIZATIONS

The Lebanese draft stipulated in its second article that the League should have the status of a permanent conference, with no international personality distinct from that of its member states, which had retained their full rights in sovereignty and independence internally as well as externally. Henry Phara'oun argued that the legal status of international bodies like the Arab League had always been subject to controversy among politicians and legal experts. Most of them had tended, however, to consider these bodies as mere permanent international conferences with no separate legal status. He stressed that

---

[1] FO 371–45237: Lord Killearn to Eden, 9 March 1945

[2] Lord Killearn was incensed at 'Azzam's championship of the full participation, in the Council of the League, of a Palestine Arab representative, and the participation in the specialized Committees of local representatives of the non-independent Arab states, as will be explained later. He admitted that 'Azzam was "generally popular" among the Arabs, but added that the Arab delegates in the Subsidiary Committee had been "frankly apprehensive of his lack of responsibility and of his amateur methods". FO 371–45237: Killearn to Ed en, 9 March 1945

[3] FO 371–19091: Personalities Report, Sir Miles Lampson, 25 February 1935

Lebanon had decided to join the League on the understanding that it would not have the status of an international organization.[1]

A divergence of views developed when the issue of the League's status *vis-à-vis* other world organizations came up for discussion. Nuri as well as 'Azzam suggested that provision should be made for the participation of the League as a regional body, or of any of its member states, in any future world organization.[2] Henry Phara'oun refused to accept this suggestion, and insisted that this would constitute an infringement upon the sovereignty of the member states. He considered it premature at that stage to include any provisions in this regard. The shape of the future world organization, he argued, had not yet been defined, and it might be decided to include Greece and Turkey with the Arab countries in a regional body. To give the League a regional status at this juncture would be undesirable, since it would create a *fait accompli* for the Great Powers. He rejected a modest suggestion made by 'Azzam that it should be stipulated that there was nothing in the Pact to prevent the League, or any of its member states, from co-operating with any future world body. He also rejected a suggestion made by Samir al-Rifai', the Transjordanian delegate, to make co-operation with any world body conditional upon a unanimous decision by the Council, and thus to give Lebanon the right to veto it if it wanted to. Henry Phara'oun was adamant and insisted that no reference should be made to the League by name. When pressed by the other delegates to accept a compromise solution, he suggested that the matter should be dropped altogether if the delegates found themselves unable to accept his views. Samir al-Rifai' stated, by way of comment, that the delegates had been eager from the very beginning to compromise in order to evolve a scheme acceptable to Lebanon. The Lebanese delegate won in the end. All reference to the League as a regional body was deleted. It was merely stipulated that the Council should decide upon the means by which the League would co-operate with any future international bodies (Article 3).[3] This rather vague clause was proposed by 'Azzam as a way out of the impasse. It left the matter to the Council to decide upon later on.

A significant addition was made by the Preparatory Committee to the provisions of Article 19 regarding the amendment of the Pact. It was stipulated that the Pact could be amended, by a two-thirds majority decision, to make allowance for, among other things, the regulation

[1] M.M.P.S.C., p. 29

[2] The Reconstruction Department of the Foreign Office recommended in December 1944 that provisions should be added to the pact of the League to ensure that the League could function within the framework of the future world organization. British representations were made to that effect to Noqrashi and Nuri, who thought the idea a good one. FO 371–39991: Eden to Killearn, 31 December 1944, and Killearn to Eden, 23 January 1945

[3] M.M.P.S.C., pp. 72–5

of the relations of the League with future international bodies. This was designed obviously to allow for a certain flexibility in this regard.

RULES GOVERNING INTER-ARAB RELATIONS

1 *The Principle of Non-Intervention in the Internal Affairs of Member States*

The Pact stipulated that each member state should respect the systems of government established in the other member states and regard them as exclusive concerns of those states. It also stipulated that each state should pledge itself to abstain from any action calculated to change established systems of government (Article 8). This was the text approved by the Subsidiary Committee. It was introduced at the suggestion of Sheikh Yusuf Yassin, the Sa'udi Delegate, who had in mind specifically the retention of the existing republican regimes in Syria and Lebanon.

Samir al-Rifai' objected, for obvious reasons, to the phrase "established at present" which was suggested by Sheikh Yusuf. He enquired whether this would preclude the member states from recognizing any future change in the form of government in any of these states. 'Azzam replied that this provision established merely the right of the people to choose their own form of government without any external pressure. Nuri suggested that this should be made clear in formulating the said provision, since this right was not recognized by some people. This was an obvious reference to Saudi Arabia and probably to Yemen. The Lebanese delegate suggested that no specific stipulation should be made in this regard, since there were still some who considered that the form of government was an exclusive right of the king, and others who argued that it was the right of the state. A compromise proposal made by 'Azzam, and accepted by the Committee, favoured the use of the phrase "as exclusive rights of these states".[1]

This was not, however, to the liking of Nuri. In a letter sent by Tahsin al-'Askari, the Iraqi Minister in Cairo, to the Chairman of the Committee on 11 March 1945 (Appendix VII), it was stressed that the choice of the form of government in any state was the exclusive right of her people. It added that this clarification was necessary since the text approved was rather vague on this point. The Iraqi Government, it stressed, could not admit any deviation from this principle, which was accepted by all the countries of the civilized world. The issue was raised by the Iraqi delegate in the Preparatory Committee meeting held on 17 March. The Committee approved a suggestion made by Al-Rifai' that it should be stated in the minutes that the interpretation of the text did not alter its intended meaning.[2] The preservation of the

---

[1] M.M.P.S.C., pp. 84–5

[2] *Mahadhir Jalasat al Lajna al Tahdiriya Lil Mu'tamar al-'Arabi al'am fil Qahira* (Minutes of the Meetings of the Preparatory Committee of the General Arab Congress in Cairo, hereafter contracted to M.M.P.C.), p. 17

status quo was therefore enshrined as one of the cornerstones of the League. This was a victory for the Cairo–Riyadh axis and for Ibn Sa'ud in particular. All his efforts in the past had been always directed towards the preservation of the existing balance of power in the area, and towards the frustration of all Hashimite attempts to establish their hegemony over the Levant.

2 *Limitations on the Treaty-making Powers of the Member States*

The Alexandria Protocol established the freedom of the member states to conclude any special treaties or agreements with other states. This was restricted, however, by the provision that these treaties should not contradict the text or the spirit of the Protocol, and that in no case would the adoption of a foreign policy prejudicial to that of the League or any of its member states be allowed. The Protocol also included among the objectives of the League the supervision of the execution of the agreements which might be concluded between the member states.

The Iraqi draft included stronger provisions in this regard. The Council was empowered to ensure the implementation of inter-Arab agreements. Each member state was obliged not to adopt an attitude or follow a foreign policy which would contradict that of the League, or of any of its member states. The member states were obliged to try, so far as possible, to unify the lines of their foreign policies through organized consultations. It stipulated, moreover, that copies of all agreements concluded by the member states must be deposited with the Secretariat.

The Lebanese draft stipulated, on the other hand, that the supervision by the Council of the implementation of treaties must not prejudice the full rights to sovereignty and independence of each member state. It stressed the freedom of each state to conclude treaties not of an "aggressive nature" towards any other member state, and that past and future treaties concluded or to be concluded by any member state did not bind or restrict the other member states. The text approved by the Committee drew from the Iraqi and the Lebanese drafts. It was stipulated that all treaties should be deposited with the Secretariat (Article 17), and that treaties should bind only the contracting parties (Article 9). This clause (Article 9), in spite of its non-controversial nature, being a mere statement of a general principle of international law, was subject to a long discussion within the Preparatory Committee.[1]

Dr Abdul Hamid Badawi, the Egyptian Foreign Minister and a well-known authority on international law, reviewed the draft proposed by the Subsidiary Committee. He suggested some changes in the wording of some articles, including that which contained the said clause. The new text he proposed stipulated that: "Nothing in this Pact shall either

[1] M.M.P.S.C., p. 77

affect the obligations already binding any member state, or preclude the member states from concluding agreements which do not contradict the principles of this Pact." Serious objections were raised by the Syrian delegates to the new text. They argued that it affirmed the sanctity of all previous obligations, which might imply either that these obligations did not contradict the Pact, or, if they were adjudged contradictory, the state concerned would have no right to seek their modification. There were two important issues involved. The first was the respect for all previous contractual obligations, which the Syrians did not like to see enshrined in the Pact. This would have been used by the French to strengthen their argument for the conclusion of treaties with Syria and Lebanon, which was based in part on the fact that the two states had accepted a contractual arrangement with France in 1936. The second was the respect for any future treaty obligations which did not contradict the Pact. This also would have fortified the French and British argument at the time, that the conclusion of treaties would not in any way prevent the two Levant states from joining the League. It would have also weakened the argument of the Arab leaders that French insistence on the conclusion of treaties would lead to the collapse of the pan-Arab movement and the Arab League scheme. The Syrians wanted, moreover, to guard against the possibility of the conclusion by any future Lebanese Government of a preferential treaty with France, quoting this clause in support of their action.

Jamil Mardam explained that the Subsidiary Committee had avoided all reference to past obligations for obvious reasons. 'Azzam agreed with the Syrian contention. He added that this was an awkward issue, since he personally believed that the Anglo-Egyptian and the Anglo-Iraqi treaties should be modified, and that obligations of this nature should not be consolidated in such an instrument of Arab co-operation. In view of these objections the text proposed by Dr Badawi was dropped, and the original clause proposed by the Subsidiary Committee was adopted.[1]

No provision was made in the Pact for the unification of the foreign policies of the member states, nor for disallowing the pursuit by any member state of a foreign policy detrimental to that of the League or any of its other member states. This was one of the weaknesses of the Pact as compared with the Protocol.[2] Neither the Iraqi nor any of the other delegates did in fact insist upon the inclusion of specific provisions in this regard.

---

[1] M.M.P.C., p. 9

[2] The provision of the Protocol in this regard was subject to sharp criticism in Lebanon. In view of this, the Lebanese President agreed with his Prime Minister and Minister for Foreign Affairs that it should be deleted from the Pact of the League, which was achieved without any difficulty in the Subsidiary Committee. Bishara Khalil al-Khouri *Haqaiq Libnaniya*, Vol II, pp. 109–10

3 *Closer inter-Arab Ties in the Future*

A special provision was suggested by Nuri Pasha, and included in the Alexandria Protocol, expressing the hope that the Arab states would be able to consolidate that step by other steps in the direction of closer inter-Arab ties. Nuri suggested also, during the meetings of the Subsidiary Committee, that the Pact should include one or two articles stipulating that the scheme devised in the Pact did not preclude the member states, if they so desired, from establishing closer and stronger forms of co-operation than those provided for in the Pact. This was necessary, he argued, in order to avoid any objections being raised in the future. Nuri's suggestion was accepted and included in the Pact (Article 9) after a tussle with the Sa'udi delegate, who insisted that it should be stipulated that any agreements designed to serve this end must not contradict the Pact or be detrimental to the interests of any of the other member states. Nuri wanted obviously to leave the door open for any future union of the Levant states, and did not want the establishment of the League to preclude his country from seeking closer forms of association with Syria, Transjordan, and Palestine.

'Azzam, who was in the chair,[1] explained to Sheikh Yusuf that the provision suggested by Nuri was intended to leave the door open for the further consolidation of inter-Arab relations. He added that the Committee had opted for a narrow and limited form of co-operation in view of the various objections and reservations made by some delegates. It would be inadvisable, therefore, to prevent those who might seek closer forms of association from realizing their objective. Co-operation, he argued, should not be detrimental to the interests of any country, since there was a prior commitment by all to respect the sovereignty and independence of each state. Henry Phara'oun was of the same view, and thought that the Sa'udi stipulation would contradict the spirit of the Protocol by implying that some forms of closer co-operation might be detrimental to the interests of some Arab states. Sheikh Yusuf insisted on the inclusion of the said clause, and stressed that each state must be reassured against the conclusion of agreements which might endanger her interests. 'Azzam managed, however, through private consultations with Nuri and Sheikh Yusuf, to get the latter to drop his objections. Nuri gave assurances that the said text was not meant to have any adverse effects on the interests of any member state, and that the idea it embodied was worthy of support from all the delegates. Sheikh Yusuf, for his part, stated that he had been instructed by King Ibn Sa'ud to favour a closer form of Arab

---

[1] 'Azzam deputized for Noqrashi in presiding over the meetings after the latter's appointment as Prime Minister, following the assassination of 'Ahmed Maher Pasha on 24 February 1945. Noqrashi, who retained the portfolio of Foreign Affairs, presided over the final meeting on 3 March 1945

co-operation, and that he would accept the Iraqi text in so far as it would serve this end.[1]

The Iraqi Government were later to reaffirm their views on the issue. In the letter of Tahsin al-'Askari referred to earlier, it was stressed that the said text acknowledged a right which each of the member states already enjoyed. It added that it should be made clear that none of the member states might object, for any reason whatever, to any arrangements which some members might make to widen the scope of their co-operation.

4 *The Peaceful Settlement of Disputes*

This was one of the most difficult issues to be discussed by the Subsidiary Committee. The divergence of views on the issue was due mainly to the fact that it touched directly on the powers of the Council and the nature of its decisions, and was therefore related to the question of sovereignty. The Sa'udi Government, as indicated in the letter of Sheikh Yusuf referred to earlier (Appendix II), was in favour of establishing strong machinery for the peaceful settlement of disputes, involving resort to conciliation, mediation, compulsory arbitration, and collective measures against aggression or the refusal by any state to accept an arbitration award. Ibn Sa'ud had serious grievances against what he considered the failure of Iraq, in particular, to fulfil her treaty obligations on border and tribal matters. He had some complaints about what he suspected to be the encouragement of anti-Sa'udi activities by the Hashimite rulers of Iraq and Transjordan. His proposals were designed to empower the Council to deal effectively with such matters. They were also designed to further consolidate the *status quo* against any attempts at its revision by force or diplomacy.

The Iraqi draft provided for the settlement of disputes between the member states through diplomatic negotiations and arbitration with the approval of the parties concerned. In the absence of such approval, the dispute must be referred either to the International Court of Justice, or to any other competent body. The Iraqi draft provided, therefore, for voluntary arbitration by the Council, and for compulsory arbitration by any competent world body. It stipulated, moreover, that in cases of disagreement between a member state and any other state, the Council might, upon the request of any Arab or foreign state, or on its own initiative, offer its mediation. Should it fail in its mediation, it would then decide unanimously on the measures to be taken to ensure the security of the Arab state involved in the disagreement, and would advise the member states to carry out these measures.

The Lebanese draft provided, on the other hand, for recourse to diplomatic means, mediation by the Council, or arbitration "with the

[1] M.M.P.S.C., pp. 76–7 and 83

approval of the legislative authorities in each state party to the dispute in accordance with her constitutional procedures". In an annex laying down the rules which should govern arbitration, the stress was laid on the necessity of concluding a written agreement by the parties concerned defining the issues involved, and setting their conditions for accepting an arbitration award. The Council was not authorized to interfere in the implementation of such an award. It was stipulated, however, that it could consider a state refusing to accept the award as having failed to fulfil her obligations under the Pact.

When the issue came up for discussion, Noqrashi Pasha proposed a text which empowered the Council to intervene in any dispute and to attempt to settle it through mediation, failing which the parties would be obliged to submit the dispute to the Council for arbitration. The Council was precluded, however, from taking any action if one of the disputants argued, and the Council agreed, that the matter under dispute fell within her domestic jurisdiction, or affected the interests of a non-member state, in which case the council would submit a report on the matter without recommending any particular solution. The proposed text excluded from arbitration, without the prior approval of the parties, all matters related to the revision of the existing territorial status of the member states. It authorized the Council to prepare draft statutes of arbitration providing for the establishment of an Arab court of arbitration to deal with disputes of a legal nature referred to it by the parties concerned. Noqrashi's text was closer to the Sa'udi proposals with regard to compulsory arbitration. The exclusion of matters falling within domestic jurisdiction, or affecting the interests of non-member states, or related to the revision of the existing territorial status, was designed obviously to make the text acceptable to the Lebanese delegates.

The first and strongest objections to Noqrashi's text were raised by the Iraqi delegate, who insisted that arbitration should be voluntary, as stipulated in the Alexandria Protocol. The Lebanese delegate stressed that compulsory arbitration would not be accepted by the Lebanese public, and that he had not been authorized to accept it. Arbitration in matters affecting the sovereignty of the state, he argued, would involve a surrender of that sovereignty. The Council, he insisted, should not be allowed to arbitrate in matters related to revision of the existing territorial status of any of its member states, even if this was done with the approval of the parties concerned. He objected also to the exclusion of matters falling within domestic jurisdiction or affecting the interests of non-member states, since this was made conditional on the Council's acceptance of an argument made by one of the parties concerned. The Sa'udi delegate insisted, however, that the relevant principle in the Sa'udi letter, referred to earlier, providing for compulsory arbitration, should be adopted.

'Azzam suggested, in view of the wide divergence of views on the issue, that a provision of a general and flexible nature should be devised. He argued that world developments might clarify many of the issues involved, making it possible in the future to evolve an acceptable protocol on arbitration. Noqrashi's text was therefore modified. The Council was empowered to mediate only in inter-Arab disputes. Its arbitration was made contingent on the approval of the parties concerned. All matters related to the independence, sovereignty, and territorial integrity of the member states were excluded altogether from arbitration.

This new text, though accepted by the Lebanese delegate, was objected to by the Sa'udi and the Iraqi delegates. Sheikh Yusuf criticized it as too weak, and insisted on the provision for compulsory arbitration. Nuri Pasha, who was not present during the earlier discussion, prepared two memoranda (Appendix V) on the subject. He argued that the Alexandria Protocol was based on two main principles, from which the Iraqi Government could not allow any deviation. The first was the retention by each member state of her sovereignty, independence, and international obligations. The second was that the decisions of the Council bound only those who had accepted them. The Council was authorized to mediate only in disputes which might lead to war, and the approval of the parties was required for its arbitration. He stressed that the Iraqi Government could not, therefore, accept any uninvited intervention by the Council in any dispute, especially if it arose over the execution of treaties and agreements concluded in the past.

The Iraqi objections brought the whole matter back for discussion. Nuri, who was ill, absented himself from the meeting, and thus avoided defending personally an argument which was more reserved with regard to the powers of the League than that of the Lebanese delegate. He obviously realized the motives behind Sa'udi insistence on compulsory arbitration, and was careful to stress that the execution of all past agreements should not be subject to arbitration. Underlying all this was the fear of isolation within the League, and the eagerness to insure against the possibility of having to accept decisions which might not serve Iraqi interests. This could only be done at the expense of weakening the authority of the League *vis-à-vis* its members.

Samir al-Rifai', who was asked by Nuri to convey his views to the committee, stated that Nuri suggested that the Council should not be empowered to mediate in any inter-Arab dispute. No role was envisaged, therefore, by the Iraqi Government for the Council in the peaceful settlement of disputes. Henry Phara'oun explained that he had been, from the start of the meetings, against the adoption of any provisions involving any infringement upon the sovereignty of a state. The modified text, he argued, provided only for the exercise by the Council of its "good offices", which did not involve any encroachment on national sovereignty. Jamil Mardam was of the same view. He stressed that mediation was voluntary in nature, especially when it was taken to mean the exercise of good offices. He explained that the Committee had chosen from the start a narrow path, preferring to evolve weak provisions accepted by all, than stronger ones to which some states would make reservations. He fully understood the special circumstances of Lebanon, but could not make secret his surprise at the attitude of Iraq, whose government had always been in favour of closer Arab ties, and whose delegate took a line more reserved than that of any of the other delegates. Tahsin al-'Askari retorted by saying that his government had only started to make reservations when it saw the Committee being flooded with reservations from its first session. Iraq, he added, was prepared to go all the way, even if this would involve the removal of all barriers and frontiers between the Arab states. Sheikh Yusuf Yassin urged the delegates to base their deliberations on the sincere desire to serve their nation, and on the assumption of good faith on the part of all the governments represented. Reservations and objections, he argued, were liable to misinterpretation. The narrow path taken by the Committee was bound to defeat the very aims which its meetings were intended to achieve. Inter-Arab relations, especially after the exchange of visits between Ibn Sa'ud, Farouq and Al-Qwatli, he added, were closer then than those envisaged in the provisions of the Pact accepted so far by the Committee.[1]

The discussion did not achieve any tangible results. The Iraqi delegate refused to change his attitude, and so did Sheikh Yusuf. Samir al-Rifai' suggested that the text should be modified. The final text embodied in the Pact provided for the mediation by the Council only in disputes which might lead to war. The Sa'udi delegate raised objections to the new text. 'Azzam replied that the Sa'udi reservations did not necessitate any further modification, since they called for the adoption of a stronger text, which it might be possible to achieve in the future. This was not to be enough for the Iraqi Government, which stressed in the letter of Tahsin al-'Askari, referred to earlier, that they could not admit any intervention by the member states, jointly or separately, in "any dispute of whatever nature" in which Iraq might be involved, except at the request of the parties concerned. Iraq, which had based her argument against compulsory arbitration on the provisions of the Alexandria Protocol, was not ready to accept the provision in the Protocol regarding mediation by the Council in disputes which might lead to war.

Ibn Sa'ud was dismayed at what he described as "the torpedoing" by Nuri of the strong provisions proposed by Noqrashi. He took this as

---

[1] M.M.P.S.C., pp. 65–7

further evidence of bad faith on the part of the Iraqis.[1] It was at that time that he started to favour the idea of a treaty of alliance with Egypt and Syria. It became obvious to him that the League would be divested of any power to deal effectively with any disputes between him and his Hashimite neighbours. The best alternative for him was to join forces with Egypt and Syria, both inside and outside the League.

The establishment of an Arab court of arbitration was proposed by the Iraqi and the Egyptian delegates. Nuri argued that this would be necessary since disputes were bound to arise between Arab companies, in view of the wide scope of co-operation envisaged by the Pact in the non-political spheres. Henry Phara'oun argued, however, that disputes between companies should be settled by the courts of the state in which the company concerned maintained its head office. The competence of the court, he added, should be confined to disputes between states. This, he stated, might provide an alternative to arbitration by the Council. He was, however, in favour of postponing the issue until a statute could be laid down for the said court. This was approved by the other delegates, and later by the Preparatory Committee. The article concerning the amendment of the Pact included a stipulation to the effect that this might be done to provide for the establishment of an Arab Court of Justice (Article 19).

5 *Action with regard to Actual or Threatened Aggression*

The Alexandria Protocol provided merely for the co-ordination of political plans with regard to the protection "by suitable means" of the independence and sovereignty of the member states against every aggression. The Sa'udi letter favoured the conclusion of treaties of alliance providing for mutual assistance in cases of aggression against a member state. The Iraqi draft ruled out the possibility of aggression by an Arab state, and confined itself to cases of foreign aggression. Unanimity was required for any decision on the measures to be taken to repel any external act of aggression. This point was left vague in the Lebanese draft. It was stated in another article, however, that unless otherwise specified, all decisions should be taken by a unanimous vote, and that majority decisions bound only those who had accepted them.

Henry Phara'oun stressed that the state concerned should be the sole judge of whether she was subject to an actual or a threatened aggression. To give the Council the right to decide on this matter would amount to an interference in the internal affairs and an

---

[1] FO 371–45237–E1992/3/65: 22 March 1945, Jedda Legation to FO. Arshad al-'Umari, the Iraqi Foreign Minister, made a confidential remark to 'Azzam, who conveyed it to Yusuf Yassin, to the effect that the reservations made in the Iraqi letter referred to were part of Nuri's intrigues. Nuri, who was not a member of the cabinet, had a great influence on Iraqi foreign policy, which was obviously resented by Al-'Umari.

encroachment upon the sovereignty of that state. This would, moreover, avoid any prolonged discussion in the Council about what constituted actual or threatened aggression.[1] The Sa'udi delegate suggested that the cases constituting an act of aggression specified in the Treaty of Arab Brotherhood and Alliance should be embodied in the Pact.[2] Most of the delegates were, however, in favour of the Lebanese suggestion, which was approved by the Committee.[3] They also agreed to drop the Iraqi specification of foreign aggression. Nuri's view was that since the Pact would disallow any use of force by any member state, and had specified that the League aimed at the protection of the sovereignty and independence of each state, any aggression by an Arab country against another Arab state would be highly improbable. Henry Phara'oun contested this thesis, and argued that history included cases of aggression by an Arab state against another Arab state. The Egyptian and the Sa'udi delegates were also in favour of including all cases of aggression.[4]

The discussion then turned to the question of unanimity. The Lebanese delegate suggested that the Council's decisions on the measures to be taken to repel aggression should be approved by all members, excluding the aggressor state if she happened to be a member of the League. This was the text approved by the Committee and included in the Pact (Article 6). The requirement of unanimity weakened the authority of the League, since any single dissenting state could render it powerless in the face of an external or an internal aggression. The Sa'udi delegate was the only one to raise objections to this clause. He enquired whether the failure to achieve unanimity would prevent any member state from extending assistance to the Arab state subject to aggression. Noqrashi Pasha replied that the provision for unanimity was designed to make any decision binding on all members, and to avoid any disagreement over such a serious matter. 'Azzam explained that the Committee had opted for a rather loose form of association in view of the cautious and reserved attitude of some delegates. To drop the stipulation for unanimity would be natural only if the intention was to evolve the strong machinery for Arab co-operation hoped for by the Arab public. He therefore argued that it would be better in the circumstances to adopt a flexible text acceptable to all, and to leave it to the states which might

---

[1] M.M.P.S.C., p. 29

[2] Aggression was defined in the said Treaty as involving a declaration of war, an undeclared war leading to an invasion by foreign troops, a military attack, or any direct assistance to the aggressor state (Article 4, clause b). Text in: *Documents on International Affairs:* 1937, ed. by Stephen Herald R.I.I.A., London 1939, p. 524

[3] In reply to an enquiry by Makram 'Ubaid during the meetings of the Preparatory Committee, Dr Badawi, who edited the Pact, explained that aggression is a factual and not a controversial matter and involves actions like actual invasion and naval blockades.

[4] M.M.P.S.C., pp. 44–5

desire to go a step further to conclude whatever agreements might serve this purpose.[1]

The Lebanese delegate then suggested that another limitation be imposed on the authority of the Council in this regard. He proposed that the decisions unanimously arrived at should be referred to the member states for implementation each in accordance with her constitutional procedures. Henry Phara'oun was determined that the Council should not be granted any special status distinct from that of its members. His suggestion meant that the Council's decisions in this case would be subject to approval or rejection by the legislature of each state. This was not accepted by the other delegates. It was stipulated in a separate article, however, that all decisions taken by the Council should be implemented in each state according to her basic laws (Article 7).

A new provision was suggested and accepted, stipulating that if aggression was of such a nature as to make the government of the state affected, or her representative in the Council, unable to contact the Council, any other member state could call a meeting to discuss the issue. Jamil Mardam, who sponsored this clause, argued that the representative of the state concerned might be a cabinet minister who had been arrested with the other members of his government by the aggressor state. Giving any other member state the right to call a meeting of the Council would provide an additional guarantee in this regard.[2]

An interesting discussion on these provisions took place during the meetings of the Preparatory Committee. Samir al-Rifai' stated that the article dealing with acts of aggression (Article 6) had been modified in order to remove the objections of some delegates. Abdul Hamid Karami, the Lebanese Prime Minister, got the impression that some delegates blamed Henry Phara'oun for the weakness of the text of this article. In an attempt to deny this, he declared that his country would be ready to go along with the other Arab states in everything they agreed upon. He expressed his hope that Lebanon would not be considered an obstacle in the path of closer Arab ties.[3] The other

[1] M.M.P.S.C., p. 46

[2] M.M.P.S.C., p. 44. This was designed obviously to deal with crises similar to that which took place in Lebanon in November 1943.

[3] M.M.P.C., p. 16. Khalid al'Azm, who was a Syrian Cabinet Minister during this period, laid the blame on Henry Phara'oun for the weakness of the provisions of the Pact as compared with the Protocol. He also blamed Karami for his deference to the views of Phara'oun, which he attributed to Karami's eagerness to retain the support of Phara'oun and the Maronites, and not to risk losing the Premiership then being coveted by Al-Sulh. Khalid al-'Azm *Mudhakkirat Khalid al-'Azm*, Vol. I, Beirut, 1972, p. 256. A British report stated that some Arab delegates seem to have complained to Karami of the rather obstructive attitude of Phara'oun during the meetings of the Subsidiary Committee, and that Karami had decided, in view of this, himself to lead the Lebanese delegation, from which Phara'oun was excluded, to the meeting of the Preparatory Committee and the General Arab Congress. It was at that time that

delegates did not wish, however, to choose a stronger text for the said article, and thanked Karami for his positive attitude. Lebanon was not, in fact, the only country responsible for the weakness of the said article, since Iraq had insisted on the stipulation for unanimity in any decisions on measures to repel aggression.

THE PARTICIPATION OF PALESTINE AND THE NON-INDEPENDENT ARAB COUNTRIES

1 *Palestine*

Strong representations were made by the British to the Arab Governments both before the Alexandria meeting and before the meeting of the Subsidiary Committee. The purpose of these representations was to ensure that the Palestine issue would not be raised in a way which might have adverse effects on British interests in the area, and that all inflammatory statements would be avoided altogether. The delegates were in fact careful to keep clear of this thorny question for as long as possible. The issue of the participation of Musa al-'Alami was settled after a long discussion in the first session. No reference was made to the Palestine problem in the subsequent ten sessions, and no contribution was made by Al-'Alami to the discussions.[1] It was in the twelfth session, held on 28 February, that the question of the participation of a Palestinian Arab representative in the meetings of the Council of the League was raised. The Lebanese delegate pointed out that it would be difficult, from the legal point of view, to provide for the participation of a non-independent country in an organization composed of independent states. 'Azzam argued for treating Palestine as a special case. He suggested that it should be left to the Council to choose a Palestinian delegate, and that it could be stipulated that his vote would not be counted in cases where unanimity was required. This meant, in effect, that the states represented in the Council would have the right to decide who represented the true interests of the Palestine Arabs. This was later to involve the League in the internal conflict and intrigues between the different Arab parties, of which the Nashashibi-led Arab Defence Party had the support of Amir 'Abdullah, and was anathema to Ibn Sa'ud. Al-'Alami described the agreement of the five

---

some extreme Maronite elements tried to raise the bogy of Islam in order to induce the Christians to oppose the government policy favouring participation in the League. A deputation composed of the three ex-presidents, Emile Edde, Alfred Naccache, and Dr Ayoub Thabit, saw the Maronite Patriarch on 17 March 1945, and tried to induce him to send a telegram to Cairo expressing disapproval of the Arab League. Their mission was unsuccessful, and the Patriarch told them that Henry Phara'oun had shown him the modifications made to the Alexandria Protocol which, in his view, constituted sufficient protection for the Maronites. FO 371–45553, Weekly Appreciation Summary (Beirut), 21 March 1945

[1] Al-'Alami was apparently disgruntled at the general tendency to compromise, and absented himself from five out of the sixteen meetings for health reasons.

Palestine Arab parties on the choice of him to represent them in the Alexandria meetings as an "unprecedented feat", which was only made possible because of their eagerness to present their case to such a prominent Arab gathering, and by the fact that he was not affiliated to any of these parties.[1]

All the delegates in the Committee confined themselves to general expressions of sympathy for the plight of the Palestine Arabs, and refrained from making any strong attack on British policy. Al-'Alami was not asked to make any statement on the subject, and did not contribute anything to the discussion of the issue. It was agreed that a special resolution regarding Palestine should be annexed to the Pact. A text proposed by 'Azzam was readily approved by the other delegates. It requested the Preparatory Committee to recognize the right of Palestine to participate in the League on an equal footing with the founding members. It suggested that the Council should be empowered to choose an Arab representative from Palestine to take part in its meetings until such time as Palestine became independent.[2]

The annex proposed by the Subsidiary Committee did not specify whether the Palestinian delegate would have any voting rights or not. It went, however, far beyond the provisions of the special resolution concerning Palestine included in the Alexandria Protocol, by establishing the right of Palestine to participate in the League "on an equal footing" with the founding members. This was to engender strong criticism from the British. They doubted the wisdom of allowing the representative of a non-independent state to participate in the meetings of the Council, and thought that the best course was to allow Al-'Alami to attend as an observer. Lord Killearn was instructed to convey these views to Noqrashi Pasha and the other Arab delegates before the meeting of the Preparatory Committee on 17 March. Noqrashi was warned against "the mistaken zeal or indeed the fanaticism of 'Azzam". He was told that the newly formed League should not try to run before it could walk. Noqrashi admitted that the position of Al-'Alami was "certainly anomalous". He thought, however, that it would be a mistake to raise the question of the technical status of Al-'Alami and added that he would leave it to the astute legal mind of Dr Badawi to develop an acceptable formula in this regard. Several representations were also made to the other Arab governments, who were told that they had no right to take such a step with regard to a country which was still under a British mandate.[3]

As a result of these representations the annex on Palestine was modified by the Preparatory Committee, which decided to delete the part providing for the participation of the Palestine Arab delegate "on

[1] Geoffrey Furlonge: *Palestine is My Country*, pp. 132–3

[2] M.M.P.S.C., pp. 78–80 and 91

[3] FO 371–45237: Lord Killearn to Eden, 8 March 1945 and 3 April 1945

an equal footing" with the founding members. Musa al-'Alami did not in fact sign the Pact on a par with the other delegates. In spite of this, the said annex was described by a Foreign Office official as "rather deplorable". Another official wondered if in the light of this annex, H.M.G. was still justified in refraining from making an official statement designed to show "for the sake of the record" that Palestine "could neither be regarded as an Arab nor as an independent state".[1]

2 *The Non-Independent Countries*

The participation of representatives from the non-independent Arab countries of North Africa in particular was proposed, and persuasively argued for, by 'Azzam. The Subsidiary Committee had received several messages from the notables of these countries calling upon its members to give them the chance to take part in the activities of the League. The general Arab nature of the League's objectives and activities was underlined both in the Alexandria Protocol and in the Preamble of the Pact. 'Azzam argued, therefore, that the League should take an active interest in the affairs and problems of all the Arab countries, regardless of whether they were independent or not. He suggested that prominent Arab personalities such as Muhammad Idris al-Sanussi should be allowed to represent their countries in an advisory capacity in the activities of the specialized committees in particular. The Lebanese delegate objected to the use of the word "participate". He agreed, however, that they should take part as advisers or experts. This was approved by the other delegates and provided for in the Pact (Article 4). The Subsidiary Committee also suggested that a special annex should be added to the Pact concerning co-operation with the non-independent Arab countries.[2]

These provisions were sharply criticized by the British on the grounds that they would prejudice the position of the peace conference with regard to the future of Cyrenaica and Tripolitania, which were under temporary British military occupation. They were also concerned about possible French reactions to the inclusion in the Pact of strong pro-

[1] FO 371–45238 Minute by Ronald I. Campbell, 13 May 1945. The Annex concerning Palestine was subjected to criticism in the Egyptian Senate on 3 April by Sabri Abou 'Alam, the Wafdist senator, on the grounds that it gave very little guarantee that the Arab countries would oppose Zionism in Palestine. Noqrashi, in reply, said that the Palestine Arabs were not dissatisfied with what had been achieved, and that it could not be alleged that Palestine had been neglected. 'Azzam added that the establishment of the League was the best possible guarantee for Palestine. Musa al-'Alami was in fact not at all satisfied with the provisions of the Pact. He told Sir Walter Smart on 23 March that the League had been reduced to a debating society, and expressed his dissatisfaction over the non-admission of the Palestine Arab representative officially to the Council on a par with the other delegates. FO 371–45930, Weekly Appreciation Summary 29 March–4 April (Cairo); and 45238: Killearn to Eden, 23 March

[2] M.M.P.S.C., pp. 78–81 and 85–7

visions in this regard. Noqrashi, when approached by Sir Walter Smart on the subject, was not responsive at the beginning, especially with regard to Libya, in which he said Egypt had special interest, and in view of the active lobbying by Al-Sanussi in the Palace. He informed the Subsidiary Committee in its final meeting of British views on the subject, but he made light of their importance. 'Azzam was in fact to make a statement to the press on 4 March in which he conveyed King Farouq's view that the League should not refuse any Arab an investigation of his problems just because he was weak, or absent from the League's Council. 'Azzam argued with Lord Killearn on 7 March that Mr Eden's statements of support for Arab unity had referred to the Arabs in general and not only to the independent Arab states. Henry Phara'oun, when approached by Lord Killearn, stated that "it was all the fault of the wicked 'Azzam Bey", and that he had told 'Azzam that he was "not prepared to sign poetry", for that was what the proposed clause amounted to. He added that he had told 'Azzam also that there was no reason to irritate the French for no purpose whatsoever. Lord Killearn thought, however, that the idea was espoused personally by King Farouq, though he attributed this to the influence of 'Azzam.[1]

Representations were also made to Ibn Sa'ud, who instructed Sheikh Yusuf Yassin to seek the deletion of the objectionable provisions, or at least the postponement of the whole matter. He instructed him also not to sign the Pact unless he obtained positive advice from the British Embassy.

The British objections were, however, disregarded by the Preparatory Committee, which approved a strong text for an annex on co-operation with the non-independent Arab states, proposed by 'Azzam (Appendix VIII). Makram 'Ubaid Pasha, who was a member of the Egyptian delegation, was to go even further than 'Azzam and to call for the formation, side by side with the League, of a popular assembly or congress in which the non-independent Arab countries could participate. He stressed that any loss of connections between the League and these countries would weaken the League itself. He added that most of the so-called independent Arab states were in fact not yet fully independent. Sheikh Yusuf sought the advice of the British Embassy on whether he should sign the Pact or not. Sir Walter Smart told him that he did not feel that H.M.G. could at this late hour prevent him from signing.[2]

---

[1] FO 371–45236 and 45237: Lord Killearn to Eden, 7 March 1945

[2] FO 371–45237–E1986/3/65. It was through Sheikh Yusuf Yassin in fact that the text of the proposed provisions on Palestine and the non-independent Arab countries reached the British Embassy even before the conclusion of the meeting of the Subsidiary Committee on 3 March. Yusuf Yassin was, in fact, together with 'Azzam, an enthusiastic supporter of the participation of Palestine in the League's Council, and of representatives of the non-independent Arab countries in the non-political

THE PACT OF THE ARAB LEAGUE: A SEQUEL

The Pact of the League was signed on 22 March 1945 by heads of delegations from Egypt, Saudi Arabia, Iraq, Transjordan, Syria, and Lebanon. A copy was sent to Imam Yehya of Yemen, who signed it on 10 May 1945. The League came officially into existence on 10 May 1945, after the ratification of the Pact by four out of the seven founding states. The Arab delegates present at the signing ceremony were well aware of the limitations of the scheme devised after laborious negotiations. They were warned during the meetings of the Subsidiary Committee, more than once by 'Azzam, and at times by Jamil Mardam and Yusuf Yassin, that the Pact, as it was then being evolved, would fall far short of the expectations of the Arab public. No mention was made of Arab unity as an immediate or an ultimate objective, which was taken by some as an admission that its achievement did not fall within the realm of practical politics.[1] The more revolutionary suggestion by Makram 'Ubaid, that the League should be supplemented by a popular assembly comprising representatives of all the Arab countries, did not find much support from the other delegates. The tone of the public speeches of all the heads of delegations was rather low-keyed and apologetic. Noqrashi stated that some people might consider the Pact a cautious step. He argued, however, that it would be much better to go slowly and to avoid overstepping events, since this might lead nowhere. Faris al-Khouri, the Syrian Prime Minister, considered it "a modest beginning", while 'Abdul Hamid Karami declared that "we know very well that this League does not achieve the

---

activities of the League. He raised objections both to the Lebanese statements about the inadvisability of allowing the participation on the Council of a non-independent state; and to a suggestion by Nuri that it should be stipulated that countries which were expected to achieve independence within five years should be allowed to participate without assuming any obligations until their independence. He did not see any force in the Lebanese argument, and did not see any reason why a time limit or a condition of any sort should be imposed in this regard. He also objected to Nuri's suggestion, which was later accepted, that the participation of Palestine should be dealt with in a separate annex. He was in favour of including it in the main text of the Pact. Ibn Sa'ud, in spite of British representations, was therefore determined to lend all support to the Palestine Arabs and to favour their participation in the League. M.M.P.S.C., pp. 79–80

[1] See, for instance, Robert W. MacDonald *The League of Arab States: A Study in the Dynamics of Regional Organization*, Princeton 1965, p. 40; Patrick Seale *The Struggle for Syria*, p. 23; Elie Kedourie *The Chatham House Version*, p. 228. The general view of the Egyptian press comments, since the initiation of the Arab unity consultations, was that in view of the fact that all the Arab states were keen on preserving their full rights in independence and sovereignty, the most that could be achieved would be the formation of a League on the model of the Pan-American Union. They noted late in 1944 that the word "unity" had been replaced in official use by the word "co-operation". See, for instance, the two articles by Mahmud Azmy and by Muhammad Zaki 'Abdul Qader in *Al Ahram*, 26 September 1944

ultimate ideals aspired to by the Arabs."[1] Dr Abdul Hamid Badawi, the Egyptian Foreign Minister, stated later that some people might argue that, in view of the various historical, geographical, racial, and cultural ties binding the Arab states, their delegates should have tried to evolve a stronger scheme than that envisaged in the Pact. He noted, however, that the past experience of other countries, especially in Latin America in this field, had shown that it would be unwise to force the pace. A union of states, he argued, has to come out as a result of a natural process of evolution, nurtured and guided by politicians and rulers, and cannot be imposed. He was aware of the weaknesses of the provisions regarding the peaceful settlement of disputes and action against aggression. He stated, however, that the prohibition of any resort to force was of itself a strong guarantee for the peaceful settlement of all disputes.[2]

The Pact of the Arab League was in fact an exercise in the art of compromise. It was an instrument which could be accepted both by the half-hearted and by the enthusiasts. In Lebanon, it was described by the Foreign Affairs Committee of the Chamber of Deputies as a great step forward, and a testimony to the soundness and sagacity of Lebanese policy. The pact, it added, provided for closer inter-Arab co-operation, and did not at the same time involve any encroachment on national sovereignties.[3] The more extreme Christian elements in Lebanon were in fact not at all unhappy about this new development, and thought that the Pact would enable their country to keep clear of any entanglements with the other Arab states. Some attributed this to the efforts of Henry Phara'oun within the meetings of the Subsidiary Committee. The Muslim elements, on the other hand, were rather disappointed, and felt that the loose form of association envisaged in the Pact would not be effective. There was a tendency, however, to consider the Pact a setback for British policy, on the grounds that H.M.G., in view of their special relations with most of the Arab states, could have found it easier to dominate a closely-knit League.[4] The Pact was subject also to some criticism from the Wafd party in Egypt, and from the extreme pan-Arab elements in Syria and Iraq.

The British, on the other hand, were impressed by the success of the inter-Arab talks in evolving a practical scheme for Arab co-operation. "A collection of European states," stated Robin Hankey of the Foreign

---

[1] Text of the speeches delivered during the public session of the General Arab Congress on 22 March 1945 in *Mahdar al Mu'tamar al 'Arabi al 'am fi Qasr al Za'faran bil Qahira* (Minute of the General Arab Congress in Za'faran Palace in Cairo), Arab League publication, Cairo 1949. Texts also in *Al Ahram*, 23 March 1945

[2] A lecture delivered on 5 April 1945, whose text was included in *Majallat al-Jami'ya al Misriya lil Qanoun al Dawli*, Vol I, 1945, pp. 8–15

[3] Bishara Khalil al-Khouri *Haqaiq Libnaniya*, Vol. II, pp. 306–13

[4] FO 371–45553: Weekly Appreciation Summary, 27 March 1945 (Beirut)

Office, "would hardly have produced anything more impressive."[1] Lord Killearn admitted that he had been a good deal surprised that an idea which had at first appeared to him in the nature of a pious hope had ended by taking such solid and serious shape.[2] The establishment of the Arab League was publicly welcomed by the British Government, as it was later by the American Government.[3] The Arab delegates were aware of the fact that the British, through their public statements, and through their representations to King Ibn Sa'ud, contributed much towards the removal of some serious obstacles from the path of Arab co-operation. Faris al-Khouri was to convey his and the other delegates' gratitude for the significant contribution of Mr Eden in particular in this regard.[4]

The establishment of the League was, however, a purely Arab initiative. It was a positive response to the genuine and strong public desire for closer inter-Arab co-operation. It was, as rightly noted by Cecil Hourani, a victory for moderate Arab nationalism, that is, for the view that union could come only as a result of evolution and a gradual surrender of sovereignty. It was also a victory for secular liberalism in Arab thought.[5] The outmoded concepts of pan-Islamism and the revival of the Arab Empire were replaced by those of co-operation and free association. Bertha Gaster, the correspondent of *The Jerusalem Post* in Cairo, summed up the measure of success achieved on the three main issues of concern to the Arab states in the following poignant statement: "Palestine: unity and defiance; the outside world: unity and hope; home politics of the Arab countries where dynastic and economic rivalries are still unsolved: circumspection."[6]

---

[1] FO 371–45237: minute dated 27 March 1945

[2] FO 371–45415: Lord Killearn to Eden, 28 February 1945

[3] Richard Law stated in the House of Commons on 9 May 1945, in answer to a question by Sir Edward Spears, that H.M.G. "have welcomed the successful formation of the League of Arab states. They will await with sympathy and interest the results of the detailed conversations which are now to be begun for reducing the various barriers which divide the Arab peoples and for promoting co-operation between them." 410 H.C. Deb., 5th ser., col. 1885

William Philips, the American Assistant Secretary of State, stated in a public speech on 2 June 1945, that the United States government welcomed the establishment of the League "and the steps which have already been taken towards unity between the Arabs in the economic, social and cultural fields". F.R. of the U.S. 1945, Vol. VIII, p. 29

[4] FO 371–45237: Lord Killearn to Eden, 24 March 1945

[5] Cecil Hourani *The Arab League in Perspective*, p. 134

[6] *The Jerusalem Post*, 25 March 1945

CONCLUSION

The Arab League was described by King 'Abdullah of Transjordan as "a sack into which seven heads have been thrust . . . with remarkable haste and at a time when Syria and Lebanon were still under a French mandate, Transjordan under a British mandate, and Iraq and Egypt bound by still valid treaties with Great Britain". The Arab countries, he added, were content "both with the veil concealing that which they wish to hide and with vainglorious boasting about what they wish to advertise".[1] 'Abdul Rahman al-Rafi'i, the Egyptian historian politician, described it as a British-inspired scheme. History had shown, he added, that the Arab governments lacked both the sincerity and the desire to co-operate with each other.[2] The Pact of the League, stated Elie Kedourie, proved to be "a device designed not so much to bring about Arab unity, as to keep the so-called Arab states at arm's length from one another".[3]

If this is so, was the flame then worth the candle? If not, did the formation of the League provide a satisfactory answer to the question of Arab unity?

From the account given in this book of inter-Arab consultations and talks from 1943 onwards, it is obvious that the loose form of association provided for in the Pact represented the most that the Arabs could agree upon in the circumstances. The alternative was not unity or union, but the recurrence of the previous unregulated and unco-ordinated state of inter-Arab relations. The establishment of the League did not remove actual or potential sources of discord between the Arab states. It did, however, provide a useful forum within which grievances could be aired, and direct contacts between high-level Arab delegates could be made more easily than ever before. The prohibition of any use of force, and the obligation to respect the independence and the existing forms of government in the member states, were designed mainly to limit the possibility of any serious future conflict between the Arab states. This did not fail, however, to give the League a rather static character socially, as well as politically. No attempt was made to supplement it by popular organizations composed of members of Parliament and prominent public figures, and thus to stimulate public interest in its ideals and achievements. The Arab League scheme was, however,

---

[1] *Al Takmila Min Mudhakkirat Hadrat Saheb al Jalala al Hashimiya al Malik Abdullah Ibn al Hussein*, Amman 1951, p. 12

[2] Abdul Rahman al-Rafi'i *Fi A'aqab al Thawra al Misriya*, p. 142

[3] Elie Kedourie *The Chatham House Version*, p. 228

readily accepted by the advocates of Arab unity as a starting-point, and a first step towards the achievement of their cherished ideal.

An attempt has been made in this book to explain the reasons behind the failure of the Arab nationalists, during the inter-war period, to transform the wave of Arab solidarity, in connection with Palestine and Syria, into a drive towards unity. The Arab nationalist movement lacked a generally accepted ideological basis and a practical plan for action. The secular elements in Egypt, Syria, and Lebanon tended to think in terms of a voluntary association which preserved for each country her identity and independence. The extreme pan-Arabs in Iraq favoured complete integration within an Arab empire for the achievement of which the Iraqi army would be the chief instrument. Arab unity as an ideal was elevated to the realm of the abstract, and meant different things to different people. To the Hashimites, it meant the unity of Greater Syria, and its union with Iraq under their leadership. To Ibn Sa'ud, it meant a comprehensive alliance system with sufficient guarantees for the interests of each state *vis-à-vis* the others. There was always an abundance of poets to extol the ideal, and a paucity of political thinkers to define it and to clarify all the issues involved.

The Arab nationalist movement lacked, above all, pervasive political organization at the grass-root level, which would have required a long process of education and socialization among the masses. The Arab Independence Party, founded in 1918 by the leading members of the pre-World War I Arab secret societies, had disintegrated, with its leaders split into pro-Sa'udi and pro-Hashimite factions. No serious attempt was made either to revive its activities or to create a similar political organ with branches all over Arab Asia. Integration requires a high level of political maturity, which was lacking in the Arab countries.

There was, however, a general consensus about the benefit, to each of the Arab countries, of closer inter-Arab co-operation. It was only in Egypt that there was general agreement among politicians as well as intellectuals about the advisability, in view of all the difficulties involved, of adopting a gradualist approach, testing the practicability of the idea first in the cultural fields. This was possible in Egypt, which had no territorial ambitions in Arab Asia, and which had a leading position in the movement towards the revival of Arab culture. Such an approach had no appeal for Nuri Pasha al-Sa'id or for Amir 'Abdullah, since it did not involve an accretion of territory or an enhancement of status. "Life is short and I have been in the background for twenty-five years and want something done," retorted Amir 'Abdullah in 1943 when urged by Nuri to tone down his agitation for the Syrian throne.[1]

A movement, in the political sense, has to have well-defined objectives

[1] FO 371–34960: Sir Harold MacMichael to the Colonial Secretary, 24 July 1943

and a strong organizational framework capable of mobilizing the masses in support of these objectives. These two prerequisites were lacking in Arab Asia in spite of the fact that all the factors conducive to the formation of such a movement were there. Of these we can mention the unifying influence of a common religion, language, cultural heritage, geographical contiguity, and the general opposition to foreign domination and Zionist ambitions, involving the need for solidarity in the national struggle. The Rashid 'Ali *coup* of April 1941 was perhaps the only movement that can be described as such in political terms. It had well-defined objectives, and was supported by the Arab masses inside and outside Iraq. Its failure was due as much to the lack of realistic assessments and planning as to the interplay of international forces in an extraordinary world situation.

These organic weaknesses were compounded by the antipathetic attitude of foreign powers, which saw in Arab nationalism a serious threat to their continued presence and influence in the area. The French had done much to consolidate the parochial tendencies, and to widen the schisms between the different sects and ethnic groups in the Levant. Turkey was apprehensive of the emergence of a strong Arab bloc which might impede the realization of her territorial ambitions in northern Syria and Iraq. The Zionists were intent on establishing a Jewish state in Palestine. Arab nationalism, weak and fragmented as it was, was no match for the dynamic and powerful Zionist movement backed by the financial and political resources of Jewish organizations in Europe and the United States. The preoccupation with the Zionist threat, which was real enough though exploited for their own internal purposes by Arab rulers and politicians, accentuated the negative aspect of Arab nationalism and sapped much of its strength.

The British had their reservations and apprehensions with regard to Arab nationalism. The pan-Arab movement had often been identified with Hashimite efforts to secure the unity of Greater Syria with Iraq. As such it represented a source of trouble for the British in their relations with Ibn Sa'ud, who was strongly opposed to such schemes, and with the French, who suspected British instigation behind the Hashimite moves. The Sa'udi–Hashimite feud did, in a way, serve them well. Ibn Sa'ud's close relations with the British were designed partly to ensure their intervention to put a stop to any objectionable Hashimite activities. The role envisaged by him for Britain in the area was that of an arbiter, and a protector of the interests of each country *vis-à-vis* the others.

Another factor weighing on the British policy-makers was the fear lest the encouragement of Arab nationalism would in the end endanger British presence and influence in the area. A memorandum on Arab federation prepared by the Foreign Office in September 1939 recognized "some truth" in the argument that a united Arab state, embracing the whole of Arab Asia, would be less amenable to British influence than a number of small and weaker states. It was therefore considered "unlikely" that H.M.G. would, of their own accord, "ever wish actively to promote and encourage pan-Arab ideas", even if the attitude of the French Government left them free to do so, and even if there were no dynastic rivalries involved.[1] The movement towards Arab federation, warned a second memorandum prepared in January 1942, whose conclusions were approved inter-departmentally and by the War Cabinet, "is likely to degenerate into an anti-British, anti-French, and above all anti-Zionist and anti-Jewish movement".[2]

The British had their apprehensions also about Egypt's increased involvement in Arab affairs. If the development of an Arab bloc in Arab Asia was of itself potentially dangerous, the consolidation of such a bloc by its inclusion of Egypt, with its larger population, wealth, and development, was naturally more objectionable. "It is probably to the interest of both Arabs and ourselves," stated Sir Miles Lampson in May 1943, "that Egypt's interest in Arab problems should remain as academic as possible." Egypt, he added, "is not really an Arab country in spite of her claims to be one".[3]

Why then did the British Government decide, in spite of these assessments, to come into the open in support of Arab unity, and to encourage Egyptian leadership of the movement towards closer Arab co-operation?

This was not actuated simply by the wish to propitiate the Arabs in a critical war situation. Eden's second statement of support for Arab unity was made at a time when the Middle East had ceased to be a major theatre for the war operations, and when the Allies had become more confident of a victorious end of the war. The roots of this policy go in fact as far back as 1915, when the decision was taken to encourage the Arabs to stage a general revolt against the Turks. There emerged, during the war and the following years, two schools of thought. The first was in favour of the encouragement of the development, under British tutelage, of an Arab union. This, it was argued, would safeguard British interests, and secure Arab acceptance of a central role for Britain in the area. Sir Herbert Samuel, the first High Commissioner for Palestine, found the British military in Palestine in 1920 strongly in favour of a settlement on these lines. His counter-proposal, which was rejected by Lord Curzon, the then Foreign Secretary, was the encouragement by H.M.G. of a "loose confederation" of the Arabic-speaking states "for common and economic purposes". The second school, which was identified up to 1938 with the Colonial Office, saw the promotion of local and separate nationalisms as the lesser danger. Arab nationalism was viewed as essentially negative in nature, and likely to drift into pan-Islamism and xenophobia.

---

[1] FO 371–23239: Memorandum dated 28 September 1939
[2] FO 371–31337: Report dated 9 January 1942
[3] Cab 95/1 (M.E.W.C. (43) 15): Memorandum dated 3 May 1943

British policy during the inter-war period was based on a combination of these two contradictory assumptions and prescriptions. King Faisal I of Iraq was discouraged in 1933 from lending his support to, or identifying himself with, any efforts designed to bring about the unity of the Arabs. He was told at the same time that H.M.G. would view with sympathy any steps taken in the direction of closer inter-Arab co-operation especially in the cultural and economic spheres. The first assumption for this policy was that pan-Arabism was a phenomenon in Middle East politics "which has probably come to stay". It was therefore considered "extremely unwise" to show open lack of sympathy with the idea it embodied, as opposed to any particular manifestation of that idea. The second assumption was that the achievement of an Arab union was anyway an impossibility, in view of the dynastic rivalries, sectarian and ethnic frictions, French policies, and Zionist ambitions. To oppose the vague aspirations of the Arabs for unity would, therefore, unnecessarily alienate and antagonize them.

Several factors tipped the balance during the Second World War in favour of the advocates of a more positive policy towards the pan-Arab movement. The first was the wide appeal which the idea of a Palestine settlement through the creation of an Arab federation began to have in British official circles, and its espousal by, among others, Churchill, Leopold Amery, Lord Moyne, and Lord Lloyd. The second factor was the mistaken belief that by realizing for the Arabs their cherished ideal of federation, their fears of Jewish domination and expansion might be mitigated, and their opposition to British policy might be removed. The third factor was the weakening of French control over Syria and Lebanon. One of the main objections raised in the early thirties, and again in 1943, to the unity of the Greater Syria states with Iraq was the fear that this would open all of these countries to French influence. The waning of the French role in world affairs, and of French influence in the Levant, seemed to offer a unique chance for the pursuit of that policy. The fourth factor was connected with the British line of thinking about post-war world organization in general. They were in favour of the establishment of regional councils composed of confederations of contiguous states with the membership, and presumably the predominance over each of these councils, of one or two of the great powers interested in the region. The fifth factor was the strong position of Anthony Eden, who was sympathetic towards Arab aspirations for unity, in the War Cabinet as a result of his special relationship with Churchill.

The change in the British attitude towards Arab unity was a gradual one. The Foreign Office memorandum of 1939 stressed that any attempt by H.M.G. to promote Arab federation, for whatever motives, would be "a very risky experiment" from the point of view of their relations with the Arab countries, France, and possibly Turkey. It was therefore recommended that a positive British declaration on the subject should be avoided as long as possible. The memorandum of 1942, while stressing the possible negative effects as far as British interests were concerned, recommended that H.M.G. should adopt a more positive policy and try to guide the pan-Arab movement "so far as possible, on lines which are both advantageous to the Arabs themselves, and not incompatible with British interests".

Some confusion was caused, however, by the gradual nature of this change of attitude and by the lack of inter-departmental co-ordination of policies towards the area. This was noticeable in particular during the discussions in London about the initiatives suggested by Richard Casey in the field of closer regional co-operation, and about the emancipation of Transjordan, then favoured by the Colonial Office. The Colonial Office cast serious doubts over the concept of the Middle East as a unit, while the Foreign Office urged the deferment of any decision on the end of the mandate over Transjordan in order not to prejudice future efforts towards the formation of an Arab federation. The Foreign Office appeared at times to be raising obstacles and creating difficulties for Nahas Pasha in his efforts to convene the Alexandria meeting. British representatives in the area had to draw attention to Eden's public statements, and to point out that this would lay H.M.G. open to the charge of inconsistency, and of having "killed the Arab seedling after ostentatiously watering it for months".[1]

By their public statements, and by raising no objections to Nahas' initiative, the British had contributed much to the evolution of the Arab League. It is true, however, that they had their serious doubts, up to the last minute, about the chances of success of this initiative. They were as surprised as anybody else at the ability of the Alexandria meeting to evolve a practical scheme for Arab co-operation. Their general reaction was one of approbation. Their expectations were, however, pitched too high and some of their assessments were rather superficial. The aim of the Alexandria Conference, stated Lord Moyne, the Minister of State in Cairo, seemed to have been to unite the Arab World in co-operation with Britain. Sir Kinahan Cornwallis, while subscribing to this view, which had been conveyed to him by Nuri Pasha, stated that many must have wondered at the time Eden made his two statements "whether the Arab World would ever unite in any practical way or direction, or still more whether they would be prepared to put themselves under the guidance and leadership of Great Britain". An invitation had been extended to Britain, he added, "to act as the guide and mentor of the Arab World", which if responded to would safeguard British imperial interests "more surely than ever before".[2]

The Arabs were ready and even eager to establish close and harm-

[1] FO 371–39988: Sir Edward Spears to Eden, 23 April 1944
[2] FO 371–39991: Sir Kinahan to Eden, 5 November 1944

onious relations with Britain after the war. They were, however, far from ready to accept British "leadership and guidance", and wanted these relations to be based on equal partnership and free association. There were many indications to that effect during the war. Objections were raised by the Arab governments in 1944 to British membership on the board of the then proposed Middle East Council for Agriculture. Egypt was already voicing her demands for the revision of the 1936 treaty, while Transjordan was pressing for the end of the mandate. The Syrians and the Lebanese were strongly against the retention by any foreign power of troops or any position of influence in the Levant. The Palestine Arabs, supported by the neighbouring Arab governments, were calling for the early establishment of self-government in Palestine.

Arab nationalism had developed mainly in reaction against foreign domination and influence. The boost given to it by the establishment of the Arab League was therefore bound to militate against, rather than in favour of, the retention by Britain of her military presence and political influence in the area. The growing interest of the United States, and to a lesser degree of the Soviet Union, in the Middle East, was likely to challenge British predominance, and to provide alternative sources of support and assistance for the Arab countries.

British representatives in the area were alive to the fact that a possible conflict of interest between Britain and the Arab states might arise. They tended, however, to over-emphasize the negative impact of a settlement unacceptable to the Arabs in Palestine, and a pro-French policy in the Levant. The fact of the matter is that, even had these problems been non-existent, this would probably have alleviated, rather than removed, the possibility of future friction.

APPENDICES

Appendix I

Test of the Alexandria Protocol, 7 October 1944[1]

The undersigned, chiefs and members of Arab delegations at the Preliminary Committee of the General Arab Conference:

Anxious to strengthen and consolidate the ties which bind all Arab countries and to direct them towards the welfare of the Arab World, to improve its conditions, insure its future, and realize its hopes and aspirations,

And in response to Arab public opinion in all Arab countries,

Have met at Alexandria from Shawwal 8, 1363 (September 25, 1944) to Shawwal 20, 1363 (October 7, 1944) in the form of a Preliminary Committee of the General Arab Conference, and have agreed as follows:

1. League of Arab States

A League will be formed of the independent Arab States which consent to join the League. It will have a council which will be known as the Council of the League of Arab States in which all participating states will be represented on an equal footing.

The object of the League will be to control the execution of the agreements which the above states will conclude; to hold periodic meetings which will strengthen the relations between those states; to co-ordinate their political plans so as to insure their co-operation, and protect their independence and sovereignty against every aggression by suitable means; and to supervise in a general way the affairs and interests of the Arab countries.

The decisions of the Council will be binding on those who have accepted them except in cases where a disagreement arises between two member states of the League in which case the two parties shall refer their dispute to the Council for solution. In this case the decision of the Council of the League will be binding.

---

[1] Translation prepared by the Arab Office, Washington D.C. (n.d.), included in a pamphlet entitled *The Arab League in Perspective* published by that Office, which contained a reprint of Cecil Hourani's article under that title, to which reference has been made in the book. Arabic text in: Sami Hakim *Mithaq al-Jami'a wal Wihda al-'Arabiya,* Cairo 1966, pp. 203–10

In no case will resort to force to settle a dispute between any two member states of the League be allowed. But every state shall be free to conclude with any other member state of the League, or other powers, special agreements which do not contradict the text or spirit of the present dispositions.

In no case will the adoption of a foreign policy which may be prejudicial to the policy of the League or an individual member state be allowed.

The Council will intervene in every dispute which may lead to war between a member state of the League and any other member state or power, so as to reconcile them.

A subcommittee will be formed of the members of the Preliminary[1] Committee to prepare a draft of the statutes of the Council of the League and to examine the political questions which may be the object of agreement among Arab States.

2. Co-operation in Economic, Cultural, Social, and Other Matters

A. The Arab States represented on the Preliminary Committee shall closely co-operate in the following matters:

(1) Economic and financial matters, i.e., commercial exchange, customs, currency, agriculture, and industry.

(2) Communications, i.e., railways, roads, aviation, navigation, posts and telegraphs.

(3) Cultural matters.

(4) Questions of nationality, passports, visas, execution of judgements, extradition of criminals, etc.

(5) Social questions.

(6) Questions of public health.

B. A subcommittee of experts for each of the above subjects will be formed in which the states which have participated in the Preliminary Committee will be represented. This subcommittee will prepare draft regulations for co-operation in the above matters, describing the extent and means of that collaboration.

C. A committee for co-ordination and editing will be formed whose object will be to control the work of the other subcommittees, to co-ordinate that part of the work which is accomplished, and to prepare drafts of agreements which will be submitted to the various governments.

D. When all the subcommittees have accomplished their work the Preliminary Committee will meet to examine the work of the subcommittees as a preliminary step towards the holding of the General Arab Conference.

---

[1] The word "Preparatory" has been used in the book since it is a more accurate translation of the Arabic word "Tahdiriya" than "Preliminary". The word "subcommittee" has been replaced by "Subsidiary Committee" which has been used in some books on the subject.

3. Consolidation of these Ties in the Future

While expressing its satisfaction at such a happy step, the Committee hopes that Arab States will be able in the future to consolidate that step by other steps, especially if post-war world events should result in institutions which will bind various Powers more closely together.

4. A Special Resolution Concerning Lebanon

The Arab States represented on the Preliminary Committee emphasize their respect of the independence and sovereignty of Lebanon within its present frontiers, which the governments of the above States have already recognized in consequence of Lebanon's adoption of an independent policy, which the Government of that country announced in its programme of October 7, 1943, unanimously approved by the Lebanese Chamber of Deputies.

5. A Special Resolution Concerning Palestine

A. The Committee is of the opinion that Palestine constitutes an important part of the Arab World and that the rights of the Arabs in Palestine cannot be touched without prejudice to peace and stability in the Arab World.

The Committee also is of the opinion that the pledges binding the British Government and providing for the cessation of Jewish immigration, the preservation of Arab lands, and the achievement of independence for Palestine are permanent Arab rights whose prompt implementation would constitute a step towards the desired goal and towards the stabilization of peace and security.

The Committee declares its support of the cause of the Arabs of Palestine and its willingness to work for the achievement of their legitimate aims and the safeguarding of their just rights.

The Committee also declares that it is second to none in regretting the woes which have been inflicted upon the Jews of Europe by European dictatorial states. But the question of these Jews should not be confused with Zionism, for there can be no greater injustice and aggression than solving the problem of the Jews of Europe by another injustice, i.e., by inflicting injustice on the Arabs of Palestine of various religions and denominations.

B. The Special Proposal concerning the participation of the Arab Governments and peoples in the Arab National Fund to safeguard the lands of the Arabs of Palestine shall be referred to the committee of financial and economic affairs to examine it from all its angles and to submit the result of that examination to the Preliminary Committee in its next meeting.

In faith of which this protocol has been signed at Faruq I University at Alexandria on Saturday, Shawwal 20, 1363 (October 7, 1944).

Appendix II

Text of a letter from Sheikh Yusuf Yassin to Ahmed Maher Pasha signifying his Government's approval of the Alexandria Protocol and stating their views on Arab co-operation[1]

19 Muharram 1363
(3 January 1945)

To His Excellency Dr Ahmed Maher Pasha, the Prime Minister of Egypt and the Chairman of the Preparatory Committee of the General Arab Congress,

Greetings

Your Excellency knows that during the last meeting of the Preparatory Committee in Alexandria in which I represented the Saudi Arabian Government, I did not put my signature on the Protocol then signed by the representatives of the Syrian, Lebanese, Iraqi, Transjordanian, and Egyptian Governments pending its review by the Saudi Arabian Government.

The Government of Saudi Arabia are desirous and anxious for the achievement of the unity of the Arab ranks. They would like this to be based on sound principles conducive to the realization of the Arab hopes pinned on the meeting of the Congress. The Saudi Arabian Government maintain that the adoption of the following principles would serve the common objective and realize the aspirations of the Arab nation:

1. The conclusion of an alliance between the Arab states designed to promote their co-operation; and to provide for mutual assistance for the security of each and all of them; and to guarantee good-neighbourliness among them. A significant step in that direction had already been taken by the Kingdoms of Saudi Arabia, Iraq, and Yemen.

2. The freedom of each Arab state to conclude with any other Arab state whatever agreements might be designed to insure her security. Such agreements should not be detrimental to any other Arab state and should foster good-neighbourliness and fraternal co-operation.

3. Arab solidarity and alliance should be devoid of any aggressive designs towards any nation, state, or group of states. It should be aimed only at self-defence, the maintenance of peace, and the promotion of justice and freedom for all.

4. The prohibition of war between the Arab states. In case a disagreement arises between two Arab states over a new issue, or the failure

[1] Text included as Annex No. 6 to the Minutes of the Political Subsidiary Committee, pp. 17–18

of one party to honour its obligations towards any other government which is a member in the alliance, attempts should be made to settle it through conciliation, mediation, or arbitration on just and equitable fraternal bases. Should either party decline to accept arbitration, or to abide by any award given, the other Arab states should advise and call upon him to admit what is right. Should that party become intransigent and resort to aggression, they may, after consultation with each other, decide on such action as would stop aggression and establish justice and equity in the Arab arena.

5. In order to avoid problems among the Arab states, it should be made clear from the start that the republican regimes in Syria and Lebanon shall be maintained, and the complete independence of the two states accepted by all.

6. The efforts aimed at the unification of culture and legislation between two Arab states and between them and the rest of the Arab countries have much to commend them. The Kingdom of Saudi Arabia represents, however, a special case in view of her circumstances and the presence of the Holy Shrines in her territory. Saudi Arabia will, therefore, refrain from adopting any principle in education or legislation which might contravene the tenets and rules of Islam.

7. The Arab states, as members of one nation with common interests, should co-operate in strengthening their economies and promoting their commercial relations. This should not, however, deprive any state of her freedom to exercise her full control over her financial and economic affairs in accordance with her special circumstances and interests.

These are the principles which, in the view of the Saudi Arabian Government, should form the bases for the unity of Arab ranks. To facilitate the achievement of this sublime objective, I, in my capacity as a representative of my government and a member of the Preparatory Committee, approve the Protocol signed in Alexandria on 20 Shawwal 1363 (7 October 1944).

Knowing Your Excellency's care for the interests of the Arab nation, I have no doubt that these principles will have your support within the committees in charge of studying this issue, which is of interest to all Arabs.

With all my respects to your Excellency.

(Signed) Yusuf Yassin.

Appendix III

Text of the Draft Pact of the Arab League proposed by the Iraqi Government[1]

The Pact of the Arab League

In order to implement the Protocol signed in Alexandria on Saturday the 20th of Shawwal 1363 (7 October 1944) by the representatives of Egypt, Syria, Transjordan, Iraq, and Lebanon, which provided for the consolidation of the close relations and the numerous ties binding all the Arab countries as well as the strengthening and the directing of these relations towards the welfare of the Arab world, the improvement of its conditions, the insuring of its future, and the realization of its hopes and aspirations in response to Arab public opinion in all Arab countries,

The signatory plenipotentiary delegates have agreed on the following:

Article 1: The League of Arab States is composed of the states which have signed this Pact and of all other independent Arab states which consent to join the League by making a statement to be deposited with the Permanent Secretariat and conveyed to all member states of the League.

Article 2: The League has as its purpose the strengthening of relations between the Arab states, the co-ordination of their policies in order to achieve co-operation between them, to safeguard their independence and sovereignty against every aggression by suitable means, and to supervise in a general way the affairs and the interests of the Arab countries.

Article 3: The League shall have a Council whose task will be to achieve the realization of its objectives. It will be composed of the representatives of the Arab member states of the League. Each state will have no more than three representatives, and will have one vote regardless of the number of its representatives.

The Council elects in its first meeting in every year a president from among the representatives of the Arab states. The Annex to this Pact names the first President of the Council.

Article 4: The Council of the League shall convene in ordinary session four times a year at the invitation of the President in any of the capitals of the Arab states. The Council shall decide at the end of each

[1] The Arabic text enclosed as Annex No. 7 to the minutes of the Political Subsidiary Committee, pp. 19–21. This draft was actually prepared by Nuri Pasha al-Sa'id, who conveyed to the British its main outlines on 1 November 1944 (FO 371–39991: Lord Killearn to Eden 1 November 1944). It was referred to by the other members of the Subsidiary Committee as "Nuri's scheme".

session on the capital in which it will hold its following session. The annex to this Pact names the first capital in which the Council shall meet.

The Council shall convene in extraordinary session at the request of two member states of the League at least. It will establish an internal regulation for its functions.

Article 5: The Council of the League shall insure the implementation of the agreements which may be concluded between the member states of the League. Its decisions shall be binding on those who have accepted them, except in cases where it has been stipulated in this Pact that these decisions shall be binding.

Article 6: The League shall have a Permanent Secretariat whose seat will be in ( ), and which will be composed of a Secretary-General, Assistant Secretaries, and a sufficient number of officials.

The Council of the League shall appoint the Secretary-General, who will be at the same time the secretary of the Council. The annex to this Pact names the first Secretary-General of the League.

The Council of the League shall appoint an Assistant Secretary-General from among the nationals of each of the member states. The name of each candidate shall be proposed by his government.

The Secretary-General appoints the necessary officials for the functioning of the League.

The Council of the League establishes internal regulations for the functioning of the Secretariat and personnel affairs.

Article 7: The Secretary-General shall prepare each year the draft budget of the League and its permanent committees, which will be submitted to the Council of the League for approval.

The share of each member state in the expenses will be specified in the annual budget.

Article 8: The members of the Council of the League and its committees as well as the officials of its Secretariat shall enjoy diplomatic privilege and immunities when engaged in the exercises of their functions. The Secretary-General shall have the rank of Ambassador, and the Assistant Secretaries that of Minister Plenipotentiary.

The buildings occupied by the organs of the League, its members, and officials shall be inviolable.

Article 9: Each member state of the League pledges to guarantee the independence and sovereignty of the other (member) states.

In case of an actual or threatened external aggression against the security, independence, and sovereignty of any member state, any other member state may ask the President to call for the immediate convocation of the Council. The Council of the League shall, by unanimous decision, determine the measures necessary to repel that aggression, and shall advise the member states of the League to carry them out.

Article 10: The member states of the League shall exchange military missions in a way to be regulated by the Council. The Council shall devise, after consultation with military experts, plans and schemes insuring, in so far as is possible, the unification of systems and (types of) arms between the military, naval, and air forces of the member states of the League. The Council shall submit these plans and schemes to these states for approval and execution.

Article 11: The member states pledge not to adopt in foreign countries an attitude which contradicts this Pact and under no circumstances may any of these states pursue a foreign policy detrimental to that of the League or any of its member states. The member states shall seek, in so far as is possible, to unify the lines of their foreign policies through organized consultations.

Each member state shall request the representatives of any other member state to represent her in any foreign country in which she has no representation.

Article 12: If there should arise a dispute between two or more member states which could not be settled by diplomatic negotiations, these states shall submit the whole issue under dispute to arbitration by giving their approval to accept mediation by any country, or the Council of the Arab League, or any personality.

Should the parties fail to agree on that, they must refer the dispute either to the International Court of Justice, or to any other body in charge of settling international disputes.

The disputants shall not, under any circumstances, resort to the use, or threatened use, of force or any other means of pressure.

Article 13: The Council of the League shall prepare draft statutes for an Arab Court of Justice whose decisions shall be binding. This draft shall be submitted to the member states of the League for approval.

Article 14: If a disagreement arises between any member state of the Arab League and any other foreign state, the Council may, at the request of any Arab or foreign state, or on its own initiative, offer its mediation to settle the disagreement. Should the Council fail in its mediatory efforts, it will decide by unanimous vote on the measures necessary to insure the safety of the Arab state party to that dispute, and will advise the member states of the League to carry them out.

Article 15: The Council of the League shall set up permanent committees to deal with the following matters:

(1) Economic and financial matters including commercial relations, customs, currency, and questions of agriculture and industry.

(2) Communications; this includes railroads, roads, aviation, navigation, telegraphs, and posts.

(3) Cultural and codification affairs.

(4) Nationality, passports, visas, execution of judgements, extradition of criminals, and similar matters.

(5) Social affairs.
(6) Health questions.

The Council may also set up other permanent committees to deal with matters not listed above.

Article 16: Each of the above-mentioned committees shall be composed of a chairman appointed by the Council of the League for a term of three years, and of a delegate from each of the member states whose name shall be suggested by his state and shall be appointed by the Council of the League. Each Committee shall in its work avail itself of the assistance of any experts as and when necessary.

Each Committee shall organize general Arab conferences to deal with matters within its competence. The technical bodies shall assist in holding these conferences.

The Council of the League shall prepare internal regulations for the functioning of the Permanent Committees.

Article 17: The Permanent Committees shall submit their proposals to the Council of the League for approval. If approved, the government of each member state shall submit these proposals to the competent local authorities for approval. The approved proposals shall not be binding on the state until the approval of the competent local authorities in each of the other states has been obtained.

Article 18: Each member state may conclude with any other member or non-member state special agreements which do not contradict the letter or the spirit of this Pact.

Article 19: All member states of the League must register in the Secretariat all treaties and agreements concluded, or to be concluded, between any one of them and any other non-member or member state.

Article 20: This Pact may not be amended except with the approval of all the states which have accepted its provisions. If a disagreement arises concerning the interpretation of one of its provisions, the interpretation approved unanimously by the Council of the League shall be binding. The Council may, by a majority vote, submit (any matter related to) the interpretation of these provisions to the Arab Court of Justice.

Annex:

The first President of the Council of the League is ——————.
The first place in which the Council shall convene is ——————.
The first Secretary of the League is ——————.

Appendix IV

Text of the Draft Pact of the League proposed by the Lebanese Government[1]

Pact of the League of Arab States

The Arab states represented by ——————— for ———————, in order to implement the Alexandria Protocol signed on 7 Tishrin al Awwal 1944, met,

And after preparatory discussions, the Pact of the League of Arab States was formulated as follows:

Article One: The League of Arab States is composed of the independent Arab states which have signed this Pact, and of the other independent Arab states which the Council of the League shall decide to accept (their admission). The Council shall decide on any application for admission within a period of six months starting from the date of the submission of the application.

Article Two: The League of Arab States shall be considered as a permanent conference of the Arab states charged with the execution of special functions specified in this Pact. This League shall not have an international personality independent of that of the governments represented in its Council, each of which has retained her full rights in sovereignty and independence internally, as well as externally.

Article Three: The Council of the League of Arab States shall be composed of the representatives of the member states of the League. These states shall be represented on the basis of absolute equality. Each one of them shall have one vote regardless of the number of her representatives.

Article Four: The Permanent seat of the Council of the League shall be in Egypt. The Council may meet during the summer in Lebanon or any other place it may specify.

Article Five: The Council shall convene in ordinary session once every six months, and in extraordinary session whenever the need arises at the request of two member states of the League. The first ordinary session shall start on 15 Kanoun al-Thani and end on 10 Shabat.

The second ordinary session shall start on 15 Ab and end on 15 Iyloul.

Article Six: The Council shall meet for the first time at the invitation

[1] The Arabic text enclosed as Annex No. 8 to the minutes of the Political Subsidiary Committee, pp. 22–5. This draft was prepared in its broad outlines by Selim Taqla, the Lebanese Foreign Minister, prior to his death in January 1945. The scheme was elaborated and expanded by Henry Phara'oun. (FO 371–45236: Shone to Eden, 19 January 1945)

of the Prime Minister of Egypt, and shall devise the internal regulations for its functions. It shall meet afterwards at the invitation of the Secretary-General.

Article Seven: The Council shall have a permanent Secretariat. The Permanent Secretariat shall be composed of a Secretary-General appointed by the Council, and of officials appointed by the Secretary-General, who defines their competence, salaries, and professional grades, with the approval of the Council. The expenses of the Council shall be apportioned between these (member) states as specified by the League.

Article Eight: The Council shall elect, by majority vote for each session, a president, who shall chair the meetings.

Article Nine: The members of the Council, as well as the officials specified by the Council, and the members of the Committees, shall enjoy diplomatic immunity and all privileges accorded to diplomatic representatives.

This immunity shall include the buildings in which the Council meets as well as the associated premises.

Article Ten: The Functions of the League:

(Firstly) Consultation and co-operation in all that would enhance the independence, full sovereignty internally and externally, and security of the borders of each of the member states of the League. Should any member state of the League be subject to an aggression or a threat of aggression, the Council shall determine the possible measures for repelling that aggression, and shall advise each state to carry them out in accordance with the established rules of her constitutional laws.

The state subject to an aggression shall alone evaluate the facts and decide whether they constitute an aggression or a threat of aggression.

(Secondly) Supervising the execution of whatever agreements shall be concluded between the states of the League. This shall be subject to the provisions of the second article of this Pact.

(Thirdly) Consolidation of relations between the (member) states and agreement on political plans designed to achieve co-operation in matters specified in this Pact.

(Fourthly) General concern with the common interests of the Arab countries.

Article Eleven: With the exception of the cases explicitly specified in this Pact, the decisions of the Council shall be taken by the unanimous vote of the signatory states of this Pact, and by secret ballot.

These decisions may be taken by majority (vote) in which case they shall be binding on those who have accepted them.

Article Twelve: Any resort to force in order to resolve disputes between two member states of the League is prohibited. If a disagreement arises, it should be settled by ordinary diplomatic means, by mediation by the Council of the League, or by arbitration by that Council with the approval of the legislative authorities in accordance with the constitutional procedures of each state.

Arbitration shall be conducted according to the rules laid down in the special regulations annexed to this Pact. Resort to arbitration is inadmissible with regard to disagreements over:

(Firstly) matters related to the sovereignty, independence, and boundaries of the state.
(Secondly) matters which affect the interests of a state which is not a member in the League.
(Thirdly) matters which fall under domestic jurisdiction.

Article Thirteen: Each state shall be absolutely free to conclude special agreements with any other member state or any other state; and to join any other League or international body provided this would not be of an aggressive nature towards any of the signatory states of this Pact.

Treaties and agreements which may be concluded between any member state of the League and any other state shall not bind or restrict the other members of the League. Treaties and agreements concluded by any of the member states of the League prior to (the signature of) this Pact do not bind or restrict the other members.

Article Fourteen: The Council shall mediate in any disagreement which might lead to war between a member state of the League and any other member or non-member state in order to reconcile them.

Article Fifteen: The Arab states participating in the League shall co-operate closely in the following matters in accordance with the principles of this pact and the rules included in its annexes as well as the special agreements which may later be concluded and ratified in accordance with the constitutional rules of each of the contracting states:

1—Economic and financial affairs, including commercial relations, customs, currency, and questions of agriculture and industry.
2—Communications; this includes railways, roads, aviation, navigation, telegraphs, and posts.
3—Cultural affairs.
4—Nationality, passports, visas, execution of judgements, extradition of criminals, and similar matters.
5—Social affairs.
6—Health affairs.

Article Sixteen: If any (member) state of the League deem it in her interest to withdraw, she will have the right to do so provided she notifies the Council of her intention to withdraw six months before her actual withdrawal.

Any state which fails to honour her obligations under this Pact shall be expelled from the League.

Article Seventeen: This Pact may be amended with a two thirds majority (vote). Any state which does not accept the amendment will, however, have the right to withdraw as soon as the amendment comes into effect without giving the notification provided for in this Pact.

Article Eighteen: This Pact has been drawn up in the Arabic language and signed by the high contracting parties, each one of whom has received a copy of it.

This Pact and the enclosed annexes shall be ratified by the high contracting parties each in accordance with her basic laws. The documents of ratification shall be deposited with the Government of His Majesty the King of Egypt. The Pact shall come into effect *vis-à-vis* each one of them as soon as these documents have been deposited.

Written in ——————— on the day ———————.

Annex No. ———

The Rules of Arbitration by the Council of the League

Article One: Without prejudice to the special provisions agreed upon in the Arbitration Agreement, arbitration by the Council of the League shall be conducted in accordance with the rules laid down in the following articles.

Article Two: The states resorting to arbitration shall sign an Arbitration agreement explaining the subject over which the dispute arose; the form and the fixed time limit for the presentation of relevant documents; the special powers to be granted to the arbitration body; and all the agreed upon terms in general.

Article Three: The Arbitration Body may undertake to devise the Arbitration Agreement if asked to do so.

Article Four: Arbitration may be entrusted to the Council of the League as a whole, or to one or more of its members, or to an international personality.

Article Five: The representative of the state in the Council shall defend its rights and interests during the arbitration (proceedings). The state may also elect (for this task) one or more legal experts.

Article Six: Arbitration shall be based on written documents only. The documents and papers including the supporting evidence shall be exchanged, within the period specified and in accordance with the terms defined in the Arbitration Agreement, either directly or through the Secretariat-General.

The period specified in the Arbitration Agreement may be extended with the approval of the parties concerned or by a decision by the

Arbitration Body if this be deemed necessary for reaching an equitable judgment.

Article Seven: The Arbitration Body may initiate any necessary investigations. These shall be entrusted to a committee of experts established by a decision specifying the subject of the inquiry and the share of each of the parties in the expenses.

The Committee of experts shall submit to the Arbitration Body a report embodying the findings of its investigation. This report shall then be forwarded to the parties for comments within a period specified by the Arbitration Body.

Article Eight: No documents may be submitted after the expiration of the time limit fixed for the exchange of documents, or after the completion of the investigation unless otherwise agreed by the parties, or resolved by the Arbitration Body.

Article Nine: The Arbitration Body may order that the documents should be produced or the necessary clarifications be given. Any refusal will be taken note of, by that Body.

Article Ten: The Arbitration Body may determine its competence in interpreting the Arbitration Agreement, and may take any decision regarding the handling of the case and the supporting evidence.

Article Eleven: With regard to the notifications deemed necessary within the territory of a state other than the one requesting arbitration, the Arbitration Body shall contact directly the government of that state. This (procedure) is to be followed also if the investigations are to be conducted.

Article Twelve: When all the above-mentioned procedures have been completed, the Arbitration Body shall announce the conclusion of the trial.

Article Thirteen: The deliberations shall be conducted *in camera*. The decision shall be taken by majority vote.

Article Fourteen: The decision must be reasoned and must be conveyed to the states which have applied for arbitration.

Article Fifteen: The decision of the Arbitration Body shall be final.

Article Sixteen: Any dispute about the interpretation of the Arbitration award shall be settled by the Arbitration Body.

Article Seventeen: The Arbitration Body may not accept any request for a retrial unless there is a new element which might have a bearing on the settlement of the case and which was not known either to the Arbitration Body or to the state presenting it not out of negligence or error on her part, at the time of the conclusion of the trial.

The Arbitration Body must, before dealing with the matter, discuss the argument made in support of a retrial, and decide on whether to accept or to reject the request.

It may request as a pre-condition for conducting a retrial that the state concerned should first implement its Award.

The application for a retrial shall be submitted, subject to refusal, within six months of the appearance of the new element. No request for reconsideration of the Award shall be accepted after ten years from the date of its issue.

Article Eighteen: The Arbitration Award binds only the states which have applied for arbitration. The League shall not interfere directly in its implementation. It may, however, resolve that the state refusing to accept the Award has failed to fulfil her obligations under the Pact of the League.

Article Nineteen: The states applying for arbitration shall bear the expenses incurred. Each of them shall also bear an equal share in the costs specified by the Arbitration Body.

Appendix V

The Views of the Representative of Iraq on the Article Dealing with the Settlement of Disputes

A *The First Memorandum* (dated 24 Feb. 1945)[1] (Full Text)

The representatives of the independent Arab governments have been engaged throughout the last year in consultations and discussions recorded in signed official minutes. These led to the enunciation on 7 October 1944 of the Alexandria Protocol, whose provisions are known to the whole world.

As is well-known, the Protocol was based on:

1. The retention by the Arab states represented in the Council of the League, of their independence, sovereignty, rights, and international contractual obligations.

2. The competence of the Council of the League of Arab States to supervise the execution of whatever agreements may be concluded by these states in order to achieve co-operation in matters explicitly stated in the Protocol. Decisions were made binding only on those who have accepted them. It was also stipulated that the Council shall attempt to settle any disagreement referred to it by the parties concerned and that it will mediate in any disagreement which might lead to war between two member states, so as to reconcile them.

The Council, therefore, was not empowered to interfere in matters related to treaties and agreements, nor to obligations established by

[1] The Arabic text included in M.M.P.S.C., p. 63

treaties concluded before the formation of the Council of the League. These responsibilities and obligations bind only the signatory states.

The Council of the League, moreover, has no right to interfere in the conclusion, in the future, of bilateral or multilateral treaties and agreements of which no mention was made in the Protocol except by requesting their registration (in the Council) lest they be detrimental to the policy of the League of Arab States, or any of its (member) states.

To include in the proposed system of the League, which we have met to discuss, any provision contradicting the above-mentioned principles, in an attempt to grant the Council of the League more powers than provided for in the text of the Protocol, would contravene what had been agreed upon in the minutes of the Preparatory Committee as well as the letter and the spirit of the Protocol itself.

The proposals and reservations made by some representatives aim at granting the Council of the League the right to intervene uninvited in the settlement of disagreements between the member states, especially over treaties and obligations concluded before the formation of the League and even before the emergence of the states participating in the present discussions. This, in addition to its contravention of the spirit and the letter of the Protocol, would weaken the sublime objective which we all seek to realize through the formation of the Council of the League of Arab States.

We maintain that all these independent states retained their full rights, on the international plane, to settle any disagreement between themselves through the customary peaceful means. The establishment of the Council of the League of Arab States will not contract these rights in such a way as would make it necessary to find means to cover this deficiency.

Being fully acquainted with the views of the Iraqi authorities on the matter, we should like to point out that it is not possible for the Iraqi Government to accept a provision which would grant the Council of the League the competence to intervene uninvited for the settlement of disagreements, especially those arising over matters related to previous agreements and conventions, except with the approval of the parties concerned.

B *The Second Memorandum* (dated 26 Feb. 1945):[1] (Full Text)

1. As an independent sovereign state, Iraq has obligations, responsibilities, and duties under treaties, agreements, and concessions to international companies some of which predate the establishment of self-government and even the last world war. It is not possible for the Iraqi Government, without their approval, to hand over their serious

[1] M.M.P.S.C., p. 64

responsibilities under these treaties and agreements to any other authority.

2. The contracting states do not lose any of their rights if they fail to agree on referring a dispute, arising over matters related to their contracts, to the Council of the League. They can resort to the usual customary peaceful means for the settlement of disputes adopted by all other independent states. The harm which may be done through the failure to agree to refer a dispute to the Council of the League can only be a limited one, which could be avoided by obliging these states to abstain from the use of force for the settlement of any dispute, however prolonged it may be. The principle of non-resort to force is one of the principles included in the Alexandria Protocol.

3. The Council of the League will be composed of the representatives of the Arab states. It is, therefore, a political organ. To authorize it to intervene in the settlement of disagreements which might arise between some member states, without the consent of the disputants, would create a serious situation threatening the structure of the League. This might also place some members in an awkward position, since they may feel inclined to avoid being implicated in matters which are not consistent with their interests.

It is not proper to introduce into the constitution of the League, which aims at co-operation and solidarity, principles conducive to corruption, contrary to our objectives.

4. If it be deemed desirable to empower the Council of the League to intervene in settling disagreements without the approval of the parties, this should be confined to disagreements over treaties and agreements concluded with its knowledge and under its supervision, in addition to all matters included in the Protocol for the realization of which the League will be established.

5. The stipulation in the Alexandria Protocol regarding the competence of the Council of the League to intervene in settling disagreements between member states has made that intervention contingent upon the approval of the disputants. In view of this, it would not be proper for the delegates in the Subsidiary Committee to come out with proposals contradicting the said provision.

Appendix VI

Text of the Draft Pact of the Arab League proposed by the Political Subsidiary Committee (14 February–3 March 1945)[1]

Draft Pact for the League of Arab States

In order to implement the Alexandria Protocol dated Saturday 20 Shawwal 1363 (7 October 1944) and signed by the representatives of Egypt, Syria, Iraq, Transjordan, Saudi Arabia, Lebanon, and Yemen, which had provided for the consolidation of the close relations and the numerous ties binding the Arab countries and the direction of these relations towards the welfare of all the Arab countries, the improvement of their conditions, the insuring of their future, and the realization of their hopes and aspirations,

And in response to Arab public opinion in all the Arab countries,

And on the basis of respect for the independence and sovereignty of the states participating in the League,

The Contracting states have agreed on the following:

Article 1 The League of Arab States is composed of the independent Arab states which have signed this Pact, and of the other independent Arab states which would wish to join the League by depositing an application in the Permanent Secretariat-General, and which the Council of the League may decide to accept in its first meeting after the submission of the application.

Article 2 The League shall have a Council whose task will be to achieve the realization of its objectives. The Council shall be composed of the representatives of the Arab states participating in the League on an equal footing and with one vote for each state regardless of the number of her representatives.

Article 3 The Council shall supervise the execution of agreements which these (member) states may conclude; hold periodical meetings designed to consolidate their ties; co-ordinate, in so far as is possible, their political plans in order to achieve their co-operation and to protect their independence and sovereignty from every aggression by suitable means; and supervise in a general way the affairs and interests of the Arab countries.

The Council shall also determine the means of co-operating with the international bodies which may be created in the future in order to guarantee security and peace, and to enhance social, economic, and other relations for the general good.

Article 4 The Arab states participating in the League shall

[1] The Arabic text in M.M.P.S.C., pp. 95–9

co-operate closely, with due regard to the organization and circumstances of each state, on the following matters:

a. Economic and financial affairs, including commercial relations, customs, currency, and questions of agriculture and industry.
b. Communications; this includes railroads, roads, aviation, navigation, telegraphs, and posts.
c. Cultural affairs.
d. Nationality, passports, visas, execution of judgements, and extradition of criminals.
e. Social affairs.
f. Health matters.

Article 5 For each of the matters listed in the previous article, there shall be set up a special committee composed of representatives of the member states of the League. These committees shall lay down the principles, and define the scope of co-operation. These shall be formulated in draft agreements, to be presented to the Council.

(The League) may co-operate in cultural, social, health, and other matters with the representatives of the local governments, or bodies, or local elements, in all Arab countries. The Council shall determine the way by which these governments, bodies, or elements shall be represented in the above-mentioned committees in order to realize thereby the national objectives included in the Preamble of this Pact.

Article 6 The permanent seat of the League of Arab States shall be established in Cairo. The Council may convene at any other place it may designate.

Article 7 The Council of the League shall convene in ordinary session twice a year, in March and in October. It shall convene in extraordinary session whenever the need arises, at the request of two member states of the League.

Article 8 The League shall have a Permanent Secretariat-General, which shall consist of a Secretary-General, Assistant Secretaries, and an appropriate number of officials.

The Council of the League shall appoint the Secretary-General by a two-thirds majority vote. The Secretary-General shall be, at the same time, the Secretary of the Council.

The annex names the first Secretary-General of the League. The Secretary-General shall, with the approval of the Council, appoint the Assistant Secretaries and the necessary officials for the functioning of the League. The Council of the League shall establish an internal regulation for the functions of the Secretariat-General and matters related to the staff.

Article 9 The Secretary-General shall prepare the draft of the budget of the League and shall submit it to the Council for approval before the beginning of each fiscal year. The Council shall determine the share of each state in the expenses, and may reconsider the apportionment of expenses whenever necessary.

Article 10 The members of the Council of the League, as well as the members of the committees, and the officials specified in the internal regulation, shall enjoy diplomatic privileges and immunity when engaged in the exercise of their functions. The Secretary-General shall have the rank of Ambassador and the Assistant Secretaries that of Ministers Plenipotentiary.

Buildings and other premises occupied by the organs of the League shall be inviolable.

Article 11 The first meeting of the Council shall be convened at the invitation of the head of the Egyptian Government. Thereafter, it shall be convened at the invitation of the Secretary-General. The representatives of the member states of the League shall in turn assume the presidency of the Council at each of its ordinary sessions.

Article 12 In case of aggression, or threat of aggression, by a state against a member state of the League, the state which has been attacked or threatened with aggression alone may demand the immediate convocation of the Council. The Council shall, by unanimous decision, determine the measures necessary to repulse the aggression. If the aggressor is a member state, her vote shall not be counted in determining unanimity.

If, as a result of the attack, the government of the state attacked finds herself unable to communicate with the Council, that state's representative in the Council shall request the convocation of the Council for the purpose indicated in the foregoing paragraph. Should this representative be unable to communicate with the Council, any member state of the League shall have the right to request the convocation of the Council.

Article 13 Any resort to force in order to resolve disputes arising between two or more member states of the League is prohibited. If there should arise among them a difference which is referred by the disputants to the Council for settlement, the decision of the Council shall then be enforceable and obligatory. Any disagreements related to the state's independence, sovereignty, and territorial integrity shall not be subject to arbitration.

The Council shall mediate in all differences which may threaten to lead to war between two member states, or a member state and another state, in order to reconcile them (i.e. the parties).

Article 14 States of the League which may desire to establish closer co-operation and stronger bonds than are provided by this Pact may conclude agreements to serve that end.

Treaties and agreements already concluded, or to be concluded in the future, between a member state and another state shall not be binding or restrictive upon other members.

Article 15 Each member state shall respect the systems of government established in the other member states of the League and regard them as the exclusive rights of those states. Each shall pledge to abstain from any action calculated to change established systems (of government).

Article 16 If a member state considers it in her interest to withdraw from the League, she shall have the right to do so provided she notifies the Council of the League of her intention to withdraw one year before such withdrawal is to go into effect. The Council of the League may consider any state which has failed to fulfil her obligations under this Pact as having become separated from the League, this to go into effect upon a unanimous decision of the (member) states, not counting the state concerned.

Article 17 Each member state shall deposit with the Secretariat-General one copy of every treaty or agreement concluded, or to be concluded, between herself and another member state, or a third state.

Article 18 Except in cases specifically mentioned in this Pact, a unanimous decision by the Council shall be binding on all member states. Its execution shall, however, take place in each state in accordance with her basic laws. Any majority decision by the Council shall be binding on those who have accepted it, and shall be implemented in each state in the manner stated above.

A majority vote by the Council shall, however, be sufficient for decisions on the following matters:

(*a*) Matters related to personnel.
(*b*) Adoption of the budget of the League.
(*c*) Establishment of the internal regulation for the Council, the Committees, and the Secretariat-General.
(*d*) Decisions to adjourn the sessions.

Article 19 This Pact may be amended with the consent of two-thirds of the states of the League. A state which does not accept such an amendment may withdraw as soon as the amendment comes into effect, without being bound by the provisions of Article 16 of this Pact.

Article 20 This Pact and its Annexes shall be ratified according to the basic laws of the contracting states and of the states whose application to join will be accepted by the Council.

The instruments of ratification shall be deposited with the Secretariat-General of the Council, and the Pact shall be operative as regards each ratifying state fifteen days after the Secretary-General has received the instruments of ratification from four states.

Article 21 This Pact has been drawn up in Cairo in the Arabic language on ——————, in one copy which shall be deposited in the safe keeping of the Secretariat-General of the Council. An identical copy shall be delivered to each state of the League.

Article 22 Until the Secretariat-General of the League has been established, the Ministry of Foreign Affairs of the Egyptian Government shall perform the functions referred to in Articles 20 and 21.

Annex I
Resolution Regarding Palestine

Considering the provisions of the Alexandria Protocol with regard to the special position of Palestine in the view of the other Arab states, and the relation of her cause to peace and stability in the Arab World.

And since Article 22 of the Covenant of the League of Nations, included in the Treaty of Versailles of 1919, has recognized the independence of the Arab countries which ceased to be under the (sovereignty of the) Ottoman state. And since Palestine is one of these countries whose independence was recognized in the above-mentioned Covenant, which gives her a legitimate right to independence. And since the Preparatory Committee resolved unanimously on 1 October 1944 to allow a representative of the Palestine Arabs to participate in its meetings and functions, the Subsidiary Committee has therefore decided to ask the Preparatory Committee to recognize the right of Palestine to participate in the League of independent Arab states on an equal footing with the founding (states).

Since Palestine has been unable so far, for compelling reasons, to exercise its recognized right to independence, and since the recognition of this right is still valid from the legal point of view and has not been changed in any way, the Committee therefore suggests that the Council of the League should take charge of the selection of an Arab representative from Palestine to represent that state in the Council of the League until that Country can achieve its independence.

Annex No. 2
Resolution Regarding the Arab Countries

Since the Alexandria Protocol has stipulated that the functions of the League shall include the supervision, in a general way, of the affairs and the interests of the Arab countries, and since this objective can only be achieved through co-operation with all these countries in all matters with possible means; the Subsidiary Committee therefore conveys to the Preparatory Committee its suggestion that a special annex should be added to the Pact of the League including the basis of this co-operation and enabling the Council to discharge its above-mentioned function.

Appendix VII

Text of a Letter addressed by Tahsin al-'Askari, the Iraqi Minister in Egypt, to the Chairman of the Subsidiary Committee of the Preparatory Committee, dated 11 March 1945[1]

To His Excellency the Chairman of the Subsidiary Committee in charge of drafting the Pact of the League of Arab States.

Greetings and respects

I have the honour to inform Your Excellency that, in view of the delay in signing the minutes of the meetings of the political Subsidiary Committee of the General Arab Congress, which was due to certain proposed additions to, and modifications of, the draft Pact of the League of Arab States about which some members have not ascertained their governments' views, therefore,

And in order to avoid any misunderstanding which may arise in this respect in the future,

And in order that I may advise my government on this matter, I have deemed it fit to inform Your Excellency that the Iraqi Government considers that the following should be made clear:

First:[2] Article 12: The member states of the League may not interfere, jointly or separately, in any dispute of whatever nature, that may arise between the state of Iraq and (other) member or non-member states of the League, except at the request of the state of Iraq and the state or states party to the dispute.

Second: Article 14: This article gives the (member states of the) League the right to establish among themselves a wider co-operation than that provided for in the Pact, should these states so desire. This authorization is, needless to say, (only) an admission of the right which is now enjoyed by the member states of the League. It should therefore be clear that none of the states of the League may object, for any reason whatever, to any arrangements which some member states may make to widen the scope of such co-operation among themselves.

Third: Article 15: The choice of the system of government in each member state is the exclusive right of the people of that state. But since the text of Article 15 of the draft (Pact) does not adequately clarify this principle, it should be made clear that the Iraqi Government cannot accept any departure from this principle, which is recognized by all the countries of the civilized world.

---

[1] The Arabic text included as Annex No. 3 to the minutes of the Preparatory Committee, M.P.P.C., p. 28

[2] The numbers here refer to those of the draft Pact proposed by the Subsidiary Committee (Appendix VI)

I shall be grateful if your Excellency will kindly inform me that you have taken note of the contents of this letter, so that I may be able to inform my government accordingly before the 15th of the current (month of) March.

With all my respects to your Excellency,

March 11 1945 (signed) Tahsin al 'Askari
Minister of Iraq

Appendix VIII

Text of the Pact of the League of Arab States[1]

His Excellency the President of the Syrian Republic;
His Royal Highness the Amir of Trans-Jordan;
His Majesty the King of Iraq;
His Majesty the King of Saudi Arabia;
His Excellency the President of the Lebanese Republic;
His Majesty the King of Egypt;
His Majesty the King of the Yemen;

Desirous of strengthening the close relations and numerous ties which link the Arab states;

And anxious to support and stabilize these ties upon a basis of respect for the independence and sovereignty of these states, and to direct their efforts towards the common good of all the Arab countries, the improvement of their status, the security of their future, the realization of their aspirations and hopes;

And responding to the wishes of Arab public opinion in all Arab lands;

Have agreed to conclude a Pact to that end and have appointed as their representatives the persons whose names are listed hereinafter; who, after having exchanged their plenary powers which were found to be in good and due form, have agreed upon the following provisions:

Article 1

The League of Arab States is composed of the independent Arab States which have signed this Pact.

Any independent Arab State has the right to become a member of

---

[1] Translation prepared by the Arab Office, Washington D.C., included in the pamphlet referred to earlier, pp. 15–20. Arabic text in Sami Hakim *Mithaq al-Jami'a wal Wihda al-'Arabiya*, pp. 227–39

the League. If it desires to do so, it shall submit a request which will be deposited with the Permanent Secretariat-General and submitted to the Council at the first meeting held after submission of the request.

Article 2

The League has as its purpose the strengthening of the relations between the member states; the co-ordination of their policies in order to achieve co-operation between them and to safeguard their independence and sovereignty; and a general concern with the affairs and interests of the Arab countries. It has also as its purpose the close co-operation of the member states, with due regard to the organization and circumstances of each state, on the following matters:

A. Economic and financial affairs, including commercial relations, customs, currency, and questions of agriculture and industry.

B. Communications; this includes railroads, roads, aviation, navigation, telegraphs, and posts.

C. Cultural affairs.

D. Nationality, passports, visas, execution of judgements, and extradition of criminals.

E. Social affairs.

F. Health problems.

Article 3

The League shall possess a council composed of the representatives of the member states of the League; each state shall have a single vote, irrespective of the number of its representatives.

It shall be the task of the Council to achieve the realization of the objectives of the League and to supervise the execution of agreements which the member states have concluded on the questions enumerated in the preceding article, or on any other questions.

It likewise shall be the Council's task to decide upon the means by which the League is to co-operate with the international bodies to be created in the future in order to guarantee security and peace and regulate economic and social relations.

Article 4

For each of the questions listed in Article 2 there shall be set up a special committee in which the member states of the League shall be represented. These committees shall be charged with the task of laying down the principles and extent of co-operation. Such principles shall be formulated as draft agreements, to be presented to the Council for examination preparatory to their submission to the aforesaid states.

Representatives of the other Arab countries may take part in the work of the aforesaid committees. The Council shall determine the conditions under which these representatives may be permitted to participate and the rules governing such representation.

Article 5

Any resort to force in order to resolve disputes arising between two or more member states of the League is prohibited. If there should arise among them a difference which does not concern a state's independence, sovereignty, or territorial integrity, and if the parties to the dispute have recourse to the Council for the settlement of this difference, the decision of the Council shall then be enforceable and obligatory.

In such a case, the states between whom the difference has arisen shall not participate in the deliberations and decisions of the Council.

The Council shall mediate[1] in all differences which threaten to lead to war between two member states, or a member state and a third state, with a view to bringing about their reconciliation.

Decisions of arbitration and mediation shall be taken by majority vote.

Article 6

In case of aggression or threat of aggression by one state against a member state, the state which has been attacked or threatened with aggression may demand the immediate convocation of the Council.

The Council shall by unanimous decision determine the measures necessary to repulse the aggression. If the aggressor is a member state, his vote shall not be counted in determining unanimity.

If as a result of the attack, the government of the state attacked finds itself unable to communicate with the Council, that state's representative in the Council shall have the right to request the convocation of the Council for the purpose indicated in the foregoing paragraph. In the event that this representative is unable to communicate with the Council, any member state of the League shall have the right to request the convocation of the Council.

---

[1] A French translation of the Pact prepared by the Egyptian Society for International Law, in which Dr Badawi, the Egyptian Minister who played a significant role in editing the Pact, was a leading member, used the phrase "bons offices" instead of "mediation", used by the said Society in its translation of the same word in the Alexandria Protocol. It is obvious that "good offices" denote a milder form of action than mediation. Henry Phara'oun, the Lebanese delegate, took great pains to stress, during the meetings of the Subsidiary Committee, that what was meant here were good offices rather than mediation, which he said might involve some encroachment on national sovereignty. The other delegates did not contest his thesis, which they seemed to accept. The Arabic text mentions only "Wasatatuh" meaning literally "its mediation". French translation in *Al Majalla al-Misriya Lil Qanum al-Dawli*, vol. I, 1945, pp. 10–25 (Documents section), and M.M.P.S.C., p. 65

Article 7

Unanimous decisions of the Council shall be binding upon all member states of the League; majority decisions shall be binding only upon those states which have accepted them.

In either case the decisions of the Council shall be enforced in each member state according to its respective basic laws.

Article 8

Each member state shall respect the systems of government established in the other member states and regard them as the exclusive concerns of those states. Each shall pledge to abstain from any action calculated to change established systems of government.

Article 9

States of the League which desire to establish closer co-operation and stronger bonds than are provided by this Pact may conclude agreements to that end.

Treaties and agreements already concluded or to be concluded in the future between a member state and another state shall not be binding or restrictive upon other members.

Article 10

The permanent seat of the League of Arab States is established in Cairo. The Council may, however, assemble at any other place it may designate.

Article 11

The Council of the League shall convene in ordinary session twice a year, in March and in October. It shall convene in extraordinary session upon the request of two member states of the League whenever the need arises.

Article 12

The League shall have a permanent Secretariat-General, which shall consist of a Secretary-General, Assistant Secretaries, and an appropriate number of officials.

The Council of the League shall appoint the Secretary-General by a majority of two-thirds of the states of the League. The Secretary-General, with the approval of the Council, shall appoint the Assistant Secretaries and the principal officials of the League.

The Council of the League shall establish an administrative regulation for the functions of the Secretariat-General and matters relating to the Staff.

The Secretary-General shall have the rank of Ambassador and the Assistant Secretaries that of Ministers Plenipotentiary.

The first Secretary-General of the League is named in an Annex to this Pact.

Article 13

The Secretary-General shall prepare the draft of the budget of the League and shall submit it to the Council for approval before the beginning of each fiscal year.

The Council shall fix the share of the expenses to be borne by each state of the League. This share may be reconsidered if necessary.

Article 14

The members of the Council of the League as well as the members of the committees and the officials who are to be designated in the administrative regulation shall enjoy diplomatic privileges and immunity when engaged in the exercise of their functions.

The buildings occupied by the organs of the League shall be inviolable.

Article 15

The first meeting of the Council shall be convened at the invitation of the head of the Egyptian Government. Thereafter it shall be convened at the invitation of the Secretary-General.

The representatives of the member states of the League shall in turn assume the presidency of the Council at each of its ordinary sessions.

Article 16

Except in cases specifically indicated in this Pact, a majority vote of the Council shall be sufficient to make enforceable decisions on the following matters:

A. Matters relating to personnel.

B. Adoption of the budget of the League.

C. Establishment of the administrative regulations for the Council, the committees, and the Secretariat-General.

D. Decisions to adjourn the sessions.

Article 17

Each member state of the League shall deposit with the Secretariat-General one copy of every treaty or agreement concluded or to be concluded in the future between itself and another member state of the League or a third state.

Article 18

If a member state contemplates withdrawal from the League, it shall inform the Council of its intentions one year before such withdrawal is to go into effect.

The Council of the League may consider any state which fails to fulfil its obligations under this Pact as having become separated from the League, this to go into effect upon a unanimous decision of the states, not counting the state concerned.

Article 19

This Pact may be amended with the consent of two-thirds of the states belonging to the League, especially in order to make firmer and stronger the ties between the member states, to create an Arab Tribunal of Arbitration,[1] and to regulate the relations of the League with any international bodies to be created in the future to guarantee security and peace.

Final action on an amendment cannot be taken prior to the session following the session in which the motion was initiated.

If a state does not accept such an amendment it may withdraw at such time as the amendment goes into effect, without being bound by the provisions of the preceding article.

Article 20

This Pact and its Annexes shall be ratified according to the basic laws in force among the High Contracting Parties.

The instruments of ratification shall be deposited with the Secretariat-General of the Council and the Pact shall become operative as regards each ratifying state fifteen days after the Secretary-General has received the instruments of ratification from four states.

This Pact has been drawn up in Cairo in the Arabic language on this 8th day of Rabi' II, thirteen hundred and sixty-four (March 22, 1945), in one copy which shall be deposited in the safe keeping of the Secretariat-General.

An identical copy shall be delivered to each state of the League.

Here follow the Signatures.

1. Annex Regarding Palestine

Since the termination of the last great war the rule of the Ottoman Empire over the Arab countries, among them Palestine, which had become detached from that Empire, has come to an end. She has come to be autonomous, not subordinate to any other state.

The Treaty of Lausanne proclaimed that her future was to be settled by the parties concerned.

However, even though she was as yet unable to control her own affairs, the Covenant of the League of Nations in 1919 made provision for a regime based upon recognition of her independence.

---

[1] The Arabic text is "Mahkamat 'Adl 'Arabiya" meaning literally "An Arab Court of Justice"

Her international existence and independence in the legal sense cannot, therefore, be questioned, any more than could be the independence of the other Arab countries.

Although the outward manifestations of this independence have remained obscured for reasons beyond her control, this should not be allowed to interfere with her participation in the work of the Council of the League.

The nations signatory to the Pact of the Arab League are therefore of the opinion that, considering the special circumstances of Palestine, and until that country can effectively exercise its independence, the Council of the League should take charge of the selection of an Arab representative from Palestine to take part in its work.

2. Annex Regarding Co-operation With Countries Which Are Not Members of the Council of the League

Whereas the member states of the League will have to deal in the Council as well as in the committees with matters which will benefit and affect the Arab World at large;

And Whereas the Council has to take into account the aspirations of the Arab countries which are not members of the Council and has to work towards their realization;

Now therefore, it particularly behoves the states signatory to the Pact of the Arab League to enjoin the Council of the League, when considering the admission of those countries to participation in the committees referred to in the Pact, that it should do its utmost to co-operate with them; and furthermore, that it should spare no effort to learn their needs and understand their aspirations and hopes; and that it should work thenceforth for their best interests and the safeguarding of their future with all the political means at its disposal.

3. Annex Regarding the Appointment of a Secretary-General of the League

The states signatory to this Pact have agreed to appoint His Excellency Abd-al-Rahman 'Azzam Bey to be Secretary-General of the League of Arab States.

This appointment is made for two years. The Council of the League shall hereafter determine the new regulations for the Secretariat-General.

BIBLIOGRAPHY

A. *Unpublished Sources*

1 *Records of Government Departments in Great Britain* (Public Records Office, London)

Air Ministry: Files 23–8–9

Cabinet Conclusions, Confidential Annexes, Papers, and Minutes of Cabinet Committees.

Colonial Office: Files 733 and 793

Foreign Office: Files 371, 793 and 800

War Office: File 32

2 *Private Papers of British Officials* (St Antony's College, Oxford). (Sir Harold MacMichael, Sir Terence Shone, Sir George Rendel, Sir Walter Smart)

3 *Records of the Arab League* (Unpublished Documents, The Arab League, Cairo, 1949)

Mulakhas Mahadir Mushawarat al Wihda al'Arabiya Ma' al 'Iraq, Sharq al Ardun, al Mamlaka al'Arabiya al So'udiya, Souriya, Libnan, wal-Yaman (Summary of the Minutes of the Arab Unity Consultations with Iraq, Transjordan, the Kingdom of Saudi Arabia, Syria, Lebanon, and Yemen)

Mahadir Jalasat al Lajna al Tahdiriya Lil Mu' tamar al 'Arabi al 'Am fil Iskandariya (Minutes of the Meetings of the Preparatory Committee of the General Arab Congress in Alexandria)

Mahadir Jalasat al Lajna al Fari'a al Siasiya Liwada' Mushru' Mithaq Jami'at al Dowal al 'Arabiya (Minutes of the Meetings of the Political Subsidiary Committee in Charge of Preparing the Draft Pact of the League of Arab States)

Mahadir Jalasat al Lajna al Tahdiriya Lil Mu'tamar al 'Arabi al 'Am fil Qahira (Minutes of the Meetings of the Preparatory Committee of the General Arab Congress in Cairo)

Mahadir al Mu'tamar al 'Arabi al 'Am fi Qasr al-Za'faran bil Qahira (Minutes of the General Arab Congress in al-Za'faran Palace in Cairo)

B. *Published Sources:* In Arabic

1 *Primary Sources*

King 'Abdullah *Mudhakkirat al Malik 'Abdullah* (Memoirs of King 'Abdullah), 2nd edn., Amman 1947

—— *Al Takmila: Min Mudhakkirat Hadrat Sahib al jalala al Hashimiya al Malik 'Abdullah Ibn al Hussein* (Memoirs completed by His Majesty King 'Abdullah Ibn al Hussein) Amman 1951

'Allouba, Muhammad 'Ali *Filistin wa jaratuha: Asbab wa Nataij* (Palestine and its neighbours: Reasons and Conclusions) Cairo 1954

—— *Mabadi' fil Siasa al Misriya* (Principles in Egyptian Politics) Cairo 1942

Al-'Askari, Tahsin *Mudhakkirati 'An al Thawra al 'Arabiya al Kubra wal Thawra al 'Iraqiya* (My memoirs of the Great Arab Revolt and the Iraqi Revolt) 2 vols., Baghdad 1936 (vol. I); 1938 (vol. II)

Al Ayyoubi, 'Ali Jawdat *Dhikrayat: 1900–1958* (Recollections: 1900–58) Beirut 1967

Al 'Azm, Khalid *Mudhakkirat Khalid al-'Azm* (Memoirs of Khalid al 'Azm) vol. I, Beirut 1972

Al Banna, Hasan *Majmu'at Rasail al Imam Ash-Shahid* (Collected Messages of the Martyr Imam) Beirut 1965

—— *Mudhakkirat ad-Da'wa wad-Da'iya* (Memoirs of the Cause and its Advocate) 2nd edn., Beirut 1966

Al Bazzāz, 'Abdul Rahman *Safahat Min al Ams al Qarib* (Pages from the Recent Past) Beirut 1960

Daghir, Asa'd *Mudhakkirati 'Ala Hamish al Qadiyya al 'Arabiya* (My Memoirs About the Arab Cause) Cairo (n.d.)

Al Durra, Mahmoud *Al Harb al 'Iraqiya al Biritaniya 1941* (The Iraqi–British War 1941) Beirut 1969

Ghusn, Dr Fu'ad *Mudhakkirati Khilal Qarn* (My Memoirs over a Century) Beirut (n.d.)

Haddad, Osman Kamel *Harakat Rashid 'Ali al Kilani 1941* (The Movement of Rashid 'Ali al Kilani) Sidon (n.d.)

Al Hasani, Abdul Razzaq *al-Asrar al Khafiya fi Hawadith Sanat 1941*
al-Taharruriya (Hidden Secrets of the Liberatory Events of 1941) 1st edn., Sidon 1958

Haykal, Muhammad Hussein *Mudhakkirat fil Siasa al Misriya* (Memoirs of Egyptian Politics) 2 vols., Cairo 1951 (vol. I); 1953 (vol. II)

Al-Husri, Sati' *Ara' wa Ahadith fil Qawmiya al 'Arabiya* (Opinions and Addresses on Arab Nationalism) Beirut 1959

—— *Mudhakkirati fil 'Iraq* (My memoirs in Iraq) vol. II (covering the period from 1927 to 1941) 1st edn., Beirut 1968

—— *Safahat Min al-Madi al Qarib* (Pages from the Recent Past) Beirut 1948

Hussein, Ahmed *Imani* (My Belief) 1st edn., Cairo 1936
Al Ittihad al 'Arabi fil Qahira *Nasha'th, Nizamh, wa aa'malh Munz Ta'sish fi 25 May 1942 Lighayet 1945* (The Arab Union in Cairo: Its Formation, Structure, and Activities from its Establishment on 25 May 1942 until 1945) Cairo 1946
Al-Jumail, Pierre *Libnan Waqi wa Murtaja* (Lebanon: Present and Future) vol. I, Beirut 1970
Al-Khardhji, Muhammad Shaker *Al 'Arab fi Tariq al Ittihad* (The Arabs in the Road towards Union) vol. I, Damascus 1947
Al-Khouri, Bishara Khalil *Haqaiq Libnaniya* (Lebanese Facts) 2 vols., Beirut 1960; *Majmu'at Khutab* (Collection of Speeches) Beirut 1951
Al-Kitab al Urduni al Abiad *Al-Wathaiq al Qawmiya fil Wihda al-Suriya al Tabi'iya* (The Jordanian White Book: The National Documents about the Natural Syrian Unity) issued by the Government of Transjordan, Amman 1946
Kurras al-Mu'tamar al Barlamani al 'Alami lil Dowal al-Arabiya wal Islamiya (A Pamphlet on the International Parliamentary Congress of the Arab and Islamic States) Cairo 1938
Majmu'at al Bayanat al Wizariya al Libnaniya (The Combined Lebanese Cabinet Statements) compiled and introduced by Jan Mulha, Beirut 1965
Majmu'at Madabit Majlis al Shiukh (The Compiled Minutes of the Egyptian Senate) 13th and 15th sessions, Cairo 1938, 1940
Al Mara' al 'Arabiya wa Qadiyat Filistin: Al-Mu'tamar al-Nisai al Sharqi: Cairo 1938 (The Arab Woman and the Palestine Question: The Eastern Women's Congress: Cairo 1938) Cairo 1939
Mudhakkirat Taha al-Hashimi: 1919–1943 (Memoirs of Taha al-Hashimi: 1919–43) ed. by Khaldun Sati' al-Husri, Beirut 1967
Al-Mu'tamar al 'Arabi al Qawmi fi Bludan (The Arab Nationalist Conference in Bludan) Damascus 1937
Al-Rafi'i, Abdul Rahman *Fi Aa'qab al Thawra al Misriya* (In the Aftermath of the Egyptian Revolt) vols. II and III, 1st edn., Cairo 1951
Al-Rawi, Ibrahim *Min al Thawra al 'Arabiya al Kubra Ila al 'Iraq al Hadith: Zikryat* (From the Great Arab Revolt to Modern Iraq: Recollections) Beirut 1969
Al Rihani, Amin *Faisal al-Awwal* (Faisal I) Beirut 1958
—— *Muluk al-'Arab* (Arab Kings) vol. II, 3rd edn., Beirut 1951
As-Sabbagh, Salah ud-Din *Fursan al 'Uruba fil 'Iraq* (The Knights of Arabism in Iraq) Damascus 1956
Safwat, Najda Fathi *Al 'Iraq fi Mudhakkirat ad-Diplumasiyin al Ajanib* (Iraq in the Memoirs of the Foreign Diplomats) Sidon 1969
As-Sayyed, Ahmed Lutfi *al-Muntakhabat* (Selections) Cairo 1937
—— *Tamulat fil Falsafa wal Adab wal Siasa wal Ijtima'* (Reflections on Philosophy, Literature, Politics, and Sociology) Cairo 1946

Al Shuqairi, Ahmed *Arba'un 'Ama fil Hayat al-'Arabiya wad-Dawliya* (Forty years in Arab and World Politics) Beirut 1969
Al-Sulh, Sami *Safahat Majida fi Tarikh Libnan 1890–1960* (Glorious Pages in the History of Lebanon 1890–1960) Beirut 1960
As-Swaidi, Tawfiq *Mudhakkirati: Nisf Qarn Min Tarikh al-'Iraq wal Qadiya al-'Arabiya* (My Memoirs: Half a Century in the History of Iraq and the Arab Question) Beirut 1969
Al-Tabi'i, Muhammad *Min Asrar al Sasa wal Siasa: Misr Ma Qabl al Thawra* (Secrets of Politicians and Politics) Cairo (n.d.)
Al-Zurkally, Khair Ud-Din *Shibh al-Jazira fi-'Ahd al-Malik 'Abdul 'Aziz* (Arabia Under King Abdul Aziz, 4 pts in 3 vols.) Beirut 1970

2 *Secondary Sources*

Al-Amrousi, Anwar *Al Jaraim as-siasiya fi Misr* (Political Crimes in Egypt) Cairo (n.d.)
Awda, Awda Boutros *Al Qadiya al-Filistiniya fil waqi' al 'Arabi* (The Palestinian Case in the Arab Context) Cairo 1970
Bahari, Yunis *Asrar 2 Mayes 1941 Aw al-Harb al 'Iraqiya al-Injliziya* (Secrets of the 2nd of May 1941, or the Anglo-Iraqi War) Baghdad 1968
Al-Barawi, Dr Rashid *Mashru' Souriya al Kubra* (The Scheme of Greater Syria) Cairo 1947
Bayham, Muhammad Jamil *Qawafil al 'Uruba wa Mawakibha Khilal al 'Usur* (The Caravans of Arabism Throughout the Ages) vol. II, Beirut 1950
Al Bazzaz, Abdul Rahman *Al-Islam wal-Qawmiya al-'Arabiya* (Islam and Arab Nationalism) Baghdad 1952
—— *Hazeh Qawmiyatna* (This is Our Nationalism) Cairo 1964
Al-Dahan, Dr Sami *Al Amir Shakib Arsalan: Hayath wa Atharh* (Amir Shakib Arslan: His Life and Contributions) Cairo 1960
Darwaza, Muhammad Izzat *Hawl al Haraka al 'Arabiya al Haditha* (The Modern Arab Movement) 4 vols., Sidon 1951
—— *Al Wihda al 'Arabiya* (Arab Unity) Beirut 1957
Ghanem, Dr Muhammad Hafez *Muhadarat 'An Jami'at al Dowal al 'Arabiya* (Lectures on the League of Arab States) Cairo 1966
Ghuneim, Ahmed and Abu Keif, Ahmed *Al Yahud wal Haraka al Suhiuniya fi Misr 1897–1947* (The Jews and the Zionist Movement in Egypt 1897–1947) Cairo 1969
Hafez, 'Abbas *Mustafa al Nahas Aw al-Za'ama wal Za'im* (Mustafa al Nahas, or the Leadership and the Leader) Cairo 1936
Hakim, Sami *Mithaq al Jami'a wal-wihda al-'Arabiya* (The Pact of the League and Arab Unity) Cairo 1966
Al Haj, Kamal Yusuf *Falsafat al Mithaq al Watani* (The Philosophy of the National Pact) Beirut 1961

Hamza, 'Abdul Latif *Adab al Maqala al Sahafiya fi Misr* (The Art of the Press Article in Egypt) vol. VIII, 1st edn., Cairo 1963

Al Hasani, Abdul Raziq *Tarikh al Wizarat al 'Iraqiyia* (The History of the Iraqi Cabinets) vols. V and VI, Sidon 1953

Haykal, Dr Muhammad Hussein *Thawrat al Adab* (The Revolution in Literature) 3rd edn., Cairo 1965; 1st edn. issued in 1933

Haykal, Dr Yusuf *Nahwa al Wihda al 'Arabiya* (Towards Arab Unity) Cairo 1943

Al-Husri, Sati' *Ara' Wa Ahadith Fil-Wataniya wal-Qawmiya* (Views and Addresses on Patriotism and Nationalism) Cairo 1944

—— *Muhadarat fi Nushu' al-Fikra al Qawmiya* (Lectures on the Origins of the Nationalist Idea) Cairo 1951

—— *al-Uruba Bain Du'atha wa Mu'ariduha* (Arabism between its Protagonists and Opponents) Beirut 1957

Hussein, Dr Taha *Mustaqbal al Thaqafa fi Misr* (The Future of Culture in Egypt) Cairo 1944

Al Jindi, Anwar *Al-Thaqafa al 'Arabiya fi Ma'arik al Taghrib wal Shu'obiya* (Arab Culture in the battles of Westernization and Parochialism) Cairo (n.d.)

Khilla, Kamil *al-Tatwur al Siasi fil Mamlaka al Urduniya: 1921–1948* (Political Development in the Kingdom of Jordan 1921–48) M.A. Thesis, Cairo University 1969

Marwa, Adib *al Sahafa al 'Arabiya* (The Arab Press) Beirut 1961

Murqus, Elias *Naqd al Fikr al Qawmi* Vol. I. Sati' al Husri (Criticism of the Nationalist Thought: vol. I. Sati' al Husri) 1st edn., Beirut 1966

Nashashibi, Nasser *Maza Jara fil Sharq al Awsat* (What Happened in the Middle East) Beirut 1961

Muzhir, Dr Yusuf *Tarikh Libnan al 'Am* (General History of Lebanon) vol. II, Beirut (n.d.)

Orfali, Jalal *Al Diplomasiya al 'Iraqiya wal Ittihad al 'Arabi* (Iraqi Diplomacy and the Arab Union) Baghdad 1944

Qarqut, Zawqan Muhammad *Tatwur al Fikra al 'Arabiya fi Misr* (The Development of the Arab Idea in Egypt) M.A. Thesis, Cairo University 1971

Ramadan, 'Abdul 'Azim Muhammad *Tatwur al Haraka al Wataniya fi Misr Mim Ibram Mu'uhadat 1936 Ila Nihayat al Harb al 'Aalamiya al Thaniya* (The Development of the Nationalist Movement in Egypt since the Conclusion of the 1936 Treaty till the end of the Second World War) Ph.D. Thesis, Cairo University 1970

Rayan, Hasan 'Ali Eid *Al 'Ilaqat al Urduniya al Biritaniya Fima bain al Harbain al 'Aalmiyatain 1926–1939* (British–Jordanian Relations between the two World Wars 1926–39) M.A. Thesis, Cairo University 1967

Sa'id, Amin *Al Dawla al Arabiya al Muttahida* (The United Arab State) vol. III, Cairo

Sayigh, Anis *Al Fikra al 'Arabiya fi Misr* (The Arab Idea in Egypt) Beirut 1959

—— *Al Hashimiyun wa Qadiyat-Filistin* (The Hashimites and the Palestine Question) Beirut 1966

—— *Libnan al Taifi* (Sectarian Lebanon) Beirut 1955

Al Shahabi, al Amir Mustafa *Muhadarat' An al Qawmiya al 'Arabiya* (Lectures on Arab Nationalism) Cairo 1959

Taqi-ul-Din, Munir *Al Jala': Wathaiq Khatira Tunsher Li awal Mara Takshif al Niqab 'An Asrar Jala' al Qwat al Ajnabia 'An Libnan wa Souriya 'Am 1946* (The Evacuation: Important Documents Published for the First Time Revealing the Secrets of the Evacuation of the Foreign Troops from Syria and Lebanon in 1946) Beirut 1956

Tarbin, Ahmed *Al Wihda al 'Arabiya bain 1916–1945* (Arab Unity from 1916 to 1945) Cairo 1959

Zuraiq, Qustantin *Al Wa'y al-Qawmi* (National Consciousness) Beirut 1939

3 *Periodicals and Newspapers*

Al Ahram Egyptian Daily Newspaper (Alexandria, then Cairo 1876–)

Akher Sa'a Egyptian Weekly Magazine (1934–)

Al Balagh Egyptian Daily Newspaper (Cairo 1923–53)

Al Bilad Iraqi Daily Newspaper (Baghdad 1929–)

Fata al 'Arab A Syrian Daily Newspaper (Damascus 1920–49)

Al Hilal Egyptian Monthly Magazine (Cairo 1892–)

Al Manar Egyptian Monthly Magazine (Cairo 1898–1940)

Misr al Fatat Egyptian Bi-weekly Newspaper (Cairo 1938–41)

Al Misri Egyptian Daily Newspaper (Cairo 1936–54)

Al Muqattam Egyptian Daily Newspaper (Cairo 1889–1952)

Al Musawar Egyptian Weekly Magazine (Cairo 1924–)

Al Rabita al Arabiya Egyptian Weekly Magazine (Cairo 1936–51)

Al Rabita al Sharqiya Egyptian Monthly Magazine (Cairo 1928–31)

Al Risalh Egyptian Weekly Magazine (1933–53)

Al Siasa Egyptian Daily Newspaper (Cairo 1922–51)

Al Siasa al Usbu'iya Egyptian Weekly Newspaper (1926–49)

Al Thaqafa Egyptian Weekly Magazine (Cairo 1939–52)

Al Zaman Iraqi Daily Newspaper (Baghdad 1937–41)

C. *Published Sources in English and French*

1 *Primary Sources*

Avon, The Earl of *The Eden Memoirs: The Reckoning*, London 1965

Ben Gurion, David *Letters to Paula* (Translated from the Hebrew by Aubrey Hodes) London 1971

Ben Gurion Looks Back (In talks with Moshe Pearlman) London 1965

Bullard, Sir Reader *The Camels Must Go*, London 1961

Casey, Lord *Personal Experience 1939–1946*, London 1962
Catroux, General *Dans La Bataille de la Méditerranée: Egypte–Levant–Afrique du Nord 1940–1944*, Paris 1949
Chandos, Lord *Memoirs of Lord Chandos*, London 1962
Churchill, Winston *The Second World War*, vols. I–VI, London 1950–54
Ciano, G. *Ciano's Diary 1939–1943*, London 1947
—— *Ciano's Diplomatic Papers*, London 1948
Cooper, Duff *Old Men Forget*, London 1953
Cust, Arthur "Cantonisation: A Plan for Palestine" in *Journal of the Royal Central Asian Society*, vol. 23, April 1936
The Diplomatic Papers of Oliver Harvey 1937–1940, ed. by John Harvey, London 1970
Documents on British Foreign Policy 1919–1939, 3rd series, 1939, H.M.S.O., London 1949–55
Documents on German Foreign Policy, Ser. D, vols. III, V, VI, VIII–XIII, London 1950–64
Documents on International Affairs, 1936, 1937, 1938, 1939–46, R.I.I.A., London 1938–51
Furlonge, Geoffrey *Palestine is My Country: The Story of Musa Alami*, London 1969
Gallman, Waldemar *Iraq under General Nuri: My Recollections of Nuri al Sa'id 1954–1958*, Baltimore (U.S.) 1964
de Gaulle, Charles *War Memoirs*, 3 vols. (Translated from the French) London 1955–9
de Gaury, Gerald *Three Kings in Baghdad: 1921–1958*, London 1961
Glubb, Sir John Bagot *Britain and the Arabs: A Study of Fifty Years 1908–1958*, London 1959
Grafftey-Smith, Laurence *Bright Levant*, London 1970
Halifax, The Earl of *Fullness of Days*, London 1957
Hansard: Parliamentary Debates: House of Commons and House of Lords, 5th series, 1937–45, H.M.S.O., London
Hull, Cordell *The Memoirs of Cordell Hull*, 2 vols., New York 1948
Hurewitz, J. C. *Diplomacy in the Near and Middle East*, vol. II: 1914–56, Princeton, N.J. (U.S.) 1956
Jackson, R. G. A. "Some Aspects of War and Its Aftermath in the Middle East" in *Journal of the Royal Central Asian Society*, No. 32 (July–October 1945) pp. 258–68
Kelly, Sir David *The Ruling Few*, London 1952
The Killearn Diaries 1934–1946, ed. by Trevor E. Evans, London 1972
Kirkbride, Sir Alec Seath *The Crackle of Thorns: Experiences in the Middle East*, London 1956
Landis, James M. "Anglo-American Co-operation in the Middle East" in *The Annals of the American Academy of Political and Social Science*, 240 (July 1945) pp. 64–72

Lawrence, T. E. *Seven Pillars of Wisdom*, London 1935
Lloyd, Lord *Egypt Since Cromer*, vol. II, London 1934
Magnes, Judah L. "Toward Peace in Palestine" in *Foreign Affairs*, 21 (January 1943) pp. 239–49
Meinertzhagen, Colonel R. *Middle East Diary 1917–1956*, London 1959
The Middle East Supply Centre *Proceedings of the Conference on Middle East Agricultural Development:* Cairo, February 7th–10th, 1944 (Agricultural Report No. 6)
Murray, Keith A. H. "Feeding the Middle East in War-Time" in *Journal of the Royal Central Asian Society*, 32 (July–October 1945) pp. 233–47
The Palestine Partition Commission Report, Cmd. 5854, H.M.S.O., London 1938
The Palestine Royal Commission Report, Cmd. 5479, H.M.S.O., London 1937
The Palestine Statement of Policy, Cmd. 5513, H.M.S.O., London 1937
Philby, H. St. J. B. *Arabian Jubilee*, New York, 1st American edn., 1953
Puaux, G. *Deux Années au Levant: Souvenirs De Syrie et Du Liban 1939–1940*, Paris 1952
Ryan, Sir Andrew *The Last of the Dragomans*, ed. by Sir Reader Bullard, London 1951
As-Said, General Nuri *Arab Independence and Unity*, The Government Printing Press, Baghdad 1943
Samuel, Viscount *Memoirs*, London 1945
Sherwood, Robert E. *The White House Papers of Harry L. Hopkins*, 2 vols., London 1948 and 1949
A Short History of Enemy Subversive Activities in Iraq 1935–1941: A Documentary Account published by the American Christian Palestine Committee, New York (n.d.)
Stark, Freya *Dust in the Lion's Paw: Autobiography 1939–1946*, London 1961
—— *East is West*, London 1945
Weizmann, Dr Chaim *Trial and Error*, London 1949
Woodward, Sir Llewellyn *British Foreign Policy in the Second World War*, 2 vols., London 1970–71

2 *Secondary Sources*
Anabtawi, M. F. *Arab Unity in Terms of Law*, The Hague 1963
Antonius, George *The Arab Awakening*, London 1938
Baer, Gabriel *Population and Society in the Arab East* (Translated from the Hebrew by Hanna Szoke) London 1944

Bar-Zohar, Michael *The Armed Prophet: A Biography of Ben Gurion* (Translated from the French by Len Ortzen) London 1967
Barbour, Nevill *Nisi Dominus: A Survey of the Palestine Controversy*, London 1946
Birdwood, Lord *Nuri As-Sa'id: A Study in Arab Leadership*, London 1959
Bullard, Sir Reader *Britain and the Middle East*, London 1951
Cachia, Pierre *Taha Husayn: His Place in the Egyptian Literary Renaissance*, London 1956
Carmichael, Joel "Notes on Arab Unity" in *Foreign Affairs*, 21 (October 1943) pp. 148–53
Chejne, Anwar G. "Egyptian Attitudes Towards Pan-Arabism" in *The Middle East Journal*, 11 (Summer 1957) pp. 253–68
Deeb, Marius K. *The Wafd and its Rivals: The Rise and Development of Political Parties in Egypt 1919–1939*, Oxford University D.Phil Thesis 1971
Faris, Nabih Amin and Husayn, M. T. *The Crescent in Crisis*, Lawrence, Kansas (U.S.) 1955
Foda, Ezzeldin *The Projected Arab Court of Justice*, The Hague 1957
Frye, Richard N. (ed.) *The Near East and the Great Powers*, Cambridge, Massachusetts (U.S.) 1951
Edelman, Maurice *Ben Gurion: A Political Biography*, London 1964
Gibb, H. A. R. "Middle Eastern Perplexity" in *International Affairs*, 20 (October 1944) pp. 458–82
—— "Toward Arab Unity" in *Foreign Affairs* (October 1945) pp. 119–29
Gray, J. W. "Arab Nationalism: Abdin against the Wafd" in *Middle East Forum* (February 1962) pp. 17–20 and 48
Haim, Sylvia G. *Arab Nationalism: An Anthology* (ed.), Berkeley, California (U.S.) 1964
Harris, Christina Phelps *Nationalism and Revolution in Egypt: The Role of the Muslem Brotherhood*, London 1964
Heyworth-Dunne, J. *Religious and Political Trends in Modern Egypt*, Washington D.C. (U.S.) 1950
Hirszowicz, Lukasz *The Third Reich and the Arab East*, London 1966
Hourani, Albert *Arabic Thought in the Liberal Age: 1798–1939*, London 1962
—— *Great Britain and the Arab World*, London 1945
—— *Minorities in the Arab World*, London 1947
—— *Syria and Lebanon*, London 1946
Hourani, Cecil "The Arab League in Perspective" in *The Middle East Journal*, vol. I, No. 2, April 1947, pp. 125–36
Howarth, David *The Desert King: A Life of Ibn Sa'ud*, London 1964
Hudson, Michael *The Precarious Republic: Political Modernization in Lebanon*, New York 1968

Hurewitz, J. C. *The Struggle for Palestine*, New York 1950
Husaini, Ishak Musa *The Moslem Brethren: The Great Modern Islamic Movements*, Beirut 1956
Ireland, Philip "The Near East and the European War" in *Foreign Policy Reports*, No. 16 (15 March 1940) pp. 2–16
—— "The Pact of the League of Arab States" in *American Journal of International Law*, vol. 39 (October 1945)
Issawi, Charles *Egypt: An Economic and Social Analysis*, London 1947
Jankowski, James P. "The Egyptian Blue Shirts and the Egyptian Wafd: 1935–1938" in *Middle Eastern Studies*, vol. VI, No. 1, January 1970, pp. 77–92
Khadduri, Majid "The Arab League as a Regional Arrangement" in *American Journal of International Law*, vol. XL, No. 4 (October 1946)
—— "Aziz 'Ali Misri and the Arab Nationalist Movement" in *Saint Antony's Papers* (Middle East Affairs) No. 17, p. 140
—— *Independent Iraq*, London 1951
—— "General Nuri's Flirtations with the Axis Powers" in *The Middle East Journal*, vol. 16, No. 3 (Summer 1962) pp. 328–36
—— *Political Trends in the Arab World: The Role of Ideas and Ideals in Politics*, Baltimore (U.S.) 1970
—— "Towards an Arab Union" in *The American Political Science Review*, vol. 40 (February 1946)
Kedourie, Elie *The Chatham House Version and other Middle Eastern Studies*, London 1970
Landau, Jacob *Parliaments and Parties in Egypt*, New York 1954
Laissy, Michael *Du Pan-Arabisme à La Ligue Arabe*, Paris 1948
Lenczowski, George *The Middle East in World Affairs*, 3rd edn., Ithaca, New York 1962
Lugol, Jean *L'Egypte et la Deuxième Guerre Mondiale*, Cairo 1945
MacDonald, Robert W. *The League of Arab States: A Study in the Dynamics of Regional Organization*, Princeton N.J. (U.S.) 1965
Majzoub, Mohamed *Le Liban et L'Orient Arabe 1943–1956*, 1956 (N. Pl.) (Typewritten copy: St Antony's, Oxford)
Marlowe, John *Rebellion in Palestine*, London 1946
—— *The Seat of Pilate*, London 1959
McBride, Barrie St Clair *Farouk of Egypt: A Biography*, London 1967
Mitchell, Richard P. *The Society of the Muslim Brothers*, London 1969
Monroe, Elizabeth *Britain's Moment in the Middle East 1914–1956*, Baltimore (U.S.) 1963
Montague, Robert "La Politique De La Grande-Bretagne Dans Les 'Pays Arabes' " in *Politique Etrangère* (November 1946) p. 489
—— "L'Union Arabe" in *Politique Etrangère* (May 1946) pp. 179–215

Quraishi, Zaheer Masood *Liberal Nationalism in Egypt: Rise and Fall of the Wafd Party*, Delhi 1967
Rose, Norman "The Debate on Partition: 1937–38: The Anglo-Zionist Aspect. II The Withdrawal" in *Middle Eastern Studies*, vol. 7, No. 1 (January 1971) pp. 3–24
Russell, Ruth B. and Jeannette E. Muther *A History of the United Nations Charter: The Role of the United States 1940–1945*, Washington D.C. 1958
Safran, Nadav *Egypt in Search of Political Community*, London 1961
Sayegh, Fayez A. *Arab Unity*, New York 1958
Seale, Patrick *The Struggle for Syria: A Study of Post-War Arab Politics 1945–1958*, London 1965
Sheffer, G. *Policy Making and British Policies Towards Palestine 1929–1939*, Oxford University D.Phil Thesis, 1970
Siegman, Henry "Arab Unity and Disunity" in *The Middle East Journal*, vol. 16, No. 1 (Winter 1962) pp. 48–59
Spears, Sir Edward "The Path to Arab Unity" in *Great Britain and the East* (April 1945)
Survey of International Affairs 1939–1946: *The Middle East in the War* by George Kirk, 2nd impression, R.I.I.A., London 1954
Survey of International Affairs: 1934 and 1936, R.I.I.A., London 1935, 1937
Toynbee, A. J. *Civilization on Trial*, London 1948
Vatikiotis, P. J. *Politics and the Military in Jordan*, London 1967

3 *Newspapers and Periodicals*
The Economist
The Times
The New York Herald Tribune
The New York Times
The Saturday Evening Post
The News Chronicle

INDEX